CRIMEFIGHTERS OF LONDON

A History of the Origins and Development
of the London Probation Service
1876-1965

MARTIN PAGE

'Brethren, warn them that are unruly,
comfort the feebleminded, support the weak,
be patient toward all men.'

I Thessalonians 5:14

Inner London Probation Service
Benevolent and Educational Trust
73 Great Peter Street, London, SW1P 2BN

ISBN 0 9516711 0 3

First published in Great Britain 1992 by
Inner London Probation Service
Benevolent and Educational Trust
73 Great Peter Street
London
SW1P 2BN

Typeset & Printed by Barnard & Crannis Ltd
Unit 30, Lea Valley Trading Estate
Angel Road, Edmonton
London
N18 3HR

TO

GUY CLUTTON-BROCK,

MERFYN TURNER

AND

ALL THOSE WHO MADE THE WORK POSSIBLE

By the same author

Britain's Unknown Genius: An Introduction to the Life-Work of John Mackinnon Robertson

Homelessness and Mental Illness: The Dark Side of Community Care
(co-editor)

The Rights of Old People
(contributor: foreword by Richard Crossman)

CONTENTS

Acknowledgments

To my knowledge, no history of the origins and development of the London Probation Service (1876-1965) has hitherto been written. Although other works have touched on various aspects of that history, I think I may safely say that most of the material presented in the following pages has not previously appeared in one volume. By the same token, so many people have contributed, and contributed generously, in diverse ways to the preparation of this work that it is virtually impossible to thank them all by name; so in case of any inadvertent omission on my part, let me take this opportunity to thank all those who have helped me in my task.

In particular, I must thank the Trustees of the I.L.P.S. Benevolent and Educational Trust for kindly awarding me a scholarship to undertake my research. I am grateful to them and to Mr Graham W. Smith, C.B.E., Chief Probation Officer of the Inner London Probation Service, for enabling me to take a period of study leave for this purpose. In addition, Mr Tony Leach and his predecessors Messrs Peter McNeal and Charles Crockford, as Secretary to the Trustees, gave me every encouragement and support. I must thank Mr Graham Smith and his head office staff for allowing me to use archival material in their care. I am also grateful to Mr John North for valuable suggestions and advice, and to Mr David Blair (Personnel Dept.) for information he provided at my request.

My sincere thanks are extended to the following former or serving London probation officers who generously granted me face-to-face interviews, often combined with the hospitality of their homes: Alison Allen; Charles Balchin; Peter Barnes; Rose Mary Braithwaite; Aline Cholmondeley; Irene Clarkson; Sally Costin; Ethel Currant; Jack and Margaret Frost; Elspeth Gray; Valerie Haig-Brown; Gunter Lubowski; Charles Morgan; Stanley Ratcliffe; (the Rev.) Nicholas Rivett-Carnac; Allen Robins; Peter Shervington; Derek Shuttleworth; Georgina Stafford; Marjorie Watts; and Lord Wells-Pestell.

In addition to many of those already named, former or serving probation officers - nearly all with experience of probation work in London - who have given me valuable information or insights through correspondence, over the telephone or in "chance" conversation are: Maud Ivy Alleyne;

Cecil Barker; Roy Barr; B.D.Beecroft; Ann Burgh; Evelyn Cleavely; Guy Clutton-Brock; Ron Conn; John Croft; Katherine Crofton; (Dr) Kathleen de Ville; Irene Edmonds; Tony Goodman; Norman Grant; W.E.Hill; Bill Hornung; Elizabeth Inman; F.V.Jarvis; Miriam Kratz; Francis Lister; Colette Maitland-Warne; Carol Martin; Margaret May; Pat Mayhew; Charlotte Mitra; Frank Monk; Jean Moore; Joe Nixon; John Oliver; Margaret Paterson; Terry Phillips; Margaret Powell; Constance Rees; Gordon Skeens; Bill Spurling; John Starke; Doris Sullivan; Ellen Ruth Susskind; and Steve Woodgate. Former London Probation Service probation officers who kindly granted me access to, and use of, various materials are: Cecil Barker; Rose Mary Braithwaite; Ethel Currant; Jack Frost; Elspeth Gray; Charles Morgan; Stanley Ratcliffe; Derek Shuttleworth; Georgina Stafford; and Marjorie Watts.

Retired London service secretarial staff who enabled me to conduct face-to-face interviews with them are: Florence Bradley; Norah Clarke; Kathleen Hoath; Josephine Knox; and Stephanie Stevens. Some of them also helped me in other ways, as did their erstwhile colleagues Lydia Blackman and Iris Pontifex with their reminiscences.

I have also received pertinent information from: Olive Cole; Marjorie Daunt; Ada Demer; Mrs Edith Farmer; Mary Farmer; Hugh Klare; Baron Mayhew; Edith Morgan; Lady Ralphs; C.H.Rolph; Dr David Rumney; Mrs Dorothy Swinney; John Treherne; and Merfyn Turner. I must also mention with gratitude the archivist and local historian Gordon Cullingham.

Organisations and institutions to which I am indebted are the: B.B.C. Written Archives Centre (Jeff Walden); British Film Institute (Anne Burton); British Library; Church Army (Elizabeth Wilford); Circle Trust (David Ward); Regimental Headquarters Coldstream Guards (Capt John Sedgwick); Golborne Rehabilitation Centre (Mrs G.Peake and Dr D.E.R.Bennett); Greater London Record Office (R.Sarnways); Home Office; Howard League for Penal Reform (Frances Crook and Emily Russell); Independent Broadcasting Authority (Kathy Turtle); Inner London Probation Committee (A.Brown); Institute for the Study and Treatment of Delinquency (Martin Farrell); Institute of Marital Studies (Evelyn Cleavely); Jewish Welfare Board (Ellis Wynick); Lambeth Palace Library; London School of Economics Library; *The Magistrate* (E.R.Horsman); Magistrates' Association (Mrs E.Halmos and Derek Howard); N.A.P.O. (Pete Bowyer); National Army Museum (Dr P.B.Boyden); New Bridge (Charles J. Paterson); Notting Hill Social

Council (Albert Tucker); N.S.P.C.C. (Annette Briggs); Privy Council (D.H.Owen); Public Record Office (Kew); Rainer Foundation (Richard Kay); Richmond Fellowship (John McCarthy); Royal Commission on Historical Manuscripts (N.W.James); St Catherine's House (General Register Office); Toynbee Hall (Helen Menezes and C. Tucker); and West London Mission (J.C.Hicks). The Berkshire, South Yorkshire and West Midlands Probation Services have also provided me with useful information.

Rose Parncutt and Jo Knox helped with the typing at various stages. Mrs C. de Silva cheerfully undertook a great deal of photocopying.

I am grateful to Rose Mary Braithwaite, Georgina Stafford and Doris Sullivan for having read the main text in typescript and making helpful comments on it. Similarly, Miss Braithwaite, Jo Knox, Edith and Bill Morgan, and Lynette Almeida assisted with the proof-reading. The index represents a necessarily selective guide to the core text.

Permission to quote from or reproduce documents or other material has kindly been granted by the Home Office, the Rainer Foundation, the executors of the Elizabeth Inman estate, Rabbit Press Ltd. of Crawley, Sussex (publishers of Leslie Thompson's *An Autobiography*), and Guy and Molly Clutton-Brock (as regards their 1972 book *Cold Comfort Confronted* and the 1987 book in their honour *Guy and Molly Clutton-Brock*).

I must thank my colleagues - in particular, Roy Barr, Dilip Gupta, Ann Jacob, Jim O'Reilly and Janice Williams - for covering my duties at work while I was on leave.

Finally, I must thank my wife for her support, encouragement and patience.

Within inevitable constraints, every care has been taken to ensure the accuracy of the facts presented by me; and any opinions I have expressed are believed to be consistent with my understanding of facts at my disposal. Needless to say, however, I alone am responsible for any factual errors or opinions attributable to me.

May 1992   MARTIN PAGE

CHAPTER ONE

Early Years of the Mission, 1876-87

In 1876, a middle-aged printer called Frederic Rainer, living in the English county town of Hertford, had a rather novel idea. Apparently as a resident of Hatton Garden in London and as a visitor to police courts in the capital (and perhaps also in Hertfordshire), he had been appalled by the number of people guilty of alcohol-related offences. With a practical scheme in mind, this sensitive and scholarly man decided to write to the Church of England Temperance Society.

Emphasising, as its name suggested, temperance rather than total abstinence, the Society had been formally established only three years earlier - in 1873 - as a response to the widespread problems associated with excessive drinking in England. This was at a time when there appears to have been a dramatic increase throughout the country, since about 1860, in the number of convictions for drunkenness and drunk and disorderly behaviour. The C.E.T.S. had three national objectives: the Promotion of Habits of Temperance, the Reformation of the Intemperate, and the Removal of the Causes which lead to Intemperance.

The Society's Chairman was Canon Henry Ellison, whose parish temperance society Rainer had joined some 17 years or so earlier in Windsor, a barracks town where the lay temperance worker probably encountered the seamy side of life for the first time. (Many years later, a memorial to Rainer would be unveiled at Windsor, as at Hertford, for his inspirational work.) In his letter to Ellison, of which the original text appears to have been lost, Rainer deplored the fact that once someone got into trouble through drink or "any other cause", there seemed no hope for that person. "Offence after offence and sentence after sentence appear to be the inevitable lot of him whose foot has once slipped. Can nothing be done to arrest the downward career?" Rainer, a family man, enclosed five shillings - which probably represented a day's pay, more or less - as the projected nucleus of a fund for rescue work which he hoped the Church of England Temperance Society would be able to undertake in the police courts.[1]

The enterprising printer's five shillings were destined to go a long way. His suggestion was promptly considered by the appropriate C.E.T.S. committee, which reacted favourably. In the Society's words:

> Feeling the great need of directing more attention to the real Mission work of the Society, the Southern Province Committee, in August last, appointed a special Missionary, whose duty it should be to visit regularly certain Metropolitan Police Courts for the purpose of dealing with individual drunkards, with a view to their restoration and reclamation.

The "special Missionary" appointed - with effect from 1 August 1876 - was a young ex-soldier, George Nelson, whom the London police court clerk Albert Lieck would remember as "in his way as heroic as Horatio of that name". The Church of England Temperance Society chose the Rochester Diocese as its testing ground and sent Nelson, as its first police court missionary, to cover Southwark Police Court, which was at that time within the diocesan area of Rochester.

This George Nelson may well have been the person of that name recorded as having enlisted in the Coldstream Guards at Newcastle on 15 November 1861 at the age of 22, and as having been discharged ten years later, on 14 November 1871, with an excellent character record and two good conduct badges.[2] Be that as it may, Nelson evidently threw himself into his new work with great energy and enthusiasm, and logged his activities with scrupulous care, for at the end of March 1877 he was able to account for his first eight months in the following impressive computation:

Homes visited	438
police court visits	293
cab-stands visited	165
pledges taken	149
prison visits	117
workshops visited	94
railway station visits	34
women sent to homes	20
lodging-houses visited	9

He also held 13 prison meetings; attended 51 "general meetings", 29 mothers' meetings, 10 open-air meetings, and 7 juvenile meetings; and handed over 72 cases to C.E.T.S. branches, so that each might be brought within the influence of his or her parish church.

The police court may well have engendered more work than the bare statistics might suggest, for clearly one police court visit may have resulted in contact with more than one person to be offered help; and Nelson's figures do suggest that he attended the court on a daily basis. From the outset home visits represented an important aspect of what the colourful London probation officer Sewell Stokes, many years later, would call "The Work". Also from the beginning Nelson was involved with prisons - mainly, it seems, through meeting prisoners at the gates on their release - and the male police court missionary was concerned about women as well as men, juveniles as well as adults. Of the women he sent to homes, Nelson would subsequently report that "seven have come under my observation again ... while others are still in Institutes, gone to service, or to their homes".

The pledges taken - thereby facilitating membership of the Church of England Temperance Society - were of two kinds: one for moderate drinkers, the other for total abstainers. And in his temperance work, if not in other respects as well, Nelson appears to have begun to exert some influence on members of the police court staff, for in relating how a court under-gaoler (whose subsequent promotion he likewise recorded) became an abstainer, Nelson stated:

> Up to the time he signed the Total Abstinence Declaration, beer was allowed to be brought in to the prisoners, after conviction, by their friends. No intoxicants are now allowed to be brought into the cells, although tea and coffee are permitted. This has done away with much noise and confusion, and it would be well if such an example were largely imitated.

George Nelson was to labour for some thirty-six years in the London police courts; but he was not destined to work alone. Early in 1877, thanks to the generosity of one of its members who undertook to guarantee the salary of another agent for five years, the C.E.T.S. appointed a second missionary, William Batchelor, who covered Bow Street and Mansion House Courts, and who would work as a police court missionary in the London Diocese until about the end of 1889, before transferring to Northampton.[3] Both Nelson and Batchelor were former Coldstream Guardsmen[4], tall and slim, with military-style moustaches

3

characteristic of the period: indeed, their appearance seemed quite impressive - a quality that no doubt helped them in their relationship with the courts and other aspects of their work, and that some 70 years later the National Institute of Industrial Psychology would consider an advantage in a probation officer. While serving soldiers at Victoria Barracks in Windsor, they in effect followed in Frederic Rainer's footsteps by attending Ellison's weekly temperance meetings; and it was probably under the Canon's influence, if not at his direct instigation, that after ceasing to be soldiers of the Queen, they became soldiers of Christ as "special missionaries" assigned to London police courts. (For an early photograph of Nelson and Batchelor, see Appendix 1.)

The C.E.T.S. historian H.H. Ayscough would later maintain that most of the earliest police court missionary cases handed over to C.E.T.S. branches were followed up, as part of the Church's network, by the local clergy or parochial mission women, with "many cases of permanent reformation of individuals, who became regular attendants at Church or Bible classes, and" - Ayscough added - "several were known to keep their pledges who did not go to Church". In 1927 Canon J. Hasloch Potter, Ayscough's predecessor (1878-81) as Secretary of the Church of England Temperance Society, would draw on his committee experience to ask: "Who among those who sat at the Board table - of whom I am one of the few survivors - and heard that first Report read, ever imagined to what dimensions the small beginnings would grow?" Certainly further seeds were sown when, during 1877, the C.E.T.S. appointed two more missionaries: Alfred Delahay to work in the Midlands, and R.R. Albin to serve Greenwich and Deptford. Indeed, London - especially the South London area - was already beginning to be fairly well covered by police court missionaries at a time when the annual report of the Metropolitan Police[5] indicated that a total of 38,748 arrests for "drunk and disorderly, drunk, disorderly prostitutes and disorderly characters" represented over 50% of reported crime in the metropolis.

It was against this background that in 1877 a judge at the Middlesex Sessions, Edward William Cox, published a book in London in which he described the practice he had developed since 1865 of releasing selected first offenders on recognizance to come up for judgment when called upon, as an alternative to sending them to prison. Factors predisposing Cox to take such a lenient course were not only if it was found or strongly believed that the criminal was truly a first offender, but also "if the circumstances of the case point to the probability of a yielding to sudden temptation or that the criminal was misled by others more wicked than he". But, declared Cox, "cases of this kind cannot be so treated without careful preliminary inquiry into the *antecedents* of the convict". To assist him at the Middlesex Sessions, he had an "active intelligent officer", a certain Mr Lockyer (presumably a policeman),

> whose business it is to make these inquiries. He takes the addresses of friends and employers named by the prisoner, sees them and obtains all the information he can, which he reports to the Court, the sentence being deferred for that purpose. The constable having charge of the case is also properly instructed to make inquiries about the prisoner, so as to be enabled to inform the Court what his past character and pursuits have been.

From Cox's book the extent to which Mr Lockyer may have supervised first offenders after the judge had released them "without punishment" is far from clear. Indeed, Timasheff (1941), King (1964), Jarvis (1972) and, to some extent, Bochel (1976), following Timasheff, all appear to have been mistaken in stating that the inquiry officer was, in Timasheff's words, "entrusted with the supervision of the behavior of probationers" (for which statement Timasheff provided no textual reference).

Certainly Cox regarded his practice as a great success, not merely because "no complaint of it has ever come to me from the Home Office". He wrote of the first offender, released after the inquiry officer had reported to the court on his (or her) background:

> The suspension only of the judgment, the knowledge that if he offends he may yet be punished - the hold which his bail thus has upon him, to a great extent guarantee that if there is in him an inclination to redeem himself he will return to a life of honesty.

> And experience has amply confirmed this anticipation. I am aware that I have been blamed for having more largely used this power than has been the practice with Judges. But the results are the best justification. No exact account has been taken of the number of convicts so treated during the last twelve years, but it must be considerable. It is a remarkable fact that of all the many cases so dealt with, in *two* instances only has it been found necessary to

require the offender to come up for judgment under these recognisances.[6]

The form of treatment championed by Cox was built on the experiment conducted by his predecessor as a pioneer of probation, Matthew Davenport Hill, who, as the Recorder of Birmingham between 1839 and 1865, had entrusted young offenders to the care of suitable "guardians" (friends, relatives, employers, etc.). Hill's experiment was based on one adopted by Warwickshire magistrates in whose court he had practised in the 1820s; but Hill refined and extended their usage through a system he devised of periodic police enquiries by "a confidential officer" and record-keeping regarding the progress of the offenders in the community. Hill reported in 1857 that out of 417 such offenders, released between 1842 and 1854, only 80 were known to have been reconvicted. However, it rather looks as though use was not made of recognizances or sureties in such cases; if so, the court had not retained any direct legal control or sanction over the offender, except in so far as Hill, for example, severely punished any such trusted offender who was again convicted before him.[7]

Hill's daughters claimed in 1878 that an attempt "made by the magistrates of the Middlesex Sessions" to introduce his experiment "in the part of London under their jurisdiction...failed from the appalling fact that scarcely one among the juvenile delinquents of the metropolis possessed either employer, parents, or friends!" Despite this claim, in 1877 at the Middlesex Sessions 86 offenders were released on recognizance, 69 of them by Edward Cox. (At the Central Criminal Court in 1877 only 7 were so treated, though this number would rise to 112 in 1912.)[8]

Whatever initial doubts some officials may have had regarding the deployment of police court missionaries, Nelson, at least, worked in the Lambeth and Southwark areas with the full sanction, support and assistance of the presiding magistrates. He wrote: "I have been treated with the greatest respect, and afforded every facility for doing good, by the Police Court Officials. Nothing has been wanting on their part to help me in the good work." The "good work" he explained as follows: "I am glad to report that hundreds of men and women have listened to that one Divine instrument, the Gospel, in its simplicity, from my lips, as well as to advice to shun strong drink." Moreover:

> Many simply sign the pledge, have a few words, and go on, refusing name and address. There are many that I have kept an eye upon, that are keeping their pledges, some are members of Parochial Branches [of the C.E.T.S.], some are attending Church and other places of

worship.

Nelson produced a statistical summary of his work for the year ending 31 March 1878 which included, *inter alia*:

Cab-stand visits	1,143
homes visited	754
police court visits	473
pledges taken	426
large works visited	172
hopeful cases handed over to C.E.T.S. branches	113
railway station visits	90
police station visits	38
prison visits	34
fire brigade station visits	19
women taken to homes	19

Apart from the newly recorded figures for police station and fire brigade station visits, Nelson's statistics, compared with those for 1876-77, indicated a marked decrease in prison visiting, and also a really dramatic increase in both cab-stand visits and pledges taken, the former no doubt providing many opportunities for the latter. Nelson's statements, and the fact that at that time virtually no other Christian denomination was attached to London police courts on a regular basis, would seem to suggest that his statistics included people who were only nominally or not at all Church of England.

Also writing in March 1878, William Batchelor declared in his first annual report for the Church of England Temperance Society that at both Bow Street and Mansion House, "I have met with the greatest possible encouragement and sympathy from the court officials, especially at Bow Street". At the Mansion House Court all visits to the cells were prohibited for six months as a result of an attempt someone had made to bribe the gaoler. This order had the effect of abruptly suspending Batchelor's work at that court.

At about this time R.R. Albin persuaded some 222 habitual drunkards to sign the pledge. Of these, thirty-two are known to have broken it, with four reappearing in court. The 190 apparently successful cases included one of a woman in the parish of St Peter's, Greenwich, who, previously well known at the police court because of several convictions for drunkenness, after signing the pledge actively tried to persuade her neighbours to give up drink and attend the Society's meetings.

Prisoners did not always recognise the police court missionary as a friend, as William Batchelor later admitted: "I have had much discouragement, for some days when I go to the cells they curse me and use fearful language." Yet Batchelor was also able to record a rewarding experience:

> One cabman said to the policeman who locked him up, when he met him in the street some time after, 'Thank God, policeman, you locked me up and brought me into touch with that Missionary. It was the best thing that ever happened to me, as it enabled me to sign the pledge. When you arrested me I was in debt and near losing my home. Besides which I had three marks on my licence; but now I have a clean one, and thank God, owe no one a penny, while my wife and family bless the day I signed the pledge, and so do I.'

The work of the police court missionaries was, in effect, extended by the 1879 Summary Jurisdiction Act, which gave police courts some powers to discharge accused persons, in trivial cases, on recognizance, with or without sureties, to keep the peace and be of good behaviour and to appear for sentence when called upon. It seems that some London magistrates asked the police court missionary to help, advise and supervise persons discharged in this way and occasionally to stand surety for them. Some courts apparently adopted the practice of granting an offender bail for a clearly defined period, so that the police court missionary, the police or the industrial schools officer could report on the offender's progress when the case came up again.

During this period it was becoming apparent that excessive drinking was often a factor in a range of crimes (such as those involving theft, violence, or neglect of children), and that the consequences, direct and indirect, of intemperance stretched far and wide. As Canon Hasloch Potter recalled in his history of the Police Court Mission:

> The Magistrates began to employ the Missionaries to visit homes, administer relief and generally act as advisers and helpers, even where no one had been charged with drunkenness. Well do I remember the searchings of heart at committee as the elder members began to realise that our Missionaries were, as it seemed, being taken off their special job, or rather put on many fresh ones. Fortunately, while the old men "dreamed dreams," some of the younger ones "saw visions."

The visionaries prevailed and both Magistrates and Missionaries were given more of a free hand as to the nature of the duties performed. This, though even we younger folk little realised it at the time, was to lead to results of vast magnitude. While the Missionary was confined to cases of actual intoxication the work was necessarily limited, but as it broadened out it began to enter into many details of life, each one of which presented a problem of its own. It appeared that there were wheels within wheels, causes of ill to be removed, opportunities of self-help to be provided. Here the policeman was useless. Official buttons could only frighten away; the power of a spiritual agency was needed to get at the back of offences, to reach the hearts of offenders.[9]

The "visionaries" no doubt advanced the claim that expansion of the scope of the work was entirely justified under the C.E.T.S. objects, particularly perhaps "the Removal of the Causes which lead to Intemperance".

By 1880 the number of police court missionaries assigned to various parts of London had risen to a total of four with the appointment of a Mr Haskett, who served Clerkenwell and Marylebone Courts. Haskett gave a vivid if depressing account of the drunkenness he encountered: "on Mondays or after a holiday the sights are beyond description. Wife appealing against husband and vice versa; children against parents and parents against children; women and men disfigured through falling about when helplessly drunk or fighting so much." He admitted to much discouragement during his year's work. But at least he was readily available, after a fashion: in January 1881 at Thames Court, where there was no such missionary, the magistrate made an enquiry about a widow through the Charity Organisation Society[10], which was in fact a precursor of modern casework, social work record-keeping and even social work use of the term "client".

In the year ending March 1881, Haskett, Batchelor and Nelson made more than one thousand visits to police courts and took at least 781 pledges between them. The Church of England Temperance Society reported that its agents' principal duty was

> to visit regularly police-courts for the purpose of dealing with individual drunkards, both charged and convicted, with a view to restoration and reclamation. They visit hopeful cases, and hand over such to Branch Societies, and work with the full consent in each case

of the presiding Magistrates.

At least one of the C.E.T.S. missionaries in London worked under an active committee (possibly a kind of embryonic case committee) at Sion College, presided over by C.E.T.S. Vice-Chairman, the Rev. Harvey Brooks. In addition to their police court duties and home visits, the missionaries continued to visit cabstands, workshops, police stations, railway stations, fire stations and addressed temperance meetings. Nelson thought that between 25% and 30% of those who signed pledges with him kept them. "Nor is this bad when we come to consider the strange kinds of people we have to deal with at our Police Courts." He believed that about a quarter of those charged with drunkenness were "to the human mind almost past redemption", and that most of those who did keep their pledges had been charged for only the first or second time.

Meanwhile a demand for the establishment of a probation system in England came not from the police court missionaries (beginning to spread to different parts of the country and numbering eight in all by the end of 1881) or from the C.E.T.S. itself, but from a different quarter. In 1881 the Howard Association (progenitor of the Howard League for Penal Reform), based in London, published a pamphlet entitled *Juvenile Offenders*, in which, with "people in authority" like the Home Secretary in mind, it commended the probation system practised in the American state of Massachusetts (where the world's first official probation officer, bearing that title, had been granted legal recognition in Boston in 1878; though a passing tribute may also be paid to the pioneering work in America of some "Pilgrim Fathers" of Massachusetts Bay, the Boston shoemaker John Augustus, who between 1841 and 1858 - more or less contemporaneously with Hill's experiment in England - had "bailed on probation" nearly two thousand people, and Augustus's successor Rufus Cook). The Howard Association suggested that a magistrate in each locality, requested by the Home Secretary to concentrate on young offenders, could be assisted by one or two policemen or, "better still", by one or more voluntary helpers, who would aim to provide "authoritative influence" and "give parents or relatives of the said children such oversight or guidance as might enable them to discharge their responsibilities aright".

It was conceivably with this Howard Association publication in mind that, in its annual report for 1882-83, the Church of England Temperance Society promised: "As soon as funds permit a special Missionary will be attached to every Police Court in the Metropolis" - a promise that, with one exception, would be fulfilled by the end of the nineteenth century.

Expansion of the scope of the service and of the numbers of police court missionaries was certainly encouraged by the kind of relationships Batchelor, for example, was able to build up. He recorded: "The officers at Bow Street and Clerkenwell Police Courts, all of them, from the Magistrates down, have given me every help possible in my work. . . Mr Barstow, the Magistrate, thanked me from the Bench one morning for the valuable help I had rendered to them at that Court." Although he found many of the outcasts he was trying to assist " a very difficult class of people", Batchelor wrote in his report for 1884-85: "One of the best parts of my work I believe is being able to meet with, and speak a kind word to, those who are charged for the first time, who do not sign, but thank me for my advice and counsel, whom I never see again." (His fellow missionary Mr A.C. Thompson, who in 1884 transferred from Rochester to Marylebone and wrote an article on "Monday Morning in the Police Court", would later describe a similar experience: a man in Battersea, whom he had forgotten, gratefully told Thompson he had persuaded him to give up drink. Such counselling doubtless helped problem drinkers to sign and keep the pledge.)

Batchelor went on to describe his work with female alcoholics and prostitutes by assisting the East London Mission in "visiting with some ladies the fallen women in the streets from 10.30 to 12.0 o'clock".[11] In helping to persuade a number of such women to go into homes, he was in effect following in the footsteps of George Nelson, who in 1883 had founded a Policemen's Christian Association, one of whose objects was apparently to achieve reclamation of the fallen without their being arrested. This was largely managed by a group of Christian ladies working in conjunction with police officers, some of whom were committed Christians and members of the Association. Nelson proudly recorded: "I am a daily witness to the grand and fruitful work of the good ladies and the work of the members of the Association among their fellow-policemen; it is quite a common thing now for policemen to bring poor girls from the streets to me to get them into Homes, etc." This was indeed a striking example of co-operation between a police court missionary and the police.

In 1884 the C.E.T.S. branch for the Rochester Diocese - which then included the South London courts of Southwark, Lambeth and Greenwich - was able to report of the missionaries working in the diocese:

> The Missionaries are all under the superintendence of experienced clergymen, who advise and encourage them, read their journals, and from time to time test and inspect their work. Even manifest results cannot easily be tabulated; but all the superintendents are able to bear thankful testimony to many persons of both sexes rescued from drunkenness, to wretched homes become happy and prosperous, to poor outcasts brought to a sense of their sin and shame, and to patient and successful efforts to deepen the influence and extend the field of Temperance Reformation.

George Nelson, in his report for 1883-84, alluded to his "brisk open air work in the evenings", in which he handed out up to three and a half thousand back numbers of the *Temperance Chronicle*, three thousand or so copies of *Fireside News* and *Hand and Heart*, and some two thousand tracts, to transport workers (such as cab drivers and railwaymen) and others. The following year, while many of Nelson's cases fell away during the hot summer weather, Batchelor attended some temperance meetings in the evening, but found this rather trying after a hard day at his two courts. (There seemed to be a growing separation between what might be broadly termed court-oriented work during daylight hours and temperance work in the evenings.) Also in 1884-85, while the C.E.T.S. spent £300 on its missionary work in the London courts, it only received £140 for this purpose - the expectation being that funds would be raised from charitable sources - yet it was doubtless gratified when its coffers were swelled by contributions such as those in 1885 and 1886, when the Clerkenwell magistrates Messrs H. Barstow and J.C. Hosack marked their appreciation of the Society's work and Batchelor's devoted labours by two successive donations of £5.

That metropolitan magistrates readily appreciated such assistance may be imagined from the frank semi-autobiographical account of Thomas Holmes in his classic *Pictures and Problems from London Police Courts* (1900), first published, according to his own account, 15 years after he became a police court missionary, assigned to Lambeth Court. Years earlier, while Thomas was a pupil at a Church school in Staffordshire, the visiting Christian missionary and explorer of Africa, Dr David Livingstone, had placed his hand on the child's head (rather as Livingstone's father-in-law and fellow missionary, Robert Moffat, would provide a camellia from his buttonhole to be pinned to the birthday frock of the child Margery Fry[12], a future friend of the probation service). At the age of eleven, Holmes had to work 14 hours a day in a local iron foundry. Then, after years of poorly paid teaching interrupted by a serious accident, he was prompted by an inspiring country parson to answer an advertisement for a police court missionary at Lambeth. Possibly influenced by the "dear old Vicar", the Bishop of Rochester and his Council selected Holmes out of a dozen candidates; and so he came to London. "There was I, up from the country, with great hopes of doing good, and not altogether ignorant of the world or the vices and sorrows of our large cities; but a revelation awaited me."

What Holmes saw and heard on his first day - a Monday - in Lambeth Police Court dazed and frightened him, "burned into my very consciousness", giving him an unforgettable "mental photograph" which he described with searing eloquence:

> I see men shorn of all glory. I see womanhood clothed in shame. I see Vice rampant. I see Misery crawling. I see the long procession of the drink- or vice-stricken as they tramped down to the place of wrecked lives and slain souls. . . I hear the unuttered cry, 'The waters have gone over me! The waters have gone over me! Out of the black depths do I cry to be delivered.' And *I* was there to deliver them!
>
> But I see and hear more. I see women with bruised and battered faces, I see their cuts and wounds and putrefying sores, I hear stories of devilish cruelty, and I hear the poor bruised women pleading that their husbands may not be punished for their cruelty. 'Don't send him to prison! Don't send him to prison! He is a good husband when he is sober!' I hear the words again and again. I see more women with poor, thin clothing. I look into their faces, and I see sorrow writ large and rings of care around their eyes, and in their hearts a weight of agony that makes them ready to curse God and die. My God! and *I* was there to comfort them.
>
> I see more. I see the children old before their time, looking up with pale and piteous faces. I see some with blighted bodies, and I know that rounded limbs and happy hearts are not for them. Still more do I see: matronly women, charged with being drunk, holding in their arms little bits of mortality . . . I see more: young men to whom obscenity is the breath of life and immorality the highest good. . . . I see young women, sometimes fair and sometimes foul to look

upon, but whether fair or foul, half beast and half human. I hear stories of lust, drunkenness, and theft. I see the smartly-dressed harpies who farm them waiting to pay their fines. I see the most despicable of all mankind, the fellows who live upon them, hovering by like beasts of prey. I see old men of threescore and ten and old women of equal age, whose tottering limbs have borne them from the workhouse to the public-house, that they might drink and forget their misery once more before they die.

I see them all; they are around me now.

Of the sexually mixed prisoners' waiting-room he declared: "All the social problems of the day were in that room, all the vices and sorrows of life were personified in it." (Later[13] he was to describe its representative occupants as having included "deformed beggars, old hags from the workhouse - or from worse places - thieves, gamblers, drunkards, and harlots, men and women on the verge of delirium tremens".)

'Rescue them,' said my employers, 'and the last day of every month a small cheque shall be your reward.' 'How am I to do it?' 'Here's a temperance pledge-book; take pledges.' 'But there are others.' 'Give them tracts.' 'But there are the hungry and homeless to feed.' 'Give them tracts.' 'There are the poor wantons.' 'Take them to rescue homes, and let them work out their own salvation at the wash-tubs.'

Then - however impotent or sceptical he may have felt when he started his missionary work - he added, doubtless with the benefit of hindsight or experience: "Verily, if temperance pledges, tracts, and wash-tubs could save humanity, we had had the millennium long ago."

At the end of his first day at Lambeth Court - which he indicated was typical of metropolitan police courts at that time - he felt so overwhelmed ("And *I* was there to save them!") that, after seeing newly sentenced men and women being loaded into the "cupboards" in the back of the prisoners' van, Holmes rushed out into Kennington Park, sat down and "cried like a child".

One of those who did their best to support practical "rescue work" in the London police courts was Frederick Flowers the Bow Street magistrate.[14] The lawyer Edmund Purcell, looking back after forty years at the criminal bar, and with reason to know, declared:

Mr Flowers was the gentlest, kindest-hearted magistrate who ever sat on the Bench. He had none of the prevailing faith in the necessity or in the efficacy of imprisonment; he constantly released young offenders long before the First Offenders Act and handed them over to the care of a man who in the course of a long career has done incalculable public service, Mr W. Wheatley, of the St Giles' Christian Mission.

William Wheatley (who had been "converted" in 1865) had been put in charge of the rehabilitation work for discharged young male prisoners which St Giles had decided to start in 1877; and he took particular care to follow up such cases by visiting them regularly, finding jobs for them and generally trying to keep them on the straight and narrow. It was scarcely surprising, therefore, that in an address delivered in 1885 at the opening of its large home at 29 Brooke Street, Holborn - ironically, formerly a public house - Flowers suggested that young male first offenders should be handed over to the care of the St Giles' Christian Mission.

Another sympathetic metropolitan magistrate was Henry Curtis Bennett, who, from the time of his appointment in 1886, started to use legislation such as the 1879 Summary Jurisdiction Act as a means of conditionally releasing offenders on bail, sometimes also with a request that a police court missionary should keep an eye on them.

Looking back at his work in 1886, William Batchelor recorded its depressing and rewarding aspects with unmistakable vividness:

> I have to thank God for giving me grace and strength to persevere in this most trying work: to meet day by day with cut heads, black eyes, cut faces, broken limbs, stabs and burns where red-hot irons have been used, etc., etc., is really past my describing.
>
> Cruelty to children by parents when under the influence of drink; two instances of women whose husbands had destroyed one eye in each case: in one the man threw a bottle at his wife; in the other the man struck his wife with the bottle in which she had fetched him some beer.
>
> The wickedness of people while intoxicated I cannot describe. Daughters witnessing against their own mothers, sons against fathers, of the cruelty they have to endure; sons assaulting parents, and fathers and mothers giving evidence of their own children's cruelty to them, when drunk, defy description. . . .
>
> The police and all the officials assist me in rescuing the fallen

ones and preventing others. Young girls, when they are without friends in London, make application to the Magistrate in the morning, and the gaolers take care of them at either Court when I am not there. This is an encouraging aspect of the work. On five occasions I have been able to restore the cases direct to their parents or relations. The worst was a case of two sisters, aged 17 and 19, who had been on the streets for five months before they got into trouble. While they were on remand I got their things from the bad house where they had been living, and asked their married sister to come and take them home, which she did. Another girl, who had been deserted in London and left in lodgings to do as best she could for herself, I sent home to Dorsetshire, and her parents wrote thanking me for rescuing their child.

Though to some extent at the expense of his regular courts at Clerkenwell and Bow Street, Batchelor was able to help out at Marylebone Court, which was without its own missionary for some time before Miss K. Dunkerton had established herself. Miss Dunkerton was apparently the first female police court missionary to be appointed in London by the Church of England Temperance Society; and her task seems largely to have been to help her male colleagues in "specially difficult female cases". But London, for once, was not the first in the field: Liverpool had already appointed one such "mission woman" by 1885, in which year there were also some female missionaries working under the Women's Union - a branch of the C.E.T.S. - in about half a dozen English provincial centres.

In 1887 Canon Ellison wrote of the C.E.T.S. police court missionaries:

> Their business is to visit the drunken cases in the cells; to influence them, if possible, to give up drink altogether, and then to hand them over to the Parochial Society of their own parish. Judges and Magistrates agree that drink is at the root of at least three-fourths of all our crime. . . . The number of Temperance Missionaries employed by the Society and its Diocesan Branches is as follows:- London, 2; Rochester, 9; Lichfield (Handsworth Deanery), 1; Liverpool, 2, of whom one is a lady; Manchester, 1; Worcester, 1; Peterborough, 1; making 17 in Police Courts. Bristol has also a special Rescue Agent. Oxford, Cambridge, Durham, and Derby, each have a Female Missionary in connection with their Branches of the Women's Union - 5 in all; making a total of 22 Missionaries actively employed amongst the lowest and criminal classes in individual

16

rescue work. Yet only a beginning has been made. The success attending those already established calls loudly for similar work at every one of the London Police Courts.[15]

CHAPTER TWO

The Semblance of Probation, 1887-1901

Some seventy years after the Probation of First Offenders Bill reached the statute book in 1887, the National Police Court Mission claimed of the police court missionaries that "the light they helped to bring to British justice led to the passing of the Probation of First Offenders Act".[1] In so far as this was true at all, it was so only in a very indirect sense. Not only were their appointments recent and their numbers small (not more than twenty-five throughout England in 1887, according to Canon Ellison's count of the C.E.T.S. missionaries), and not only was their distribution uneven; but also there seems no evidence that the police court missionaries, individually or collectively, influenced or attempted to influence the reforming M.P. Howard Vincent, whose Probation of First Offenders Bill (resulting in the Act) specified no role for the police court missionary. Vincent had been much impressed by the probation system in Boston, Massachusetts - which he had seen for himself - but, rather curiously, his Bill did not advocate the creation of a class of probation officers in England. Instead, he envisaged police supervision of first offenders (Vincent was a former Director of Criminal Investigations at Scotland Yard); and after the Assistant Commissioner of the Metropolitan Police and members of the judiciary, supported by the Home Office, had challenged the appropriateness of the police assuming this responsibility, the offending proposal was dropped - but without any clearly defined alternative supervising authority or agency being officially designated - in order to get the Bill through Parliament. Thus the Act which introduced the term "probation" to the statute book of England signally failed to introduce any system of statutory supervision of first offenders in the community (or, indeed, to make any formal provision for pre-sentence enquiries).

However, the Probation of First Offenders Act did aim to encourage the reformation of first offenders by avoiding resorting to imprisonment, and by extending the use of recognizances. The Act enabled the courts to release "on probation of good conduct" any first offender convicted of larceny, false pretences or any other offence punishable with not more than two years' imprisonment, having regard "to the youth, character, and antecedents of the offender, to the trivial nature of the offence, and to any extenuating circumstances under which the offence was committed": such a course entailed the offender's release "on his entering into a recognizance, with or without sureties, and during such period as the court may direct, to appear and receive judgment when called upon, and in the meantime to keep the peace and be of good behaviour". (It has been estimated that by 1893 thousands of offenders were being released in this way.)

The Act continued: "The court, before directing the release of an offender under this Act, shall be satisfied that the offender or his surety has a fixed place of abode or regular occupation in the county or place for which the court acts, or in which the offender is likely to live." As many offenders likely to benefit under the Act were, according to Anthony Babington, "homeless vagrants", this requirement regarding a fixed address appears to have acted as a catalyst: the new Act facilitated the residential work of the St Giles' Christian Mission (as the Mission itself later acknowledged) and seems to have stimulated the provision of similar accommodation by the Church of England Temperance Society, which was no doubt anxious not only to retain but also to develop its links with the courts, particularly perhaps in London, where homelessness seemed a real problem.

At the time the Probation of First Offenders Act received the Royal Assent on 8 August 1887, the C.E.T.S. London police court missionaries -unlike the St Giles' Christian Mission - did not manage any hostels or homes for clients. Doubtless largely for this reason, a number of judges and magistrates committed boys at risk to the care of William Wheatley of the St Giles' Christian Mission; and some four years after the Act initiated by his friend Howard Vincent came into force, St Giles reported that "Mr Wheatley is daily called to the Sessions Houses or Police Courts by Judges or Magistrates on behalf of some boy who has been charged with a first offence". According to the social historian Kathleen Heasman, writing in 1962:

> His method was to visit the courts, select the more hopeful cases and suggest that they should be placed in his charge. The boys came for one or two years, and after a short period of trial were sent to jobs found specially for them. In the evenings classes or organised recreation were provided for them, and they had to pay part of their

wages for board and lodging. Few of the lads who passed through his homes committed fresh offences, and by the first decade of the twentieth century this had become the usual way of dealing with them. In this work he anticipated methods such as a congenial atmosphere with strict discipline, organised occupation for all free time, and training in an honest way of living, which were later incorporated by Sir Evelyn Ruggles-Brise in his Borstal system. His homes are also suggestive of the approved hostels of today to which lads on probation, who have unsatisfactory home surroundings, are sent.

Between 1888 and 1891 the St Giles' Christian Mission opened up to three homes for "lost women", rescuing hundreds of them during that time. In 1888 the Women's Union of the C.E.T.S. opened a shelter for women, as a means of supporting the police court rescue work in London.

In 1891 the Church of England Temperance Society established a home at Ealing for the reception of some of the male offenders employed in its nearby labour yard; it soon operated a similar home at Bethnal Green; and in 1896 the C.E.T.S. opened a boys' shelter home at Camberwell, where (to judge from a contemporary picture) a dozen or so lads could work simultaneously in its wood-chopping yard. These male-orientated facilities clearly seem to have been modelled on the labour homes for "honest men in distress", with wood-chopping as their principal activity, set up from 1889 onwards by the Church Army, which had affiliated in the summer of 1887 to the C.E.T.S. ("this sister Society", as the Church Army would call it). Of its own labour yards the Church of England Temperance Society would report:

> these Yards may truly be called "character factories", for in them, as the years go by, many a one who has fallen from the effects of drink, has found the Labour Yard and Home to be the first step on the up-grade of restoration to social position and integrity. Homes are attached to most of these Labour Yards, so that the chances of shielding the inmates from temptation are increased, and a permanent rescue is rendered more probable.[2]

In the late 1880s more than 75,000 people a year passed through the London police courts - more than the combined populations of Oxford and Cambridge in those days - and the rescue work undertaken may well have seemed like a drop in the ocean. But that at least some success was possible was acknowledged by the Lambeth magistrate Mr Chance, who declared: "Many drunkards have been reclaimed, some of whom had been given up as hopeless by others"; and at about this time the magistrates gave approval for the opening of a Temperance Refreshment Bar within the precincts of Lambeth Police Court. John Bridge and James Vaughan, magistrates at Bow Street, also expressed appreciation of the service provided by the police court missionaries; and at a meeting at the Mansion House on 18 October 1889, the Bishop of London, Dr Frederick Temple, pointed out:

> In many cases the Magistrates find that they are able to trust the Police Court Missionaries from the beginning, and, instead of sending the poor creatures to prison, they defer judgment, and let the Police Court Missionary try his best; and it happens again and again that, before judgment is passed, the unhappy prisoner has completely changed, and the Magistrate inflicts no punishment.

Apparently encouraged by such successes and declarations of approval and confidence, the Church of England Temperance Society decided to embark on a vigorous programme of expansion of its police court missionary work. In September 1889 its London Police Court Mission Secretary, the Rev. James Dennis Hird, wrote in his special report on its progress in the London Diocese, covering an area north of the Thames:

> During this year six Police Court Missionaries have been appointed, so that now we have Missionaries in seven of the Police Courts. There only remain two to be supplied, and we hope also to appoint Missionaries for the more important Petty Sessions in the Diocese. Many of these men have had considerable experience in Temperance work, and are prepared to address meetings of the various branches throughout the Diocese.

These men included some "District Superintendents"(perhaps embryonic seniors), with William Batchelor (Bow Street) among them; the list of seven also featured Thomas Holmes (Dalston) and William J. Fitzsimmons (Thames Street).

Dennis Hird added that the sole "mission woman" in the Diocese was "a mere drop in the ocean. As funds increase it is hoped that each Police Court Missionary may have the assistance of a Mission Woman to

21

take up her special part of this work." A year later, in 1890, the C.E.T.S. employed some 36 police court missionaries throughout the country; and Hird reported that the London Diocese now had two "mission women" and seven new male police court missionaries in post (making a total of 13 male missionaries, Batchelor having left in the interim), and had opened two wood-chopping yards. Much of the credit for this work in London seemed to be due to Hird, as a tribute to his apparent initiative and drive. Ironically, Hird had a crisis of faith, of a kind that beset many Victorians, and would be "cast out" of the Church of England in 1896 on account of his satirical book *A Christian with Two Wives*. But Hird (who was a graduate of Oxford University, where he had also been a tutor) had an undiminished belief in education and social progress which led him to write and lecture for the Rationalist Press Association, and to become Principal of Ruskin College, Oxford, and of the Central Labour College, London, speaking at the opening of the former and helping to found the latter College. Remaining conscious of men, in his own words, "cursed with the squalor of slums and starvation", Hird does not appear to have made any public attack on his erstwhile colleagues in the London Police Court Mission.[3]

Meanwhile, after the Probation of First Offenders Bill reached the statute book, some magistrates became increasingly accustomed to asking the police court missionary to exercise what was in fact voluntary supervision of offenders bound over for a specified period. As the London Police Court Mission reported:

> Many of these cases are visited in their homes - others at a distance are handed over to the parochial clergy, with the details of the circumstances. The aim is to offer sympathy at a time when sympathy is most needed - to try and find a pathway for those to whom life offers only despair.

When the home was unsuitable or non-existent, a person at risk could be placed in an institution.

Similarly, men - including ex-prisoners - without a trade or any regular employment could be referred to the labour yards which the C.E.T.S. set up to test "their willingness to strive to reform", and to act as a link with employers who might at some stage offer them jobs. In these labour yards, which operated with the blessing of the magistrates, the men engaged, under supervision, in firewood-chopping or other paid occupations which enabled a man to earn enough to keep body and soul together (this scheme could be considered a kind of forerunner of the supported work programme provided by Bulldog Manpower Services Ltd., which came into being in October 1975 under the auspices of the Inner London Probation and After-Care Service). During 1890 the C.E.T.S. opened two labour yards in the London area - the first at Ealing (on 6 January), the second in Chelsea. At the Ealing Wood Factory, workshops were constructed for the men referred from the various London police courts; and its success led not only to its enlargement, but also to the establishment of a yard at Lots Road, Chelsea, which received fifty men during its first three months of operation, though it was closed in 1891 - the year in which yards were opened in Croydon and further afield.

During 1891 the police court missionaries, between them, in the London Diocese (which covered the Greater London area north of the Thames) visited the homes of 5,387 people, wrote a total of 3,442 letters about their cases, made 2,165 visits to police courts and Sessions, and took 2,111 pledges, in addition to meeting prisoners on their release, placing persons at risk in homes, arranging for boys to be sent to sea, providing children with free dinners, and so forth. In one case, for example, the police court missionary lent a young butcher at Edmonton ten shillings to enable him to pay his forty shillings court fine (for stealing when drunk), avoid the taint of prison, and get married a fortnight later as originally planned. Within a week the missionary had received his ten shillings, together with a letter of thanks, followed a fortnight later by another letter from the couple, informing him that their teetotal wedding had taken place, and inviting him to visit the matrimonial home, which he subsequently did, to discover one of the happiest households in North London.

By 1892 George Nelson was working north of the Thames, at Marylebone Court, while William Batchelor was working in Northampton (where the atheist crusader - and former soldier - Charles Bradlaugh had been a legendary M.P. for years before his death in 1891). The extent to which Nelson and Batchelor saw each other after this date is not known. Not only had they been comrades in arms, brothers in Christ, and, indeed, pioneers in a common cause over many years; but also, according to a story given credence by Canon Ellison's daughter Dorothy and son John,

Batchelor had saved Nelson from throwing himself out of a barracks window - in an apparent suicide attempt through drink - during their soldiering days at Windsor.[4] If true, this incident may well have been instrumental in persuading either or both of them to take up police court missionary work, to rescue the fallen, and no doubt cemented the bonds of friendship between them. (Ada Demer, who joined the London Police Court Mission staff at about the time of Nelson's death, would independently recall hearing that he had been an alcoholic.)

1893 was quite a significant year in the development of the London Police Court Mission. The C.E.T.S. preventive and reformatory work in the courts in the London area was extended during the year, so that "now every Police Court, Sessional Court, Sessions and Criminal Court in London and Middlesex is provided with a Missionary". R.D.M. Littler, Q.C., Chairman of the Middlesex Sessions, was quoted as having said: "The London Police Court Mission does more to reduce crime than any device which has yet been found."

During the year a succession of drawing room meetings on behalf of the London Police Court Mission was addressed by the Rev. Dennis Hird (who seemed a skilful administrator), prominent police court missionaries such as George Nelson, Thomas Holmes and John Massey, and some metropolitan magistrates. A concert in Bycullah Athenaeum, Enfield, by the Chitty Orchestra raised a substantial sum for the Mission which was much needed, as John Massey, for example, was receiving a salary in the region of only £50 a year. In the course of 1893 Massey encountered failures interspersed with "splendid successes": he received and sheltered 13 girls in his own house, some ultimately being restored to friends of theirs in the country; and his other work included making arrangements for a young female defendant to get married to "a very respectable young man", resulting in the happily married couple frequently visiting the missionary and his wife. Massey also escorted from door to door one of the first lads to be sent by the London courts to the Mission's boys' shelter in Bethnal Green; and the lad made such encouraging progress that within two months Hird appointed him temporary foreman in the workshop. "As the years go on", Thomas Holmes recorded, "the work accumulates upon the Missionary. Poor wretched people cannot be taken in hand one week and cast off the next, so the burden increases." The missionary Peter Carradus was highly commended for his efforts at West London Police Court by a magistrate there, Henry Curtis Bennett, who maintained that out of the 10,000 people he had bound over, not more than a dozen had fallen back into crime, so far as was known. From Brentford Police Court, the missionary Robert Marshall reported that, to his knowledge, not a single case under his care during the year had reappeared before the bench. (For a photograph of the London Police Court Mission staff in 1893, see Appendix 2.)

On 4 December 1893, the C.E.T.S. London Police Court Mission opened its boys' shelter at 467 Bethnal Green Road, a double-fronted house equipped with workshops, roomy bedrooms, and a large enclosed yard where it was hoped to erect a gymnasium for the residents. The shelter was intended to help those boys who really needed and wanted to be helped and do better in life; and the scheme apparently had the full support of the magistrates. It was expected that, on average, some 20 boys (bound over by the courts) would be accommodated at the shelter for between three and six weeks each, after which they would be transferred to other homes, "placed in situations", or sent to work on farms or at sea. Mr John Dickinson, magistrate at Thames Police Court, declared at the opening ceremony: "It has been my idea that we ought to have between the dock where the boy stands and the home where we can send him, some kind of probation - a sort of test-house." Dickinson went on to infer that a boy's protestation of penitence could be tested by the police court missionary on behalf of the magistrate, who "has in the court the police court missionary - and all the magistrates are deeply indebted for the work they do in fighting this battle with crime, and the most valuable assistance they render every magistrate, and they are skilled judges of character". Within a very short time the shelter was full of lads handed over to the Mission.

Similar gratifying progress was discernible in police court rescue work south of the river. The Rochester Diocesan Branch of the Church of England Temperance Society had a total of seven police court missionaries: five for the whole of London south of the Thames, one for Rochester and Chatham, and one for Kingston, Richmond and district. The scale of their activities, gleaned from the C.E.T.S. Annual Reports for 1894-95, may be understood from the following summary in tabulated form:

	1894	1895
Total number of interviews with persons accused of drink-related offences	9,259	9,317

	1894	1895
cases visited at their own homes	6,868	6,303
visits to Courts and Sessions	2,040	2,003
handed over to Parochial Clergy	1,172	738
pledges taken	1,093	1,188
visits from cases to Missionaries	885	1,173
total number of persons placed in homes or restored to friends	496	440
(males	203	143)
(females	293	297)
cases attended to at magistrate's request	488	494
jobs provided	188	155
prisoners met on discharge	84	66
loss of employment averted through Police Court Mission	74	71
number of breakfasts to discharged prisoners	53	74

Having declared the previous year that the Rochester Branch's Police Court Mission work had been conducted "with vigour", the C.E.T.S. Annual Report for 1894 commended the Branch's missionaries for a job well done with very limited resources: "That the Missionaries are doing a much-needed work, and with very beneficial results, there is no doubt. . . . Even to maintain the present strength of the Mission, pecuniary help is greatly needed. Extension is necessary, but at present impossible for want of necessary funds." If expansion was not always a reality, it was at least an aspiration, no doubt reflecting a growing self-confidence on the part of the missionaries. By 1895 nearly all the police courts in the London Diocese were said to be served individually by a missionary from the London Police Court Mission, which also provided work, food and shelter for starving men, and kept families from the workhouse while the husbands were in prison. During this same year the Mission's two labour homes in the Diocese - at Ealing and Bethnal Green - had to be closed for sanitary reasons; and this situation probably prompted or reinforced the suggestion of police court missionaries to Evan Griffiths, Secretary of the C.E.T.S. Rochester Diocesan Branch, that it would greatly assist them if they had a home of their own in South London where young male offenders could be sheltered until other homes, institutions or work could be found for them. The missionaries had great difficulty in finding accommodation for boys who were homeless or charged with petty offences, or both, and whom the magistrates were unwilling to send to prison. Yet scores of such boys used to be remanded in prison until they could be reunited with their parents or suitable accommodation could be found for them.

After a number of rebuffs from unsympathetic property owners, Evan Griffiths found dilapidated old premises at 134 Camberwell Road, which had long been used as a boys' school. On a rented basis, these premises were opened by the C.E.T.S. on 20 February 1896, as a boys' shelter home. Within about a year, 83 boys over fourteen years of age had been admitted, and 59 boys under fourteen taken care of while on remand. It appears that quite a few such boys were first offenders in the eyes of the law, and that many were "street arabs" (of the kind mentioned by Dr Conan Doyle in a Sherlock Holmes story). During their stay at the home - where the Diocesan Secretary had his office - the boys were mainly occupied in sawing, chopping and bundling firewood. During 1897, the first complete calendar year in the home's life, 32 lads were found jobs, 26 left of their own accord, 22 had permanent homes found for them, 12 were restored to friends, 7 enlisted in the Army or Navy, 3 were expelled, 2 were sent to sea, and one was adopted.

It seems that police court missionaries often felt it was more difficult to find homes for boys than for girls. If so, this may have been largely because of a greater number of boys appearing before the courts, and partly because of a greater tendency by boys to form troublesome gangs or commit offences involving violence. Be that as it may, the London shelter home (1 Gratton Road, Kensington) for inebriate women apparently followed a practice of not admitting females known to be over 40 years old, dishonest or immoral. The referrals - including self-referrals - came from police courts, prison, employers, relatives, temperance workers, and organisations like the Church Army. It is not clear how far religious affiliation was a criterion of admission.

To help female alcoholics, the London Police Court Mission had obtained the services of six "mission women" by 1896 (whereas the Rochester Diocesan Branch - which, in London, covered Southwark, Lambeth, South Western, Greenwich and Woolwich Courts - apparently acquired its first temperance mission woman in 1897). In London, at least north of the Thames, the missionary interviewed at court women charged with drunkenness, who were visited at home and followed up by a mission woman. The mission women sent some inebriates to the Gratton Road home, several of whose ex-residents returned on Boxing Day 1897 for tea at the home and expressed their gratitude for the kindness and help they had received there.

But it was not always tea and sympathy, or sweetness and light. The lawyer Edmund Purcell remembered an incident from about this time in which a police court missionary - apparently George Hall from Bow Street - was beaten up to prevent a girl he was escorting from reaching such a home:

> A pretty girl, looking even younger than she really was, appeared before Sir John Bridge on a charge of street robbery.
>
> She had been charged once before, but was not recognized. I prevailed on the kind-hearted magistrate to give her an opportunity of leading a better life, and the experienced and respected missionary agreed to look after her. Directly she got a little way from the court two men set upon the missionary, assaulted him, and rescued the girl. Both men were well known, and soon I had to defend them. Unluckily it was Sir John Bridge before whom they came. I could do nothing, and they went to prison for two months. It was well deserved, for their violence to the benevolent missionary was quite gratuitous. If the girl was bent on her evil ways, as the sequel proved, she had only to walk away from the Home. Many years later I was taken to Bow Street to defend three women who had been repeatedly convicted, and were consequently charged under the Prevention of Crimes Act. One of them was this irreclaimable girl. The missionary was there, and reminded me of the chance she had thrown away.

She was sentenced to nine months.

The work of the police court missionaries with female clients was further extended as a result of the Summary Jurisdiction (Married Women) Act, 1895. This Act conferred wide jurisdiction in matrimonial disputes upon magistrates, and its scope and usefulness in helping to alleviate the distress of oppressed married women were succinctly described by the London missionary Thomas Holmes:

> As soon as this Act came into force our police courts became thronged with women applying for protection. Briefly, the Act provides that any woman having a persistently cruel husband may leave him, and, having left him, may then apply to the magistrate within whose jurisdiction she lives for a summons against her husband for separation and maintenance. These the magistrate is empowered to grant, provided the woman proves her case, that the cruelty has been persistent. An order being made upon the husband, he must pay or go to prison. A large number of women have been protected by this Act; men have learned the power of the Act. . .

Magistrates increasingly referred such matrimonial problems to the police court missionary, whom they asked to carry out any necessary enquiries and, more especially, to consider an attempt at domestic reconciliation by way of guidance and assistance to the court before a decision was made on a woman's application (documentary evidence and the testimony of probation officers interviewed for this study indicate that matrimonial work of this kind in the police or magistrates' courts was quite a significant function of police court missionaries and, later, of probation officers in London from about this time until at least 1965). Moreover, it was sometimes found expedient for the husband to hand over his maintenance payments for his wife to the court missionary, who was thereby encouraged to maintain contact with both parties and, indeed, mediate between them.

Thomas Holmes was quick to claim that the law, and through the law the state, gave no relief or redress to husbands "possessed of drunken wives . . . though their goods and clothes are pawned, though their children be neglected, and though their homes be turned into veritable hells". At least some of these women, he added, "were too much for me, and so far as I know I was powerless to influence them for good. I never could find out whether their peculiar mental condition was due to drink, or their drinking was due to their mental condition, and either way I was helpless."

The women's shelter home in Gratton Road received drunken women from the police courts free of charge, and others at 7 shillings per week. By the end of 1895 it was reported that out of the 165 women who had left the home since it opened, news had been received of 100, of whom 68 were doing well. By the end of 1898 some 260 or so "patients" had passed through the home since it opened, but the report from the home for that year suggested no cumulative figure for quantifiable successes in recent years. Indeed, it admitted "there are many discouragements", though the report for 1898 added in Biblical style: "there has been much in the past year to make us see that the bread cast upon the waters has been found after many days." In the London area north of the Thames, although many females were "induced" to sign the pledge at the police court before they came under the care of the "mission women", the latter were successful in many cases in persuading employers to reinstate persons discharged for drunkenness, and also through these ladies many neglected and deserted children were rescued and placed in schools or homes. The Rochester Branch declared: "There is a great need of several more Temperance Mission Women in the Diocese; the Committee would at once appoint more were the necessary funds forthcoming." By the following year (1899) the Rochester Diocesan Branch had appointed a second temperance mission woman.

The Inebriates Act of 1898 gave the courts power to detain habitual drunkards in an inebriate reformatory, as an alternative to repeated short-term prison sentences. Although the Home Secretary's interpretation of the Act led *The Reformer* to conclude that "in this case 'reformatory' is simply prison 'writ large'", a need for improved residential facilities for alcoholics seemed to be highlighted as a result of Canon Wilberforce's eloquent speech in London on 19 December 1898, in which he claimed that there had been an enormous increase in intemperance during the preceding thirty years, and that he knew one home for inebriates where three thousand women were refused admission the previous year because of its limited accommodation.[5] (The Gratton Road home admitted 26 females during 1898, the usual period of residence being between two and three months, with some "patients" moving on to "long homes".) In May 1899 the high-quality journal *The Contemporary Review* featured an article by Holmes which gave both a useful account of his London experience of difficulties in dealing with alcoholics, particularly female ones, and his evaluation of the repercussions of the Inebriates Act of 1898, which had been welcomed by the Howard Association (of which he was to become Secretary), although Holmes would be more critical of the Act, charging that "the really inebriate go uncared for".

Conscious of the homelessness, destitution and alcoholism well known to Britain's "submerged" population, the London Police Court Mission opened a boys' shelter home in Gunnersbury in June 1898. By the end of that year eleven lads were still in the home out of the total of 62 who had been admitted. Of the 51 who had passed through, unspecified numbers of those placed in work were believed to have appreciated their new start in life and to have given satisfaction to their employers. During their stay at the home, the boys engaged in basket-making, wood-chopping, and mat-making, as well as doing most of the housework. Discipline, religion and worthy leisure pursuits were seen as complementary components of the régime: discipline among the residents was maintained by severe reprimands where necessary, apparently backed up by the cane and, for more serious offences, the birch; and in July authority was given for the home to acquire 40 prayer and hymn books combined, a bagatelle board, draughts, dominoes, a cricket set and garden utensils. Although, according to Mark Monger[6] many years later, the shelter home was "unsuccessful", the staff were gratified that during Christmas week of 1898 they were visited by six "old boys", including one who walked from the City to Gunnersbury because he could not afford the railway fare.

It was not uncommon for police court missionaries to offer their own accommodation to vagrants and others in need. In his *Pictures and Problems from London Police Courts* (first edition, 1900), Thomas Holmes described a number of tragic alcoholics offered "the shelter and protection of my own house"; and he and his family did their best to care for others in the same way ("some of the most notorious women of London have formed part and parcel of my family circle"). In this stable home environment offenders of both sexes quite often seemed to make encouraging if sometimes unsustained progress, in terms of regular employment, abstinence, improved appearance and manners, etc.; and at such close quarters some close relationships were formed (when Holmes's only daughter died, a male recidivist who had been helped by the family attended her funeral and afterwards placed his offering of flowers, without card or name, among those on her grave; and when "poor demented Jane Cakebread", who had proposed to Holmes, died in Claybury Asylum, the missionary attended her funeral in Chingford

Mount Cemetery in December 1898). The London Police Court Mission Report for 1898 recorded how an unnamed missionary - quite probably Holmes himself - took a woman of 35, with a record of repeated prison sentences and at least one suicide attempt, who would otherwise have been on the streets, into his own house, where she stayed for seven months before becoming a valued servant in a good family.

At the same time the police court missionary was seen as an authority figure, viewed with suspicion by some - not so much, it seems, by waifs and strays as by parties directly involved in matrimonial discord. In one instance, Holmes provided material assistance and moral support for the pregnant "battered drudge" of a wife and the deformed child of a lazy, arrogant man, with a weakness for drink, who had been sent to prison for assaulting his spouse. On the man's release, Holmes continued to visit the home: "I could see that he suspected me, and looked at me with a cunning eye. I found afterwards that he thought I was watching him, and believed that I should give evidence against him in case he ill-used his wife again. I encouraged this belief, for it helped to protect the wife, and he kept to his work."

Holmes related how he had gone into many homes wrecked by the violence of alcoholic husbands and had seen the wives cowering in a corner, with little children creeping from their hiding-places to shelter behind the missionary:

> I have stood in front of these men, and have been horribly afraid for my own safety, for with a poker or hatchet in his hand, a man of this kind needs wary dealing. I know these men are mad, but I know that no doctor will certify them as such. . . . Temperance pledges and tracts are worse than useless, for who or what can minister to a mind diseased? Drink in their case is only a symptom of a deeper-seated trouble. Cruelty in their case is not a natural condition, but the outcome of their delusions.

Undoubtedly some of Holmes's ideas placed him in the forefront of contemporary opinion regarding the causes of crime and the treatment of criminals. He believed that, whilst serving to protect society and punish the criminal, prisons should be "hospitals or asylums for the study and cure of moral disease". The prison staff should be carefully selected and trained with the welfare of prisoners in mind. To destroy "the long-continued soul-and-mind-destroying monotony" of prisoners' lives, there should be: "Short sentences; abolition of ticket-of-leave; interesting work and more of it; less time alone, and more with the schoolmaster; gradual improvement in conditions as a reward for industry and good behaviour; some relaxation at intervals, such as lectures with magic lantern, concerts, etc." To enhance their chances of rehabilitation, prisoners should be discharged with decent clothing and with the experience of rewarding work. Holmes was highly critical of labour homes: "these places are as pitiless as commercial life itself, for no one over forty need apply." He referred to ex-prisoners working ten hours a day "for nothing" in labour homes (where wood-chopping was apparently undertaken largely because it was seen as a much-needed source of income[7] at a time when wood was commonly used for heating from fires).

He came to the conclusion that

> the great majority of boys and girls go wrong . . . because of the indifference, idleness, or worthlessness of their parents. I am persuaded that it is not the poverty of the parents, not the environments of the children, not the possession of criminal instincts, that lead the great bulk of boys to wrong, but the utter indifference and incapability of parents.

He later[8] maintained that the Probation of First Offenders Act "has undoubtedly kept thousands of young people from prison, for which everyone ought to be supremely thankful", but that the Act failed to enforce financial compensation for stolen property: "Hundreds of times I have tried to persuade young persons, who have been charged with dishonesty and dealt with as first offenders, of the duty and necessity of paying back the money dishonestly obtained, but I never succeeded. The law had done with them; nothing else mattered."

In his Victorian masterpiece Holmes wrote of "respectable" and "decently married" women charged with theft:

> Such offenders, if offenders they can be called, are considerately and even tenderly dealt with, and the First Offenders Act is invariably put in operation with regard to them. A knowledge not only of law and human nature, but also of physiology, is essential for the proper consideration of many cases that come before police court magistrates, and they often remand prisoners for a few days that medical opinion may be obtained.

Regarding the incidence of attempted suicide among women, he observed:

> Numbers of such women are rescued from it, and are charged with attempted suicide before our magistrates. . . . But, whatever the method or the mode, when the law has released its hold upon them, such poor creatures become a sacred charge upon the police court missionary. There is only one way of 'giving Christ' to these, and it means weeks or months of kindly sympathy and the consecration of brain and self. I do not for one moment wish it inferred that most of our female 'attempted suicides' are driven to it by their husbands' drunkenness or cruelty, for this is not so; but quite a number of them are, and a sufficient number to make them an important part of any police court missionary's work - at any rate, they have been an important part of my work.

Holmes used proceeds from the sale of his book to set up a home of rest at Walton-on-the-Naze, Essex, for worn-out London women "home workers". He sometimes went down to spend a week-end with these poor women, who had often tottered into his "little home at Walton" with their bodies frail and bent, their faces pale and wrinkled, and their pathetic bits and pieces wrapped in brown paper parcels, but who responded positively to its happy community atmosphere. This project for the care of "sweated drudges" - supported from within the Royal Family and also by a London women's "Farthing League" and donations from far-flung outposts of the British Empire - had been prompted by the plight of "a weary-faced, bloodless woman" who had stolen to feed her children and then attempted suicide. She was subsequently discharged by a kindly magistrate at North London Police Court who told Holmes, "Do what you can to help her".

The help given by the missionaries - including Holmes at North London - of the London Police Court Mission during 1900 (see Appendix 3) was summarised in the Mission's report for that year. This report also related, *inter alia*, the case of a chemist who took to drink after his wife's death and was thereby reduced to penury; but this resulted in his being placed by a missionary in a labour home, and he "has now finished his probation", having earned the commendation of his labour-master and regained the confidence of his relatives. Towards the end of 1901 the C.E.T.S. opened a home at 40 Filmer Road, Walham Green, for "the reception of cases which might be considered as being upon probation from the Courts, or who might be waiting to have situations found for them".

Meanwhile the Howard Association - for example, in its Annual Reports for 1896 and 1897 - had been pressing for the introduction in England of a probation system based on that in Massachusetts. The Association addressed a memorial to the Home Secretary, inviting him to take a number of measures in the fight against crime, including the establishment of special courts and probation officers (as in Massachusetts) for young delinquents. Soon afterwards a Youthful Offenders Bill, supported by various lords, was introduced at Westminster. It seemed to take some account of the principle of probation, but it was later dropped in the Commons on account of its controversial provision for birching delinquents rather than sending them to prison. The Howard Association concluded in 1900 that the Bill "would probably have done much to check the violent 'Hooliganism', so mischievous and even murderous, which has, subsequently to the lapse of the Bill, proved such a plague in East and South London, in particular". The C.E.T.S. Rochester Diocesan Branch believed in 1901 that its boys' shelter home at Camberwell provided a solution to "the problem of so-called 'Hooliganism' ".

In a modified form the Youthful Offenders Bill was finally enacted in 1901, having among its objects the checking of juvenile imprisonment. Although the new Act contained no provision for birching or for the committal of youthful offenders to the care of probation officers, its section 4 seemed to mark at least a step in the direction of probation (once again advocated by the Howard Association in its pamphlet *Probation Officers and the Gift of Guidance*, published in 1901). Section 4 of the Act stated:

> A court of summary jurisdiction, on remanding or committing for trial any child or young person, may, instead of committing him to prison, remand or commit him into the custody of any fit person named in the commitment who is willing to receive him (due regard being had, where practicable, to the religious persuasion of the child), to be detained in that custody for the period for which he has been remanded, or until he is thence delivered by due course of law, and the person so named shall detain the child or young person accordingly.

It seems strange that accounts of the evolution of the English probation service, written in English during or after the Second World War - including those by Timasheff (1941), the United Nations (1951), King (1964), Jarvis (1972) and Bochel (1976) - should have paid no attention to the Youthful Offenders Act, 1901, and its progress as a Bill through Parliament.

CHAPTER THREE

The Coming of the Act, 1902-8

The reclamation and rescue work continued apace, partly through the development of residential care. The London Police Court Mission had publicly acknowledged its gratitude for the co-operation and assistance of the many managers of "Homes and Institutions" who threw open their doors to receive promising cases from the missionaries. The Mission moved its Bethnal Green home for boys to Yiewsley, West Drayton, where, under the name of "Padcroft", it was opened in June 1902 by the Chief Metropolitan Magistrate, Sir Albert de Rutzen, who maintained: "There are other Homes, it is true, there is ample room for more, but the advantage of the Mission's own Home is that the missionaries are in constant touch with the boys, they know when they are sent out, and where, and are able to follow up each individual case as he struggles on in his new sphere of life." That Sir Albert's claim was overstated was indicated by the fact that of the 116 lads admitted to the new home during the last six months of 1902, 15 absconded, while 62 were placed in work and 2 returned to their parents' home, leaving 37 as longer-term residents. However, the metropolitan magistrates at about this time contributed at least £350 towards paying off a £1,000 debt on the boys' home; and the continuing interest of the bench would be illustrated by the annual inspections of Padcroft conducted by the Middlesex Justices of the Peace (two of whom would sit on the management committee) and by the metropolitan magistrates.

The Chief Metropolitan Magistrate also showered praise on the London police court missionaries themselves. Speaking at the Mission's Annual Meeting on 7 November 1902, Sir Albert de Rutzen declared:

> The reason I was asked to speak at this meeting probably was because I am the oldest magistrate on the metropolitan bench, having had 25 years' experience in the courts, which goes back to the time when there were no missionaries in the court. Having, therefore, been at the birth and watched the development of the mission, I unhesitatingly say, that a better thing was never started in this world, and a more noble work it is impossible to conceive. The missionary

attends each day at the court, is looked upon as the magistrate's friend, with whom he confers, as case after case arises demanding his attention. The work is admirably done, no trouble is too great for the missionary, no time demanded too long. No person is too old, no person too deeply steeped in crime, for the sympathy of the missionary to be withheld. No finer thing was ever started, and it has been productive of more good than any single thing I know of.

By the end of 1902 the position of the London Police Court missionaries was such that - in the Mission's own words -

> at the present day the Society has a Missionary and a Mission Woman attending each Police Court, Metropolitan and Petty Sessional, in the Diocese of London. There is also a Missionary working part of his time at the Central Criminal Court and the Middlesex Sessions. There are now no fewer than 13 Police Court Missionaries, who, by the kindness of the Magistrates, have a *locus standi* in all the Courts. These are assisted by 8 Mission Women and 2 Ladies, who work amongst the women charged there.

After noting that a majority of the 200,000 or so people passing every year through the London police courts did so as a result, direct or indirect, of abuse of drink, the London Police Court Mission's Annual Report for 1902 continued:

> The Missionaries are at the Courts for some time before the Magistrate takes his seat on the Bench, and during this time they make acquaintance, in the cells or in the prisoners' waiting room, with those that are about to be charged. Then, as each prisoner stands in the dock, the Missionary being in his place in the Court, the Magistrate will constantly ask what can be done for this or that case. At the suggestion of the Missionary many cases are put back till the afternoon, or remanded for a longer period for the purposes of investigation, and Magistrate and Missionary often consult together on the various cases. The Magistrates have constantly expressed their high appreciation of the work and the great help the Missionaries are to them every day. In every way, by subscription, by advocating the cause at meetings, and by personal kindness to the Missionaries, the Magistrates as a body have done all in their power to stamp the work with their approval. The Officials of the Courts and the police force generally have rendered the Missionaries every assistance in their power. The Magistrates attribute the unique success of our workers

to the fact that we send the right men to the right place, and just at the right time. The missionaries help all classes of persons, not those only who are charged with the abuse of intoxicating drinks, but any case that may be handed over to their charge by the Magistrate. They deal principally with first offenders, but they have, by the Grace of God, reclaimed many from the depths of sin and woe - one man, for instance, who had been charged over 500 times at various English Police Courts.

At Padcroft, the boys (many of whom had apparently been charged with offences like theft and vagrancy) were taught mat-making, boot-repairing, gardening, etc., with evening classes to improve their general education, church attendance on Sundays and Bible classes once a week, and the provision of indoor games, as well as football in winter and cricket in summer on the recreation field. The C.E.T.S. Annual Report for 1902 maintained: "The lads are kindly treated, shown that they are no outcasts, and have friends who consider their best and highest interests. When the time comes for leaving, occupation is found for them, and also an outfit; they are also commended to the clergy of the parish in which they work." Out of the 168 boys received at Padcroft in 1903, North London Police Court - where Thomas Holmes was the male missionary - sent ten, of whom none was believed to have reappeared in court.

By 1902 the freehold of the boys' shelter home at 134 Camberwell Road had been purchased by the C.E.T.S. Rochester Diocesan Branch, whose activities in Rochester, Chatham and Gravesend were, in effect, transferred in 1905 to the new, amalgamated Canterbury and Rochester Diocesan Branch, leaving its work in the South London area and in Kingston, Richmond, Wimbledon and Mortlake the responsibility of the emergent Southwark Diocesan Branch. In addition to providing a total of four male missionaries to cover Tower Bridge, Lambeth, Greenwich, Woolwich, and South Western (Battersea) Police Courts, the Southwark Diocesan Branch arranged for its missionaries to visit the Surrey and South London Sessions. In 1905 this emergent Branch also had three temperance mission women, whose individual geographical spheres of influence do not appear to have been publicly explained.

In October 1904 the London Police Court Mission suffered a severe blow when Padcroft was almost entirely destroyed by fire. The story - however embellished by time - was told that after the fire broke out, a boy was found to be trapped on the third floor, his means of escape cut off by the burning staircase, and that, without a moment's hesitation, Frank Green, the home's recently appointed manager, made a perilous climb up the stackpipe and ivy-covered walls to the roof, releasing the boy and bringing him safely to the ground. Frank Green had been a miner in Wales and had served in the Anglo-Boer War. While the burnt-out section of the home was being rebuilt, he was attached to one of the London truant schools. If Green appears to have had little directly relevant training for his work at the boys' home, he had a breadth of life-experience and qualities that were to stand him in good stead in his new role: courage, resourcefulness, and faith; a wealth of common sense allied to a sense of humour; and a belief in orderliness and discipline tempered by a ready sympathy. He would prove to be an outstanding superintendent whose selfless devotion would earn the trust and affection of countless Padcroft boys in his care. After some 45 years at Padcroft he would appear to have established a record as not only the longest serving social worker in the annals of the London Police Court Mission, but also the one in its history with the longest period of continuous employment at one centre.[1]

The freehold having apparently been secured by 1903, Padcroft would rise phoenix-like from the ashes, with the implementation of plans for a new and even more commodious house on the same site to provide short-term accommodation for up to 45 boys at a time between the ages of 14 and 18. The boast was that Padcroft was "a home in fact, as well as in name". The same could be said of the women's shelter home, which moved in 1903 from 1 Gratton Road to larger and better maintained, rented premises at 40 Filmer Road, Fulham, which had been a home for working girls under different auspices. The Church Army provided one assistant matron for the women's shelter home; and "our kind doctor", the ever faithful Dr Andrews, continued to come from Hammersmith to see his patients at the home. Of the 59 patients resident in 1904, 30 came from the police courts, 14 from C.E.T.S. workers apart from the courts, 11 from other temperance workers, 3 from their own relatives, and one from her employer - "4 of these had been with us before". The aspect of the work that the staff seemed inclined to find most encouraging was reconciliation between quite a few of the married patients and their respective husbands. As a result, grateful husbands, in their spare time, were often anxious to help the staff and do work for the house which would save much expense. Some former residents kept in touch with the home (and perhaps with one another) by correspondence; while at Christmas many returned to see the staff and brought presents for the home, with old and new residents and staff alike crowding into the brightly decorated rooms to play games and enjoy music performed by an "old friend" who was a first-rate pianist.

To judge from the London Police Court Mission's Annual Reports for 1904 and 1905, workhouse, infirmary, hospital and prison visiting was undertaken by its "mission women" rather than by its male missionaries, who none the less continued to place women and girls in homes, restore them to friends and find work for them. In 1904 these London missionaries handed over a total of 2,139 women inebriates to mission women (but in subsequent years this category was absent, for some reason, from the missionaries' published aggregated summaries of their work). Of the handful or so of mission women working for the London Police Court Mission in 1904, the most dynamic appeared to be Miss Jaggs, who covered Bow Street, Marlborough Street, and Marylebone Police Courts and Middlesex Sessions, and who made a total of 2,410 visits to clients, although she took only 3 pledges in all, thereby combining the highest recorded number of such visits with the lowest number of pledges taken during that year by any of the C.E.T.S. mission women working in the London area north of the Thames: Miss Jaggs was exceptionally active in all the other specified areas of work undertaken by these mission women (homes and jobs found for clients, letters written, police court visits, etc.).

"The Mission Woman, too, in common with her colleagues, has been most helpful, her services being marked by tact, persistence, and sympathy." Thus declared Thomas Holmes (who had worked at North London Police Court since 1895) some 18 months before he resigned in the summer of 1905 as a police court missionary. In this public expression of esteem for his female co-worker (Miss Robeson), as in other respects, Holmes was a rather remarkable missionary. The role of the mission women certainly seemed ancillary and secondary to that of the male missionaries. The London Police Court Mission's annual reports of this period regularly included case histories from the courts which highlighted the successful intervention of its male missionaries, but rarely that of its mission women. By the end of 1907 the untrained male missionaries received an annual salary of at least £100, rising to about £160 - which seemed to place them at least in the upper working-class income group - whereas the mission women were apparently paid not more than £60 a year for what seemed to be broadly comparable work. The fact that the Mission, closely associated with a male-dominated Church, called the men "missionaries" and their female colleagues "mission women", with the initials of their Christian names habitually published for the former and rarely for the latter, also suggests that the women had an inferior status, as in many spheres of social life.

Moreover, the mission women received scant attention in H.R.P. Gamon's *The London Police Court To-day and To-morrow* (1907), which yet was a book without which no history of the origins of the London Probation Service could truly be compiled. Hugh Gamon was a young Oxford graduate and student of law who was invited by the Trustees of Toynbee Hall, Whitechapel, to undertake a study of the London police courts. Resident at Toynbee Hall for about a year in 1904-5 in preparation for his work[2], Gamon visited various London police courts, concentrating, it seems, on the East End and Tower Bridge, and apparently accompanied the police court missionary on his rounds. His account had a pleasing style, though less intensity than Thomas Holmes's book (which it briefly mentioned), no doubt largely because it was not autobiographical, but was the work of a more detached and transient observer. As Gamon appears to have provided the only extended contemporary study by an outsider of the London police court missionary in the period immediately preceding the passing of the Probation of Offenders Bill, no apology is needed to focus on his book at some length.

Gamon examined the missionary's work, his position in court, his relationship with magistrates, "clients" and the police, and speculated about his future role, "the metamorphosis of the missionary". Noting that the C.E.T.S. police court missionary made "periodical reports" to the diocesan branch which employed him, Gamon remarked:

> He is not in orders, but he affects not infrequently a semi-clerical costume, and his wife, like the rector's wife, affords her husband gratuitous assistance, when some special need for a woman's help arises. He is liable to be called upon by his branch to be a propagandist, to aid in the general work of the society by delivering lectures and addresses on temperance and his special experiences, which form an inexhaustible fund of anecdote and terrible warnings.
>
> But his proper sphere is the police-court to which he is assigned,

and there he does the great body of his work.

After pointing out that while the missionary "has a special commission to work in the cause of temperance . . .he has also a general
commission of philanthropy and social enterprise", Gamon declared:

His aim is to obtain a grip upon prisoners passing through the
court's hands, and tó influence them permanently for good. He has
grand opportunities. Many who find themselves in a court for the
first time are in a peculiarly malleable frame of mind; ready to grasp
at any outstretched hand, grateful to any one who will bring them a
little comfort, penitent enough to listen to sober and sane advice. The
very incongruity of his presence and methods on that scene redoubles
their efficacy. He can do much to lift them out of the slough of
despond, and bring back confidence and hope; while he overcomes
their distrust by doing a hundred and one little services for them. His
good word with the magistrate is much solicited; for the magistrate,
in giving sentence, may allow himself to be influenced by the
representations of the missionary, and be lenient to one who has
promised faithfully to amend. Even old offenders may at last accept
the assistance constantly proffered, but always before rejected.

But the missionary will not put up with mere promises. He gets a
knowledge of men, their minds and their moods, in his work; he
expects response, and uses his discretion when he believes the
offender to be merely making overtures, that his sentence may be
lightened. He will not willingly put himself at the service of the
absolutely worthless.

The prisoners are not his only clients. The applicants, who have
come to see the magistrate, may find their way to him, and pour their
trials into his ear, taking comfort from such advice or promise of help
as he can give them; and sometimes he will explain their stories to the
magistrate for them.

Women ill-treated by their husbands, and husbands afflicted
with drunken wives are sure of his sympathy, and, where any good
can come of it, a visit to their homes. Often, when husband and wife
are separated by a police-court order, the missionary is installed as
the wife's chief confidant, and undertakes to receive and pay over to
her the weekly sums of maintenance money, payable by the husband.
It prevents the chance of friction between the separated pair, and may
ensure a more punctual payment; the husband will at least feel that

his derelictions are known in authoritative quarters.

The missionary is always to be found at the police-court by those who wish to consult him. He is accessible to all and a good listener. Not a few who go to the police-courts, never go inside the court at all; they have come to call upon the missionary during office hours, to acquaint him with fresh developments in their story, or to ask for further help, monetary or other.

Although the Charity Organisation Society had used the term "client" in a general social work sense at least as early as 1885, Gamon appears to have been one of the first British writers specifically to refer to the police court missionary's "clients". Moreover, the early London police court missionaries did not have offices at the courts - a sign of their apparent impermanence and lack of status - and their positive results may well have seemed the more remarkable in view of the almost complete absence of privacy or confidentiality with which they had to conduct many interviews at court. Gamon's detailed description of Tower Bridge Police Court - "one of the most recent of those at present in use" - did not mention any room at that court set aside for the use of the police court missionary; and according to Elspeth Gray's understanding, Marlborough Street was to become the first London court to have a room for police court missionaries incorporated in the architect's plan.

Whereas in later years home visiting would generally tend to take place in the afternoon or evening, this did not appear to be the case at the time of Gamon's investigation:

And before the court sits, perhaps as early as eight o'clock in the morning, the missionary will go his rounds, visiting the homes that one cause or another has made dependent upon him; here a separated woman or grass-widow struggling to get a livelihood for herself and her children, lodged in some dismal back garret; there, a street or two away, a man who has lost his job by going to prison and is now looking hard for work, or a family troubled with sickness and so poverty-stricken, that the children had had no boots to go to school in, and the attendance officer had intervened. The missionary pays surprise visits. At eight o'clock in the morning he can tell, whether his clients deserve help. If the good man is seen scurrying into the back yard, leaving the missus to say "Not at home," when he should have been up and away seeking work, or a woman comes half dressed, bearing all the marks of a slattern about her, to answer the knock on the door, the missionary will know that he can do no more. When slothfulness or despair has killed energy and self-respect, there is nothing left to which the missionary can appeal.

Thomas Holmes had indicated that he was "a constant and not unwelcome visitor" in thousands of homes as a result of his police court work. Likewise with no statutory powers at his disposal, Gamon's missionary presumably made appeals sincere enough, and had a personality attractive enough, to avoid or minimise any resentment by his clients and their families over his surprise home visits at eight o'clock in the morning. As Gamon explained:

> In the London courts, at least, he holds a semi-official position, which both widens his sphere of usefulness and clothes him with greater authority . . . his position in the courts is definitely recognised, and he has the privilege, accorded to no one else, of moving freely behind the scenes, and interviewing prisoners in the cells and waiting-rooms. In no other way could he find a means of talking with many of those who are charged at the courts.

Gamon added that the police court missionary's functions included those of "court almoner", advising the magistrates on disbursements from the police court poor-box ("replenished by voluntary subscriptions from City companies and private persons"), both in response to approaches from the magistrates and on his own initiative drawing attention to deserving cases. Such donations to clients were generally made "in kind" - in the form of boots and clothing for children, blankets, coal, groceries, etc. - as was the case with the Old Street Court Montagu Williams Fund, named after the Q.C. who in 1891 had praised the "great assistance" London magistrates received from the police court missionaries, who were "in touch with all the philanthropic institutions". Montagu Williams had then recorded that the missionary at Worship Street Court (John Massey), "who has permission to go into the prisoners' rooms and cells", had taken some 230 pledges within a period of about a year following his appointment to that court in January 1890, and had procured clothes, food, lodgings and work for many male offenders, including those sent to prison.

During 1903 the missionary and mission woman at Marylebone

Police Court provided 702 destitute families with food, clothing and coal. In 1904 Frederick W. Barnett, the missionary at Westminster Police Court, helped 474 persons with tools, stock, food, clothes, rent, etc., and William J. Fitzsimmons, the missionary at Thames Police Court - whose district had no public park - assisted in distributing over 2,000 toys and dolls, "as a means of brightening even a few children's lives". During 1905 the Bow Street missionary, George Hall, distributed eight tons of coal, 680 pounds of bread, one hundred pounds of meat, and large quantities of groceries "amongst poor cases recommended to the Court, the means being placed at his disposal by the Magistrates" (the recipients apparently included impoverished "immigrants from the Provinces").

Gamon commented generally on this kind of practice by the London missionaries:

> No few of the homes, that are thus kept together, are the homes of men, who have been sent to prison, and have left their wives and families without food or money. . . and if a man return from prison to find his home intact, he is more likely to settle down again to a steady life. It is curious to find the Law, in the person of the magistrate, thus toning down the blow that itself has inflicted.

Indeed, the police court missionaries clearly seem to have encouraged poor people to have faith in the criminal law system, when "mercy seasons justice" (as the Rev. H.H. Ayscough of the C.E.T.S. would maintain) or a combination of "hard" and "soft" methods of social control applied.

Moreover, Gamon believed that the police court missionary was in an excellent position to enable the magistrate to keep abreast of local developments:

> whether the magistrate wishes to obtain certain information in a particular case, that is before him, or to replenish his own stock of local information, he can, as a rule, apply to no one better fitted. The missionary has a wide knowledge of the seamy side, and is constantly visiting the homes of his patients in the neighbourhood of the court; nor are people inclined to be so reticent with him as with a policeman.

In this context:

> A magistrate may remand a man or a boy, or bind him over to

come up for judgment, when called upon; the missionary will call at the home to encourage and to restrain, to make the defaulter feel that there is a sword of Damocles hanging over him, and to reassure him that it will never fall, so long as he behave well; and by the missionary's reports the magistrate will know, whether his leniency was justified or not.

In some courts it is the practice to allow the missionary on occasion to go bail for the person thus bound over; in one of the courts the missionary told me that he was bail to the amount of £200 and over. In this way perhaps the missionary gets a greater hold upon the supervisee, who may feel some gratitude towards him and in a sense dependent upon him; and the magistrates find it otherwise so difficult to give the missionary a legitimate authority over one, who has shown himself incapable of protecting his own best interests. But it savours of farce. For should the man prove unfaithful to his bond, the missionary, who by its terms is surety for its due observance, would in no case be called upon to pay the forfeited money. The practice is hardly justifiable; it has a weakness of moral tone, that is of bad example. The law, which necessitates such a subterfuge, must be in need of alteration. It should be possible for a magistrate to put into proper hands a stronger control, directly and in due legal form.

When personal supervision is not feasible, and it has been decided to send some boy away to a home, it not infrequently falls to the missionary's lot to find the home for the magistrate, take care that the boy is decently clothed and equipped, and travel down with him into the country, to see that he reaches his destination safely; or if it is a girl, who is thus sent off, the same office will naturally be undertaken by the missionary's wife.

The legal historian and London stipendiary magistrate - later a judge - Anthony Babington declared in 1968 that the earliest police court missionaries were "all appointed on an unofficial basis"; whereas Gamon - a direct observer of police court missionaries at work, unlike Babington - repeatedly referred in 1907 to their "semi-official" position. When all due allowance is made for the growth and expansion in the scope of the work undertaken by the police court missionaries between 1876 and 1907, Anthony Babington's description may still need to be qualified to the extent that although C.E.T.S. missionaries had no role in court defined by law and no statutory powers, they were official in the sense that they were authorised representatives of the still powerful State Church, working in court on a regular basis with the public blessing and sanction of the magistrates.

Gamon went on to consider the police court missionary's relationship with the police:

> His work at court lies chiefly in the domains of the warrant officers and gaolers, and it is with them that he chiefly consorts. His salary and circumstances, perhaps his education, hardly make him the superior of a police-sergeant. On his first entrance in the police-court he was regarded with suspicion and distrust, as an intruder in police domains. He has now made himself a home in the court, and overcome much of the dislike; he may even have warm, sympathetic friends among the police, who gladly help him in his work, where they can; but he suffers from his anomalous position in the court. His uncertain rank, lacking its proper dignity, renders him liable to be disregarded, and by the majority of the force he and his office are little appreciated.

> He is even dependent on the police. The gaoler controls the cells and waiting-rooms; and if the gaoler be in a surly humour or out of temper, the missionary's morning behind the scenes may well be spent in vain. He may hear remarks and jests made by some of the police there, which he cannot rebuke, and which yet render his work more difficult. The scant respect paid to him is not calculated to raise him in the eyes of the prisoners. Perhaps an evilly disposed detective may even attempt to counteract his influence. No doubt he could appeal to the magistrate against the police; but only in very exceptional circumstances would he dare to do so. He is in a wholly subordinate position, as they are, perhaps ignored even by the clerks . . . .

> The missionary is wise enough to prevent such collisions by avoiding all interference with the police. Again, it may be questioned, whether his dependent position and association with the police do not damage him. He runs the risk of imbibing police notions and prejudices, of losing sight to some extent of his ideals, and taking an almost cynical view of human nature. He is content with his position, and regards himself as the butt end and not only the thin end of the wedge; he does not see the latent potentialities of his office. Nor is the close juxtaposition of police and police-court friend likely to redound to the latter's public credit. Those, who distrust the police, would naturally incline to distrust him; they, who distrust the police most,

can least discriminate.

It is certainly true that heavy dependence on "good terms" with the gaoler would be a *sine qua non* in London police courts until at least the Second World War (as would be illustrated by the inimitable Sewell Stokes, assigned to a court which had virtually the longest association of any with police court missionaries: Bow Street). But it is not clear from Gamon's account how far any disparaging remarks or public display of scant respect by the police towards the missionaries could be reconciled with the risk of the latter "imbibing police notions and prejudices". In its Annual Report for 1893, the London Police Court Mission had attributed to Sir Edward Bradford, Chief Commissioner of Police, New Scotland Yard, the view that "he sympathizes very sincerely with the work of the Mission, as he believes it to be a really valuable one"; and his Assistant Commissioner of Police, Dr Robert Anderson, head of the C.I.D., New Scotland Yard, was quoted as saying:

> There is a constant tendency in the weak and erring to go wrong; they need a helping hand to enable them to go right, and in the work of the London Police Court Mission we find that encouragement. The police are absolutely dependent on efforts of this kind. . . . when a Society like the London Police Court Mission steps in and gives a guarantee of help, and advice, care and watchfulness, then it becomes safe and it becomes a pleasure for those who have to deal with crime in its punishment, to stand aside and allow the exercise of this help by the Mission.

Bradford and Anderson may well have been expressing personal views rather than official policy; and, of course, pronouncements by top officials were not necessarily reflected in practice or attitudes at grassroots level, particularly perhaps after the passage of years. While Gamon's comments on relations with the police no doubt reflected his perception of the current situation at the London courts with which he was most familiar, they did not appear to be equally applicable to all police courts in the metropolis. The Bow Street missionary, George Hall, recorded the case of a young man who in 1903, on his release from a long term of penal servitude,

> as a result of a promise made came back to the Missionary, whose efforts to obtain work for him were nobly seconded by a police-officer. This work was persevered in till his health failed, and he sank to the lowest depths of poverty, though without a return to

his old crimes. Infected by his tenacity, the Missionary again took him up, and he is now learning a trade, though at low wages.

George Nelson, the very first police court missionary, seems to have had a particularly fruitful relationship with the police, as reflected, for example, in his efforts at Marlborough Street to rescue girls from a life of vice and degradation. Of his activities in 1903, it was recorded: "Work which seems strictly to lie outside the province of a missionary is sometimes undertaken by him, thus 21 girls were sent to Marlborough Street Police Court by police officers and others. These girls tired of their life of shame were placed in Institutions or sent to their parents." Two years later, Nelson and colleagues attached to Marlborough Street Court "issued invitation tickets (with which police officers are supplied) to those anxious to give up a life of sin": this produced 41 women and girls who got in touch with the Mission, and he reported "with joy on the happy results achieved". In 1907 a London police court missionary apparently advised on employment for a destitute young married man who had attempted suicide, but was snatched from the Thames by "that splendid brigade, the River Police"; and in that same year Nelson's work was enriched by the fact that, as he noted, "thirty-four women and girls from Hyde Park came voluntarily and sought the Missionary's or the Mission Woman's help to start a better life. The Police co-operated in these cases. One was emigrated to Canada."

Also in 1907, Gamon declared that the London police court missionaries' semi-official status "placed them awkwardly", and he added:

> Perhaps, if the missionary had been a man of culture and social standing, he would have risen unharmed above the difficulties that beset his position. The magistrates would have extended to him a more cordial welcome and freer companionship, and the police would have been obliged to recognise him as a superior. But the missionary is, at his best, a self-educated man with no pretensions to a high rank in the social scale. Temperance is the primary object of his society; and the society chooses its instruments in conformity with its ideas. But a police-court missionary of the highest type must possess qualities, that a temperance advocate can afford to lack. What wonder then, that sometimes the police-court missionary is well-intentioned but narrow-minded, zealous but inclined to preach, and apt to derive a sense of self-importance from the condescending

friendship of magistrates and the deference of the humble people, with whom he has to deal. As agents of a denominational society they are tarred with the sectarian brush. They do not confine their attention to members of the Church of England; though, as a courtesy title, it covers the majority of their patients.

In commenting on Gamon's book, his contemporary, C.H. Denyer, a highly experienced London police court clerk, admitted that the police court missionary "is not always well educated", but suggested that "even if he were a University man he might easily be out of touch with his patients". Denyer thought "that the Missionary's position is anomalous; that he has only with difficulty achieved his present status; that he still exists on sufferance". But he also claimed that "many of the magistrates think with me that were he an official he would lose much of his influence" (Gamon had declared that the missionary "must have the dignity as well as the duties of a public servant" and "must be in the courts of his own right as a state friend"). Denyer acknowledged that the police court missionary "represents a religious body". But, he added, "his religion gives him unselfishness and a spiritual power which we, who represent the secular arm, would do wrong to despise", and "were he not an earnest Christian man his work would sink to a lower routine level". All in all, Denyer's assessment of the police court missionary was a favourable one: "he is a surprising success. His duties compel the exercise of tact . . . His work is most important. If well done, it would be cheap at three times his present salary."[3] Although any notion that only representatives of the Church of England - or, indeed, of any denomination or religion - should be able to practise social work in the criminal courts would be discarded, Denyer, stimulated by Gamon, at least raised some issues that would concern observers of the London police court scene for a long time.

Anthony Babington maintained: "The Metropolitan magistrates might have reacted with a curt refusal to accept the uninvited help of the Temperance Society's agent." It may be added, however, that the Church of England had long been the established Church, that outward respect in England for Anglicanism and its institutions was almost certainly more widespread during the closing decades of the nineteenth century than it would be a century later, and that even the most "case-hardened" (to use Thomas Holmes's term) magistrate would have been aware of personal and social problems daily manifest in court, and may soon have seen the missionary as a kind of support figure, adviser or mediator in the disposal of cases.

The early police court missionaries, apparently regarding remuneration as secondary, were enthusiasts - no strangers to the spirit of "muscular Christianity" - sustained by their religious faith and strong sense of vocation, with the pledge card as their principal tool and a ready recourse to prayer and the Bible (soon after Elspeth Gray became a London police court missionary in 1925, she heard of a female colleague at Thames Court who used to take her Bible into the court cells; and as late as about 1963 Gunter Lubowski was told about a South London senior probation officer - originally a police court missionary - who conducted prayer meetings with his staff at the start of each working day).[4] As George Newton, an able Assistant Principal Probation Officer in London, would explain:

> These founder fathers were missionaries in the true sense of the word and they used the methods of missionaries - changing behaviour by changing feeling - through 'conversion'. Their methods were persuasion, exhortation and support. They strengthened weak resolution by administering solemn pledges to renounce drink; they gently admonished the sinner while at the same time they offered him the helping hand of friendship; they advised him for his own good; they assisted him in many ways to improve his social and economic condition; and finally they prayed for guidance for him and for themselves. These men believed in the supreme importance of the individual to God and the parables of the lost sheep and the prodigal son were their casework manuals.[5]

In 1907 Gamon looked forward to the day when, in the work of the Police Court Mission, "religion is no longer invoked to sanctify it, but simply that common spirit of humanity, which needs no commending". Of the missionary, or "police-court friend" (as he preferred to call him), he thought that, in addition to a "sunny smile and warm heart, overflowing with the milk of human kindness", he needed certain essential qualities:

> He must have the breadth to sympathise with frailty, but he must also have the firmness, that can alone be of real help. He must be able to see the picture from his patient's standpoint, but with other

eyes; he must find hope in the gloomiest outlook. He must exhort without cant, and disarm his candour by his earnest goodwill. He must be respected no less than liked. The missionary wants all the attributes of a true friend. In no few cases the missionary has taken a patient, perhaps a woman given to drink, into his own home and sheltered her among his own family. Such actions of self-denial are more eloquent than words.

Thomas Holmes, for example, had admitted quite a few disturbed clients to his own home, where, on one occasion, he felt compelled to seize an aggressive, unsettled woman by the throat and shake her vigorously, and where, in another case, he locked a violent male dipsomaniac in his room, in which Holmes himself was later imprisoned by this same man, who threatened to kill him. On the other hand, when a wild and bitter woman appreciatively said to Holmes, "You must be the missionary from North London", he thought those words the greatest compliment ever paid him.

Playfair and Sington (1965) maintained, without supporting documentation, that the police court missionaries of this period "dealt exclusively with relatively minor offences".[6] Even if many of the offences were "relatively minor" in the eyes of the law, it would not follow that the same was true of many of the problems experienced or perceived by the offenders (annual reports indicated that attempted suicide cases, for instance, were quite a regular feature of the work of London police court missionaries, and Montagu Williams in 1891 had suggested that the London police court missionary could play an important part in rehabilitation in such cases). The metropolitan magistrate Frank Milton declared in 1959 that "the missionaries were warm-hearted and generous-minded men and women, who often did excellent work although without any technical qualifications". The London probation officer Marjory Todd also wrote (1963) of the early untrained police court missionaries: "Few theories about crime or criminals could have come their way." She was almost certainly right: neither Holmes's book nor Gamon's mentioned any such theories encountered by the missionaries; and by 1907 - in Lombroso's lifetime - Dr Charles Goring had largely completed his massive statistical survey *The English Convict* without any reference, it seems clear, to the police court missionaries, who worked with criminals before and after, if not during, their prison sentences.

Meanwhile the Home Office had been studying aspects of probation in the United States and New Zealand fairly intensively since about 1903. In 1905 the metropolitan magistrate Frederick Mead told the London Police Court Mission: "The Missionaries are very efficient probation officers for the juvenile offender, and being free from official suspicion are warmly welcomed in the homes of the poor." Mead - who had been a magistrate since 1889 - would be regarded by Frank Milton as "founding father of the probation service . . . who put into effect something very like the future system long before it received official recognition". Moreover, in the Howard Association's Annual Report dated October 1905 its Committee (whose membership included Thomas Holmes) earnestly expressed "hope that it will not be long before a beginning is made with Probation in this country". On 21 March 1906, Holmes, in his new role as the Secretary of the Howard Association, met the new Liberal Home Secretary, Herbert Gladstone, in an interview at the Home Office; and according to the contemporary Home Office record of their meeting, Holmes told Gladstone that he

> has practically acted as probation officer for 20 years. He had supervised and made reports on very many persons released under the First Offenders Act but a police court missionary's duties are heavy and he cannot give time enough to the work. He advocated a change of the law to empower payment of salaries to probation officers.

Holmes proposed to Gladstone that a first offender should be placed under a probation officer, so as to "establish a system whereby he should be fully discharged on the probation officer's recommendation".[7] The Home Office record was not clear concerning the extent to which Holmes believed that probation officers could or should be drawn from the police court missionaries, in the light of such factors as numbers of staff and assessment of duties.

The Chief Metropolitan Magistrate, Sir Albert de Rutzen, wrote to the Home Office on 9 January 1906:

> I am of opinion that the appointment to each Metropolitan Police Court of a Probation Officer, properly so called, and with statutory powers to enable him to carry out his duties, would be of great service to the State and would in the end lead to a diminution of crime . . . the Police Court Missionaries who are no doubt of very

great use in many Courts to which they are attached, have done so to the best of their power, but they have neither the time, the opportunity nor the necessary powers for doing the work which would and ought to be done by an efficient Probation Officer.[8]

He seemed to favour the idea that probation officers should be selected from those who had served with the police force, whereas Edward Richard Henry, Commissioner of the Metropolitan Police, apparently thought that the most suitable probation officers would be "men and women of higher class, such as now give their services gratuitously to the Charity Organisation Society". On the other hand, strong support for the appointment of police court missionaries as paid probation officers came from the metropolitan magistrate Henry Curtis Bennett, who made great use of the missionaries, and whose wife would serve for over thirty years (from 1908 onwards) as a patroness of the Police Court Mission Needlework Guild, founded in 1895 to raise funds.

On 7 May 1906, a C.E.T.S. deputation to the Home Office offered to co-operate, if possible, with whatever arrangements the new Liberal Government envisaged for the introduction of probation officers; and it claimed that, funded largely from church collections, its Police Court Mission had functioned for years without any sectarian bias. In his soothing and blandly reassuring reply, the Under-Secretary, Herbert Samuel, thanked the Society for offering to place its police court missionaries at the service of the Government and added his appreciation of their valuable work; but he made no specific promise or commitment regarding the Society.

Having resolved at the end of May "That officers may be offered to the Government as 'probation officers' trusting to grants for remuneration", the Church Army sent a deputation in July to meet the Home Secretary, who was flanked not only by Samuel, but also by the Chairman of the Prison Commission, Sir Evelyn Ruggles-Brise, who had already reported to the Home Office on the "invaluable service" to magistrates provided by an agency like the C.E.T.S. In the context of a projected probation system, the Church Army offered, in the words of the *Church Times*, "the free services of twelve experienced officers to inaugurate the system. ... The undoubted difficulty of providing suitable probation officers could be got over by employing trained Church Army officers, who would have at their backs the whole Church Army organization, including the labour homes, etc." In the deputation's discussion with the Home Secretary and his colleagues, the advantages of a probation system were described as including individualised treatment, avoidance of the stigma of prison and of the sufferings of the innocent, preservation of homes and of an offender's employment, development of self-respect, and substantial saving of public money vis-à-vis the cost of imprisonment. Samuel said he hoped the matter could be dealt with by legislation "during the present session". The Church Army shortly afterwards advertised a "Probation Department", whose aim was "to prevent the imprisonment of early offenders, our representatives acting as outside guardian-warders for persons committed by Magistrates or Judges".[9]

By 1907 the Church of England Temperance Society had a total of 124 male missionaries and 19 mission women. Of these, 17 missionaries and 10 mission women were employed by the London Police Court Mission, and 7 missionaries (excluding the superintendent of the Camberwell Road boys' shelter home) and 2 mission women were employed by the Southwark Diocesan Branch. Their court work was supplemented by a few agents from some other religious bodies. Gamon commented:

> There are men who would gladly join in social work, but the need of a livelihood presses upon them. The Church, it is true, offers them the opportunities of social service that they covet, but there are dogmas, to which they cannot honestly subscribe, and a narrowness and deadness that repel them. Some subscribe to tenets that they doubt, in order that they may be hired to do the work in which they do believe; while many others, shrinking from such a step, find some outlet for their enthusiasm in boys' clubs and lads' brigades.

Gamon declared that "in London the British Women's Temperance Society also has women missionaries at some of the courts; this society is undenominational and works peculiarly for the reclamation of women and children." He also mentioned N.S.P.C.C. officials, "dressed in what at a glance looks like the uniform of a police inspector". He suggested that police officers were not suitable to be appointed as probation officers, and that there should be special courts for children, served, in London, by London County Council representatives who "must be better educated than the missionary", and of the calibre of "such men as the secretaries of the Charity Organisation Society": as Gamon believed that "the care of a probation officer lies primarily with children", his views in this context were in some respects, no doubt coincidentally, distinctly similar to those, already noted, of Commissioner Henry of the Metropolitan Police.

Just as some groups seemed to be vying for support in their bid to provide probation officers, so there seems to have been some kind of competition between the Government machine and Howard Vincent (now knighted) concerning legislation on probation and related matters. In 1905 he introduced a Bill in the House of Commons to empower magistrates to exclude the public from trials of defendants under sixteen. He supported a more far-reaching Bill presented by John Tennant, who proposed the establishment of separate courts for children with the power to order supervision by "an official of the court, the court missionary or some society willing to undertake the work". In late June 1906, only days after Tennant's Bill had been withdrawn, Vincent brought before Parliament a Bill to permit police authorities to appoint probation officers. None of these three Bills was carried into law - and Vincent himself would soon be dead - but they at least helped to prepare opinion in Parliament, and exert some kind of pressure on a reform-minded Government, for the introduction of a probation system.

In December 1906 the Home Secretary, Herbert Gladstone, presented the Liberal Government's first Probation of Offenders Bill. After one or two hitches, the second reading in the Commons of a revised version of the Bill took place on 8 May 1907, when out of the ten M.P.s who spoke, only three referred to the police court missionaries. George Cave, M.P. for Kingston, Surrey - a future Solicitor-General, Home Secretary and Lord Chancellor - said that he knew of "very many cases where the assistance of the Police Court Missionaries had been the saving of prisoners released under the First Offenders Act", and he asked for an assurance that there would be no objection to the appointment of such missionaries as probation officers. Welcoming the Bill, the Bethnal Green M.P. Edward Hare Pickersgill (who would be appointed a metropolitan police magistrate in 1911) declared that "the principle of the Bill had been already to some extent carried out, because the Court missionaries had largely performed the duties which it was the object of the Bill to regularise". A third M.P. revealed that he had no particular objection to the Bill "if it was merely a benevolent measure to provide and pay somebody like the Court missionary, with no legal powers, to look after the offender".[10]

During the Commons debate on the third reading, on 26 July 1907, when various amendments were agreed to, only six M.P.s, including the Home Secretary, spoke - and of these, three had spoken in the second reading debate. On 8 May, Samuel had maintained that the Bill was "of a non-controversial character"; on 26 July, Herbert Gladstone, seeking to fend off an amendment (which was finally withdrawn) that police officers could not be appointed as children's probation officers, declared: "This Bill was an experiment. They wanted to feel their way . . ." During the third reading debate the Member for Cambridge University mentioned "the work which was so well done at the present time by the police court missionaries". But in neither the second nor the third reading debate did any M.P. claim to speak on behalf of the Church of England Temperance Society, which does not appear to have supported any legislative proposal by Howard Vincent or the Howard Association, for example, as a possible means of strengthening the position of the missionaries in the police courts.[11]

Although the Bill attracted little discussion in either House, its passage through Parliament was not entirely without protest outside. On 6 July the Parliamentary Committee of Middlesex Quarter Sessions passed a resolution that the Bill was unnecessary

> so far as the County of Middlesex is concerned, in view of the fact that the Court makes ample use of the First Offenders Act, both for young and old, in binding prisoners over to come up for judgment, and that the Court is well served by voluntary officers and Missionaries, who carry out the wishes of the Court, and that it is not necessary to saddle the county with the expense of paying the Probation Officer.

The Act, which applied to the whole of the United Kingdom (including Ireland), received the Royal Assent on 21 August 1907 and came into operation on 1 January 1908. It repealed the whole of the Probation of First Offenders Act, 1887 - to which the Middlesex resolution referred - and parts of the Summary Jurisdiction Act, 1879, and Youthful Offenders Act, 1901.

The new Act would be summed up nearly thirty years later in a Home Office report (Cmd. 5122): "Supervision was given statutory effect. Probation was distinguished from binding-over, and Courts were enabled to appoint paid probation officers, who might be the agents of voluntary societies." The Act was also significant in that its application was not confined to first offenders.

The most relevant aspects of its ten sections may be briefly summarised and assessed. *Section 1* enabled the courts to release any offender (including a child) "on probation", "having regard to the character, antecedents, age, health, or mental condition of the person charged, or to the trivial nature of the offence, or to the extenuating circumstances under which the offence was committed". This would be "without proceeding to conviction" in the case of a court of summary jurisdiction, and "in lieu of imposing a sentence of imprisonment" in the case of a higher court. Courts were also empowered to order probationers to pay costs, damages for injury or compensation for loss. (In a typed letter of 8 April 1908 to the penologist William Tallack, Holmes welcomed Herbert Gladstone's assurance in Parliament that under the Act a compensation order for loss could include restitution of stolen money: "I think I may say that this is entirely due to the efforts of the Howard Association," declared Holmes, who had got Percy Alden, his progressive local M.P. (for Tottenham), to ask Gladstone about this. In Gladstone's view, it would be "undesirable" in any way to encourage the offender to regard the probation officer as a debt-collector rather than as a friend or adviser.[12])

Section 2 introduced "a probation order" to ensure supervision of the offender by "such person as may be named in the order". It also permitted conditions "prohibiting the offender from associating with thieves and other undesirable persons, or from frequenting undesirable places", to encourage abstention from intoxicating liquor, and/or "generally for securing that the offender should lead an honest and industrious life". The court making the probation order had to furnish the offender with "a notice in writing stating in simple terms the conditions he is required to observe". (It was not stated that the offender had to consent to being placed on probation. Nor was any minimum period of probation specified, though section 1 had indicated that the maximum was three years. Although the Home Secretary in a memorandum anticipated "that the ordinary term of probation will be six months, and that orders for more than a year will be rare and exceptional", the practice in London in 1908, for example, was rather different. In that initial year of operation, the Central Criminal Court and the North and South London Sessions, between them, placed a total of 386 people on probation for over six months but not more than one year, and put two people on probation for over three months but not more than six. In the same period, the metropolitan police courts placed a total of 492 persons on probation for over six months but not more than one year, and put a total of 185 on probation for over three months but not more than six. Also in 1908 the metropolitan police courts placed a total of 58 people on probation for more than a year, though the already mentioned higher courts in London did not make any probation orders at all in this last category during 1908.)

Section 3 introduced "probation officers", who could be of either sex and would be appointed for a petty sessional division. Once appointed, a probation officer would be "subject to the control of petty sessional courts for the division for which he is so appointed". To supervise offenders under sixteen, "there shall be appointed, where circumstances permit, special probation officers, to be called children's probation officers". Probation officers could be paid a salary or some other form of remuneration - as well as "out-of-pocket expenses" - to be determined by the authority controlling the fund from which the salary of the justices' clerk was paid. (The concept and appointment of "special" children's probation officers - followed by the establishment of separate juvenile courts under the Children Act, which received the Royal Assent on 21 December 1908, and which consolidated the role of probation officers in the supervision of children and young persons - marked the beginnings of a long-standing separation between juvenile court and adult court probation officers that, in London, persisted until the end of the period covered by this study.[13] Hugh Gamon's book was published before the Probation of Offenders Bill received its second reading; but in an article published in August 1908 he indicated that the creation of "special probation officers" was "regrettable" and "incongruous with the general breadth of the Act". Gamon also pointed out - as would the London police court clerk Albert Lieck thirty years later - that under the Act the supervisor named in a probation order did not have to be a formally appointed probation officer at all. In retrospect this may be seen as an acknowledgement of the probation officer's lack of professional status, and also of the range of voluntary workers willing to assist in the courts: in his memorandum on the Act, the Home Secretary suggested that "much valuable assistance in carrying out the Act will be given in London by volunteers". No age restriction for probation officers was prescribed.)

Section 4 specified a probation officer's duties and, in so doing, introduced the now famous phrase, "advise, assist, and befriend". These duties included: "to visit or receive reports from the person under supervision . . . to report to the court as to his behaviour . . . to advise, assist, and befriend him, and, when necessary, to endeavour to find him suitable employment." (There was no legal requirement for a probation officer, before any probation order was made, to conduct any background enquiries - a deficiency that would be remedied by the Probation Rules issued in 1926.)

Section 5 enabled the appropriate court to vary the conditions of an offender's probation "upon the application of the probation officer", and also to discharge the order if the offender's conduct no longer warranted supervision. *Section 6* made provision for the court to convict and sentence an offender for the original offence in the case of a breach. *Section 7* empowered the Home Secretary to make rules relating to the implementation of the Act. (The first such Probation Rules, issued by the Home Office to coincide with the Act's coming into operation, required probation officers, *inter alia*, to visit schools attended by their probationers, to supply the clerk of the court with statistics of their work, and not to wear uniforms or use courts or police stations as reporting centres. Some difficulty associated with this last condition was perceived by the metropolitan police magistrates at their quarterly meeting on 2 January 1908, and their feelings were conveyed by Sir Albert de Rutzen, who pointed out to the Home Office that "in many cases the offender either has no home at all, or lives in a common lodging house - which would probably not be considered a suitable place for the probation officer to visit him".[14])

Under the Probation Rules, probation officers would be appointed, or reappointed, on an annual basis by the justices, except in the metropolitan area, where they would be appointed by the Home Secretary. A Home Office committee - set up to advise the Home Secretary on implementation of the Act - proposed that the metropolitan magistrates should be provided with a list of diverse probation officers, appointed to their courts, from whom they could select those thought most suitable for particular cases. In its report of 18 November 1907, this committee declared that the C.E.T.S. police court missionaries were

> well suited to be Probation Officers: they are in constant attendance at the courts, have had much experience, and are in touch with other philanthropic societies, with whom they work harmoniously. They communicate with Nonconformist or Roman Catholic Agencies when the case of a Nonconformist or Roman Catholic prisoner is brought to their notice. The Church of England Temperance Society are willing that, for the present at any rate, the services of the Missionaries should be given without payment.

The Under-Secretary of State, Herbert Samuel, and his colleagues on the committee (including Edward Troup, a future Chairman of the London Police Court Mission Committee) recommended that the C.E.T.S. police court missionaries should be appointed probation officers for adults (defined as persons over the age of 16); and, in London at least, this was done.

Some other distinctly religious organisations also offered the services of their agents as probation officers, as did the Reformatory and Refuge Union and the National British Women's Temperance Association; and their offers were accepted. Initially the Home Secretary appointed about half a dozen probation officers to each metropolitan police court, with many of these officers covering more than one court. According to a printed Home Office list (stamped 4 March 1908) of London probation officers, every metropolitan police court was served by one representative of the Westminster Diocesan Education Fund (for Roman Catholics). In addition, there were male C.E.T.S. police court missionaries at 13 London police courts (i.e. excluding Old Street, where John Massey had broken away from the Church of England Temperance Society to act as an independent missionary employed by the court). There were C.E.T.S. mission women at 11 or so police courts (i.e. excluding Old Street, where John Massey's wife acted as an independent missionary, South-Western and also Woolwich). There were Reformatory and Refuge Union representatives at 13 police courts (i.e. excluding Westminster). There were Salvation Army representatives at 12 courts (i.e. excluding Greenwich and Woolwich). There were Church Army representatives at 6 courts (with some 17 other officers - nearly all managers of Church Army London labour homes and women's homes - being appointed probation officers on a stand-by basis for the metropolitan police courts generally); and there were National British Women's Temperance Association representatives at two courts (Greenwich and Lambeth, where the Association had agents at work before the Act came into operation).[15]

Thus, to judge from this list of probation officers *per se*, the organisation which at this time had official representatives as probation officers specifically assigned to all of the London police courts on an individual basis appeared to be one identified with Roman Catholicism. But in practice - certainly in the metropolitan police courts - as the civil servant John F. Henderson had noted at the Home Office on 8 February 1908, "it looks rather as though the tendency is to employ the Police Court Missionary in all cases". This was no doubt mainly because the male and female C.E.T.S. missionaries were the best known, most numerous and most readily available of all the appointed probation officers, and perhaps partly because the very diversity or restricted appeal of groups offering alternative probation officers may have deterred some magistrates.

According to the printed Home Office list, William Wheatley and Miss Jane Sargent of the St Giles' Christian Mission "have been appointed Probation Officers for all the Metropolitan Police Courts, for the special purpose of taking cases at the London Sessions". It also seems that three Jewish probation officers were appointed, each dealing with Jewish cases throughout the metropolis: one lady to take Jewish girls, another to take Jewish women, and a man to take Jewish boys and youths - responsibility for Jewish men was not specified. Five women children's probation officers had been superintendents of play centres, and appear to have been recommended by the well-known novelist and philanthropist Mrs Humphry Ward (whose religious views seemed rather unorthodox).

While many probation officers were to be paid fees and expenses for successfully completed probation orders, in London the Home Secretary approved two ladies as "specially appointed Children's Probation Officers at fixed salaries, giving part of their time to their duties": they were Miss Ethel Maud Croker-King (aged about 37) and Miss A. Ivimy. Miss Croker-King was assigned to Old Street, Clerkenwell, Thames and North London Police Courts; Miss Ivimy to Westminster, Lambeth,

South-Western and apparently also Bow Street and Marlborough Street Police Courts. Miss Ivimy (of 82 Vincent Square, Westminster) had been strongly recommended to the Home Secretary as "a lady who had much experience of work among the poor". Miss Croker-King was a colonel's daughter (her father served in the 78th Highland Regiment); and an Armed Forces background may well have helped this pioneer children's probation officer, as well as George Nelson (the first police court missionary who became one of the first London probation officers, appointed to Marlborough Street) - and, indeed, many later probation officers - in organising their work or in their efforts to encourage a sense of discipline in offenders in their care.[16]

In early January 1908 the metropolitan police magistrates expressed regret that the C.E.T.S. police court missionaries had not been appointed as probation officers with power to act in cases of offenders under the age of sixteen, with whom, they felt, the missionaries had already done "admirable work". Perhaps partly for this reason, for over a year until separate juvenile courts were officially established as from 1 April 1909 (under the Children Act, 1908), Miss Croker-King and Miss Ivimy had very few cases referred to them; and they were disappointed at the little use made of their services by the police courts. However great their sense of commitment, they seem to have received quite a low salary in recompense for devoting about one-third of normal working hours to probation duties.[17]

It seems clear that both the Home Office and the Receiver for the Metropolitan Police District wanted to keep down the unknown cost of the new probation service, by paying poorly, encouraging part-time work and using voluntary workers, both in London and the provinces. Moreover, the Probation of Offenders Act had a number of blemishes and deficiencies, some of which have already been noted, and some of which could perhaps only be acknowledged with the benefit of hindsight and the wisdom of experience: there was no legal requirement for any court to appoint any probation officer, there was no national machinery for co-ordinating the work of probation officers (except to a distinctly limited extent through the Probation Rules issued by the Home Secretary under the Act), and there seemed no recognition of any need for training, to take three examples. Yet the Act marked a step in the transition from a voluntary to a wholly public service, and in softening the religious image suggested by the title "police court missionary". Herbert Samuel's contribution to the Commons debate on the second reading, the Act itself, and the subsequent Home Office memorandum, all made it clear that the Act was largely intended to provide an alternative to imprisonment: this it would do, as well as offer countless offenders the chance of rehabilitation. A sense of personal commitment and purpose, as suggested by signing the pledge, could now also find expression in a probation order. The new legislative measure may have been, as the Earl of Meath indicated in the Lords, a small measure.[18] But if so, it was the small acorn from which a mighty oak would grow.

CHAPTER FOUR

In the Crucible, 1908-21

During 1908, its first year of operation, the incipient probation service under the Probation of Offenders Act, 1907, seemed to make relatively encouraging progress in London. In its Annual Report for 1908, the C.E.T.S. London Police Court Mission stated that it now employed 17 male missionaries and 10 mission women. During the same year, C.E.T.S. missionaries continued to visit the Surrey and South London Sessions, in addition to their work as outlined in March 1909 by Evan Griffiths, C.E.T.S. Southwark Diocesan Secretary, who said that his Diocesan Branch deployed six men and also two women workers - neither of whom was an appointed probation officer - to cover, between them, five police courts within the metropolitan area south of the Thames: apparently unlike their female colleagues, these missionaries were basically attached to one court each. Of the men working north of the Thames, two were trained at Stepney Training College, their intention being to take up Church of England parochial work; others had been captains in the Church Army; and one had been a businessman. Of their female co-workers in the same area, one was the wife of a doctor; two were thought to be the daughters of farmers; and two others were presumed to be from the artisan class.

Although it now seems impossible to know for certain, it does seem likely that a high proportion of the C.E.T.S. police court missionaries, and accordingly of the probation officers, in London came from the artisan class. Long before working-class children in Britain were able to go to University in any appreciable numbers, the university of Victorian artisans in London was their workingmen's club, which was often a mutual improvement society providing education in literature, history, political economy, religion or public speaking.[1]

The metropolitan police magistrate John Rose (who placed 58 people on probation in 1908 - slightly above the average for the fourteen metropolitan police courts that year) approvingly described the Tower Bridge Court missionary, whom he used as a probation officer:

He is of the educated artisan class, a man of intelligence and a clear cold mind, who investigates cases without sentiment, but thoroughly and efficiently. I found him a most useful check upon myself, because I investigate the cases of the poor people who come for help from the poor box. They persuade me that they are very poor and very deserving. I cross-examine them as far as one reasonably can in court. I remit them to the missionary, who comes afterwards to me after having closely examined them, and I find my first view of the applicant is modified very often. And yet the missionary is a sympathetic man. He is altogether an excellent man for the post, because, being of the artisan class, he knows what questions to put, he knows the sore places, and his judgment is good.

Not so good, according to Thomas Holmes, was the judgement in July 1908 of Rose's colleague Mr Hutton, whose leniency on at least one occasion incurred Holmes's criticism. A "lady missionary" at Tower Bridge Police Court conveyed to the magistrate the humble apologies of a young woman who had dishonestly obtained money from different people. "Mr Hutton bound the prisoner over under the Probation Act!" -whereas Holmes would have preferred that this "accomplished artist in deception" received six months' hard labour. The views, if any, of the lady missionary were not revealed by Holmes.

Hugh Gamon referred to the situation, apparently at Old Street, where

> one London court has for some time past possessed its own missionary at a salary found for him by the magistrates of that court, because when the missionary had to choose between the C.E.T.S. and the magistrates, he chose the service of the latter. So even before the Act, in one court at least the missionary had become an official of the court, a probation officer in the chrysalis.

The London Police Court Mission was relieved to announce, in its Annual Report for 1908, that "Old Street Court, which for some years had ceased to be under the control of the Mission, was restored to its original position in the early part of the year". Perhaps it was partly because of this experience that its Secretary insisted in 1909: "We have practically given our workers to the magistrate to use, and it has always been an understood thing that a man's police court work comes before anything else", including, he added, C.E.T.S. deputations for evening-speaking on temperance in various parts of London.

Yet the question of dual control remained. The Mission had offered its services to the Government without charge and committed itself to continuing to accept responsibility, in London at least, for the salaries of its police court missionaries appointed as probation officers under the 1907 Act. This remained the position, throughout 1908, of the C.E.T.S. London police court missionaries working north of the Thames, though their Secretary would maintain in March 1909 that from the outset "it was understood that if other people received payments we should not feel ourselves bound to continue to do the work without". Meanwhile, C.E.T.S. Southwark Diocesan Branch missionaries - in the words of Evan Griffiths - "finding that other probation officers outside our own Society were receiving fees from Scotland Yard, went and presented their papers; so that south of the Thames we have received the fee authorised by the Home Office through Scotland Yard." However, the Home Office fees, low as they were, were not added to the missionaries' salaries, but handed over by them to the Society employing them: on whose initiative this was done seems unclear. The C.E.T.S. police court missionaries working in the London area apparently received higher salaries than their colleagues in the country - the basis for this was not explained - and the Mission indicated that the fees were quite inadequate for the time spent on the work; but the Mission did not appear overtly to question the ethical basis of a probation officer being paid a fee for satisfactory supervision of each probationer. (A copy of the official printed form, used in London at the time, for a metropolitan police magistrate to give certificated authority for a probation officer to be paid fees and out of pocket expenses under the Probation of Offenders Act, 1907, is attached as Appendix 4.)

Attached as Appendix 5 is a copy of the aggregated statistics on the work of the London Police Court Mission - north of the Thames - from 1901 to 1908 inclusive, presented by the metropolitan police magistrate Henry Curtis Bennett to a Home Office Departmental Committee in 1909. As it is not clear to what extent the statistics for 1908 may have included work done on probation cases, there may have been some overlapping in relation to figures for probation orders made in the London area in 1908, publicised by that same Committee and attached as Appendix 6.

When the Home Office figures in Appendix 6 for 1908 are compared with those in the London Police Court Mission Annual Report for the same year, some interesting pointers emerge which at first sight may seem surprising. The court that issued most probation orders in London in 1908 was not a police court with a long history of C.E.T.S. missionary involvement, but the North London Sessions. Other things being equal, a smaller number of probation orders than in a London police court would in fact have been expected in view of the more serious cases the Sessions had to deal with. Yet 289 persons were placed on probation by the North London Sessions that year, compared with 151 by Acton and Willesden Petty Sessions (outside the Metropolitan Police District), 115 by Lambeth Police Court, and 102 by Tower Bridge Police Court, during the same period.

The 1909 Home Office-appointed Committee, set up to review the working of the Probation Act in England and Wales, found that localities with similar socio-economic characteristics and crime-rates often revealed a remarkable disparity in the number of probation orders made by their respective courts. The Committee, on investigation, attributed limited use of the Act "partly to misapprehension of the scope of the Probation Act, partly to its novelty and partly to objections that have no solid foundation". Conversely, though the Committee did not explicitly say so, the high incidence of probation orders made by the London Sessions, Lambeth and Tower Bridge Police Courts seemed to owe a tremendous amount to the pro-probation commitment and pioneering zeal of two rather remarkable men: Robert Wallace, Chairman of the London Sessions, and Cecil Chapman, magistrate at Tower Bridge and Lambeth. In their evidence to the Committee, Wallace and Chapman both said that they had made a considerable number of probation orders under the 1907 Act. John Rose, Chapman's colleague at Tower Bridge, said of him and of the situation at that court in 1908: "I think he at once began to apply this Act with considerable vigour, and the really large number placed under probation officers was due to him rather than to me." Years later Chapman himself wrote: "I have heard several complaints from police officers against Sir Robert Wallace for putting 'old lags upon probation,' as it seemed a waste of time to catch them. I was at first inclined to sympathize with them, but I believe I was wrong."

It is also interesting to note that the probation officer in the Metropolitan Police District with the highest number of probation orders in 1908 was not a C.E.T.S. court missionary, but William Wheatley, head of the St Giles' Christian Mission. Wheatley declared: "During the year 1908, 414 cases were bound over on probation under my care." It seems clear that most of these originated from Wallace at the London Sessions. Wheatley had up to about 15 helpers, including Jane Sargent who attended to the women clients and any children placed on supervision to St Giles. More or less inevitably in the circumstances, the focus of his work was material assistance or charitable relief, for which he would be strongly criticised by the Committee:

> The methods adopted by Mr Wheatley, to whose care large numbers of probation cases are committed from the London Quarter Sessions, seem to us to be open to objection, for his evidence gave the impression that he regarded the personal influence of the probation officer upon the probationer as quite secondary to the relief, in money or in goods, which might be given to him, and which was in fact given to a very large proportion of the probationers in his charge. Except in unusual and urgent cases, it is in our view desirable that probation should be kept distinct from charitable relief, and that where charity is necessary, the probation officer should rather put the probationer in touch with one of the benevolent institutions of the neighbourhood, or with some person charitably disposed, than himself play the part of a relieving officer.

Notwithstanding Wheatley's position at the London Quarter Sessions, the C.E.T.S. missionaries dominated probation work in the metropolitan police courts. For example, at West London Court, which boasted ten probation supervisors, the C.E.T.S. police court missionary, assisted by one female colleague, apparently supervised all but 7 of 79 probation cases emanating from that court in 1908. At Thames Court, the missionary, William Fitzsimmons, assisted by one male and one female colleague, apparently took on 65 of the 82 probation orders made there that year, despite the fact that there seem to have been four named probation supervisors assigned to that court who were unconnected with the Church of England Temperance Society. In this instance at least, the lion's share of probation orders allocated to the C.E.T.S. London Police Court Mission was doubtless related to the reputation and personality of William Fitzsimmons, of whom the police court clerk Albert Lieck, who knew him well at Thames, wrote: "If ever a man could be said to be 'called' to his task it was he." Fitzsimmons had toiled selflessly for years at Thames Court and in the mean streets beyond. Not the least of his successes was the case of an "old lag" who, with 480 drink-related charges and many periods of imprisonment behind him, left prison for the last time at the age of 63 in December 1898, when he applied to Fitzsimmons at Thames and never looked back. Times without number Fitzsimmons had tried to help him; but on this occasion he saw that the man was in earnest, he furnished a room for him, stood by him and encouraged him. The alcoholic recidivist became "a respectable man and useful citizen - a Temperance worker and lecturer", and in 1909 he was apparently among the first of Britain's newly honoured old age pensioners.

If the probation officer's contribution was highly individualistic, his role certainly seemed fluid in the early days of the 1907 Act. This was allied to a degree of uncertainty or confusion regarding the advantages of a probation order over a bind-over combined with voluntary supervision, and even regarding the difference between the two options - a situation reflected in a case that came up at the Central Criminal Court. In his oral evidence to the 1909 Home Office-appointed Committee, the Hon. Treasurer of the Church Army stated that the Common Serjeant, Sir Frederick Bosanquet, had made a probation order in respect of an ex-soldier guilty of highway robbery, placing him under the care of Captain Walter Spencer of the Church Army (which apparently had twelve captains and eleven sisters officially appointed as probation officers in London). Captain Spencer's own account of the same case - in *The Other Side of the Prison Gate* (1938)[2] - also suggested that the ex-soldier had been placed on probation to him, whereas he had in fact been bound over and placed under the voluntary supervision of Captain Spencer, whom the Treasurer called "our principal probation officer". Indeed, no one was placed on probation at the Old Bailey in 1908.

Whereas at the North and South London Sessions combined, almost exactly nine times as many men as women were placed on probation that year (a ratio that probably very broadly corresponded to that of males and females in court), this ratio became nearly three to one in the metropolitan police courts, on the basis of probation orders made by those courts in 1908.

According to the Secretary of the London Police Court Mission, the Mission supervised relatively few children under the Probation Act. Such work would in fact become increasingly undertaken by children's probation officers, recruited and appointed by the Home Office without recourse to the Police Court Mission. The magistrate Cecil Chapman felt that female rather than male probation officers were suited to supervise boys up to 16 years of age; and apparently his male missionary took the same view. The developing practice - reflected to some extent in the Criminal Justice Act of 1925 and enshrined in that of 1948 - of female clients being supervised by female probation officers would appear to have been largely the brain-child of Miss Nettie Adler (in so far as the idea can be traced back to any one individual); though up to a point it may be said to have been implicit in the emergence of the C.E.T.S. "mission women". When the Probation Act was born, Miss Adler influenced the Home Office in the view that women officers should be appointed for boys and girls of school age and for female probationers over 16, and that probation officers should be persons of good education and with some knowledge of local social and industrial conditions. The Chief Rabbi's daughter, a member of the London Education Committee, Hon. Secretary of the Committee on Wage-Earning Children, and author of the pamphlet *Probation and Probation Officers* (dated February 1908), Miss Adler also collaborated at about this time with both Gertrude Mary Tuckwell (later President of N.A.P.O.) and Richard Henry Tawney (later a leading British economic historian).[3]

Early in 1908 a third Home-Office-appointed children's probation officer in London started work: she was Miss Evelyn Lance, a friend of the religious scholar Baron Friedrich von Hügel, who introduced her to Cecil Chapman as a lady anxious to do work for police courts as a volunteer. With no previous experience of working amongst poor people, she was, in her own words, "looking out for something which might be useful to do". She was assigned to Tower Bridge and Lambeth Courts, receiving work at both courts from Chapman, and acquiring at least 34 probation cases by April 1909; although she felt this number was too high for her to supervise adequately - and she was working virtually full-time -she also thought about 30 of them were progressing satisfactorily. During and after remand enquiries she was apparently a regular visitor to the C.E.T.S. boys' home at Camberwell, while C.E.T.S. police court missionaries sometimes used William Wheatley's boys' home when their own was full up.

A voluntary probation officer at Tower Bridge Police Court seemed less impressed with the Camberwell boys' home. In April 1909, in stressing the importance of medical examinations at remand homes, he related how a poor boy, after being remanded to the Camberwell home but not medically examined there, was placed on probation before the volunteer discovered that the boy was epileptic. The volunteer who helped Cecil Chapman at Tower Bridge was also warden of the Oxford and Bermondsey Boys' Club and looked after Bermondsey boys out of borstal. He was to become a major figure in the treatment of delinquency in Britain, influencing men like Basil Henriques and Guy Clutton-Brock, of whom more later, and on friendly terms with Clement Attlee - author of *The Social Worker* (1920) and a future Prime Minister - with whom he discussed his book *Across The Bridges*. The honorary probation officer's name was Alexander Paterson.[4]

Based on his Bermondsey experiences, Paterson's *Across The Bridges* (first edition, 1911) presented a well-written and quite vivid account of aspects of working-class life in South London. He noted the lack of attraction of religion for contemporary youth; and predictably he outlined treatment programmes for juvenile delinquents, with a fair amount of attention devoted to boys' clubs and their role. In a brief section on the use of probation he said of "this new system of probation": "It is the recognition by the State of such certain facts in daily life as personal influence and genuine repentance. Many boys take full advantage of their period of probation, and never appear again in the police-court." Paterson illustrated this with the history of a youth whom he called "Stump" - probably drawn from his own caseload of about ten -who had a poor home, had never worked since he left school, and had no "decent" friends. "Stump" had engaged, with a gang of which he was the worst offender, in repeated acts of petty larceny. Brought to court as, technically, a first offender, he found himself at 17 on twelve months' probation. A job was found for him (ten hours a day in a factory), and he became a steady workman; he was made a member of a boys' club, where he learned to box and run, and was introduced to summer camp. Some evenings he could be seen running in club colours, past the street stalls where he used to snatch and pilfer. "Stump is now a pillar of society"; and the future Prison Commissioner added: "This natural and friendly supervision has done far better for him than the expensive machinery of prison." As regards probation, Paterson's book was descriptive of actual situations rather than suggestive of ways in which the work of probation officers could develop in relation to juvenile delinquency.

In commenting on "the Moral Drift" among boys between 15 and 18 years old, the London Police Court Mission's Annual Report for 1909 declared: "Various methods of stemming the tide have been suggested; apprenticeship, compulsory military service, higher school age. One of the most effective remedies is undoubtedly emigration." The Mission then elaborated on this last point with the case-history of a fifteen year old vagrant whom a police court missionary helped to emigrate to "one of our colonies, where such lads have plenty of elbow-room; room to grow and develop in an environment which does not drag down". In another case where a youth seemed to be saved from a life of crime, a ragged, dirty and ignorant waif of the South London streets was brought to the Camberwell boys' home. After a few weeks the boy was sent to work in the Yorkshire coal-mines - a favourite field for Southwark boys, forty-four of whom were visited in Yorkshire in 1908 by the C.E.T.S. Southwark Diocesan Branch Secretary, Evan Griffiths. Within some four years the boy had become not only a man earning full wages, a Sunday-school teacher and a Band of Hope worker, but also a successful candidate in two examinations of the course that would lead him to receive a science degree at Leeds University and a qualification as a mining engineer. Another "delinquent solution" was marriage: in the summer of 1909 a London Police court missionary - apparently the veteran George Nelson at Marlborough Street - was invited to the wedding of a young woman who some years earlier had abandoned her child after being deserted by her lover and turned out by her parents.

Difficulties for clients struggling to triumph over their environment were sometimes highlighted by a probation officer's home visits, which in fact evoked diverse and changing responses. Referring to Miss Lance as "indefatigable in her visits to the homes of the children", Cecil Chapman declared:

> An amusing illustration of the general effect of probation may be given in this, that when it first started we were warned to avoid making the visits of probation officers too conspicuous because the families receiving them would be jeered at by their neighbours. That seems to have been true at the outset, but by degrees the jeering changed into a feeling of envy that one family should be favoured rather than another by the helpful visits of so nice a lady.

Soon after probation started, the Bow Street missionary, F.A. Herbert, was going up the staircase of a tenement house when he heard some expletives in reference to himself: "There goes that so-and-so missionary - the ginger-haired missionary from Bow Street. I wonder who he is looking after upstairs!" On the other hand, Frank Brown, probation officer and C.E.T.S. police court missionary since the day the 1907 Act came into force, found in his work from Thames Court that clients had no objection to his visiting them at home and were not "marked down" by neighbours on account of such visits. The Police Court Mission in London maintained that "the missionary is accepted everywhere as a sort of peacemaker", and that this "gives him the entry anywhere". Moreover, the Mission added, a police court missionary often had to rely on the neighbours to find out where a man was if he did not appear to be at home.

Factors which added to the time probation officers in London spent on home visits no doubt included one or more of the following: an officer attached to a court in the East End of London, for example, could be asked to supervise an offender charged at that court whose home was in South or West London; the probation officers seem to have had no offices at the courts; and offenders could be deliberately allocated for supervision to an officer sharing their religious affiliation.

In his oral evidence in April 1909 to the Home Office-appointed Committee, set up to review the working of the Probation Act, Jack Myers, who had worked as a children's probation officer in London, emphatically expressed the view that he had been assigned too large an area to cover it properly: taking only boys up to 18, he was not only attached to Old Street, Thames, Clerkenwell and Tower Bridge Police Courts for "ordinary cases", but also allocated supervision of Jewish youths by courts throughout London. He found it impossible to supervise adequately a boy living in South London: "Although I visited every week I could not expect a boy living in Lambeth to join my boys' club in East London."

Of the total of five London probation officers (including Myers, who had by then resigned his position) appearing as witnesses before the Committee, none mentioned that he or she had an office at court. William Wheatley said he had an office in Brooke Street, Holborn (where St Giles' Christian Mission had opened a boys' home); the C.E.T.S. Southwark

Diocesan Branch Secretary revealed that "with regard to one of our missionaries the cases come to see him at a room he has borrowed for the purpose" (presumably on C.E.T.S. premises); Miss Lance made it very clear that she had no office at all.

With the advent of the 1907 Probation Act, John Rose, and no doubt other metropolitan magistrates, received a list of names of probation officers, including some for Roman Catholics and Jews. From about this time dated the practice of probationers, particularly if they were Catholics or Jews, being supervised by officers of their own faith or church - a practice that, in London at least, was to last for many years. As William Wheatley, for example, was a Protestant, if some Roman Catholic clients objected to being supervised by him, they were transferred to a Roman Catholic (who was not in fact an officially appointed probation officer). The Police Court Mission in London indicated that if its missionaries wanted a club, recreation centre or person in authority to look after a probationer, they would consider contacting a clergyman or "somebody belonging to his own faith, should it happen to be a lad of a different religious point of view from ourselves". The London Police Court Mission sometimes used a Church Army home, but did not come into contact very much with the Church Army, according to the Mission's Secretary. However, the Church Army would, in effect, provide a number of notable probation officers in England[5]; and that the Church Army in London was active in the field of delinquency was illustrated by the resolution, recorded in its Women's Committee Minutes for 4 February 1908, "That the upper floors of 133 Edgware Road be taken for Probation and Rescue Workers for 3 years".

The metropolitan magistrates who gave oral evidence to the Home Office-appointed Committee seemed generally satisfied with the services provided by their probation officers. However, in their evidence Evelyn Lance and Jack Myers expressed regret that they were not able, as a matter of routine, to conduct preliminary enquiries in probation cases: such enquiries would have enabled them to establish an empathic relationship with an offender and/or the family, and identify cases which seemed unsuitable for probation. Of Miss Lance's four cases brought back to court (by April 1909) for fresh offences, she reported two to the magistrates, and the police reported the other two. Of Myers's total of about 18 cases, he brought two boys back to court himself, and he knew of a third boy who was arrested.

In its recommendations the Committee did not address itself to the question of office accommodation, whether at court or elsewhere, for probation officers. But its 36 or so recommendations, aimed at supporting and consolidating the work of probation officers under the Act, did include: an annual directory of probation officers prepared by the Home Office (implemented from 1911 onwards); the designation of one official at the Home Office to monitor the development of probation work; the appointment of at least one paid probation officer at each court; cases should be "supervised by a probation officer in the district where the offender lives, as is frequently done now when a probationer moves from one part of England to another"; payment by salary rather than by fee; formation of a "Probation Officers' Society"; a probation officer's caseload should be limited to about 60 (the London Police Court Mission's Secretary had suggested between 50 and 70); the probation officer should keep case-records and inform the court of an offender's progress; probation officers should not collect fines or generally engage in charitable relief; legislation should be introduced to permit the inclusion of a condition of residence in a probation order for an offender over 16 (permitted under the Criminal Justice Administration Act, 1914,s.8).

The Committee expressed its appreciation of the work done by probation officers enlisted from "the carefully chosen and experienced staff of the police court missions". Probation was

> a system in which rules are comparatively unimportant, and personality is everything. The probation officer must be a picked man or woman, endowed not only with intelligence and zeal, but, in a high degree, with sympathy and tact and firmness. On his or her individuality the success or failure of the system depends. Probation is what the officer makes it.

As the question of client motivation was not examined in any detail, arguably the Committee laid undue emphasis on the officer's individuality, "on which everything depends"; while its rejection of a supervising and co-ordinating "Central Probation Commission" and proposed "chief probation officer" (because the assumed cost was expected to be disproportionate to the volume and value of work engendered) suggested the Committee was less prescient than the Penal Reform League, for example, and was only vaguely aware of the potentiality of probation as a profession.[6] On the other hand, formal involvement of the Home Office

77

and increased participation by magistrates in oversight of the service, and the formation of a probation officers' association, were all recommendations in the Committee's report that sowed the seeds of important developments in London and elsewhere.

In 1910 there was a truly dramatic increase in the number of probation cases allocated to the London Police Court Mission compared with those so allocated the previous year: 1,132 as against 692 in 1909. This increase - no doubt related to the interest aroused by the Committee's hearings and published report - suggested a broadly comparable increase in pressure of work for many of the police court missionaries and mission women, as over the same period the Mission's complement of staff rose by only one male missionary to 18 missionaries and 10 mission women by the end of 1910. This increase of one was apparently caused by the appointment of a missionary to the London Sessions, Newington Causeway, which promptly rewarded him with 184 probation cases (161 men, 23 lads) within about six months. As the London Police Court Mission explained, with reference to the report of the Home Office-appointed Committee:

> As a result of this Report the Missionaries at those Courts used as Children's Courts were made Children's Probation Officers, at the Magistrates' special request, and the Home Office asked us to appoint a worker at the London Sessions. This was done, and on July 1st, Mr F.A. Cooper began his work there.

Within a year or so, following representations by Judge Wallace and the Home Office, the Mission sent a second missionary to join Cooper at the Sessions.

The Home Office-appointed Committee, chaired by Samuel, had concluded that the scale of fees provisionally fixed by the Home Office for probation officers in the metropolitan police courts was too low, and that the likely maximum of £75 a year which a probation officer with 60 probationers would receive under that scale was "obviously too little to attract the class of person that is needed". In the light of this conclusion and the Home Secretary's responsibility for the appointment of probation officers in the metropolitan police courts, new rates of remuneration for London probation officers were introduced in April 1910. It was also decided to follow the Committee's recommendations by replacing the method of payment by fee per probation case (except for those who took an occasional case) with fixed annual payments. Under the new arrangements all C.E.T.S. male missionaries received £40 a year from the State and the mission women £20 (inclusive of expenses, according to Bochel; exclusive of expenses, according to Jarvis). The Home Office had presumably calculated on the basis that probation work was expected to be part-time in most instances, even in London, and that the C.E.T.S. London Police Court Mission already paid its male missionaries an average salary of £157 a year. Thus the State was contributing about one-fifth of what a C.E.T.S. London Police Court missionary could earn if the two sources of income were added together. In spite of, or because of, this possible income of about £197 p.a. for a man, there was some dissatisfaction within the Mission when it became known that the children's probation officer Miss Ivimy (whom a Lambeth Police Court magistrate had called "a most excellent lady") was now receiving a salary of £200 a year, her official working hours having increased from one-third to full-time, following the coming into operation of the Children Act, 1908. She and Miss Croker-King would appear to have had independent means (like Thomas Holmes and the Howard Association, neither gave evidence to the Home Office-appointed Committee).

Perhaps thinking of the Committee's description of a probation officer as "a man or woman chosen for excellence of character and for strength of personal influence", at least one Home Office official felt that "the salaries given in London will serve as models elsewhere, and it is desirable that local authorities should strive to obtain the services of really good people". In 1911 the London Police Court Mission established a staff pension fund which enabled its missionaries to take voluntary retirement at 65 with a pension of £1 a week for men and 12s.6d. for women.

After referring to demands upon the court poor-box, an unnamed Middlesex magistrate of this period declared:

> A police-court missionary of the right stamp is the Justice's most valuable auxiliary in a host of matters of this class. He acts under private appointment, of course, but he is really indispensable. Latterly he has obtained *quasi*-official recognition. A room should, if possible, be set apart for his use, and as a matter of course he should be given free access to prisoners coming before the Bench prior to their appearance in the dock. Even when the Court is cleared for the hearing of juvenile cases, etc., he (or she it should be said, for the

missionaries are of both sexes) should always be allowed to remain. In cases of a peculiarly loathsome kind, when women are ordered out, the presence of a female missionary is valuable to give countenance to a woman who, as prisoner or witness, would otherwise be compelled to pass through a painful ordeal in an assembly consisting solely of men. A missionary's business is to make himself acquainted with the collaterals of a case - with circumstances which the police do not know, or cannot well bring forward, and which would very likely remain outside the cognizance of the Justices but for his intervention. He is *amicus curiae*, and still more he is the sagacious counsellor of the feckless, the friendless and the unfortunate. When an applicant seeking redress, for example, is quite unable to give an intelligible account of his or her difficulty, he will act the benevolent interpreter. He can seldom do anything for the full-fledged criminal, but it is often the case that his kindly interest in a lad or a girl who has lapsed into crime makes all the difference between ruin and reformation.

(Appendix 7 explains in tabulated form what happened to boys admitted to Padcroft, the London Police Court Mission home at Yiewsley, Middlesex, between 1902 and 1908. On 3 January 1908, Sir Albert de Rutzen, reflecting the views of the metropolitan police magistrates, wrote to tell the Home Office that at Padcroft "the work of reforming juvenile offenders has been most successfully carried on. I am informed that success has attended the treatment at that Home in 80 per cent of the cases dealt with."[7] Padcroft was inspected in 1908 by the Chief Inspector of Industrial Schools and in 1909 by the metropolitan magistrate Horace Smith, both of whom left with favourable impressions.)

Noting that the independence of the police court missionaries (latterly probation officers) enabled them to act as mediators in family disputes with considerable success, the Middlesex magistrate added:

> They have just the right admixture of authority, knowledge and sympathy. Obviously in this relation it is personality that counts. The Probation Officer has to win the confidence of his charge by showing a genuinely human as distinguished from professional interest in his welfare. He will lead rather than drive him along the path of virtue, and his success mainly depends on the moral force he can exert on his subject. A little pecuniary help may be necessary - to buy a suit of clothes or a few tools, or to send a young man out of the reach of influences that are harmful. The Probation Officer looks to the Justices to support him, and they will not waste their time if they

examine carefully the reports he has to furnish. While they do all in their power to encourage him, they will be wise to discount his natural optimism. Finally, if his endeavours are baulked by the contumacy of the offender, his authority must be sternly vindicated by the Bench. . . .They will deem it not beneath their dignity to see and confer with the Probation Officer as to his work, knowing how greatly he may be aided by their encouragement and advice. If they are helping to maintain the peace of the kingdom when inflicting punishment, they are working for the same object when they bring their experience and sympathy to bear on the more difficult task of checking the manufacture of criminals. The probation system, though still young, marks an epoch. It offers the best means yet devised for giving artificial support to those whose weakness rather than wickedness has brought them within the power of the Law. The conscientious Justice . . . will rejoice to assist that preventive and curative action which gives hope of arresting the development of the criminal in the earliest stages.

The magistrate further suggested that however successful the probation system might be with persons convicted of dishonesty, habitual drunkards and prostitutes often seemed irredeemable.

The London Police Court Mission's Annual Report for 1911 highlighted cases in which drink contributed to offending behaviour. One concerned a Surrey girl who, adrift in London, resorted to soliciting, theft and drink, for which she was placed on probation for three years to the mission woman, who sent her straight home to her mother "after many a serious and earnest word". The girl found contentment in nursing her sick parents and happiness in her own marriage, and maintained contact with her probation officer after successfully completing her period of probation. In another case the missionary arranged the admission to a home of a secret drinker and drug-taker who, after a great struggle with her addiction, rose to become the lady superintendent of an institution with a staff of several matrons. Similarly, Fred Barnett, the Westminster Court missionary, and Padcroft boys' home, between them, rescued a sixteen year old badly influenced by the "picture-palaces and cheap music halls" he had daily frequented.

According to Albert Lieck, Fred Barnett "could draw money from a skinflint, and goodness from a wastrel. One who knew him well described him as a mixture of saint and genius with a touch of madness. His missionary work was wonderful." Barnett had already earned an enviable reputation. In one of the earliest probation cases at Westminster Police Court, he found a window-cleaning job for a man who, on completing his twelve months' probation, wrote to the magistrate Curtis Bennett: "I have gone straight, and now I am starting to go in for motor-driving, and I shall do my best to get on, and I also wish to thank Mr Barnett, the court missionary, for his kindness to me. I think he has been more than kind to me. It was my first offence and it will be the last." Also in 1909, the London Police Court Mission Secretary said of Barnett: "He has been remarkably successful in finding work. I do not know how he does it, but he does it."

Helping men to find work was a key concern of the Discharged Convicts Department which, at the urgent request of the Central Association for the Aid of Discharged Convicts, the London Police Court Mission set up in February 1912. The Mission detached one officer, Frank Brown, and provided him with an office at 120 King's Cross Road (a kind of precursor of the after-care unit in Borough High Street which the London Probation Service would open in January 1965), so that he could devote himself full-time to men released from penal servitude. Of the 143 men "credentialled from prison" who passed through his hands during eleven months in 1912, he found jobs for about 113. One of them, according to the C.E.T.S. *Temperance Chronicle*, was "a middle-aged ex-convict, who is now in His Majesty's Prison Service", and at whose wedding in December Frank Brown was the 'best man'.

The London Police Court Mission's booklet *Handed Over to the Police Court Missionary* related many cases in which a missionary's intervention had proved successful, including an unusual case where a missionary, convinced of a man's sincerity and innocence, was instrumental in tracing a farmer in Kent for whom the man had worked at the time of his alleged burglaries in London, and who was able to establish an alibi which prevented a miscarriage of justice. At the same time positive relationships between police court missionaries and their clients sometimes took the form of the latter helping the former. The Mission's Annual Report for 1912 mentioned a young man who, after attempting suicide, was placed under the care of a missionary, who arranged seaside convalescence and then employment as a foreign correspondence clerk for him: "to-day he is a happy and contented man and frequently assists the Missionary in his work." Six years earlier, the Mission had recorded the history of a family man who, when destitute, had been provided with tools, stock and other assistance by the Mission, so that "now he gives employment to two men, in addition to helping the Missionary by providing temporary employment for others similarly situated".

During 1912 the London Police Court Mission appointed a supernumerary missionary to help staff "in times of sickness and during the holiday months"; and it also took over missionary work at Hampstead Court at the suggestion of the Hampstead Women's Union. But neither the Mission itself, nor even any individual probation officer or missionary, nor the Home Office, seems to have taken the first step towards the formation of a national society "comprising and managed by the probation officers themselves", recommended by the 1909 Home Office-appointed Committee "to assist in the dissemination of information and in the development of probation work".

The first known step was taken by a justices' clerk, apparently acting on his own initiative, though in his official capacity he would presumably have been one of the first to study the Committee's report after it was made publicly available in 1910. The initiator was Sydney Edridge, Clerk to the Justices at Croydon and a former Mayor of Croydon. He had not appeared as a witness before the 1909 Committee; but at his instigation a preparatory meeting to establish the proposed association was held at Croydon Town Hall on 22 May 1912, attended by some 40 probation officers, mainly from courts in or near London. To take the necessary steps towards the formation of a national association, a provisional committee was set up. Its membership, which was largely drawn from probation officers attached to London courts, included Fred Barnett (Westminster), Mrs Eleanor Cary (Thames), Mrs C. Curtis (Tower Bridge), William Fitzsimmons (Thames), T. Harwood (Tower Bridge), Miss A. Ivimy (Bow Street Juvenile Court), G. Phillips (Guildhall), and George Warren (Croydon). The committee's zeal and hard work resulted in the first official meeting of the National Association of Probation Officers being held in London (at Caxton Hall, Westminster) on 11 December 1912. At this meeting, at which officers from the London area understandably predominated, some 70 probation officers adopted a constitution for N.A.P.O., whose objects comprised: the advancement of probation work; the promotion of a bond of union amongst probation officers; and the provision of a forum for collective suggestions on probation work and the reformation of offenders. Edridge was elected Chairman, George Warren Secretary, and Fred Barnett Treasurer. Although the new-born Association faced an uncertain future - some police court missionaries declined to join as they felt it was symbolic of a move towards secularism - membership of N.A.P.O. would at least provide a rare opportunity for children's probation officers like Miss Ivimy and Miss Lance to discuss matters of common interest with their police court missionary colleagues manning the adult courts.[8]

Six years earlier the London Police Court Mission had reported that it often discovered "another kind of victim, the short-witted lad, the innocent girl, the helpless wife, who from force of circumstances and many strong influences join with those who are expert in crime". This point seemed to be illustrated by the indignation aroused in Britain - and reflected in London Police Court Mission literature - in 1912 by the "white slave" traffic. At Old Street the magistrate Chartres Biron permitted a middle-aged single woman to foster a destitute orphan as an alternative to sending the child to the workhouse; and the entirely satisfactory results were monitored by the police court missionary John Massey, "a Lancashire man with an agreeable burr, a great sense of humour and a large heart".[9] At Tower Bridge Cecil Chapman presided over the juvenile court established there under the Children Act of 1908. He recalled:

> I was very fortunate at the start in having for my assistance an exceptionally good probation officer in Miss Evelyn Lance, who not only loved the work but had a natural genius for influencing children to self-mastery, which solved many difficult problems. I decided to entrust her with all cases of boys and girls up to sixteen instead of sending children of fourteen and fifteen to the male missionary, which was the practice in most Courts. The result was in every way satisfactory.

Chapman added that, with serious offences, he remanded children for reports from the probation officer, the school attendance officer, and the industrial schools officer: if they all agreed, he invariably followed their advice; if they differed, he was inclined to follow the recommendation of the probation officer, who had specially studied the home conditions. Some weekends Miss Lance took the children on outings to Epping Forest, and on one or two occasions she invited Chapman to join them for tea at Lyons (these restaurants long provided an informal venue for London probation staff[10]).

Of the grand total of 2,166 persons placed on probation in the Metropolitan Police District during 1912, the overwhelming majority had committed offences of dishonesty in one form or another: offences involving violence against the person and sex offences were relatively rare (see Appendix 8 for details).

In some respects 1912 and 1913 were the golden years of probation in London, if not nationally, before the outbreak of the First World War. In 1912 N.A.P.O. and the London Police Court Mission's Discharged Convicts Department were established, and more people (1,374) were placed on probation to the Mission than in any other year before the First World War. In 1913, the boys' home at Camberwell was rebuilt and reopened, the number of jobs found by the Discharged Convicts Department rose to 126, the number of missionaries at the London Sessions rose to three, and N.A.P.O. launched its journal. It was during this period of growth and expansion that, in 1913, George Nelson, "the Senior Missionary, loved and respected by all", retired. He had addressed the London Police Court Mission's Annual Meeting in 1910, and he would outlive the 50th anniversary of the day he started work as Britain's first police court missionary (he was at least 86 when he died on 6 November 1926[11]).

At the Mission's Annual Meeting in November 1913, the Chief Metropolitan Magistrate, Sir John Dickinson, said that he and his colleagues on the bench were unanimous in their high regard for the Mission and its work. He praised the missionaries for offering adolescent girls, in court for drunkenness, a home and shelter and saving them from the "white slave" traffic and the depths of degradation. At Tower Bridge Court Cecil Chapman, against his better judgement and the advice of his "assistants", provided three unruly teenage girls - a well organised gang of shoplifters - as the nucleus of the Little Commonwealth, which would in fact be closed down within a few years, though its name, and that of Homer Lane, would live on in the literature of education.

Soon after Britain and Germany found themselves at war in August 1914, a former "citizen" of the Commonwealth who had left to enlist in the British Army wrote (apparently from France, where he was later killed) to a probation officer (quite probably Fred Barnett) that "the Little Commonwealth has made a man of me". More than 200 Padcroft "old boys" quickly joined the colours, and some were soon at the Front. By the end of 1915 about 1,100 recent clients of the London Police Court Mission had joined the Army or Navy since the War began. A magistrate at Westminster Court said, in a letter to the *Times*, that he was proud of the men who had appeared at that court - including those placed on probation - but were now in H.M. Forces. By the end of 1917 the number of Padcroft boys known to have joined the Forces stood at 726, of whom one had been awarded the Military Cross, five had won the Distinguished Conduct Medal, five had won the Military Medal, eighteen were 'mentioned in despatches', and four had gained Commissions.

As some of the London Police Court Mission staff were of military age, the Mission was anxious to know whether duty should release them for the armed forces. In the case of the metropolitan courts, the Home Office declared that the missionaries were exempt from military service as their contribution was "indispensable" to the work of the police courts. In the case of three missionaries attending Middlesex courts - also manned by the Mission - an appeal was made at a tribunal, with a like result. Despite these rulings, two of the staff were keen to volunteer for military service, for which the Mission was able to release them in 1915 -before the coalition Government introduced conscription for single men -with their work covered by colleagues. The two were P.S. Wilson (Acton Court) and C.F. Browne (Old Street Court), both of whom would survive the War to return as missionaries with the London Police Court Mission (similarly, Bennett Bailey's court missionary work in Mortlake and Richmond would be undertaken by his wife during his active service in 1917-18).

In 1915 the London Police Court Mission appointed the Reverend Harry Pearson as its Secretary. Educated at Repton and Trinity College, Oxford, Harry Pearson was ordained in 1898 and held curacies in Scotland (1898-1900; 1903-1906) - which included a slum area of Glasgow - and London (South Hampstead, 1900-1903; Kensington, 1907 onwards). Following the outbreak of war he became a Chaplain to the Forces and served in the Middle East (he would return to the Mission from the Army in 1919). Pearson would prove to be not only an able administrator, but also a good friend and counsellor of the missionaries, whom he was said to receive with sympathy and courtesy when they turned to him for advice in their problems. A similar need for support was felt by N.A.P.O. members who, late in 1915, formed a London and Home Counties Branch; anxious, in William Fitzsimmons's words, "to break the crust of isolation", these members then held their first meeting, as a branch, at the British Museum, where they attended a lecture on "The Romans in Ancient Britain"![12]

When Pearson took up his appointment the Mission's financial position gave cause for considerable concern. As the Annual Report for 1915 gloomily explained:

> From the nature of our work and the large staff of Missionaries now employed, it must be obvious that the responsibility of providing for the heavy expenses is a very serious burden.
>
> The yearly cost of the Police Court Mission is about £6,000, and the Boys' Home costs £1,300 more.
>
> Towards these expenses the Home Office contributes £1,160 in consideration of duties performed by our Missionaries as Probation Officers, and for similar work in the Petty Sessional Courts the Middlesex County Council contributed last year £292. Apart from these two sums we have to provide for the whole of the expenses by voluntary contributions.
>
> Collections in Churches in 1915 yielded £288, while £2,615 came from private subscriptions and donations; and £1,163 from other sources.

The following year the Annual Report identified several factors impeding the Mission's financial recovery: the higher cost of food, clothes and other necessities; the loss, through death, of support from the Mission's most generous subscribers; the switching of assistance by many erstwhile subscribers in favour of "war funds"; and the record number of boys admitted to Padcroft in 1916. Indeed, although the Annual Report understandably did not say so, it was feared that some of the missionaries might have to be discharged as there clearly appeared to be insufficient funds available to pay their modest wages. In spite of war-time difficulties, Pearson immediately set about raising additional funds so that the work could continue, and he was so successful that he was able to persuade his committee to begin a process of expansion which would lead to an increase in the number of the Mission's probation officers working in the London courts from a total of 32 in 1915 to 90 in 1938.

According to Sir Chartres Biron, writing in 1936: "The war had a curious effect on the work of the London police courts. It almost disappeared. There was little or no crime. This was partly due, no doubt, to high wages and abundance of employment. The early closing of public houses undoubtedly helped; but the criminals, to do them justice, stood by their country." He then went on to quote some comments "my old friend and missionary at Old Street", John Massey, had made to him during the War: "There has been a change in the district. The old gangs of ruffians you broke up have not returned. Some of them are in the Army and have done well."[13] Referring to recent claims that "there has been a decrease in crime", the London Police Court Mission's Annual Report for 1915 maintained that, with one or two exceptions, the missionaries were as busy as ever - a situation "due partly to the increase in the number of women charged at the Courts for all kinds of offences, and partly to the startling increase of juvenile crime".

The Mission and its "sister Society" the Church Army, between them, suggested that this increase in reported crime was due to a number of factors, including: the absence of fathers from the home; the sorrows and anxieties of many women left behind, with their resorting to drinking; and the concentration of soldiers in and around London attracting a large number of women to the neighbourhood of the camps. Throughout the War Miss Croker-King kept open the "Club" for "unclubbable" or working boys and girls which she had operated from her small Bethnal Green flat since 1909 as a social and reporting centre; although there were many nights when she and Miss Cheshire, her colleague and companion, experienced anxious moments in getting their young clients safely home during air raids.[14]

At a time when juvenile delinquency appeared to be increasing, there was published a noteworthy book which stressed the value of probation for juveniles. This was *The State and the Child* (1917) by the metropolitan magistrate William Clarke Hall, who was based at Old Street, and who -like Basil Henriques and John Watson in London - would become well-known for his great interest in the welfare of children. In his book, the future Chairman of N.A.P.O. presented figures which indicated that of the 297 children placed on probation at Old Street Juvenile Court in 1915 and 1916 taken together, about 87% proved "fairly satisfactory" in the sense that they seemed to clear their period of probation without being recharged. As the total number of children charged at this court in these two years combined was 1,955, on average just over 15% of them were placed on probation (this compared with an average of 13% placed on probation out of the total number of juveniles proceeded against in the Metropolitan Police District in 1911, for example). It also seems that metropolitan magistrates were ahead of other parts of the country in the extent to which they used probation.[15]

Clarke Hall recognised that even "unsatisfactory" probationers may have benefited in some way from a period of probation and may improve their behaviour: "The very experienced Old Street Missionary, Mr Massey, tells me that many of the boys who have been most troublesome while on probation, have later on settled down to steady work and done well. One of the worst of them has recently won the D.C.M." The magistrate felt that a children's probation officer could not efficiently supervise more than about 70 children; and that accordingly it would be impossible "under present conditions" in East London in general, and at Old Street (with just two children's probation officers) in particular, to place any more children on probation, although many more could benefit from it.

He noted that the children's probation officers in London had been carefully chosen by the Home Office "from ladies who had had experience in the social work of charitable societies", but thought that professional probation officers "should be selected and trained with the utmost care" (in acknowledging the need for effective training, Clarke Hall was, in effect, responding to a call already made by the Birmingham probation officer Cecil Leeson and by the Howard Association, for example). He explained that, in London at least, unruly fifteen year old boys were placed "under the Court missionary, who is also the probation officer in all adult male cases". He paid tribute to the "zeal and efficiency" of the C.E.T.S. missionaries with whom he had come into contact, and he praised their Secretary's "great tact and ability". But Clarke Hall none the less felt that a situation, as in London, where three separate authorities - the C.E.T.S. London Police Court Mission, the Home Office, and the court itself - were all involved in the administration of probation was a "curiously complicated one and eminently calculated to lead to friction". He went on to declare that "ultimately it will be necessary to place the whole matter upon a more systematic basis and under one direct control". As a parallel or preliminary process Clarke Hall pointed to a need for improved intersectoral co-operation and co-ordination - for example, between probation officers and N.S.P.C.C. inspectors - though he added:

> It is true, no doubt, that many Police Court missionaries are, in fact, in intimate personal touch with all such agencies. This is so to my own knowledge at Old Street, where Mr Massey, with twenty-seven years' experience of the district, knows exactly to whom to look for assistance in each individual case.

Clarke Hall advocated the appointment of chief probation officers to co-ordinate probation work in London, supervise and deploy interested volunteers ("often fresh from the Universities"), and facilitate the organisation of would-be case committees.[16]

The work of the London police court missionaries increased appreciably during 1917. A considerable amount of their time was taken up in making enquiries when the wives and dependants of soldiers and sailors were charged or brought charges in the courts. In the case of pensions and allowances for the wives and children of servicemen, missionaries were appointed "guardians", receiving the "ring-paper", drawing the money and seeing that it was properly used. The absence of so many fathers from home was thought to be a major reason for the rising number of probationers supervised by the London Police Court Mission: 937 in 1915; 1,328 in 1916; and 1,472 in 1917 (rising to 1,780 in 1918).

At the same time there was an unprecedented demand for admission to "Padcroft": 299 were admitted in 1917, while many applications had to be turned down. In his report for the previous year, the manager, F.A. Green, had declared: "A great number of the boys admitted are the sons of sailors or soldiers. The lack of parental control is the chief cause of their downfall." In 1916 William Fitzsimmons and Eleanor Cary - like the Church Army - stressed the harmful effects on children of improper film exhibitions.[17] In his report for 1917 as manager of Padcroft, Frank Green stated that cinema-going was "not by any means the sole or the chief cause of the trouble", but that "the present state of the labour market, which necessitates paying enormous wages to boys" was a contributory factor in increased juvenile delinquency. Of the jobs found for 182 boys from Padcroft during 1917, 34 were in engineering or munitions work, 30 were on farms, and others were as carpenters, grocers, glassworkers, house and garden boys etc., while 12 lads joined the Army or Navy. Some Padcroft boys were sent out to assist neighbouring farmers, and their earnings contributed towards the upkeep of the home, while a certain proportion was given to them as pocket money. Some "old boys" on leave from the Front spent it at Padcroft, "their only home".

The London Police Court Mission responded to the pressure on Padcroft by opening an additional home - suggested by some magistrates - in the summer of 1917 for the reception of first offenders. This was in fact a large mansion lent by a Hampshire landowner and intended to furnish accommodation, as a "temporary experiment", for some 20 boys who were to be employed in farm and field work during the summer and harvest-time. Frank Green provided the necessary staff and selected the most suitable boys from Padcroft to undertake the field work. This venture was so successful that it led to a nearby house on the outskirts of Basingstoke being rented by the Mission so that it could offer accommodation and horticultural training to some 27 boys from the London police courts. The Boys' Garden Colony, as it was called, was managed by a joint committee of the London Police Court Mission (which accepted financial responsibility) and of magistrates and others representing the metropolitan courts. With the aid of a motor-cycle, Green managed to dash around and temporarily combined oversight of these projects in Basingstoke and discharge of his existing duties in the Uxbridge area. The Boys' Garden Colony (which opened in September 1917 and acquired a resident "master" in November) owed much not only to the Mission but also to its instigator and Treasurer, Henry Lannoy Cancellor, a metropolitan magistrate who gave, in the Mission's words, "unstinted time and labour to promote the success of the scheme". Sadly, the Boys' Garden Colony would not long survive Cancellor's death in 1929.

In 1918 occurred the death of John Edward Massey, who had been a police court missionary in London for 30 years. According to the Church of England Temperance Society: "He was said to have had more criminals through his hands than any other Police Court Missionary except the late Mr. Thomas Holmes." According to Chartres Biron: "He had an uncanny instinct for a rogue and was a very difficult man to humbug." But what was almost certainly the finest and most extensive tribute to his memory came, so to speak, from beyond the grave, in H.L. Cancellor's posthumously published *The Life of a London Beak*. Referring to his time at Old Street, Cancellor wrote:

> At the court I had one great friend, and I think he was one of the best men I ever met. John Massey had been missionary at Old Street for many years, and also at the time when the court was held in and known as Worship Street. He possessed a great personality. In appearance he was very like John Hare, the great actor of that period, and he possessed John Hare's winning manner and whimsical smile.
>
> Massey was a man who liked freedom and independence, and he believed that every police court in London should run its own missionary staff and work without having to submit to any control from a directing or organising society. That sort of independence had been tried at Worship Street when Haden Corser was the senior magistrate and Massey the missionary at the court, but it had not lasted after Haden Corser's time.
>
> I agreed with Massey that it would be a fine thing for the missionary work of the courts to be run on those lines.
>
> Later experience and the advice of older magistrates showed me it would be impossible. Money would be a difficulty. The magistrates would have to beg hard and incessantly. Changes often occur on the Bench, in the office and in the missionary's room. Moreover, there are two magistrates at each court, and they might not be in accord about the organisation of missionary work. In later days, too, the Home Office has taken an active part in the supervision of missionary and probation work, providing a large proportion of the money necessary to pay the salaries of the men and women who do this splendid work in the police courts. I feel sure the controlling authority in Whitehall would not approve of a free state for missionary and probation work being created at a particular court.

Then, with more than a hint of emotion, Cancellor continued:

> The memory of John Massey lingers in my mind. I doubt if I shall ever meet a man for whom I shall feel more regard or admiration. He died in harness, worn out by hard work for his fellow-men. If ever a man laid down his life for his friends, that man was John Massey, the missionary of Worship Street and Old Street.

The police court clerk Albert Lieck added his own appreciation of "the Masseys at Old Street, husband and wife, persons of quiet personal charm, with persuasion in their tongues".

By 1917 the "mission women" had become "missionaries", at least in the London Police Court Mission's literature. This change may have been connected partly with the relative depletion of male officers in wartime (a third London male missionary, C.A. Turner, was now on active service), partly with the related fact that the coming of "total war" had highlighted the contribution, and would do much to raise the status, of women generally, and partly with a perceived need to close ranks within the Mission and present a united front in the face of mounting criticism nationally of the quality of police court missionaries' work and the system of dual control. Books like Cecil Leeson's *The Probation System* (1914) and William Clarke Hall's *The State and the Child* (1917), for example, clearly seemed to imply a diminished role or status for the representatives in the criminal courts of a religious organisation like the C.E.T.S. (which established a Central Police Court Mission to safeguard its position during and after the War); and the State Children's Association claimed that all too often an appointed probation officer was "an elderly police court missionary, fully occupied with other work, uninstructed in child psychology and with little, if any, knowledge of modern reformative methods". Soon after receiving this complaint from the Association, the Home Office issued a circular in August 1917 which suggested - apparently for the first time in a Government communication - that police court missionaries were not necessarily always well suited to supervise juveniles. This resulted in a Church of England Bishop protesting to the Home Office about this "outrageous" statement in the circular. Moreover, the London magistrate Ralph Bankes declared in 1919 that "my Lady Probation Officer . . . is walking in the footsteps of Christ"[18]; and Buckingham Palace sent a message of support in 1916, and a donation in 1917, to the Mission.

As early as 1914 Cecil Leeson, in *The Probation System*, had remarked: "It is too often the custom of professional probation officers in England to look askance at the use of volunteer probation officers"; and he favoured the appointment of carefully selected and supervised voluntary workers to help provide "the intensive work which makes probation real". Leeson's book was studied by William Clarke Hall, who then master-minded an experiment that showed an imaginative use of volunteers in an attempt to increase the number of delinquent children in the Old Street area who could be placed on probation at a time of rising juvenile crime, with an inadequate number of probation officers available. The Juvenile Organization Committees of the eight Boroughs covered by Old Street Juvenile Court - viz. Finsbury, Shoreditch, Bethnal Green, Hackney, Islington, Stoke Newington, Stepney and Poplar - were asked to appoint sub-committees for juvenile delinquents. Each sub-committee had a secretary whose duty it was to find volunteers within the particular Borough willing to supervise one or more delinquent children each. The work of these sub-committees was co-ordinated by a general secretary, supplied by the Home Office and equipped with a room at Old Street Court. A probation order was made out in the probation officer's name, but the case was forwarded by the general secretary to the appropriate sub-committee secretary, who selected a voluntary worker to take the case. The experiment started in October 1918 - virtually at the end of the War -and although some probation officers apparently suspected that the scheme could undermine their own position, remarkably few of the supervised children relapsed and most of the volunteers' progress reports to the court proved admirable. A similar venture for children over 14 was operated by Fred Barnett at Westminster Court, but without a committee - much as Miss Croker-King, for example, believed that working for a secretary or through a committee was no substitute for close personal contact between probation officer and voluntary worker.[19]

At the London Police Court Mission's Annual Meeting in October 1919, Clarke Hall paid an eloquent tribute to the work of the missionaries and especially emphasized the value of the women's shelter home, which he seems to have used, with considerable success, as a remand home alternative to Holloway Prison for girls charged with street offences. (This home, intended for inebriate women, was distinctly closer to Old Street as a result of its relocation, completed by 1918, from 40 Filmer Road, Fulham, to 59 Leigh Road, Highbury.) Very few of these remanded girls apparently attempted to abscond, and the week's remand enabled the sister in charge to make valuable suggestions regarding the sentences to be imposed. The cost of the remands was borne by the home or the court poor box.

In 1919, in England and Wales as a whole, the total number of persons placed on probation represented 1.77% of those brought before the courts; whereas in the same year, 2.27% of those appearing in the London police courts - i.e. 3,148 defendants - were placed on probation. It is also noteworthy that of the total of 580 probation orders made at Quarter Sessions throughout England and Wales in 1919, no less than 465 were made by the County of London Sessions under the Chairmanship of Sir Robert Wallace. In the words of the metropolitan magistrate J.A.R. Cairns: "Sir Robert Wallace and his colleague Mr Allan J. Lawrie are emphatic that in the interests of both the prisoner and the community the probation order is the most beneficial and beneficent treatment of the criminal."

This confidence in London in probation seemed to be matched by the "very substantially increased" salaries which the London Police Court Mission announced its missionaries received in 1919, when in fact their salaries were fixed at £200 a year, rising to £250, for men, and £120, rising to £150, for women. Of these amounts the Home Office contributed two-thirds (with a similar commitment by Middlesex County Council regarding the Petty Sessional Courts in its area), while the C.E.T.S. paid one third. None the less, to meet its expenses, the Mission had to sell £1,000 worth of invested stock. The women children's probation officers in London appointed direct by the Home Office were normally paid a salary of £120 a year, rising to £150, though some of them received a maximum of £200 before the new salary was fixed; and in addition they were eligible for war bonus on the same scale as civil servants, with the result that at least some of these children's probation officers actually or potentially commanded appreciably higher salaries than their colleagues staffing the adult courts.[20]

Another issue that remained unresolved in 1919 was training. Adding his voice to an appeal made by the Penal Reform League some two years earlier, Cecil Chapman recommended that intending probation officers should take the social work course offered by the London School of Economics. Also in 1919 Fred Barnett, who had served as a police court missionary for twenty-seven years, called for permanent training centres for probation officers, declaring that, self-taught as he was, he would have avoided known mistakes had he had the advantage of a training centre.

However great their need for training, the experience of the police court missionaries no doubt stood them in good stead in their matrimonial reconciliation work, in which they seem to have been largely successful. The London Police Court Mission claimed that during 1920 -the first year in which its Annual Report gave any general statistics for this kind of work - reconciliation was effected in 710 out of 1,449 would-be separation cases referred to its missionaries. Over a period of two years before his death in 1921, the metropolitan police magistrate Ralph Bankes collected the figures for the matrimonial cases which came before him at South Western Police Court. He referred every case of this description immediately to the police court missionary; and of the total of 747 such applications in which the missionary was consulted during the two years, there were no subsequent proceedings in 655 cases. Indeed, over a period of one year from October 1917, the probation officer at Bankes's court in Battersea had been instrumental in amicably settling out of court 381 of the 414 cases there in which judicial separation had been sought. Apparently at Tower Bridge Police Court the missionary persuaded a husband to try to maintain the home himself on 32s. per week housekeeping money on which the husband had insisted his wife could manage; but within a week the husband had relented and agreed to give his wife thereafter the 38s. per week which she had insisted was the minimum required. Bankes's colleague H.T. Waddy described this as "the missionary's, not the magistrate's, wit".[21]

A metropolitan police magistrate who, rather like Bankes, had a positive experience of missionary work at South Western Court, Lavender Hill, just after the War was H.L. Cancellor, who recorded:

> My experience there was much the same as it has been at Old Street and North London. I found a missionary who had been permitted, with the consent of the magistrate of the court, to run his own show in his own way, without paying much heed to the direction of the controlling society. Close to the court there was an excellent club for police court boys. The missionary also had a cricket ground for South-Western boys at Raynes Park. He got money for these purposes from men of business and shopkeepers in the district, and the work done to reform lads and boys by wholesome recreation was wonderful.

Cancellor was indefatigable in his endeavours to raise funds for the Boys' Garden Colony, which in 1920 admitted 44 boys, 32 from "Padcroft" and the rest direct from the courts. All of these were on probation, and their period of residence at the Colony was usually twelve months. It was normally three months at "Padcroft", which aimed to provide training, care and discipline in cases where a long period of detention was unnecessary, but where the home conditions were unsatisfactory. The London magistrate Cecil Chapman believed that "for all things human the simpler the rules and the broader the margin of discretion the better", and that this was what he found at "Padcroft". If, at Westminster Court, he wanted to steer a middle course between prison and reformatory, he often put an offender on probation to Fred Barnett -"my genius for the purpose" - with a condition of residence at "Padcroft" combined with a requirement that he should thereafter get work and reside where directed: "It was an admirable arrangement, and was attended with marked success, and to some extent resembled what I have often advocated, namely, an indeterminate sentence."

Chapman cited the case of a teenager (convicted of stealing about eight pounds from his employers) whom he placed on probation to Barnett for eighteen months, with a condition of three months' residence at "Padcroft" and repayment of the money he had stolen. Chapman later saw one of the lad's letters to Barnett, which read:

> Thank Gawd this is the last letter I have to write to you on probation. You will be glad to know that I have now repaid the whole sum which was ordered by the magistrate. When I says I am glad this is the last letter I have to write to you I don't mean that I want to forget you or you to forget me and when I can get the time off some day I mean to come and see you at the court and perhaps the magistrate too.

No doubt near the other end of the social scale was a refined-looking wreck of a man whom Chapman also placed on probation to Barnett for eighteen months for theft, and who turned out to be the heir to a peerage. Chapman recorded that he and Barnett

> both persuaded him to take the Normyl treatment for his drug propensity. He followed the advice and in a very short time became a new man; he resumed his favourite pursuit of painting in water colours and presented Mr Barnett and myself with charming specimens of his art. He subsequently succeeded to the peerage.

On the debit side was the "notorious" Netley Lucas: "deceived in believing him to be the victim of misfortune", Chapman was "so impressed by his innocent appearance that I released him on probation to Mr Barnett, the best of missionaries, but he proved incorrigible". Before long the young man had breached his probation by reoffending; so Chapman sent him for residential training to "Padcroft", from which Netley Lucas very soon absconded and, in Chapman's words, "sounded all the depths of crime".

The reprobate had a counterpart in the London juvenile courts of that time who, under the pseudonym of Mark Benney, would also publish his autobiography and other works dealing with aspects of crime. But whereas Netley Lucas would be tight-lipped about his experience of probation under Fred Barnett, Benney would be much more revealing. Benney vividly described how, as a first offender, he was arrested for house-breaking and then released to appear at the Dean Street Juvenile Court a week later (apparently in 1920):

> The affair brought a deluge of social workers upon the home. Black-coated gentlemen came to ask questions about my interests, attitudes, proclivities. Big-bosomed ladies in fur coats came to inquire of me - out of Mother's hearing - if my parents ill-treated me or were neglectful. All went away with a good impression, for I praised my parents as highly as they praised me; and Mother had taken care to remove all beer bottles from sight against their coming.

> The day came when I had to appear before the magistrates.

> I sat beside Mother in a large hall annexed to St Anne's Church. Big double doors indicated the room where the magistrates were sitting, and every now and then important people would pass to and from the room with hands full of documents. Once or twice somebody came across and asked me, cheerfully, how I was feeling. . .

> I would be placed under the care of a Probation officer for twelve months.

> As I left the Court with Mother, I began to cry with relief. In the hall outside, the Probation officer, a kindly little man with an irritatingly brisk way of speaking, bade me dry my tears, I was under his care, and he wasn't an ogre. He was going to see that I had no need to break into empty houses to amuse myself. He was going to make me a member of a boys' club, where I could do gymnastics and box and play draughts and billiards in the evenings. And once a month I must come to see him, and he would lend me books and

jig-saw puzzles. And I'd soon forget all this silly clambering over roofs.

... I, for my part, spent most of my evenings in the boys' club to which the Probation officer had introduced me. Here I learned to box, to play chess and billiards, to handle an air rifle and dance the hornpipe. And in these engrossing pursuits I gradually forgot my late misadventure. Fear of the police receded to the back of my mind; tentatively I began to steal again; my visits to the Probation officer became irregular. Within four or five months I was responding to the invitations of the streets as freely as ever.

Meanwhile the Society of Juvenile Courts Probation Officers had been formed, apparently at a meeting on 31 March 1920, attended by probation officers serving London juvenile courts, including Miss Nina Blyth (Tower Bridge), Miss Cheshire and Miss Croker-King (Old Street), Miss Ethel Crosland (Bow Street), Miss Grayson-Smith (Westminster), and Miss Martin (West London). One of the new Society's leading members was Miss Blyth, who had begun work in this field in 1915 as a helper to Miss Lance at Tower Bridge. According to Miss Blyth, "Miss Lance had developed a scheme of treatment for young offenders, then known among the Magistrates as 'The Lance Method', which was the seed of the great plant of to-day". Miss Blyth did not elaborate on Miss Lance's methods, but went on to suggest that the Society had as its basis "the need of fellowship and of free discussion of differences - no easy thing. And it seemed to us that without such discussion and co-ordination no work could stand." (The Society would be addressed by Mark Benney in April 1948 on "Probation from my angle".[22])

During the remainder of 1920 the fledgling organisation held some half a dozen further meetings at which it was agreed, *inter alia,* that: voluntary workers in the juvenile courts should work under the probation officers; after two years' service probation officers should be made permanent (i.e. should not indefinitely be subject to annual appointment); probation officers in both juvenile and adult courts should be persons of education; caseloads could, on average, be at least 60; there should be a pension scheme to ensure a compulsory retiring age; and no probation officer for adults should also act for juveniles. Yet at no stage was there apparently any discussion of relations with, or attitudes towards, the National Association of Probation Officers.

The Juvenile Courts (Metropolis) Act of 1920 - which came into force in July 1921 - laid down that in London the juvenile courts were to be held in a room or building quite separate from the police court, and that they were to be presided over by a stipendiary magistrate assisted by two lay justices, one of whom was to be a woman. Female probation officers in the London courts, however, opposed the employment of newly-appointed and inexperienced women magistrates in this field.[23] The London Police Court Mission commented:

> Although in theory children charged at the Juvenile Courts hitherto have come under the care of the Probation Officers appointed to those Courts by the Home Office, in actual fact it has been customary in most Courts for our Missionaries to be given the care of children over 14 years of age. Thus, in 1920 the number of children on probation under our Missionaries was 211, and in 1921, 135.

It was at this time of concentrated interest in the young offender that the house used by the Boys' Garden Colony at Basingstoke was purchased and much improved following its being offered for sale to the management committee, during the summer of 1920, at an attractively low price.

During 1921, 1,490 persons were placed on probation to the London Police Court Mission, compared with 1,745 the year before. The Mission noted that probation, as such, was very little used in some courts, where there was a tendency for offenders to be bound over and placed under the missionaries' voluntary supervision. No one was placed on probation by the Central Criminal Court during the years 1917 to 1919; though in 1921, for example, there materialised at least 40 "probation cases" (36 men, 4 children) at the Old Bailey and Middlesex Sessions. Where probation was used, it appeared to be largely successful in producing a real change in the moral attitude of probationers. According to statistics for London provided by the metropolitan police magistrate J.A.R. Cairns:

> *Thames Police Court:* 1919- 75 men and lads over 16 placed on probation (9 lapsed and were recharged). 1920- 86 men and lads over 16 placed on probation (13 lapsed and were recharged). 1921- 76 men and lads over 16 placed on probation (8 lapsed and were recharged).

> *West London:* 1919- 50 men and lads over 16 placed on probation (4 lapsed and were recharged). 1920- 57 men and lads over 16 placed

on probation (7 lapsed and were recharged). 1921- 43 men and lads over 16 placed on probation (2 lapsed and were recharged).

Old Street: 1919- 117 men and lads (of all ages) placed on probation (13 lapsed and were recharged). 1920- 128 men and lads (of all ages) placed on probation (20 lapsed and were recharged). 1921- 112 men and lads (of all ages) placed on probation (8 lapsed and were recharged).

North London: 1919- 80 men and lads (of all ages) placed on probation (9 lapsed and were recharged). 1920- 85 men and lads (of all ages) placed on probation (10 lapsed and were recharged). 1921- 103 men and lads (of all ages) placed on probation (8 lapsed and were recharged).

The statistics of nine police courts within the Metropolitan Police area: 1919- 601 probation orders, 78 unsatisfactory. 1920- 608 probation orders, 89 unsatisfactory. 1921- 532 probation orders, 46 unsatisfactory.

It was not clear, from Cairns's account, whether "unsatisfactory" probation cases and even "lapses" were defined solely in terms of fresh offences committed during the calendar year in which the orders were made, or over a longer time-scale.

Cairns - a former Presbyterian minister who, in Lieck's words, "found his church too narrow" and tried his hand at politics before becoming a magistrate at Thames in 1920 - also gave some figures for the use of probation in respect of "girls on the threshold of a prostitute's career":

At the Thames Court during the year October 1920 - October 1921, seventy-five women and girls were put on probation. Of these seventy-five the preponderating majority were young girls and the charges chiefly related to street offences. Fifty-two have proved satisfactory, nine have disappeared and left no trace, nine have been charged again, five have warrants against them awaiting execution.

Thus about one-third have broken the terms of their recognizances to lead an honest and industrious life and report changes of address to the Probation Officer.

He described how a police court missionary - presumably Miss Perry at Thames - had tried to save a girl from prostitution in the Chinatown area by arranging training for domestic service, providing a set of clothes for her, etc. (Seldon Farmer's widow would remember Rosa Perry as "a sweet old lady"[24]); but the girl responded by disappearing, only to re-surface in court many months later as a disorderly prostitute, debauched and degraded beyond recognition.

Some indication of the social and family disruption associated with the World War may be discerned in the fact that the recorded incidence of bigamy and petitions for the dissolution of marriage had been appreciably higher in 1919 than in 1913, for example. On the other hand, whereas 139,060 persons had been sent to prison in 1913, this figure had declined to 49,712 in 1920-21. The London Police Court Mission attributed this "astonishing" reduction partly to the restricted hours for sale of intoxicating drink, partly to the extended provision, under the Criminal Justice Adminstration Act of 1914, for the payment of fines, and partly to the increasing use of probation. In *The Social Worker* (1920), Clement Attlee, conversant with conditions in London, crisply referred to the probation officer's task as one "requiring knowledge, patience and experience in dealing with very difficult cases".

CHAPTER FIVE

Mightier than the Sword, 1921-30

The London Police Court Mission received encouragement from the Home Secretary, Edward Shortt. In a letter read out at the Mission's Annual Meeting on 2 November 1921, Shortt declared: "by appointing your Missionaries as Probation Officers in the Metropolitan Police Courts, successive Home Secretaries have shown in the clearest possible way that they recognise how carefully you choose your Missionaries and how well these devoted men and women perform their difficult tasks."

A few months later, the Home Secretary received the report of the small Departmental Committee he had set up in November 1920 to enquire into the training, appointment and payment of probation officers. The 49 witnesses who gave evidence to the Committee included: Sir Robert Wallace, Chairman of the London Sessions; six metropolitan police magistrates (Sir Chartres Biron, H.L. Cancellor, Cecil Chapman, William Clarke Hall, C.K. Francis, and H.W. Wilberforce); Harry Pearson and Evan Griffiths, Secretaries of the C.E.T.S. London and Southwark Diocesan Branches, respectively; and eight probation officers working in the London area (as well as a female "voluntary probation worker" attached to Old Street Police Court). These probation officers were, on the male side: S.G. Boswell of Marylebone Police Court (later an Assistant Principal Probation Officer in the London Probation Service); William Fitzsimmons (Thames); G.E. Franey of Greenwich (much appreciated by Cecil Chapman); F.A. Herbert (Bow Street); C.F. Wrigley (South Western); and R. Russell (a Roman Catholic probation officer covering metropolitan police courts north of the Thames). On the female side, Miss E.D. Cheshire (Old Street) and Mrs B.M. Stead (Tower Bridge) were the children's probation officers who appeared as witnesses.

At a time when it seemed that in many areas the Probation Act had hardly consolidated itself, the Committee acknowledged the importance of "missionary work" in the courts, the "religious conviction" and "high character and qualifications" of many of the C.E.T.S. police court missionaries. "We have, however, received a good deal of criticism of the organisation of the Church of England Temperance Society." Accordingly, the Committee suggested: complete separation of the Police Court Mission from the temperance work of the Society; organisation of the Mission on county rather than on diocesan areas, with magistrates and experienced social workers prominently associated with its control; "the selection of Probation Officers should not be limited to members of the Church of England"; and there should be one Police Court Mission for the whole of London.

Somewhat cryptically the report declared: "Some of the Societies who furnish Probation Officers - for instance, the Church Army and Police Court Mission - already undertake the training of candidates." Referring to the C.E.T.S. London and Southwark Diocesan Branches, the report continued: "We understand that both branches of the Police Court Mission hold regular meetings of their staff, but many of the magistrates who attach much importance both to probation and to missionary work have little knowledge of what is being done outside their own Court." Although the Committee did not recommend any obviously fundamental changes in the organisation and administration of the probation service generally, it recommended that the Home Office, in its oversight of probation work nationally, should be assisted by an Advisory Committee, comprising about a dozen members, including representatives of local authorities, magistrates and probation officers. The Departmental Committee also felt that some members of this Advisory Committee should be chosen from London and could deal specifically with the organisation of the work in London, including the selection of probation officers.

The London Police Court Mission had awaited the Departmental Committee's report with much anxiety. In the Mission's own words: "It was known that persons of influence had made great efforts to obtain the separation of this work from the hands of any religious or voluntary society and to provide that it should be carried on as a State department." While the Mission felt largely reassured by the published report, it decided to respond positively to the criticisms and suggestions it contained regarding the work of the C.E.T.S. in London. Accordingly, the Church of England Temperance Society - including representatives of its London and Southwark Diocesan Branches - decided to amalgamate the two branches of the Police Court Mission in London. A Joint Committee was formed, comprising: nine members nominated by the London Diocesan C.E.T.S.; three members nominated by the Southwark Diocesan

C.E.T.S.; three metropolitan police magistrates (nominated by the Chief Magistrate); and two Middlesex Justices of the Peace. It was also agreed that the conduct of the new Police Court Mission should be separated from the temperance work of the Society. The Mission added: "it was hardly to be expected that a Church Society would renounce her *right* to appoint as her agents only persons of her own creed"; yet the C.E.T.S. reluctantly conceded that it would not necessarily appoint as missionaries only those subscribing to the tenets of the Church of England, but would be prepared to consider each case on its merits.

On the question of remuneration in London, the Departmental Committee revealed that the C.E.T.S. police court missionaries received a bonus - £15 for men, £7 10s. for women - in 1921 "in view of the continued high cost of living", and that the Police Court Mission had a scheme of insurance under which the missionaries became entitled to an annuity of about £60 a year on retirement, the missionaries contributing a proportion of the premium. Their travelling and other incidental expenses incurred in the course of their probation work were paid by the Mission. The Committee suggested that full-time male probation officers, appointed at the age of 30, should receive not less than £200 a year, rising to £350 at the age of 45. "Women Probation Officers might begin at a salary of £150, and rise to a maximum of £250." (Miss Blyth described how during or just after the First World War the women children's probation officers drew their weekly cheque from their district police court chief clerk, as did the police.) The Committee's report briefly mentioned "the report of a Departmental Committee on the Remuneration of Probation Officers in the Metropolitan Police Court District (1913)" -though copies of this pre-War report have not come to light, it presumably took account of evidence from Mrs C. Curtis.[1]

Whatever their feelings about their actual or expected remuneration, probation officers working in London and elsewhere were doubtless encouraged by Sir Robert Wallace's address to the 1922 N.A.P.O. Annual Conference in London. In his address, Wallace described their work as "the most glorious work in which any man or woman can be engaged"; and in identifying qualities and virtues that he felt probation officers should possess (if they did not already), he stressed above all that "the probation officer should be inspired with missionary zeal". He drew attention to the frequency with which offenders, with whom he had had to deal at a late stage in their criminal careers, had been sent to prison for a first offence, "without any helping hand held out to them"; and prison, he suggested, had failed to exert a reforming influence upon them on this or any subsequent occasion. By contrast, he claimed, regarding the use of probation at the London Sessions, that "out of every 100 probationers for years past, the average of those who have never returned to criminal life and never come back to prison has been 96" (a claim derided by Lieck).

Wallace admitted:

> I know the anxiety that was felt originally in regard to the action of the judges at the London Sessions touching the workings of the Probation Act. My dear old friend, who was then the Under-Secretary of State, Sir Edward Troup, stated at one of our gatherings that the Home Office, when first our work began, were alarmed as to what it was going to lead to . . .[2]

Such misgivings appeared to survive Wallace's speech. In 1936 Sir Chartres Biron drew public attention to a case at Bow Street in which an offender, guilty of soliciting an innocent boy for immoral purposes, was sent to prison for six months, but, on appeal to the London Sessions against sentence, was put on probation. Chartres Biron angrily commented that "such an abuse " of the Probation of Offenders Act "merely brings the law into contempt". Lieck mentioned what seemed to be a similar case.[3]

Meanwhile, in the summer of 1922, the Home Secretary, in accordance with the Departmental Committee's recommendations, appointed an Advisory Committee, including representatives of magistrates, local authorities and probation officers, to assist in the development of the probation system. The sixteen members of this Advisory Committee included two London probation officers (Ethel Crosland of Bow Street and William Fitzsimmons of Thames), three metropolitan police magistrates, Alexander Paterson, and the Rev. Harry Pearson. A small committee -which became known as the London Probation Committee -was set up specifically to supervise the organisation of probation work in the Metropolitan Police Court District, where the Home Secretary was responsible for appointing probation officers. To secure co-ordination, this committee was composed of seven persons (all male) who were also members of the Advisory Committee: its Chairman was S.W. Harris of the Home Office, and among its other members were the Rev. Harry Pearson, and the three metropolitan magistrates, including Clarke Hall.

The Mission welcomed Pearson's appointment and at the same time announced that he had been appointed Secretary of the new Committee in its revamped organisation - now officially known as the London Police Court Mission - with effect from 1 January 1923, with Evan Griffiths as Assistant Secretary, Sir Edward Troup as Chairman of the Committee, and the Lord Chancellor, Viscount Cave, as President.

Following the Departmental Committee's report, the Home Secretary decided to adopt in London the salary scales it had suggested; and the Home Office used its influence to secure similar arrangements with Middlesex County Council. Of these salaries the Metropolitan Police Fund contributed two-thirds and the London Police Court Mission one third. The Home Office also undertook to pay two-thirds of the police court missionaries' official travelling and incidental expenses. (The new salaries involved £10 annual increments for men and women alike.)

As from the beginning of 1923 the London Police Court Mission covered the following courts, most of which had been covered by C.E.T.S. police court missionaries since before the World War: Bow Street, Clerkenwell, Greenwich, Lambeth, Marlborough Street, Marylebone, North London, Old Street, South Western, Thames, Tower Bridge, West London, Westminster, and Woolwich; the Central Criminal Court; the London and Middlesex Sessions; Acton, Brentford, Ealing, Enfield, Hampstead, Hendon, Highgate, Tottenham, Uxbridge, Wealdstone, Willesden, and Wood Green Petty Sessional Courts. The total number of persons placed on probation to the London Police Court Mission in 1923 was 2,104: 1,506 man and "lads", 390 women and "girls", and 208 children. (Figures for offenders put on probation in London - including those supervised by the "special" children's probation officers - between 1908 and 1919 are included as Appendix 9.)

During 1923 the London Police Court Mission had 47 missionaries, of whom 20 were women. In its Annual Report for 1923 the Mission tersely announced: "Much to our regret, Miss Porter was obliged, through illness, to resign." Behind this seemingly innocuous announcement lay the story of a scandal which had largely gripped the nation's attention in 1921. John Wakeford, Archdeacon of Stow, Precentor of Lincoln, and a married man, had been found guilty of improper conduct with a woman in the Bull Hotel, Peterborough, on two occasions in March and April, respectively, of 1920. Wakeford appealed to the

Judicial Committee of the Privy Council against the verdict which the consistory court announced in February 1921. At the ensuing appeal hearing, presided over by the Lord Chancellor (Lord Birkenhead) in Downing Street in April 1921, the London police court missionary Evelyn Porter was named in court as the person suspected of having been Wakeford's alleged companion at the hotel. She was named by Wakeford's clerical brother-in-law, who had previously claimed that a former Bishop of Lincoln had alleged the existence of a scandalous relationship between Wakeford and Miss Porter, the devout daughter of a brigadier and Wakeford's secretary while he was Precentor of Lincoln.

Shortly before the appeal hearing, the manageress of the Bull Hotel in Peterborough had gone to Evelyn Porter's room at Marlborough Street Police Court, where she had worked as a court missionary since 1917, and had pointed her out to the Bishop of Lincoln's solicitor. This incident was described by Miss Porter in the restricted evidence she was permitted to give to the Judicial Committee, which upheld the earlier verdict and confirmed that Wakeford would be deprived of all his ecclesiastical promotions within the diocese of Lincoln. Evelyn Porter was the only known probation officer in the history of the Privy Council to appear before its Judicial Committee.[4]

The Wakeford Case was highly embarrassing for the London Police Court Mission, the more so as the scandal received immense publicity in the middle of the Home Office enquiry into the training, appointment and payment of probation officers, and the Mission clearly seemed anxious as to what the Home Office-appointed Committee might recommend. More than half a dozen factors, taken together[5], suggest that Wakeford may well have been guilty of an improper relationship with at least one woman (in April 1922 Wakeford, who had continued to proclaim his innocence, took his monster petition, addressed to the King, to the Home Office, without success). But Miss Porter was almost certainly innocent. Birkenhead's friend Horatio Bottomley, through *John Bull,* of which Bottomley was the founder and editor, tracked down another woman as Wakeford's companion in Peterborough. Ironically, Douglas Hogg (later twice Lord Chancellor), who, representing the Bishop of Lincoln, led for the prosecution at Wakeford's appeal hearing, became President of the London Police Court Mission, a position he would hold between 1928 and 1950. Elspeth Gray, who joined the Mission in 1925, believed that the

Mission handled the case well by keeping Miss Porter on until illness forced her resignation, although the mothers of some of the Mission's clients apparently made rather caustic comments in relation to the case; and Mrs Gray seems to have been advised not to use a particular hostel which had been used by Miss Porter and was run by one of the latter's friends.[6] Miss Porter denied the allegation about her.

On a happier note, "Padcroft" celebrated its twenty-first anniversary in the summer of 1923, when the boys put on an interesting display of physical drill, gymnastics, and organised games, after which J.A.R. Cairns presented prizes to the lads who won them. This spirited metropolitan magistrate had just written that Padcroft and the Boys' Garden Colony were not institutions with warders, cells or uniforms, but homes "in the true sense of the word", and that "a Sunday spent *en famille* at the colony is one of my happiest recollections".[7] Frank Green reported that Padcroft had admitted 4,630 boys and given them another chance since it was opened. Indeed, by 1922 an A.C. - or "Another Chance" - Club had been formed by a group of ladies anxious to help Padcroft, and its funds, by making shirts for the lads.

What was officially described as "the Inaugural Conference" of the Guild of C.E.T.S. Police Court Missionaries was held on 4 October 1923. Although held in Leicester - not far from the famous Secular Hall - the Conference was largely dominated, at least in terms of the number of missionaries present, by those from the London and Southwark Dioceses. The outgoing Secretary traced the history of the Guild (which was apparently founded in 1919), and the Conference participants proceeded to revise the Constitution. Paradoxically, the objects in the revised Constitution stressed a religious inspiration as distinct from the secular basis of N.A.P.O. while, at the same time, they seem to have been at least partially modelled on those adopted by N.A.P.O. in 1912. Thus, the first object of N.A.P.O. was "the advancement of probation work", whereas the Guild's first object was: "To deepen and strengthen the spiritual life of each member and to keep alive the true Missionary spirit among C.E.T.S. Police Court Missionaries." N.A.P.O.'s second object was the "promotion of a bond of union amongst Probation Officers, the provision of opportunities for social intercourse, and the giving and receiving of friendly advice". For theme and wording it bears comparison with the Guild's second object: "To assist the members in any difficulty and to promote brotherhood in every Diocese and throughout the Society, particularly by providing opportunities of social intercourse and friendly comparison of work." The Guild's fourth object included "To improve the status and welfare of all C.E.T.S. Police Court Missionaries". Despite a later, honeyed claim by the N.A.P.O. leader Gertrude Tuckwell that "the objects of this Guild are quite different from those of the N.A.P.O.", they did seem to be partially competing organisations.

Messrs F.A. Herbert and S. Burgess - both from London - were elected Hon. Secretary and Hon. Treasurer, respectively; and the new Guild Executive included Fred Barnett (though he would soon resign on medical grounds). The Rev. Harry Pearson witnessed the Conference's discussion and approval of a proposed new C.E.T.S. pension scheme[8], which the London Police Court Mission Committee used to provide a "fair" pension for all future members of staff as well as a supplementary pension for the missionaries who were too old to be brought under the terms of any new scheme. The retiring age was fixed at 65 - apparently for men and women alike.

The London Police Court Mission declared:

> It is the policy of the Committee to pay such salaries as will enable the Missionaries to perform their duties without harassing anxieties, but at the same time not large enough to attract persons who only desire to make a living and have not given their hearts to social and religious work.

In 1924 the Mission's expenditure amounted to almost exactly £20,000; and the Home Office contributed nearly £6,000 and Middlesex County Council just over £2,000. As previously, the Mission's income was derived from such sources as subscriptions and donations, sales of work, and collections. In July 1924 William Fitzsimmons and Mrs B.M. Stead represented London in a N.A.P.O. deputation to the Home Office, where they pleaded for adequate pensions and Fitzsimmons claimed that the revised salary scales had still not been fully implemented in London.

Meanwhile the Probation Rules, 1923, had come into effect: these prohibited the appointment of serving police officers or school attendance officers as probation officers, made provision for the establishment of probation committees (composed of at least two magistrates), required probation officers to keep records on all their probationers, and also abolished the practice of annual appointment of probation officers, about which N.A.P.O. had long complained. At the same time the seeds of a system of "confirmation" were sown, for the Rules provided for appointment for one year in the first instance, to be followed by confirmation of the probation officer's appointment by the Home Secretary or the justices, after which the appointment would be allowed to continue.

In some areas of the country there were still probation officers supplied by bodies like the Church Army, the Salvation Army, the N.S.P.C.C., and the Discharged Prisoners' Aid Society. Some indication of the heterogeneous nature of the probation service was provided by the racy London court reporter who adopted the pseudonym "R. E. Corder": in his description of proceedings at Marylebone Court at about this time he referred to " a tired-looking youth who had been put on probation at the Church Army Labour Home", and, in another case, to a juvenile thief (from a large motherless family) whom the magistrate turned over to "the Roman Catholic probation officer". The journalist's reports habitually mentioned the metropolitan police magistrates by name, sometimes named the police court missionaries, and appeared to publicise the names of offenders, while he declined to use his own. Of one case at Clerkenwell Court which seemed to require social work intervention he wrote: "Mr Gill looked towards the woman missionary of the court, who throughout was busy crocheting, and said: 'Remand this case.' The woman missionary nodded. Here was the other side of the police court."

Publicity sometimes appeared to be beneficial: in about 1924 a destitute man who had been gassed and wounded in the War was contemplating suicide when he casually glanced at a copy of *John Bull* which he had picked up in Hyde Park, and he read of a man being helped by the probation officer at Westminster Court, in which direction he himself then turned and received help - no doubt from Fred Barnett - in getting a responsible job.[9] (Rather ironically, *John Bull*'s Horatio Bottomley - a former court reporter - had been sentenced in 1922 to seven years' penal servitude for fraud, and years earlier the paper had accused the Church Army of exploitation in its employment schemes.) Barnett, wrote Cecil Chapman, "has constantly proved himself to be a genius at reformation"; and the magistrate provided some evidence of this by publishing the text of two affectionate letters which a former probationer who had made good in Canada wrote to his "old friend" Barnett in the summer of 1924, nearly a year after "I left old England and said good-bye to you and Mr

Francis", who had placed the boy on probation to Barnett.

Cecil Chapman was not, of course, the only metropolitan police magistrate at this time to publicise good work unobtrusively done by London police court missionaries. In 1925 Henry Turner Waddy revealed how, one Saturday afternoon towards the end of the War, the missionary at Tower Bridge Court successfully approached the magistrate for some emergency money from the poor-box for a local woman to visit a military hospital in Birmingham in time to see her dying son. In *The Police Court and Its Work*, Waddy claimed that at least 80 per cent of matrimonial applications magistrates referred to the missionary were "happily settled". He added that the children's probation officers for the Southwark and Lambeth districts had combined to provide an office for the reception of their probationers, and that married women with young families still came week by week to this office to see the children's probation officer years after their probation had expired.[10] If the office was away from the court, this may have encouraged such continuing contact. Waddy did not say where this office was situated, though it did not appear to be at court - which hardly seems surprising in the light of William Fitzsimmons's reported comments that in any metropolitan police court at about this time "the worst accommodation in the building is, as a rule, allotted for Probation work, and some Courts provide no accommodation whatever for the work of the Probation Officer". Fitzsimmons also deplored the fact that, in London at least, respectable women and their innocent children were obliged to witness "sordid scenes" when they came to the courts to collect their maintenance allowances; though at Thames, for example, he had unsuccessfully suggested they could use a separate part of the building.[11]

Waddy pointed out that the joint Southwark-Lambeth probation office was equipped with a free lending library that was much appreciated by the children. At Westminster Court Fred Barnett - who had read Smollett and Hume when he was eleven, and who was concerned about the effect of "pernicious" literature on the young - apparently also supplied his boy clients with books, though he seemed to find that most of them wanted to read *The Autobiography of a Crook* (1925) by his former probationer Netley Lucas! Miss Blyth drew attention to the case of a boy who had apparently been influenced by a film in an assault on his mother; and in December 1924 the London and Home Counties Branch of

N.A.P.O. discussed a film, being shown at some cinemas, called "Big Brother", which gave such an unfavourable representation of probation officers that the Branch decided to approach the cinematograph trades society. Probation officers would long be conscious of the influence of films; and the interest of London probation officers in the cinema was also illustrated by the fact that Ethel Crosland was allowed to be present at the "shooting" of a film she did not name.[12]

If a film were to be made about some of the more colourful metropolitan magistrates of the period, it would probably include Forbes Lankester of West London Court whom "R. E. Corder" described as "looking more and more like Mr Pickwick", and who spoke of his juvenile court as a "farce" because on one occasion he had found no young offenders there to try. For this remark he was rebuked by the penological investigator Sydney Moseley (on the staff of *John Bull*), who commented: "if juvenile crime is disappearing in West London, the Children's Courts, with their cleaner, kinder atmosphere and the Probation Officer, their good genius, are entitled to public gratitude." Moseley was much impressed by Clarke Hall and the way he conducted his juvenile court at Shoreditch Town Hall, where, in Moseley's words, "a casual visitor could hardly associate this gathering with a Court of Justice". He then recounted the story of Charlie - a destitute and abandoned boy found wandering - "as told to the Court by the very human Probation Officer"; and Moseley praised "what the Probation Officers in connection with the Children's Court are doing every day with success"[13] in redirecting the energies of juvenile delinquents.

At Shoreditch Juvenile Court Clarke Hall placed all child probationers - including boys over 14 - under the care of the three lady probation officers appointed by the Home Office. He also felt that if there were several children in one family, or many children in one street, on probation at about the same time, it was undesirable in principle and unduly time-consuming in practice for them to be supervised by different probation officers, particularly if the supervisors included probation officers from the adult courts. (Appendices 10 and 11 show the nature of the charges, and how they were dealt with, at Shoreditch Juvenile Court between 1912 and 1924.) He maintained that while "success" and "failure" were difficult to measure in probation work, "the Courts which place the greatest confidence in their officers will inevitably tend to entrust them with more difficult cases and thus lower the percentage of successes". He believed the probation "failures" were due in nearly every case to the employment of "the wrong type of probation officer". He devoted some time to sitting in on client interviews conducted by his probation officers, and he found the experience "most illuminating". On one occasion a woman brought her husband with her: he had given her two black eyes, and she hoped that the "probation lady" would talk him into a better frame of mind. To her husband's great surprise, he got a severe "dressing down" from Clarke Hall instead, and thereafter, by all accounts, treated his wife properly.

Although the probation officers at Shoreditch were regularly assisted by a number of ladies, "usually down from the Universities or studying at the London School of Economics", Clarke Hall decided to discontinue his own experimental use of volunteers, partly because the number of cases heard at Shoreditch Juvenile Court had fallen dramatically since the end of the War while the number of probation officers there had increased. At the same time he felt strongly that probationers, whether men, women or children, should be placed under probation officers of the district in which they *lived*, not in which they *happened to be sentenced* (unless, of course, the two areas coincided). He knew of youths from East London who went into the country - almost certainly Kent - to engage in fruit- or hop- picking for a short while and, on getting into some kind of trouble there, were often put on probation to the local probation officer, only to return to "the Smoke" very soon afterwards, without any East London probation officer being informed of the situation until the youths reoffended and came before a London court. Conversely, if Clarke Hall sent such youths to jobs or situations in the country, he often had no assurance that the local probation officer would take any interest in them: indeed, he knew of cases where such assistance had been definitely refused. (In 1938 London juvenile court probation officers would agree that when a probationer moved to a new district, the probation officer of that district should be informed, in case the child were recharged.[14])

Clarke Hall also criticised the "waste of time, inconvenience, and failure" of the arrangements whereby five Roman Catholic and two Jewish probation officers in London were not attached to any particular court, but had peripatetic duties, with clients of their own faith scattered over the whole of London. He knew of a case where at least two remands were necessary to secure the attendance in court of a Catholic probation officer. He suggested that the Catholic authorities nominated at least one officer who would ensure that a Catholic delinquent placed on probation "was brought in touch with Catholic influences", perhaps through the use of Catholic volunteers or even, indirectly, of non-Catholic probation officers; and he pointed out that the two Jewish probation officers in London were "content to give assistance to the regular officers of the Court, leaving the actual order to be made out in the name of the latter".

Our London magistrate spoke briefly, but with his usual vigour, at the N.A.P.O. Annual Conference held in London in May 1925. At that Conference the other notable guest speakers included the serving metropolitan police magistrates J.A.R. Cairns and H.L. Cancellor, and retired metropolitan magistrates Cecil Chapman and Sir John Dickinson. Cairns paid tribute to "the devoted work of Mr Fitzsimmons and his colleague" and said that a reformed woman had just conveyed her gratitude to Fitzsimmons for the kindness he had shown her when she was a "terror" in East London, and had seemed a habitual criminal, over 25 years earlier. Cairns added that others were also recalcitrant or slow in responding to the offer of help: he had very recently heard of a lad who had been put on probation eight times; and as regards eight lads on probation whom he had brought into his own home, Cairns found that "it is futile to think they want the chance you offer or your standard of living. What they want is freedom." Sir John referred particularly to "the excellent work of Mr Fitzsimmons and Mrs Cary, from whom he received every possible assistance". Cancellor stressed the importance of pre-sentence enquiries by probation officers concerning the environment, state of mind and susceptibility of the offender.[15]

A potential facility for such enquiries was provided by the London Police Court Mission's Speedwell Club, which was formally opened on 15 April 1925, as a hostel for girls and young women between the ages of 18 and 25 who had been charged in the courts and were without money, work, friends or accommodation. Some beds were reserved for girls on remand whom it was thought undesirable to send to Holloway. The Speedwell Club (situated at 4 The Terrace, Old Ford Road, Bethnal Green) was apparently the Mission's first hostel for girls (as distinct from a home for female inebriates). Established at Clarke Hall's instigation, it originated in a secret meeting he had in a disused coal cellar in the slums with 20 to 30 young women of dubious repute who had invited him to tell

115

him about their accommodation problems. By 1926 the hostel staff commented: "The past year had proved at once the difficulty and the hopefulness of the undertaking. Most of the girls have been quite undisciplined and their management has been a constant problem." By the end of March 1926, a total of more than 100 girls had been admitted. Of these, 69 were described as on probation, 32 were quite homeless, and 20 were on remand at the hostel while enquiries were made about them. (naturally, these were not necessarily mutually exclusive categories). Employment was found for 43 girls; 24 were returned to their homes or friends; 12 were transferred to other institutions; 8 were sent to hospital; 5 got married; 1 emigrated to Australia; 1 absconded; and 15 remained in the hostel. The recreation room was used every evening by former residents; and the Speedwell Club's successes included a woman who had spent the previous ten years on the streets, in hospital and in prison, but who, after a period of residence at the hostel, settled down as a nurse.[16] (In 1929 the Speedwell Club would become an "approved" hostel, eligible for Government grants, after Dr A.H. Norris and Mr S.W. Harris of the Home Office had carried out "a very thorough inspection" of the premises.)

As a result of an invitation from the Governor of Holloway Prison, the Mission appointed a number of lady volunteers - reduced from six to two by 1926 - who, after a period of service in the courts by way of preparation, were sent to visit all women and girls on remand at Holloway, irrespective of any visits paid by probation officers. The London Police Mission Committee was represented at the International Prison Congress, held in London in August 1925; and the Rev. Harry Pearson, who addressed the Congress on the subject of probation work undertaken by voluntary and religious societies, no doubt heard Lord Hewart, the Lord Chief Justice of England, tell the same audience that probation was "a method the value of which could hardly be exaggerated - and its opportunities had by no means, as yet, been fully explored".

One problem faced by those outside prison with criminal records -whether or not they were on probation - was unemployment, particularly at a time when very approximately two million people were out of work in Britain. At the invitation of the Home Office, the London Police Court Mission Committee (which included three metropolitan magistrates) appointed one of its police court missionaries as a full-time "employment officer" with effect from September 1925: this was Alfred J. Pilgrim[17], who was detached from his work at Clerkenwell and North London Courts (in which connection he had been mentioned, by name, by "R.E. Corder" in *Tales Told to the Magistrate)* and given an office at 27 Gordon Square, the headquarters into which the Mission had moved at about the time that Pilgrim was appointed a missionary in 1923. No doubt the courts he had to leave were assisted by some of the Mission's many voluntary workers. In a sense Pilgrim's new task represented a variation and a continuation of the work undertaken before the War by Frank Brown (who had subsequently moved to Chelmsford). Finding thousands of jobs for offenders over the years, Pilgrim and his Employment Department would long be remembered by probation staff in London.

Probation officers were also concerned about their own conditions of employment. This was a matter that was taken into account by the Criminal Justice Act of 1925, which received the Royal Assent on 22 December 1925 and came into force the following summer. The Bill had been introduced by the Home Secretary, Sir William Joynson-Hicks, who in 1925 addressed the Annual Conferences of both N.A.P.O. and the London Police Court Mission. More than thirty years earlier he had been treasurer of the C.E.T.S. Canterbury Diocesan Police Court Mission - he called himself "an old Temperance worker and Police Court Missioner" -and in his speech to N.A.P.O. he strongly indicated that promoting the probation service was his dearest wish and goal as Home Secretary. He said he wanted to establish a system of superannuation and pensions for probation officers; and the N.A.P.O. Chairman, Sydney Edridge, asked him not to forget the older officers "who had borne the burden and heat of the day". One such veteran, the metropolitan children's probation officer Miss Croker-King, had made a similar heartfelt appeal five years earlier; and in October 1925 her London colleague Ethel Crosland spoke with equal sincerity about the need for a fair and comprehensive pension scheme.

Under the Criminal Justice Act of 1925 the Home Secretary was empowered to arrange for the introduction of a superannuation scheme for probation officers. The Act was no less far-reaching in its provisions that at least one probation officer had to be appointed for every probation area; that probation work in the designated probation areas would in general be the responsibility of a probation committee (composed of magistrates); that local authorities could make contributions regarding officers' remuneration direct to voluntary societies providing agents to act as probation officers; that local authorities could contribute towards the maintenance of persons released on probation with a condition of residence; and that the cost of probation would be shared between the local authorities and the Treasury. Edridge, for N.A.P.O., welcomed the Act for enabling probation officers to be seen as an integral part of the country's criminal justice system. The London Police Court Mission commented on the expected effects of the Act: "In London, however, the results are less marked than elsewhere, because the main provisions have already been in existence here since 1923."

In the summer of 1926 the Home Office introduced the super-annuation scheme for which the Criminal Justice Act provided. Under this scheme for full-time probation officers, the retiring age was fixed at 65 for future appointments, and for future service, pensions would be calculated at the rate of £6 for every completed year of service for men and £4 for every year of service for women. The Home Office undertook responsibility for the entirety of the pensions due to the probation officers it appointed direct, and for two-thirds of the pensions of police court missionaries and such probation officers who were agents of voluntary societies, on the basis that as these societies were already responsible for one third of the salaries, they should assume a similar responsibility for one third of their agents' pensions. With perhaps a hint of self righteousness combined with lack of diplomacy vis-à-vis the Home Office, the London Police Court Mission publicly declared:

> The Home Office scheme has been adversely criticised in respect of the small pension it provides for officers who are now over 60 years of age and who have spent practically a life-time in the work. Fortunately in the case of our own Missionaries in this category we have invested a considerable sum to secure that they will be adequately provided for when their working days are done.

Ethel Crosland (a London member of N.A.P.O. who was also a member of the Home Office Committee which reported on this matter) told a N.A.P.O. conference in London in October: "The Committee which investigated this question had under consideration the position of officers appointed very late in life, as for example between 57 and 67 years of age, and decided that such officers should not be pensionable." In the

118

case of serving officers who were eligible, back service would produce a pensionable benefit at the rate of £3 for men and £2 for women for each year already served.

No doubt Miss Crosland, who was the only woman on that Home Office Committee, spoke *de facto* for many women when she told N.A.P.O.: "She was very pleased to think they had the advantage of a woman's membership, because she thought the women were quite lost sight of; whenever they were spoken of they were called female officers and she did dislike it so much. (Hear, hear.)" The question of equal treatment for women was raised, in the context of homelessness, by Mrs Cecil Chesterton - G.K. Chesterton's sister-in-law and author of *In Darkest London* (March 1926) - when she addressed N.A.P.O.'s Autumn Conference in London in October 1926 on her experiences as a voluntary "dosser" in the metropolis. She pointed out that "of the total sleeping accommodation, licensed by the L.C.C., only 9.42 per cent was available for women, the rest was for men"; and she appealed to the probation officers for support in her plan to open a lodging-house in Central London for homeless and destitute women.[18] The extent to which, at the time, London probation officers, for example, actively supported her plan seems unclear; but soon afterwards she started the first of her Cecil Houses for such women in London and would continue to take a close interest in them until her death in 1962.

A year before Mrs Chesterton's speech, the London probation officer Clemence Paine, who worked in the East End, had drawn N.A.P.O.'s attention to "the housing question", which, she said in her characteristically forthright way, "made her boil". At the same time Miss Paine reported that Clarke Hall had offered to give free advice to members of the public who wished to consult him privately, and that this often meant more work for the probation officer, including, in her case, supervision - apparently on a voluntary basis - of a high-ranking police officer's son who was "a perfect imp". Clarke Hall's colleague H.L. Cancellor told the 1926 N.A.P.O. Annual Conference in London that "the gulf between the Magistrate and the prisoner was bridged over by the Probation Officer" -a somewhat similar point would be made 40 years later by the metropolitan stipendiary magistrate Anthony Babington, who, in discussing the assistance of pioneers of the probation service, would refer to "the tremendous gulf which seems to separate the dock from the bench at the moment of judgment".[19]

Just as Anthony Babington's *The Power To Silence* (1968) would be "Dedicated to The Officers of the Probation Service with admiration and respect"; so Clarke Hall's *Children's Courts* (1926) was dedicated "To My Probation Officers in grateful recognition of their services to delinquent children". Possibly bearing in mind that, as the Rev. Harry Pearson had pointed out, the London Police Court Mission provided probation officers for both the juvenile and the adult courts in Middlesex, Clarke Hall, in his book, strongly attacked the religious tests imposed by the Mission:

> At present the Police Court Mission *does* impose tests. It is necessary that every "missionary", and this implies every probation officer, appointed by it, should be "a communicating member of the Church of England." Such a test applied to men and women assisting in the administration of justice, and paid largely, and to be paid still more largely, out of public funds, savours of the seventeenth rather than the twentieth century....In London at the present time there is no male probation officer attached to a Metropolitan Police Court who has not been subjected to this religious test....it cannot seriously be urged that it is any part of the duty of a probation officer to give dogmatic religious teaching to the delinquents under his care....If a probation officer's duty involves the inculcation of the dogmatic beliefs of those who appoint him, no part of his salary should be paid by the State. If it does not involve such teaching there is no point whatever in a dogmatic test.

Concerning the Mission, Clarke Hall added:

> It is to the great honour of this society that it has succeeded so wonderfully in discovering men and women imbued with the right spirit, and I cannot imagine any of the many whom I have known using their position as probation officers for the purpose of dogmatic propaganda.

He went on: "This fact, however, serves only to strengthen my plea for the abolition of a test which is mischievous and unjust, which serves no useful end, and which is to my own knowledge disliked and resented by many of those who are compelled to submit to it."[20] (Clarke Hall's line of argument appeared to receive some reinforcement when the 1935 N.A.P.O. Annual Conference voted by a large majority for the probation service to be divorced from the Mission. Support for Clarke Hall's approach to religious tests, as well as for his use of volunteers at Shoreditch, was expressed by Fenner Brockway in *A New Way with Crime,* published in 1928.)

Clarke Hall may have noticed from the London Police Court Mission's Annual Report for 1926 that at Padcroft the new Chapel was dedicated "in the presence of all the boys....all the lads attend the Yiewsley Parish Church for worship on Sunday". In the same report Frank Green, the manager of the home, declared that before they came to Padcroft most of the boys were reluctant to enter a boys' club, library or church: "The literature they have been accustomed to read before being admitted to Padcroft is of the most pernicious character, but once they read the good books we possess and are forbidden to read the others, they in time thoroughly appreciate our action." Green believed that "cinemas and Music Halls were once the principal causes of the boys' downfall (because they stole money to go to them) but unfortunately, a greater evil has recently appeared - that of Greyhound Racing" - a visit of observation to the White City Stadium strengthened his conviction that "this sport - if it can be called by such a name - is beggaring our homes". The boys were very difficult to handle, "but once they realize that they have to do as they are told and settle down to work they become quite at home, and very often the most unruly lad on admission becomes the leading lad on discharge". There was much emphasis on wholesome food, healthy recreation, regular habits and a stable environment, backed up by the provision of a spacious gymnasium, open-air sports like football and cricket, and the services of a doctor and dentist.

When Green heard that Pilkingtons, the famous glass-makers of St Helens, Lancashire, had decided to close their boys' hostel with effect from the end of 1926, he found that a number of Padcroft "old boys" there would be homeless and out of work unless help was forthcoming: consequently, every one of them was found a position - whether in civilian life or in H.M. Forces - and five were emigrated to Australia. Green felt, in his own words, that "the Missionaries and Probation Officers have sent the better class boy to the care of Mr Pilgrim, and only sent to Padcroft those that badly required discipline and training".

Pilgrim, through his Employment Department, found that some of those he was able to assist had been out of work for up to four years. He placed a number of youths as apprentices in various skilled trades and industries, partly as a result of co-operation between the Home Office and the Ministry of Labour since at least 1925. Pilgrim also found employment for women and girls - including some unmarried mothers - in such areas of work as the catering trades, hotels and hospitals. At the Speedwell Club in Bethnal Green (which did not operate rigid rules as to the length of residence), 151 stranded and homeless girls were admitted during 1927, including two Irish and 12 Welsh girls; and Elspeth Gray would remember how in the 1930s - and conceivably earlier - she put a lot of Welsh girls (brought to Marlborough Street Court for Hyde Park offences or wandering abroad) onto the train at Paddington for Wales. (In the 1950s the emphasis would change to her putting foreign 'au pair' girls, who had been caught shoplifting, onto the train for the Hook of Holland.)[21]

Her work with prostitutes enabled her to give evidence - as did her friend Miss Langton, probation officer at Bow Street - to the Street Offences Committee, appointed by Sir William Joynson-Hicks in October 1927. "R.E. Corder" wrote in a newspaper article that Miss Macpherson (as Mrs. Elspeth Gray then was) "probably knows more about the streets problem than any member of the committee now sitting". In her summary of evidence for the committee, the Marlborough Street missionary and probation officer declared:

> At Marlborough Street, Probation is used almost always for girls under the age of eighteen, with fairly good success, but such cases are very few in number.

> I see all girls from the age of eighteen upwards, who are charged for the first time, and in many cases useful work has been done in
>   1. getting the girls off the streets.
>   2. placing them in hostels.
>   3. providing employment.
>   4. restoring them to relations.
>   5. arranging for treatment where necessary.

> In such cases they are usually bound over, under the Probation Act, but no order is made....

> Experience at Marlborough Street has shown that the best results are obtained from those girls who are
>   1. in the early stages of prostitution.
>   2. getting tired of the life.

Whilst "a very large proportion of the prostitutes are drawn from the servant classes", "I feel very strongly that the causes that lead a girl to adopt a life of prostitution are psychological rather than economic". She suggested that most of the prostitutes using Hyde Park did not solicit elsewhere, and that from the Park came "most of the girls charged who are found to be pregnant" as well as older women who were "often methylated spirit addicts".[22] She did not apparently perceive what in 1927 Canon Hasloch Potter (supporting a provincial police court missionary) called "the extreme desirability of rendering the hopelessly morally polluted, or the half-witted evil-doer of either sex, incapable of propagating offspring, only too likely to be as diseased as themselves".[23] Be that as it may, one of the magistrates who gave evidence to the Street Offences Committee, Henry L. Cancellor, seems to have drawn on his knowledge of young prostitutes appearing before him at Marlborough Street when, at about this time, he conceived the idea (which failed to materialise) of a scheme for girls similar to that embodied in the Boys' Garden Colony at Basingstoke.

"The Boys' Home at Yiewsley, maintained by the London Police Court Mission, and the Farm Colony at Basingstoke, subsidized in part by the same body, are used...by the London courts with much success." Thus declared the London-based psychologist Professor Cyril Burt in his book *The Young Delinquent* (1925), in which the sections on treatment had been read by Ethel Crosland as well as by Elspeth Gray's immediate predecessor at Marlborough Street Court. Burt proposed that "probation should be employed with larger freedom, and at the same time with finer discrimination", and that there should be improved multi-disciplinary co-operation in the treatment and management of juvenile delinquency. He also indicated in *The Young Delinquent* that probation officers in London had "recently referred many cases of juvenile delinquency" to the Vocational Section of the National Institute of Industrial Psychology for "psychological examination in order to discover what form of employment may be most suited to the child's particular needs" (a generation later, in 1946, the National Institute would advise the Home Office on desirable qualities of probation officers). Burt recommended that children's probation officers "should have received, wherever possible, an intensive training in the psychology of delinquency and child-life".[24]

Although many years later he would appear to be discredited, Burt's book was largely influential in the establishment of the London Child Guidance Clinic in Islington in 1928 (seven years earlier, the first birth control clinic in the British Empire had opened in Islington); in 1927 the East London Child Guidance Clinic was founded by the Jewish Health Organisation; and interest in the question of juvenile delinquency was also stimulated by the publication in 1927 of the Report of the Departmental Committee on the Treatment of Young Offenders. This Committee had been set up by Sir William Joynson-Hicks, and the Rev. Harry Pearson had submitted to it the views of the London Police Court Mission Committee and of its missionaries. The witnesses examined by the Home Office Departmental Committee included: Pearson; Cyril Burt; London magistrates Sir Chartres Biron, Clarke Hall and Basil Henriques; and the London probation officers – all attached to juvenile courts – Nina Blyth (Tower Bridge), Ethel Crosland (Dean Street) and Miss M.A. Warner (Shoreditch). The Departmental Committee observed in its Report: "Our scheme of treatment contemplates the fullest use of probation in suitable cases"; and in that context "a woman or girl should always be placed under the supervision of a woman probation officer. Boys over school age should be placed under the supervision of a man." The Committee also indicated, among its many conclusions and recommendations, that there was a need for greater use of hostels, there should be closer co-operation between probation officers and Home Office schools and other institutions, the Home Office Children's Branch (established just before the onslaught of the World War) should be strengthened, and the Probation Advisory Committee might be reconstituted.

The Home Office would certainly come to play a more active part in the development of the probation service, not least in the London area. At Padcroft (where training in carpentry was added to the facilities), Frank Green obtained the assistance of the Home Office in checking on the progress of the 360 boys admitted to Padcroft during the years 1926 and 1927. He received encouraging replies from 297 of these 360 boys, to each of whom he had written for up-to-date information. At the same time he sent a list of all the boys' names and addresses to the Home Office, which subsequently informed him that only 27 out of the 360 boys had been reconvicted. Of these 27, 10 had been in residence at Padcroft for three months, 7 for about ten weeks, and 10 for periods ranging from four weeks to two days. Though he did not say so, Green may have suspected some kind of link between reconviction and shortness of residence or boys' relative lack of qualitative experience at Padcroft. Certainly, "after making liberal allowance for doubtful cases", Green claimed that over 80% of the boys admitted during 1926-7 had benefited from their time at Padcroft - which he considered a very good result, bearing in mind that many of the boys could well have been sent to borstal as an alternative.

Discipline and training clearly had a more military complexion at the Boys' Garden Colony, Basingstoke, where all the boys were made members of the Cadet Company attached to the Territorial Brigade of the Hampshire Regiment, with access to the Regiment's drill hall and gymnasium. At the Colony the boys at work received between 17 and 30 shillings a week, depending on diligence, experience and capability. The management committee made a deduction from each boy's earnings as a contribution to the cost of his clothing and maintenance; the rest was banked for him and given to him in cash, as need arose, for personal expenses. Up to the end of December 1928, the total number of boys admitted was 352, of whom some 69 joined H.M. Forces, 55 became gardeners, 28 found other jobs in the Basingstoke area, and 8 went to farms, while 192 returned to their homes, where most of them behaved well. In some cases at least, "after care of old boys" was found to be difficult, as no kind of official control could be exercised on completion of the period of probation (which appears to have been not less than twelve months).

In 1920 William Fitzsimmons had warned N.A.P.O. that the "officialisation of Probation work will enthrone bureaucracy, paralyse individuality, initiative and enterprise, stereotype methods of work", and that accordingly probation officers "would, in time, degenerate into mere statistical recording officials". Yet, assisted by such measures as the Criminal Justice Act of 1925 and the 1926 Probation Rules, the probation service was beginning to establish a national identity, as illustrated by legal or administrative changes to facilitate the extension of the use of probation in the higher courts, the transfer of cases from one area to another, and the introduction in all probation areas of a standard form of record-keeping, including "followers". This method of record-keeping had been used, on a pioneering basis, since early 1925 in at least some parts of London, where probation officers did not apparently have any typists.[25] An interesting example of a London probation case-record dating from this period is attached as Appendix 12 (intact except for the fact that the probationer's name and address have been deleted for the purposes of this study): the case-record contains brief hand-written entries on the officially prescribed cover (printed in 1926) and forms (printed in 1926 and 1927). As the record - which gives some personal and family information as well as details of official contact - is of a boy who was placed on twelve months' probation by the Guildhall Court in June 1927, it is no doubt one of the oldest probation records of supervision to have survived in England in the officially prescribed original form. By 1929 the London Police Court Mission covered 14 metropolitan police courts, the Central Criminal Court, the London and Middlesex Sessions, and, indeed, every criminal court in the County of Middlesex, but not the Guildhall Court in the City of London (where, in the nineteenth century, the Chamberlain, in his semi-private court at the Guildhall, had given generally effective advice or warnings to delinquent City apprentices[26]).

During 1928 the London Police Court Mission's Employment Department, under A.J. Pilgrim, managed to find positions as apprentices in "all trades" for boys and girls, though most of his applicants were found jobs as unskilled labourers. Perhaps the greatest tribute to Pilgrim's endeavours came from Mrs Cecil Chesterton, who in the final chapter (entitled "The Way Back") of her book *Women of the Underworld* (1931) described his Department as "the strongest bulwark against a return to crime", adding: "The manager, Mr A.J. Pilgrim, has a most comprehensive knowledge of human nature. . . Nothing perturbs, nothing upsets him, he remains eternally interested, unflaggingly eager." Mrs Chesterton believed that "a formidable-looking building, emblazoned with vast lettering and a host of minions" would have put off the prospective applicant for work, whereas Pilgrim's office, being a "quiet and unpretentious little place, easy of access and unfraught with any terrifying form of ceremonial, brings its own atmosphere of hope and healing".

While Pilgrim's office was welcoming and homely, at least some London probation officers seemed to prefer the home - their own or the client's - to any office they might have had. The Roman Catholic probation officer Mary Stopford (who covered three police courts in South London and the London Sessions for six years until she became Mary Ellison on her marriage in 1933) asked: "Is there anything more cold and cheerless than the sight of a locked office door, to the penniless and lonely, who have trudged wearily to the only friend they possess? Disappointment sometimes breeds despair: those wounded spirits may never come your way again." She pointed out that "Jewish and Roman Catholic offenders were, and are still, supervised by itinerant workers of their own faith in the Metropolitan area" who were approved by the Home Office. Her experience convinced her (as, she said, the colleagues in the service whom she most admired had learnt long before) that "one gets very near to the homeless, the difficult and the unhappy, by opening one's home to them". Accordingly, to 32B Ebury Street, S.W.1 (her home address was published in *Probation*), came all manner of men and women seeking help, and she marvelled at the progress many of them made.[27]

Nearby, at 90 Claverton Street, lived Miss Hester Leaver, who was a police court missionary between 1919 and 1933 at Westminster Court, where she had the use of a cell before a room was made available. Georgina Stafford, who knew her well, remembered Miss Leaver as middle class, with no degree, but intelligent and direct, with a deep concern for people in trouble (according to other sources, Miss Leaver was a clergyman's daughter and a friend of Dean Inge[28]). Miss Leaver once changed clothes, at very short notice, with a bedraggled woman with a drink problem so that the client could keep an appointment for a job, which she got, leaving Miss Leaver eventually to slink home. Moreover, she had her name on her front door at home, where the police, instead of charging some drunks, apparently used to bring them to her, resulting in the drunks sleeping in her bed and the police court missionary sleeping on the floor.

The veteran children's probation officer Miss E. Croker-King felt that one advantage of visiting children in their homes, compared with their reporting at an office, was that, although more time-consuming, "it gives a far better insight into what the troubles and difficulties are in every individual family". She added: "To have your probationers to visit you at your home is far more ideal, though not always possible." She may well have had in mind the "Club" she had operated from her Bethnal Green home (which she shared with Miss E.D. Cheshire) to welcome her little clients and keep them safely occupied, often while their parents were manning their street stalls in the evenings - some boys reported to her flat as late as 10 p.m. on their way home from work. Her "Club" was a kind of precursor of East End youth projects that would be associated with

Derek Shuttleworth and Merfyn Turner, rather as Evelyn Lance's "club" for boys in Deptford seemed a forerunner of the Bermondsey Children's Flats.

Between 1921 and 1929 Miss Croker-King worked at Westminster Juvenile Court, whose area in those days included Chelsea, Pimlico, and parts of South Kensington, Lambeth and Kennington; and home visits sometimes involved long walks in districts beyond the reach of buses or trams. In 1925 the metropolitan magistrate H.T. Waddy declared that the women children's probation officers "make their way unobtrusively, unprotected by uniform, into some of the darkest places in London, and find themselves welcomed wherever they go". Miss Croker-King concluded: "The 'office' is very well in its way, but if it becomes the centre of importance in the probation work, not the home, then it is a very grave menace to the ideal and spirit of true probation work."

Just as the recommendation by the metropolitan magistrate John Dickinson of an assistant for Miss Croker-King resulted in the appoint-ment of Miss Cheshire; so his later realisation that Miss Blyth needed an assistant resulted in the appointment of a succession of dedicated and talented women juvenile court probation officers from Ethel Crosland to Rose Mary Braithwaite, and including Clemence Paine and Laelia Sander, all of whom had the benefit of working with or "under" Nina Blyth. When, towards the end of the Great War, it became clear that Miss Blyth's tiny office in the Old Kent Road - which she seems to have inherited from Evelyn Lance - was quite inadequate for her needs, Nina Blyth (assigned to Tower Bridge) and Ethel Crosland (assigned to Bow Street) decided to look for a bigger room in a central district which they could share. As the Home Office at that time would only cover a very small rent for this purpose, the best the two probation officers could manage was a room at the Library, 179 Blackfriars Road. Yet this address was almost ideal: anyone could visit a public library without attracting undue attention - and for the reporting children there was often the bonus of being given a sweet, shown a picture, told a story or lent a book from her own collection by Miss Blyth, whose love and understanding of children, combined with her unfailing humour and vivid personality, made her an effective and influential probation officer. Some measure of her success is suggested by the fact that her Saturday reporting book for 1923, for example, recorded visits from 421 "old boys" and 60 "old girls", as well as 1,491 visits from probationers, 504 by parents, 287 from other relatives, and 121 from others.[29]

When Miss Elizabeth Inman became a London juvenile court probation officer in 1929, at the age of about 31, she had to find an office from which to work, and she, too, managed to secure a room at Blackfriars Public Library. The rental (up to a maximum of £40 a year) was paid, like her salary, by the Receiver for the Metropolitan Police. However, she had to pay for furniture herself (rather as Elspeth Macpherson, later Gray, at Marlborough Street Court discovered that neither the London Police Court Mission nor even the Home Office provided furniture). It was a six day week job for Miss Inman, and on Saturdays she held a "surgery" at her room in the Library, where youngsters reported to her and parents dropped in for advice. "It was a lovely job, no organisation, and so independent," she recalled. She spent one day each week at Lambeth Juvenile Court, where initially the stipendiary used to read her reports aloud for all to hear. Before the court sat, she could see the magistrate in his room and privately discuss her report and its recommendation (usually probation or Home Office schooling: later she would be allowed to act as an escort to approved schools - formally established under the 1933 Children and Young Persons Act - and thus got to know many of them). Apart from her court day and Saturday "surgery", her time was spent visiting the children at home. One year after her appointment, she had a caseload of 80 and was writing two or three reports a week; her sole clerical assistance for her first ten years or so was an old typewriter. "Nobody told you what to do, you had to find out for yourself." Her predecessor, who had retired aged 72, had a reputation for shouting at the children under her supervision while they stood rigidly to attention. This lady's daughter, who used to help out, told Miss Inman: "if mother and I can't haul them straight then nobody can." Miss Inman decided to adopt a different approach (illustrated by her short story attached as Appendix 13).

How did she come to join? When the World War ended, Miss Inman (who left school in 1915, before working in naval intelligence) took a job at Girl Guides headquarters, and her interest in juvenile delinquents was aroused by the realisation that she "always liked the naughty guide the best". Despite the low pay there was fierce competition to join the probation service, and applicants had to pay for their own training. Having saved enough money, she decided to enrol at the London School of Economics for the two-year Social Science Certificate course. When she finished her course, she discovered that there were no probation vacancies; but she kept writing to the Home Office at regular intervals, and after some two years she was offered a post at a salary of £200 a year. (A rather similar experience befell Elspeth Macpherson, who became a London police court missionary and probation officer some four years earlier at a salary of £150 per annum, after obtaining an M.A. and Social Study Certificate at Edinburgh University, surmounting her middle-class parents' horror that she should be contemplating police court missionary work, and making repeated approaches to the London Police Court Mission and the Home Office.) Though at the Girl Guides headquarters she was earning twice the salary, Miss Inman quickly accepted the Home Office offer; and before taking up her formal appointment, she did six weeks' holiday relief work for Clemence Paine at Old Street Juvenile Court, where having access to Miss Paine's case-papers was, she believed, the most valuable part of her training and an inspiration in her future work.

The Home Office, which appointed Elizabeth Inman and had also apparently supported Elspeth Macpherson's appointment at the age of 25, seems to have set store by education and perhaps relevant experience rather than age as such. But, according to Elspeth Gray's recollection, the London Police Court Mission at this time appeared to operate a general rule of not appointing as missionaries single women (or widows) who were under the age of 40, with the additional condition that if they got married they would have to sacrifice their police court missionary work. If there was such a restriction, Miss Macpherson may well have been the first London female police court missionary to overcome it, for after she told Harry Pearson in 1929 that the man she proposed to marry was very critically ill she retained her post at Marlborough Street on her marriage.

Matrimonial and domestic work still represented an important part of the caseload of the probation officer or police court missionary. In 1929, 5,370 applications for separation orders were referred by magistrates to London Police Court missionaries, and in 2,570 cases reconciliation was effected (in 1928, 4,844 such applications had resulted in reconciliation in 2,449 cases). Such work was given some emphasis by Mrs Cecil Chesterton in the penultimate chapter of her book *Women of the Underworld* (1931). In this chapter, appositely entitled "Guide, Philosopher and Friend" - devoted to the London Police Court Mission and largely based, it seems, on a morning with the missionary at Old Street - she declared:

> The missionary, like an Eastern Cadi, is the father of his people in all the poorer districts of London. ...The secrets of psychology are open to him, nothing surprises, nothing appals. ...Matrimonial differences are adjudicated in the missionary's room. ...The missionary listens, reasons, and in a large majority of cases sends man and wife away with a better understanding of each other. The unbearable contiguity bred of overcrowding is responsible for many of the fracas that so often end in a separation order. ...There is such a narrow line between these matrimonial squabbles and a summons for assault. ...The Court Missionary is the safety valve of matrimonial high pressure.

Across the Thames, similar unobtrusive rescue work was being undertaken, as the metropolitan police magistrate J.B. Sandbach testified of the situation in Lambeth (where he worked from July 1928 onwards): "most of the work consisted of family squabbles and rows between neighbours, a state of affairs attributable to overcrowding more than anything else. In the majority of cases a talk with the probation officer kept the case out of Court." The court clerk Stanley French, who arrived at Lambeth not long after Sandbach, would remember the probation officer and missionary there, S.C. Fidgen, as

> a portly, soberly dressed, bespectacled man, solemn of visage and measured of tone. He was very good with young criminals, who respected him for his obvious sincerity and Christian principles, and he also managed to keep a great many quarrelling husbands and wives out of court, sometimes by a method which would not be approved of by modern theorists.

Fidgen was deaf and used a hearing-aid. According to French, he would allow husband and wife to pour out their troubles and complaints about each other in the privacy of his room, with a look of rapt attention on his face, then he would shake his finger at both of them and roughly tell them to go away and make it up - after which he would switch on his hearing-aid.[30]

CHAPTER SIX

Towards a Professional and Unified Public Service, 1930-38

In accordance with the letter and spirit of the Report (1927) of the Home Office-appointed Committee on the Treatment of Young Offenders, the Home Office was beginning to take a more active part in the administration and development of the probation service. In response to an invitation from the London Police Court Mission, Home Office officials carried out careful inspections of Padcroft and the Speedwell Club, both of which were "approved", with Government grants being made in 1929 for inmates between the ages of 16 and 21 sent to these institutions under a probation order with a condition of residence.

Then, in 1930, the Home Office started its own training scheme for probation officers. Apparently it selected five trainees - three men and two women - out of some 600 applicants. Both the women became London probation officers. One of them, Miss Cecil Barker, originally thought that her training would last for about six to twelve months, but in fact it drifted on for a couple of years while she acted as an assistant and "stop-gap" in London and the Home Counties. She did not have to attend lectures because of her History degree; and although she did go to one or two law lectures, she found them extremely dull. Her first placement seems to have been at Bow Street, where she worked as an assistant probation officer with the lady police court missionary, Miss Langton, for about three months, during which time she encountered a more or less representative cross-section of seamy cases (when there were any cases of indecency, the women were supposed to leave the court). Thereafter the young trainee - she was almost 30 when she started, no one over 30 apparently being accepted at that time - went to some five other London police courts before being appointed in November 1932 to West London Court (succeeding Miss E. Brown, who had just died after 26 years' service at that court, listening to stories of broken lives and devoting her life to mending them). The other female trainee, Miss Joan Potter, had a background of children's nursing. (The letter of 6 October

1930 to Miss Cecil Barker - giving details regarding her training - is attached as Appendix 14.)

Evidently very flexibly structured, the training scheme was considered to be a success and was continued, partly under the guidance of Elizabeth Macadam, long-time Secretary of the Joint University Council for Social Studies and a pioneer of professional training for social workers. Certainly the concept of the scheme was an improvement on the situation that had faced a police court missionary like Elspeth Macpherson, who had received no formal training, though she would later credit her senior colleague Tommy Mills (who had worked in the London police courts since 1911) and the veteran metropolitan magistrate Frederick Mead with having taught her everything. (In a message to the Police Court Mission Jubilee meeting in York in 1926, the then Home Secretary, Sir William Joynson-Hicks, referred cryptically to those "selected and trained by our Mission".) Apparently a number - probably a majority - of these early Home Office trainees were appointed to the juvenile courts, where the Home Office had already deployed "women of education".

The Home Office course seems to have represented a small and hesitant first step towards the provision of common training for probation officers in the juvenile and adult courts. There was already some contact between officers of the two wings of probation. The four London Branch members of N.A.P.O.'s Executive Committee in 1929, for example, comprised three police court missionaries and Ethel Crosland (who also served with two of her three adult court colleagues on a pensions subcommittee of N.A.P.O.). The advertised speakers for N.A.P.O. London Branch meetings during 1930 included both adult court and juvenile court probation officers. Moreover, in the words of Cyril Burt[1] (1925): "In London, the police-court missionaries ...deal with male and female adults and with older unruly boys; and special women officers, appointed by the Home Office, deal with children and (in a few instances) with adult females." But relations were not always cordial (one of the London police court missionaries complained to the Home Office about one of the earliest Home Office trainees); and whereas the juvenile court officers -totalling 12 in London in 1929[2] - dealt with all religious denominations, this was not always, or even usually, the case with their counterparts in the adult courts. Such differences seem to have fostered the development of a perceived dichotomy not only between adult and juvenile court officers, but also between God-fearing missionaries and supposedly godless children's probation officers appointed direct by a secular authority (the Jewish settlement warden Basil Henriques, who had been a London J.P. since 1924, would be "horrified" when told by a probation officer that a boy's religion was no concern of the officer's[3]).

The London Police Court Mission was shaken and angered by the proposals in a private member's Bill, introduced in the House of Commons in July 1930, that no voluntary society should form part of the probation system, and that in the appointment of probation officers no questions should be asked about their religious views. Declared the Mission: "Thus the great voluntary principle, responsible for so much excellent work in our country, and the religious faith which has brought such fine men and women into the probation service, would be swept away by the Bill." The Mission was on the point of participating in an "influential" deputation to the Home Secretary when the Bill was withdrawn - but it was a straw in the wind; just as the appointment in 1933 of Morley Jacob, who never became ordained, as the Rev. Harry Pearson's deputy would in a sense mark a move away from the Mission's clerical background.

The beginnings of a move away from a religious basis were discernible not only in the field of administration and organisation of the probation service (a process associated with greater involvement by secular authority in the form of the Home Office), but also in the realm of ideas regarding crime and its treatment. There was a growing interest among probation officers in England in psychology, psychological aspects of crime, and some connections between medicine and the work of probation officers. Thus towards the end of 1929 Dr Charles Burns of the Children's Department, Tavistock Square Clinic for Functional Nervous Disorders, gave a talk on "The Psychology of the Criminal" to N.A.P.O. London Branch, which was addressed in December 1930 by Dr I. Feldman on "Problems of Adolescence" and in January 1931 by Dr H.C. Miller on "Psychology and Probation". One London probation officer who appeared to see probation work largely in scientific terms was Grace Harrison, a Roman Catholic. She declared: "Probation officers who are attempting to do their work thoroughly are rendering service to the nation synonymous with that of a doctor." She added: "the probation officer must have sufficient time to make such investigations as will enable him to form a careful diagnosis...The magistrate looks to the probation officer to search for the causes which have led to an offence and then looks to him to suggest a definite plan of treatment." Similarly, the London juvenile court probation officer Laelia Sander expressed the hope that probation officers' "investigation, upon which treatment depends, may be carried out in an increasingly intensive manner and gradually help to secure a more scientific approach to crime and treatment of offenders".[4]

In October 1930 *Probation* advertised a course of eight lectures at the Tavistock Square Clinic (on aspects of mental health, developmental psychology, sexuality and sex perversions), as well as another series of lectures to be given in London under the auspices of the National Council for Mental Hygiene. London probation officers were invited by the staff of the Tavistock Square Clinic to attend a meeting there in November "to consider whether, and in what form, the joint discussions held last winter, shall be continued". The well attended meeting duly decided to form a distinctive Discussion Group. Stimulated by such lectures and discussions, some probation officers and police court missionaries in London may have begun to modify or expand some of their ideas. Yet the metropolitan police magistrate Claud Mullins, who became a member of the London Police Court Mission Committee in 1931, resigned from the Committee not long afterwards because he wanted it to consider a general scheme for providing the service of medical men in all the London courts who could help married couples with sexual problems; but the Rev. Harry Pearson refused to put his proposal on the agenda: "presumably, he feared lest his members would dislike the subject." Mullins found the atmosphere "stifling" at the Committee meetings of "this well-meaning but then somewhat old-fashioned body".

It may have seemed like the end of an era in 1931, when two of the London Police Court Mission's veterans, Frederick Barnett and William Fitzsimmons, retired (on pension) virtually simultaneously.[5] Barnett, who had been with the London Police Court Mission for some 40 years, had worked at Westminster Court since 1897. Cecil Chapman, who knew him there, would remember him - in *From the Bench* (1932) - as

> a wonderful missionary, Frederick Barnett by name, who never despaired of getting a boy or man a job if he was sure that they were anxious to get one. He must have worn out many pairs of boots in

doing it, but his success was such that he created in me a new sense of confidence which lasted until I left the Bench.

Barnett was also an effective speaker: almost as a lad, he was a noteworthy local preacher in Somerset; and later - in the words of A.C.L. Morrison, Clerk to the London Juvenile Courts - "he would talk of the Police Court Mission and the work among the poor, the fallen and the hopeless, until people gave him all the money they had in their pockets, and many a woman gave him a ring or a bracelet to make it more... though sometimes his talk of saving souls jarred on sensitive ears!" Fiery as Barnett was, "he never gave up, and perhaps that is why he wore himself out before his time". (His colleague at Clerkenwell, Henry Robinson, lived to be 87.)

Fitzsimmons had been police court missionary at Thames since 1889. Perhaps, as the court clerk Stanley French (who apparently never met him) believed, Fitzsimmons's accountancy was "very slap-dash". But the finest tributes to his life-work came from those professionals at the court who knew him best, Sir John Dickinson and French's colleague Albert Lieck. According to Dickinson, who knew him for at least 23 years, Fitzsimmons was

> a pioneer in the work of Probation, for in 1893 he conceived and worked out a "Lads' Shelter" in the Bow Road, for placing young offenders under care, where they were looked after and obtained some training until they could be sent out to various employments... William Fitzsimmons was a big hearted, unselfish and devoted man. No trouble or task was ever too great for him if it would help the well-being, spiritual or temporal, of his loved East-Enders.

According to Lieck, Fitzsimmons was

> a big fellow in physical stature, and a bigger in his work. If ever a man could be said to be "called" to his task it was he. He gave up an excellent job in a Belfast linen firm where he had every prospect of one day drawing a large salary, and he took a pittance to work among the drabs and ruffians who were the day-to-day occupants of the old Thames Police Court cells.
>
> I never saw him once showing signs of discouragement or lassitude. A straightforward word for the felon or the fool, a bit of homely advice to husband and wife who could not get on together, patient help for the young who had tripped. On occasions he took them to his own home. Sometimes he was deceived, or rather he took

chances with his eyes open. Sometimes he failed. But the recording angel was likely to be tired of making credit entries for Fitz before Fitz wearied of doing his good deeds; and he did them all, not as efforts of goodness or magnanimity, but just in the ordinary course of the ordinary day... I often had a feeling that he did more useful work than all the rest of us put together, from the magistrate downwards. I told him so, but you couldn't spoil a fellow like that...

He had a thousand stories of the people he dealt with, some of them against himself. I can hear his good-natured laugh now.

In 1925 Cyril Burt had concluded that juvenile delinquency in London was most rife in the most crowded areas north of the City, but that the long line of slums immediately south of the Thames from Battersea to Woolwich formed "a region fairly prolific in juvenile offenders". *In the Heart of South London* (1931) by Cyril Forster Garbett, the Bishop of Southwark, stated that 40 per cent of young offenders brought to court were placed under a probation officer; and it also referred to the Camberwell boys' shelter home,

through which no less than 3,000 boys have passed. It was originally intended for Police Court "First Offenders," but many other lads have been admitted to it; some are orphans or the sons of unsatisfactory parents. The Home is a large substantial building, with good rooms and a small gymnasium and workshop. It can hold thirty boys at a time and is usually full. The boys stay any time from a few weeks to two years. Work is found for them if possible; four are porters, two work in saw mills, three are shop assistants, one is an engraver, another a wireless assistant and so on. Those for whom no employment can be found help in the Home and work at a shoemakers' bench. At one time they were employed at cutting wood, but this was abandoned as a monotonous and unintelligent occupation for lads who are naturally full of life and energy.[6]

Meanwhile it had become clear that with abundant local labour available in the Basingstoke area, it was no longer possible to obtain employment for more than half the boys for whom accommodation had been arranged at the Garden Colony, which was forced to close in 1931. But if one door closed, another opened. In January 1931 the Society of Saint Vincent de Paul, to assist its probation officers, opened a hostel -approved by the Home Office - at 21 Breakspears Road, Brockley, S.E.4, for Roman Catholic boys (aged 16 and upwards) in the metropolitan area.

It seems it was sometimes more difficult to find accommodation for female clients: Mary Ellison (a Roman Catholic probation officer who had been a nurse) would record the problem she had at about this time in getting a hostel place for a female alcoholic in London. It was probably with this kind of problem in mind that the Catholic Prisoners' Aid Society arranged in 1931 for its women probation officers to form a probation committee, resulting in monthly meetings between such officers and male probation officers appointed by the Society of Saint Vincent de Paul to the London area.

The need for support and exchange of ideas and experiences was also highlighted by the debate at the N.A.P.O. Annual Conference in London in May 1931 on how far probation officers should undertake responsibility for the after-care of discharged prisoners. (In 1925 the metropolitan magistrate Cecil Chapman had proposed that the prisoner "should be released before the expiration of his sentence on probation to some trained officer, whose business it would be to see that he is assisted till he finds some remunerative work", and he added that Fred Barnett "has done this work successfully for years". In 1932 Chapman would reiterate his proposal in the form that prisoners should be released "on licence some time before the end of their sentence"[7]: thus Chapman may be considered to have been a pioneer of parole in England, as well as, in effect, "the children's magistrate" in London years before Clarke Hall.) In the N.A.P.O. debate, the respected Chairman of the London Branch, Sidney Gardiner Boswell, maintained that, in London, probation officers "have done important work with Borstal boys", but that, much as a probation officer no doubt wished to help ex-prisoners, his first and time-consuming duty was to his probationers, whom he did not want to be in contact with ex-prisoners. Boswell was supported by E.W. Watts, who had worked for the Church Army Discharged Prisoners' Aid Society for years before becoming a London probation officer and police court missionary in 1920. During the 1930s probation officers would be invited on a more or less regular basis to act as after-care agents by the Central Association for the Aid of Discharged Convicts, the Borstal Association, and the Aylesbury Association; but until the Criminal Justice Act of 1948 such arrangements were entirely voluntary as far as the probation officer was concerned.

Pressures on probation officers were further indicated at this time by the missionary at Old Street, who claimed that he had 203 men and youths on probation, with over 50 women under his female colleague, quite apart from the domestic and other work they had to do (in 1934 Mary Ellison would mention that "at the request of the Commissioner of Scotland Yard, cases of 'attempted suicide' are investigated by probation officers"). At first sight at least, the situation did not appear to be helped by the London police court magistrate Mr W.J.H. Brodrick, who, in a speech in March 1932 to the Royal Society for the Assistance of Discharged Prisoners, claimed that: every year there were thousands of crimes which would not have been committed "were it not for the use which we have made of the Probation of Offenders Act"; "members of the criminal classes are trading on the use that we make of the Probation of Offenders Act"; and "we have run the Probation of Offenders Act to death".[8]

In May 1932 N.A.P.O. and the London Police Court Mission, as cited in the Commons, appeared to be on opposing sides regarding the proposal in the Children and Young Persons Bill, then at Committee stage, that the age limit for juvenile courts should be raised to seventeen.[9] Then in October, before the Bill became law, death came to Sir William Clarke Hall, the virtual architect of the Children and Young Persons Act, 1933 (which seemed to be largely welcomed by Laelia Sander, for example). Indeed, the London juvenile courts probation officers issued a fine tribute to him (probably penned in whole or in part by Nina Blyth); rather as, many years later, Miss Blyth's last student, Rose Mary Braithwaite, would write a no less eloquent, unsigned obituary (also published in *Probation*) of her magistrate, Basil Henriques, who said that Clarke Hall "was a great master and taught me all I know"[10], and who may well have been influenced by Clarke Hall in developing his wonderful gift of communicating with the children who appeared before him.

The London Police Court Mission reported that, on the day the new Act came into force, one of its male missionaries

> was transferred from London Sessions to the Home Office Service for work in Juvenile Courts under the terms of the Children and Young Persons Act, 1933. ...The Act enables appointed persons to bring before the Court children and young persons who need care and protection. This is a most valuable provision. Already it has enabled interested persons to take measures for the training and protection of those who had not committed an offence but who were living in circumstances of moral danger or in other unsatisfactory

conditions...This will not seriously affect our Missionaries in the Metropolitan Police Court Area as they do not normally attend the Juvenile Courts, but it will bring a great deal of additional work to those who serve the Petty Sessional Courts in Middlesex.

Earlier in 1933, Nina Blyth was awarded the M.B.E. for her services as a juvenile court probation officer. According to Margery Fry, she was the first probation officer of either sex to receive an official honour of this kind for probation work, though others would follow ("Jack" Frost, for example, would receive the M.B.E. in 1965, after some 22 years at the Old Bailey). Miss Blyth had been appointed in 1915; and on Evelyn Lance's retirement in 1916, she took over her work in the large riparian area in South East London, where - fully supported by the philanthropic Cecil Chapman - Miss Lance had several reporting rooms and used to run a club for some of her boys in Deptford to keep them off the streets. Miss Blyth, with her keenness and zest - indeed, the joy she brought to her work - had proved a worthy successor to Miss Lance.

Not long afterwards, Miss Croker-King, then the longest serving juvenile court probation officer in London, retired because of ill-health, after some 25 years' dedicated service. Rather as Nina Blyth had delighted many children with the photos she had taken of them; so a valedictory "snapshot", taken at a tea-party that summer in Ethel Croker-King's small garden, showed a happy group of boys who had satisfactorily completed their probation, and recalled the tea-party held in Miss Croker-King's flat so many years earlier to celebrate the successful termination of the supervision of the twelve year old boy who had been her very first probationer. Just as Evelyn Lance was remembered in Southwark and Bermondsey some 20 years after her retirement; so parents, now grown old, in the Thames Court area, where Miss Croker-King had started, still enquired after "the fair-haired lady, the kind lady".[11] Many years later, Elizabeth Inman, turned 86, would still receive regular letters from six former clients, all in their sixties; and after his retirement in 1972, Charles Morgan would unexpectedly receive an appreciative letter from someone he had helped about 30 years earlier.

Miss Croker-King disliked the fact that at some juvenile courts there was no proper place where the probation officer could talk to a boy or girl alone. She had also hoped that, before her retirement, a simpler probation order would have been designed, suitable for serving on young children.

However, Claud Mullins was one metropolitan police magistrate who made a point of explaining a probation order to would-be probationers in the simplest terms which they could understand, as he felt the success of probation could partly depend on this.

Another factor that often seemed to contribute to the success, or otherwise, of probation was employment. Mullins related how he and a probation officer had tried to sustain in employment a middle-aged man who was unfortunately dismissed after being asked by his employer where he had learnt his boot-mending craft, and after giving the "unnecessarily honest" reply that he had learnt it in prison. Cecil Chapman had recorded in 1932 that some men for whom he had found work - probably through Fred Barnett - subsequently lost their jobs when their fellow-workmen became aware of their past. (That this would be a continuing problem would be illustrated by Mary Ellison's account of an incident that occurred about 1960, when an ex-prisoner was found a job by a probation officer, only to have his chances spoiled by the press revealing his previous convictions to his would-be workmates.) Laelia Sander, a juvenile court probation officer working in South East London, in 1933 found unemployment in 44% of the homes she knew, and definite signs of depression in 52% of these. Alfred James Pilgrim, who directed the London Police Court Mission's Employment Department, considered that in 1933 the difficulty of finding work had been greater than in any previous year, although, he wrote, "special cases are dealt with from the Juvenile Probation Officers. Help has been extended in many instances to youths on licence from the Home Office Schools, and quite a number of ex-Borstal lads have been placed in employment."[12]

This task of helping clients with employment was included in "The Work of a Probation Officer", a radio programme of half an hour's duration, broadcast by the B.B.C. on 2 May 1934. Focusing on work with individual probationers rather than on matrimonial or domestic work or activity involving institutions (though "the probation home", prison and borstal were mentioned), the programme gave a largely admirable description of the kind of work undertaken by a probation officer at that time. The speaker declared:

> I feel absolutely sure, after twenty-two years' experience and after dealing with all sorts of offenders, that the probation system has long passed its period of probation, and is a demonstrated success...

When I think of the army of men and lads who have passed through my hands, and the high percentage of them who have made good, I shudder to think of a Court without the probation system, the probation officer, and all he stands for.

He added that the probation officer "works to bring about a change *within* the man, without which there can be no lasting success".

Although the B.B.C. referred to the speaker simply as "A Probation Officer", he was in fact Tommy Mills[13] of Marlborough Street Court; and the programme may well have been the very first B.B.C. domestic radio broadcast by a personally identifiable, serving London probation officer and police court missionary. Charles Morgan, who would begin his long career as a probation officer at Marlborough Street in 1937, would remember Tommy Mills not only as a link with George Nelson, but also as "a marvellous character who had a tremendous affection for human beings". During Mills's many years at Marlborough Street occurred the retirement at the age of 86 of the notable metropolitan magistrate Frederick Mead, whom Elspeth Gray would remember as "wonderfully kind and patient"; and Mead's correspondence clearly indicated his high regard for her. Mead, a magistrate since 1889 who served at Marlborough Street between 1908 and 1933, was later hailed by the magistrates Chartres Biron, J.B. Sandbach and Frank Milton as a pioneer of the probation system.[14] But according to Mrs Gray's recollection (which certainly proved reliable in other respects), he hardly ever put anyone on probation: he used to bind defendants over and advise them to listen to the probation officer; and both Biron and Sandbach stated that Mead used to remand a defendant on bail for his or her behaviour in the interim to be assessed by the court missionary, who reported back.

"Every London magistrate consults the police court missionary, whose advice and information invariably influence the sentence," declared a newspaper article by "R.E. Corder", who asserted that court missionaries and probation officers "take in hand the woman without hope and the man without work, and they pick their disciples [*sic*] from the dock". Although Sandbach considered her methods "far too subtle for me", he paid tribute - as would Charles Morgan - to the quality of Mrs Gray's work with prostitutes. This work seems to have attracted the attention of Harold F. Davidson, notorious as the Rector of Stiffkey, preoccupied with vulnerable girls in London and proclaiming himself "a second Wakeford".[15] After he was unfrocked, Davidson visited Marlborough Street Court to see her and then sent her a copy of his pamphlet *The Reason Why* in early May 1934.

The resourcefulness of court missionaries was illustrated by a rather remarkable incident that occurred in about 1934. A visiting London police court missionary found his young male probationer dejected and alone at home:

> Interrogated, he said: "I am courting the daughter of a gipsy; the mother objects, she has cursed me; her curse was that the MOGGERS (evil spirits from the nether world) should be set upon me. They are on me now. I am done! I am done!"
>
> The Missionary caught him by the coat collar and stood him on his feet, saying: "Look at me. Do you know who I am?" "My Probation Officer." "Yes! but more." "A Police Court Missionary." "Yes! but more." "What then?" "I am a man of God. No Moggers can stand a man of God. Stand close to me. Press tight, man, shoulder to shoulder. We must be as one. Now the Moggers will flee." So they stand together, in silence for three minutes by the clock."Ah! See!" says the Missionary, "they are gone. You are free. A new man." "Yes! Yes!" replied the other, "I am already different."

The probationer subsequently found regular work, married the gipsy's daughter and started a family.

Meanwhile, discussion in Parliament concerning matrimonial conciliation in the courts developed into the appointment by the Home Secretary in October 1934 of a committee, chaired by his long-serving Assistant Secretary Mr S.W. Harris, to enquire into the work undertaken by probation officers in courts of summary jurisdiction and the organisation of probation services. This wide-ranging enquiry was to have far-reaching consequences for the probation service. (Harris - like Miss A. Ivimy - had been on the 1920-22 Home Office Committee on probation officers.) The London Police Court Mission reported: "apart from the Chairman, who holds a neutral position, there was not one of this Committee who had ever been known as a friend of the Police Court Mission."

In its preparatory notes of evidence to be submitted to the Harris Committee, the Mission mentioned that training for prospective missionaries was provided by the National Police Court Mission - not by the London Police Court Mission itself - under the auspices of the London University Extension and Tutorial Classes Council. This took the form of a part-time Course in Social Science, which included "Social Economics", "Problems of Poverty", "Psychology of Criminal Tendencies", and "Criminal Law and Administration". The London Police Court Mission's notes did not reveal the identity or status of any of the lecturers, or how long the course had been running. Nor did the notes refer to the series of seminars for probation officers given in 1934 by Dr Denis Carroll of the recently founded Institute for the Scientific Treatment of Delinquency (based in London). Dr Carroll would be involved with the training of probation officers for some 20 years, and the seminars would be repeated regularly until at least 1938. In 1935 Dr Carroll's course, much appreciated by probation officers, was extended and divided into three parts: "Organic Factors in Delinquency" by Dr Rowland Hill; "Mental Deficiency and Delinquency" by Dr C.J.C. Earl; and "Psychiatry, Psychotherapy and Delinquency" by Dr Carroll himself. Some two years later, the Institute found that, "largely as a result of our educational activities", probation officers tended to refer more cases of the type suitable for treatment. At about this time Claud Mullins seems successfully to have used the probation officer as an intermediary in a number of cases to facilitate psychiatric or other specialist treatment - apparently through the Institute - for men who faced charges of a sexual nature.

Also involved in the training of probation officers from 1935 onwards was Hermann Mannheim, a distinguished refugee from Nazi Germany who lectured in criminology at the London School of Economics, where one of his early students was the future London probation officer Rose Mary Braithwaite, who would remember him with affection. A small part of Mannheim's massive study *Social Aspects of Crime in England between the Wars* (1940) was based on an investigation he carried out at two London police courts; and his chapter on recidivism, based on examination of the records of 1,197 men and 77 women sentenced by the Central Criminal Court or Quarter Sessions between 1915 and 1935 (with the exception of 1918), seemed to suggest that probation was insufficiently used in cases where a long record of imprisonment or penal servitude had been built up. Claud Mullins related how a probation officer persuaded him to place an old recidivist on probation, which had apparently never been tried before in this man's life. This was Mullins's "first adventure in gambling on 'old lags' ": through the probation officer, he kept in touch for some years with this apparently successful case.

Mullins also remembered the case of a lad whom he committed to Quarter Sessions at about this time with a recommendation of borstal training, after prolonged enquiries by a probation officer and a full report from the remand prison. Quarter Sessions accepted the recommendation, but when the boy appealed to the Court of Criminal Appeal, the Lord Chief Justice, Lord Hewart, and two judges altered the sentence and placed him on probation to Mullins's probation officer, who had earlier told the magistrate that probation would be useless. Mullins added: "The judges in the Court of Criminal Appeal acted without any fresh social enquiry and without any reference to the Probation Officer who was to be responsible for him....The lad came gloating to the Probation Officer. No doubt the latter did his best, but conditions were next to hopeless." Claud Mullins did not elaborate on the boy's subsequent career, criminal or otherwise.[16] But in his Clarke Hall Lecture, delivered in May 1935, Lord Hewart spoke of both borstal training and probation in positive terms, declaring, for example: "the right-hand man, the indispensable handmaid, of the Juvenile Court, is the probation officer. The men and the women of this service are as remarkable as they are unknown." He added that "the Home Office have now arranged for the attendance of a probation officer at Quarter Sessions and Assizes".

Lord Hewart's lecture was the second in a series intended both as a tribute to Clarke Hall and as a continuation of his work. Another, if less obvious, sign of Clarke Hall's influence was N.A.P.O.'s publication in 1935 of *A Handbook of Probation and Social Work of the Courts,* the preparation of which had in fact been initiated under Clarke Hall's chairmanship. Those contributing to the production of this composite work included the London probation officers Nina Blyth, Mrs Grace Harrison, and Messrs S.G. Boswell and F.W. Whaits (the last two of whom had supervised probationers in London since 1908), as well as A.J. Pilgrim, who was not attached to any court. Although widely commended on its publication, and still useful as a descriptive historical document, the *Handbook* seems disappointing in a number of respects. It was reticent, indeed unimaginative, in its comments on probation officers' training needs - for example, in interpreting information and making recommendations in the context of written court reports. Moreover, whilst it acknowledged the impact of psychology, and although the Birmingham probation officer who, in 1930, had made one of the earliest known references in British probation literature to "case-work" was a contributor to the *Handbook*, it contained only one brief reference to casework.

The *Handbook* was followed by the blueprint: this was the *Report of the Departmental Committee on the Social Services in Courts of Summary Jurisdiction*, published in March 1936. The Harris Committee had heard evidence from 126 witnesses, including the London probation officers Miss C.M. Astle (Edmonton), Miss C. Barker (West London), S.G. Boswell (Marylebone), Sydney Burgess (Highgate), G.E. Franey (Greenwich), Miss Hamilton-Hunter (North London), Mrs Grace Harrison (peripatetic Roman Catholic probation officer), Miss Elizabeth Inman (representing the Society of London Juvenile Court Probation Officers), T.W.C. Marsh (Westminster), A.E. Shields (South Western), Miss M.H. Tallerman (representing the Society of London Juvenile Court Probation Officers), and E.W. Watts (Clerkenwell). In other words, apart from spokesmen for organisations like the London Police Court Mission, National Police Court Mission and N.A.P.O., serving London probation officers accounted, on average, for about one in ten of the witnesses. Another witness was Miss M.A. Warner, who until comparatively recently had been a London probation officer, but who was now H.M. Inspector in the Children's Branch (whose responsibilities included probation work) of the Home Office: no doubt she was one of the first to progress from the probation service in London to the Home Office inspectorate.

The Committee's Report, which recognised the value of probation work, recommended that the Home Office should play a larger role in the direction and supervision of the probation service, but that, in the country as a whole, the appointment of probation officers should be left in the hands of magistrates, acting through the probation committees. The Police Court Mission representatives, including the Rev. Harry Pearson, argued that the voluntary societies attracted men and women with a sense of vocation based on religious conviction who might not be attracted by secular public authority, and that the funds of these societies constituted, in effect, a form of saving on public expenditure. The Committee, however, concluded that the time had come for the system of "dual control" to end, and for the probation service to become a wholly official and unified public service, separated from any denominational or sectarian voluntary society. The Committee believed the probation officer should be a trained and well-qualified full-time social worker of the courts. To improve probation service training, supervision and administration, it recommended the establishment of a Central Training Board and the appointment of principal and senior probation officers, with assistant or deputy principal probation officers "in some of the larger areas". Whilst the range of duties had widened, "the religious and voluntary spirit in probation work should not be lost. This spirit has no doubt been manifest in the work of the Police Court Mission... the London Courts can ill afford to lose the assistance and inspiration which it has given for so many years." The Committee declared that "the pioneer work of the early police court missionaries forms a splendid chapter in English social history. The example they gave of devotion and self-sacrifice has inspired the work of successive probation officers in later years." Accordingly the Committee suggested that the Police Court Mission could still be fruitfully associated with the work of the probation service in various ways, such as through the provision of probation hostels and homes.

Elizabeth Inman - who appeared as a witness before the Committee -had ably expressed the opinion of a large section of probation officers when she told the 1931 N.A.P.O. Annual Conference:

> I am sure that we are all agreed that a sense of vocation is the first essential for a probation officer, but many of us feel very strongly that adherence to any particular religious body is not a test of sincerity or of vocation. A sense of vocation is a spiritual thing and cannot be measured by an outward test. Such a test may, indeed, debar people of deep sincerity of purpose and honesty, whilst admitting those who may be, if not less sincere, at least less thoughtful.

A few years later such a view seemed to be shared by a majority of those probation officers and N.A.P.O. representatives who gave evidence to the Home Office-appointed Committee. Harry Pearson had warned his own Committee that the results of the Home Office enquiry could threaten the very existence of the Police Court Mission; and, according to S.W. Harris's later testimony, the Departmental Committee's Report "came at first as a shock to Pearson who naturally thought that much of his past labour was brought into jeopardy".[17] Rather ironically, this period of anxiety coincided with the Police Court Mission's celebration of its Diamond Jubilee (for a copy of the scroll of appreciation Elspeth Gray -

then Stormont - received in 1936 from the Police Court Mission, see Appendix 15).

While Pearson and the London Police Court Mission were considering their response to the Report, the Government was acting swiftly to implement its recommendations which did not require legislation. By December 1936 the Home Office had set up a special Probation Branch under B.J. Reynolds. Miss D.M. Rosling (who had been a London Police Court Mission probation officer at Willesden in 1932-33 and at Old Street in 1934-35) was appointed as the first inspector specifically for the new probation service; and she was later joined in 1937 by two male inspectors. Their aim was, in the Government's words, "to fulfil functions of advice, encouragement and stimulation". (In March 1920 Miss Croker-King had pointed out that probation officers were not inspected.[18])

The Home Secretary appointed the London Probation Committee; and its members, who were designated to serve for three years from 1 January 1937, included the Rev. Harry Pearson, Sir Rollo Graham-Campbell (a metropolitan magistrate member of the London Police Court Mission Committee), Claud Mullins and Basil Henriques. A month later the Home Secretary brought into being two more bodies: the Probation Advisory Committee (whose members included H.E. Norman, Secretary of N.A.P.O., and Alexander Paterson) and the Probation Training Board (whose members included Professor A.M. Carr-Saunders and Miss Elizabeth Macadam). The purpose of the Advisory Committee was "to advise on questions relating to the administration of the probation system and the other social services of the Courts", while that of the Board was "the provision of facilities for the training of candidates for appointment as probation officers and of persons serving as probation officers and for the selection of persons for training". S.W. Harris's influence and status were indicated by the fact that he was appointed Chairman (or, as Annie Besant had said in 1889[19], "chair-person") of all three bodies, of which Mr B.J. Reynolds was also a member.

In the light of the Harris Committee's recommendations, it was decided to appoint a Principal Probation Officer for London. Half a century later, the Central Council of Probation Committees would declare that the appointment of Principal Probation Officers "represented the first move towards the setting up of a professional supervisory hierarchy".[20] According to Harold M. Morton (who was a London Police

Court Mission probation officer at Marylebone between 1935 and 1938), it had been apparent for some time that such a post was needed in London to organise probation work and supervise generally its administration in the courts of the Metropolitan Police Court District. In fact, London was by no means the first area to have such a post in Britain. The concept of Chief Probation Officers - apparently derived from America -had been espoused by Clarke Hall in *The State and the Child* (1917) and by William Fitzsimmons in 1923, to take two examples. A Chief Probation Officer had been appointed in Liverpool in 1920; issues of *Probation* in 1934 carried a report of an address by the Chief Probation Officer for the City of Glasgow, Mr W.G. Buchanan (who died, in harness, in 1948), and an advertisement for the job of Principal Probation Officer for the City of Manchester; and in 1935 Alfred Leeding in "Manningfield" discovered that the "chief probation officer" was "a recent and resented new appointment". By 1936 about a handful of areas had appointed Chief or Principal Probation Officers.

According to Harold Morton's testimony, it was decided that, for this challenging new job in London, "personality and education were more important than practical experience of probation work".[21] Certainly the man chosen had not previously been a Chief or Principal Probation Officer, or indeed a probation officer or police court missionary at all, though he had personality and education combined with social work experience. His name was Guy Clutton-Brock, and he was 30 years old when he received the call. After reading history at Cambridge University, Clutton-Brock lived and worked for four years as a full-time social worker in the slum area of Notting Dale in London, where he ran a hostel for unemployed youths from Wales, and where he spent some of his days "in police courts trying to rescue boys and girls who appeared there all too often, in prisons to visit them when we failed". Then, under the influence of the charismatic Alexander Paterson (who had "a deep love for the outcast"), he joined the prison service, working as a housemaster at Feltham Borstal and at Wormwood Scrubs boys' remand prison before becoming Deputy Governor at Portland, which took the toughest borstal boys. A few months after this promotion, Paterson intervened again and, as Clutton-Brock would recall in 1987, "pushed me into the probation job" (rather as Paterson - "a marvellous man" - was instrumental, in about 1938, in persuading Jack Frost to become a Home Office probation trainee instead of a borstal housemaster). Clutton-Brock's move from

Portland Bill to London to become Principal Probation Officer in January 1937 is best described in his own words:

> Alec Paterson summoned me to the Home Office: 'We want you to start the London Probation Service. It's a tough pioneering job. Can you stand on your feet and speak in public?' After diffident thought I agreed and became the first Principal Probation Officer for the Metropolitan Police Court District. We leased a small house in Chelsea and I was given offices in St Stephen's House, adjoining the police headquarters at Scotland Yard. I bought a dark suit, stiff collar, black hat and two false teeth to stick in my gaps in front. I was given a civil service brief-case, pencil and paper and sat at my office desk, wondering what to do.
>
> The Home Office was starting to take control of the Probation Service, to develop probation more fully as an alternative to prison for the courts. In London there were Children's Courts, Metropolitan Police Courts with stipendiary magistrates and higher courts at the Old Bailey with judges. They were all served by professional Probation Officers. Some, particularly in the Children's Courts, were highly qualified and came directly under the Home Office. Others were under various Police Court Missionary Societies. Some, with social science diplomas, who had perhaps also done mental health courses, did careful case work and were conscious of their professional status; some spent long hours in their back-room offices in slums, befriending their probationers through their sentence and far beyond; others, more casual and full of faith, from their offices in the courts said: 'Here's five bob and a Bible, my boy. Go and behave yourself and don't come back.'
>
> All were over-worked, deeply dedicated to their task and dealing with criminals, down-and-outs, matrimonial disputes and every sort of case which came before the courts and was beyond the magistrate or police to deal with. 'Refer to the Probation Officer' was often an easy way out and the over-worked officer was left with the problem. I, as the Principal Probation Officer, was the least qualified of all. In social science, I had neither degree, diploma nor training; I was one of the last of the great untrained.[22]

Clutton-Brock's first few months in post may have been largely taken up, as Harold Morton believed, with finding office accommodation, which was eventually found at St Stephen's House, Westminster, overlooking the Thames by the Embankment, in rooms provided by the

Receiver for the Metropolitan Police District. The P.P.O.'s duties included establishing a system of clerical assistance for probation officers, confirmation of appointments, and attending to arrangements for sick leave, expense allowances and the provision of equipment (this may be compared with Alfred Leeding's recollection that in 1935 in "Manningfield" the chief probation officer's main duty was the keeping of the register of probation cases, and that one of his "minor" duties was to instruct trainees like Leeding himself).

Much as Clutton-Brock felt he needed to give support, encouragement and reassurance in spearheading the development of the new service, he needed to find friends and allies on whom he could rely within the service. Apparently by April 1937 he had made contact with George Neve, who, according to Jack Frost and others, was a key figure in the evolution of the London Probation Service. After serving in the First World War, George Neve was with the London Police Court Mission for a short time in 1925 before it appointed him the following year as a missionary attached to the Central Criminal Court, where he worked until 1943, becoming the senior probation officer there in 1937. His colleagues remembered Neve with affection as a very capable, loyal and supportive officer, charming, dapper and well-groomed. Clutton-Brock -who referred visiting foreign dignitaries, such as a Director of Prisons in Ceylon, to Neve - had by June formed such a good relationship with him that Neve suggested that the Old Bailey "should come directly under the Principal Probation Officer as being in every way a separate institution to the rest of the Probation Service".[23]

Meanwhile the London Police Court Mission, in February, had sent a Memorial to the Home Secretary, stressing the importance of the "missionary spirit" and of flexibility in probation work, and urging continuance of the Mission, while offering to negotiate the complete separation of the London Police Court Mission from the Church of England Temperance Society (the Harris Committee's Report pointed out that such distinct separation - proposed in 1922 - of the two bodies had not indisputably taken place). The Memorial also suggested the appointment of Home Office inspectors to ensure adequate supervision of probation officers, though it made no comment on training. While the Mission was waiting for a reply to its Memorial, the Probation Training Board was pressing ahead so that the first selection of trainees under the new system could take place in June. Under the Home Office's original training scheme for probation officers, 39 men and 9 women had completed a course of training between 1930 and 1936. Among these early Home Office probation trainees was Miss Audrey Williams, who would work in the London area for a quarter of a century and who "would go to great lengths and spare no effort in the service of her friends and charges".[24] Her attitude seemed to reflect a still strong sense of vocation (traditionally associated with a religious outlook) among probation officers; whereas the element of training was redolent of a more professional approach to the work.

During the period 1937-39, no less than 117 men and 40 women would be trained under the new scheme. In London at least, it seems that male probation officers were being appointed increasingly to the juvenile courts, as a result of the Children and Young Persons Act, 1933 (s.48), extending the jurisdiction of those courts to persons aged 17. From November 1936 lay justices replaced stipendiaries as presidents of the London juvenile courts (which thereby became aligned with such courts outside London); though a preference for stipendiary magistrates in juvenile courts was expressed in February 1937 by the London children's probation officer Miss Ethel Currant, who had worked under Clarke Hall, and whose colleague Laelia Sander had been appointed Clarke Hall's secretary. Miss Currant felt that "whilst the Juvenile Court is a Court of Law", the trained lawyer should not be replaced by the lay justice, who might try to do the work of a probation officer or intervene in the life of a delinquent to a far greater degree than a stipendiary ever would:

> For instance I have a Jewish boy on probation to me who was attending a Mission for the conversion of the Jews. I was asked by one of the Justices who is also Jewish to forbid him to have anything to do with this Mission, in fact to use the power of the Court to forbid him attending the Mission. I said that the boy's religion was his own personal affair and that I could not forbid him to attend.

She thought that an apparent decrease in the number of juvenile cases heard at Toynbee Hall seemed to reflect "a prejudice on the part of the Police against the appointment of Lay Justices". On the other hand, she believed that lay justices tended to show more interest in the remand homes and approved schools, and more desire to change and improve conditions, than some stipendiaries. She also had a warning in February 1937 for the probation service: "There is a danger that we as Probation

Officers would tend to become a body of Social Workers, stereotyped, and red taped, the beginning of a miniature L.C.C. with its rules and regulations."[25]

An increasingly frequent visitor to the London courts at this time was Guy Clutton-Brock, with his abiding passion for "life at ground level". As he explained:

> John Darcy joined me as chief clerk. He built up a competent office, and so freed me to get out around the courts. There, I met probation officers, police, magistrates and judges. They were friendly but suspicious of Home Office interference...I was part of the civil service establishment. Magistrates sometimes invited me onto the Bench or to a chat in their rooms. Deep within I felt critical but tried to be diplomatic. It seemed that too often they thought they were God.

In June the Rev. Harry Pearson reported that his Mission was still paying the two missionaries who were being "taken over" as Assistant Principal Probation Officers, and he presumed that the Home Office was still considering the difficult question of pensions. The following month the two missionaries Pearson was alluding to - Sidney Boswell and E.W. Watts - were appointed as Assistant Principal Probation Officers assigned to head office at St Stephen's House. They were joined there by the first woman A.P.P.O. to be appointed in the London Probation Service: Miss Ethel Crosland, who had run a very successful school at Westerham, Kent, in the Great War before becoming a probation officer.[26] Interviewed in 1987, Guy Clutton-Brock said he thought he had chosen his Assistant Principal Probation Officers - presumably based on his assessment of staff as a result of his tour of the courts. It seems likely that at very least he was consulted about these appointments. Be that as it may, the appointments appear to have been felicitous and well-merited: all three A.P.P.O.s were experienced officers (each with a minimum of 16 years' experience) who seemed to be respected, trusted and liked by their colleagues, as well as by magistrates and clerks. At least two of them had also been active or prominent in the ranks of N.A.P.O.; and the three of them provided quite a nice balance - no doubt intended - between adult court and juvenile court probation officers as represented by their respective numbers, and also, if to a lesser extent, between male and female officers. Apparently Boswell assumed responsibility for adult courts south of the river, Watts for those north of the river, and Miss Crosland for all the juvenile courts in the Metropolitan Police Court District.

These appointments almost coincided with the long-awaited response, in July, to the London Police Court Mission's Memorial. Although presumably not necessarily bound by views previously expressed by others in his Department, the new Home Secretary, Sir Samuel Hoare, gave a reply that by now the Mission must have expected: he saw no reason to disagree with the Harris Committee's conclusions; but he suggested a meeting between a few members of the Mission and Home Office representatives to discuss the Mission's future activities. Such a conference accordingly took place at the Home Office in October, when the following points were made: the very recently passed Summary Procedure (Domestic Proceedings) Act, 1937 - which, *inter alia,* extended the statutory duties of probation officers to include domestic conciliation work - embodied those recommendations of the Committee which had required legislation; the Home Secretary had definitely decided that all the probation officers engaged in the metropolitan courts should in future be appointed and employed only by the Home Office; the Mission could none the less assist the probation service and the Home Office by continuing its existing homes and hostels and opening new ones, including an urgently needed hostel in London for probation officer trainees (in fact, the genesis of Rainer House), by reconstituting and extending its Guild of Police Court Missionaries so that all probation officers could become members, by providing voluntary workers, where necessary, to assist probation officers, and by establishing a "Good Samaritan Fund" to supplement the resources of the court poor-box. The date suggested for the Home Office take-over was 1 January 1938, but this had to be postponed because of difficulty in resolving the pensions problem.

It seemed like the end of a chapter when, by the end of 1937, two of the Mission's veterans had retired: Mr F.A. Herbert after 34 years' service (the last 30 at Bow Street), and Mr G.E. Franey after some 32 years' work in South London. But the tradition of long and devoted service - which may be regarded as part of the "missionary spirit" - was to be perpetuated by Miss Georgina Stafford, who in September was appointed as a missionary by the London Police Court Mission with effect from 1 November 1937, when she would have reached her twenty-fourth birthday, the minimum age at that time for entry to the service. Miss Stafford is understood to have been the last known police court missionary to be appointed by the London Police Court Mission to the Metropolitan Police Court District, and certainly the last such person, appointed initially as a missionary and serving continuously in the metropolitan area of London, to retire after more than 40 years' service. (Before her appointment she did six weeks' holiday relief work at various London courts for the Mission, which paid her £3 per week: apparently this basic rate had remained unchanged since at least 1932.) A copy of Georgina Stafford's letter of appointment is attached as Appendix 16: her starting salary of £220 a year, rising to a maximum of £320, was in accordance with the minimum and maximum salaries for full-time women probation officers laid down in 1937 by the Home Office, whose scale for their male counterparts was from £220 to £400. She remembered that at her interview it had been clearly enough indicated to her that she was unlikely to be appointed unless she gave up her Sunday School teaching -a surprising condition on several counts, not least as by that time the writing was plainly on the wall for the London Police Court Mission as an appointing agency of salaried social workers in the courts. On the other hand, the provision of four weeks' paid holiday a year - which Elspeth Gray recalled - was by no means ungenerous for those days; and Charles Morgan, who related that Sir Samuel Hoare had personally signed his probation officer's card, certifying his appointment, felt that, for him at least, the starting salary was "not so bad" in view of the general economic climate at that time.

Whereas both Charles Morgan and Georgina Stafford had been appointed in 1937 by the London Police Court Mission (before being formally appointed as probation officers, in effect by a Home Office board, after three months' "apprenticeship"), their colleague C.W. ("Bill") Hornung, who started his duties only some seven months after Miss Stafford, symbolised the new, intensified involvement of the Home Office. Bill Hornung joined the Home Office training course for the probation service in September 1937. Based at Morley College in South East London, the course comprised lectures, visits of observation, and practical placements. According to his recollection, there were lectures on law by the notable London court clerk A.C.L. Morrison, on court procedures by a number of other officials, and on psychology by an Oxford professor. Experienced probation officers like Sidney Boswell, E.W. Watts and Tommy Marsh took Bill Hornung and his fellow students through the role and work of probation officers. Visits were organised to a wide variety of penal institutions, hostels, hospitals, and every type of court. Hornung vividly remembered how one Monday morning at about the end of September - his very first morning in a London police court as an observer - he found Tower Bridge Court in turmoil as a result of breaches of the peace and related charges arising out of clashes in the local streets between Communists and Mosley's Blackshirts the previous weekend. (Similarly, Margaret Frost and Georgina Stafford recalled that, at one time shortly after the Second World War, North London Court was flooded with defendants following clashes in the Ridley Road area of the East End between Mosley's supporters and Jewish people.[27])

After two practical placements, first at Croydon, and then at Old Street Court under "that grand old warrior A.E. Cox", Hornung worked for three months full-time at Clerkenwell Court, where "the formidable Miss Hamilton-Hunter was senior, and it was said that even the magistrates went in awe of her. But to me she was kindness itself." At the end of his training, he was interviewed in May by the Home Office and then appointed to Marylebone Police Court, where he started work in the summer of 1938. Again according to his recollection, he was among the very first appointments to the London service which were sanctioned by the Home Office under the new training arrangements. The new probation officer followed in the footsteps of Sidney Boswell, who had worked for decades at Marylebone Court, where "S.G.B." had often co-operated with the magistrate Alfred Plowden in appealing to offenders to mend their ways.

By this time the London Police Court Mission Committee had concluded that "however the Mission and its friends may regret the changes proposed, they have no power to oppose them" and could only "bow to the inevitable". The way ahead had been cleared by December 1937, when the Mission was informed that the Home Office now had sufficient information to prepare a scheme to preserve the pensions of missionaries taken over. Moreover, virtually simultaneously with the appointment of London's first Assistant Principal Probation Officers, senior probation officers were appointed in the metropolitan criminal courts. In the main, these seniors were appointed according to the length of their service in the courts they already served. As Miss Stafford later pointed out, on the basis of that criterion, the appointed senior was not necessarily the best person for the job. But these were pioneering days;

and according to the recollection of Miss R.M. Braithwaite (who joined the London service in February 1939), Miss Clemence Paine was not the only children's probation officer who reluctantly accepted the rank of senior but declined to take the pay differential (some £50 a year extra), apparently on the grounds that she had nothing special to offer her main-grade colleagues and felt it was rather demeaning to supervise them (it seems that senior probation officers were appointed in the juvenile courts at roughly the same time as in the adult courts in London).

In 1920, for example, the Rev. Harry Pearson had referred to "the Senior Police Court Missionary". Whilst the precise meaning of this description was not clear from the context, in the Mission's literature "the Senior Missionary" seemed to relate to length of service. There seems little doubt that the Home Office bureaucratization of the service - as illustrated by the appointment of assistant principal and senior probation officers - was a major factor in the London Police Court Mission's feeling, expressed in its Annual Report for 1938, that the probation system would now become "a machine without a soul". Mrs Elspeth Gray, in 1987, did not recall any great feeling by the London police court missionaries (who were not very assertive as a group) against the Home Office take-over; and Charles Morgan testified that the police court missionaries saw the take-over as inevitable and evidently did not strongly resent it, though there was a feeling of regret that the missionary background and outlook would fade away. Georgina Stafford remembered that some missionaries feared that the service would become more "materialistic".

Similar feelings were expressed by the London lay magistrate Basil Henriques in 1937:

> There is a danger that the treatment of the young offender to-day is becoming so scientific that we may lose sight of something which was of outstanding importance in the old method, though we may not approve of the manner in which it was applied. I am referring to the religious spirit of the court missionaries.

Charles Morgan remembered that at Marlborough Street Court his "chief" Tommy Mills had a beautiful crucifix on the wall by his desk and started each working day with private prayers in front of it, regardless of anyone who might be around. In December 1938 Mr F.W. Whaits (who had received his first probationer at 10 a.m. on 1 January 1908 - apparently the first known probation officer and police court missionary in inner or outer London to do so under the 1907 Act) was ordained at the exceptional age of 64; and the London probation officers A.J. Pilgrim and Nicholas Rivett-Carnac, for example, would also become Church of England priests, in 1955 and 1964 respectively (whereas the London juvenile court probation officer Miss K. de Ville would leave the service in 1943 to study medicine).[28] Charles Morgan recalled that on the last Friday of each month all the missionaries of the London Police Court Mission took their lists of expenses to the Mission's head office, where the Treasurer, without raising any queries, paid them in cash on the spot, and this was followed by a meeting with the Rev. Harry Pearson, concluding with a prayer meeting which all the police court missionaries were expected to attend.

Morgan felt that the gender separation largely operating in probation work in London tied in with the theological background of the Mission. Some women probation officers - Miss Croker-King, for example - had gained (or would gain) preparatory social work experience through University or religious settlements, which tended to reflect concepts of gender segregation. Clutton-Brock recorded: "Welding the collection of interests and individuals together into a new service was largely a human job. Probation staff meetings were sticky at first; like African men and women, the males and females would not sit together." Later, in 1987, Clutton-Brock declared that although the probation officers provided by the London Police Court Mission and the female juvenile court probation officers provided by the Home Office initially sat separately at staff meetings convened by him, "I had to bring them together".

Clutton-Brock's attempt to bring different groups of probation officers together may be compared with his subsequent attempt to bring blacks and whites together in Rhodesia, and with the matrimonial conciliation work of police court missionaries and probation officers themselves. Such matrimonial work received some prominence in the account of the London Police Court Mission which appeared in Mrs Cecil Chesterton's book *Women of the London Underworld* (1938). Mrs Chesterton added: "Attempted suicide is a charge on which many women, and indeed young girls, are brought to court...In most cases the offender is put on probation, and the healing work of the mission begins." (Although Mrs Chesterton did not say so, an examination of London Police Court Mission annual reports indicates that, over the years, attempted suicide cases were quite a regular feature of the work of London police court missionaries, who, in this respect if in no other, seemed to serve as would-be psychiatrists.) She recognised the diverse and often difficult cases tackled by the Mission:

> All sorts and conditions of wrecks, physical and emotional, come for help to the offices of the society. Borderline cases on the brink of mental instability or crime, with a tendency to become hopeless drunkards or dope addicts: one and all they are sure of counsel and forbearance from the man in charge.

Mrs Chesterton believed that, through the Mission's Employment Department, A.J. Pilgrim "has saved countless lives from utter shipwreck, and brought hope and healing to thousands of little homes".

It was fitting that the major part of the final chapter (entitled "The Helping Hand") of *Women of the London Underworld* was devoted to a tribute to "the magnificent work of the London Police Court Mission": although readers would scarcely have known from the book itself, its publication virtually coincided with the Mission's relinquishing direct involvement with the criminal courts and ceasing to employ police court missionaries in the metropolitan area of London. Indeed, Mrs Chesterton paid what was probably the last independent tribute to the London Police Court Mission to be published in book form in England before its London missionaries were taken over: for the British Museum received its copyright copy of her book on 30 June, and, as a result of negotiation between the parties, all the London Police Court Mission's missionaries in the metropolitan courts became Home Office employees, with no official responsibility to the Mission, as from 1 July 1938 (not 1 January 1938, as indicated by William McWilliams, misled by Jarvis). Some 60 police court missionaries were thus taken over (with the Mission still employing missionaries in the Middlesex courts). Also absorbed into the Home Office system at about this time were half a dozen Roman Catholic and Jewish probation officers who supervised probationers of their particular faith in London. Including the children's probation officers, the total number of probation officers working under the aegis of the London Probation Service at its inception was in the region of one hundred. Only when the foot-soldiers, so to speak, had joined their commanders could the London Probation Service be considered truly operational.

In London it seemed that, for virtually all practical purposes, the

Mission had been replaced by the Service, "spiritual power" had given way to "strength of personality", redemption to re-education[29] of offenders; and a vocation which dedicated individuals were "called" to follow was, in effect, becoming a profession which they were trained to enter. As Ada Demer (who had worked for years as a secretary at the London Police Court Mission's headquarters) would recall, the change-over suggested that probation officers' status in court and associated effectiveness would be enhanced by their being members of a unified public service. She felt -as did Elspeth Gray - that the Mission could not have coped financially with an expanding probation service; but also that the Mission had provided "very diverse personalities" or, in Elspeth Gray's words, "such a marvellous variety of people" as probation officers.

The London Police Court Mission did not apparently submit evidence to the Departmental Committee on Courts of Summary Jurisdiction in the Metropolitan Area, which had been appointed in July 1936. But the 43 diverse witnesses examined by the Committee included the London probation officers Ethel Crosland and W.G. Minn (both representing S.J.C.P.O.), S.G. Boswell, E.W. Watts, and Grace Harrison. Concern for the status and effectiveness of probation officers was reflected in its report, published in 1937 (reprinted in 1959). It admitted that the accommodation provided for probation officers at many metropolitan courts was "not good", adding: "It is impossible for satisfactory probation work to be carried on when two or three interviews of a confidential nature are being conducted in one small room" (para. 66). The Committee acknowledged the importance of making arrangements to enable magistrates and justices "to exercise proper supervision over the probation service". In an attempt "to avoid duplication of work and to ensure proper co-ordination", the Committee suggested that juvenile court probation officers should assist the court dealing with cases in which "parents are charged and the real issue is the welfare of the child". In effect, the Departmental Committee thereby seemed to point towards the "integration" in probation work that would become a reality in London several decades later.

CHAPTER SEVEN

The Service's Baptism of Fire, 1938-48

The London Probation Service was born at a time when there was a strong sense of social awareness and commitment to political causes. There was much concern in Britain about such matters as poverty, unemployment, bad housing, and slum clearance, and a keen desire (at least in some quarters) to get to grips with these problems. Guy Clutton-Brock and Derek Borboen, who were members of the London Probation Service from its inception, appear to have absorbed much of this atmosphere of social concern while they were students at Cambridge in the inter-war period.

In recalling his work as a youth and community worker in the East End of London, Kenneth Brill (who became a probation officer with the London Probation Service, later first General Secretary of the British Association of Social Workers, and then Director of Barnet Social Services) seemed to capture much of the spirit of the age:

> In my patch of East London, throughout the nineteen-thirties many welfare workers and volunteers helped youngsters to form clubs and responded to their need to talk, individually and in groups. They housed and fed the hunger-marchers; looked after the sad possessions of old people in the "institutions", shared the grief of the bereaved, averted suicide, marched against Mosley and the means test. They spoke up for defendants in court, helped tenants' defence leagues to tackle bad landlords; sought better jobs for school-leavers and for unemployed people...

Probably few London probation officers, in what was, after all, a more authoritarian and bureaucratic role, committed themselves to the whole range of such welfare tasks enumerated by Brill. Probation officers could hardly remain entirely impervious to the social conditions and influences of the times in which they, and their clients, lived. Mr F.T. Watts, probation officer at Thames Police Court who (in the words of the court clerk Stanley French) "succeeded the legendary Fitzsimmons and achieved an even more enviable reputation", once told French that an older woman, knowing her married son sometimes hit his wife, said to her daughter-in-law: "It's all right for his father to do that to me, I'm used to it. But you're a different generation; that sort of behaviour's not good enough from my son. You go along to Aylward Street and see the probation officer." Yet sometimes doubt was cast on the extent to which probation officers understood the nature of the society in which they lived. Kenneth Brill, in his account of the socially conscious and active East London priest, John Groser, vicar at St George-in-the-East between 1929 and 1948, maintained that Groser had a good working relationship with Watts and Reginald Pestell (who worked together as police court missionaries and probation officers at Thames Court between 1934 and 1937, Pestell becoming Mayor of Stoke Newington and quite prominent in Labour Party politics after the War): "But Groser never found common ground with Watts about the complicated motivations under-lying criminal behaviour. ...'The trouble', he would say, 'with a man like Watts is that he doesn't see that half his probationers wouldn't need his help at all if they had decent jobs and decent houses'."

Similarly, Alfred Leeding remembered his sense of shock as a probation officer when a theological student on placement to him in about 1935 or 1936 told him that offenders were created by social conditions, and that, to combat juvenile delinquency, much more had to be spent on clearing the slums, building good houses, relieving poverty, and promoting health and education: "I was too stunned to question how he squared his theories with his theology." Thus some Church people seemed more scientific than some probation officers at about the time that most of the work of the London Police Court Mission was on the point of being subjected to a process of secularisation.

It was against this background that during 1938 Guy Clutton-Brock, W.G. Minn, Miss A.E. Beasley, Miss B. Bromley and Miss M.L. Tabor represented the London Probation Service at conferences, also attended by officials from the Home Office and London County Council, at the London School of Economics to discuss with Professor Alexander Carr-Saunders, Dr Hermann Mannheim and Dr E.C. Rhodes the investigation into juvenile delinquency - first in London, later in the provinces - which the three academics were planning to conduct on behalf of the Home Office. The collection of data began in London on 1 October 1938 and was completed in rather more than six months (the assembly of data from provincial cities began later, but was completed at about the same time), valuable assistance being given by probation officers and the education services in all the cities concerned. As regards London, the investigators analysed the cases of a total of 989 "delinquents" and 1,000 "controls" (out of a national total of 1,953 and 1,970, respectively), drawn from the courts at Toynbee Hall, Woolwich Town Hall, Caxton Hall, Stamford House, Islington Town Hall, Southwark, and Springfield Hall. Completion of the analysis of the results of the national investigation would be delayed by the outbreak of war in 1939 and the consequent upheaval; and the investigators' report was finally published in 1942 as *Young Offenders* (which took account, *inter alia,* of Dr M. Fortes's study of sibship, derived from some 750 probation records of the Toynbee Hall Juvenile Court between 1926 and 1930). The Home Office was disappointed with *Young Offenders,* which Sir Alexander Maxwell, the Permanent Under-Secretary of State, seemed to regard as more or less inconclusive. Ironically perhaps, the Home Office had prohibited Carr-Saunders and his colleagues from including any psychiatric examination of delinquents in their enquiry, which focused on social factors. Although most London probation officers apparently dealt with only a few "mentally defective" delinquents at any one time, the Society of Juvenile Courts Probation Officers expressed its concern in 1938 at the "lack of accommodation in M.D. residential schools" and the paucity of alternative methods of treatment in practice for such delinquents.[1]

At about this time, Clutton-Brock visited the experimental Hawkspur Camp for lawless youth run by W. David Wills[2] (a future biographer of the educationalist Homer Lane, the tragic visionary of the Little Commonwealth). If Wills found Clutton-Brock challenging, others found him reassuring. Bill Hornung vividly remembered his first interview with Clutton-Brock at St Stephen's House:"He was friendly, down to earth and most reassuring and encouraging to me as a novice probation officer. My appointment was confirmed 12 months later. ...I started with a caseload of 70 ... Records were kept by hand by each individual probation officer." Florence Bradley recalled being interviewed by Clutton-Brock, E.W. Watts, and Darcy the chief clerk, for the post of "clerical assistant" at St Stephen's House; she was offered and accepted the job, though it entailed a drop in salary, as the job sounded more interesting than the one she had been doing. She started work in May 1938 and, in so doing, became the first full-time, official secretary in the history of the London Probation

Service, which would acquire "an extraordinary mixture" of staff. Working mainly for Clutton-Brock and intermittently for Watts and Boswell, she found the former charming and the latter two very considerate and helpful. She appreciated the "friendly family atmosphere" and rapidly became part of the very enthusiastic team of pioneers at head office. According to Miss Bradley's recollection, the second probation "clerical assistant" (or secretary) to be appointed in London was Miss West, assigned to West London Court.

Then, towards the end of August 1938, Miss Bradley was joined at St Stephen's House by Miss Iris M. Pontifex, who appears to have been the third such secretary. As Miss Pontifex was only 21 at the time, and as the work was considered unsuitable for anyone younger than 25, there was a great deal of discussion as to whether she could be appointed. Finally it was decided that she could go to head office, where the work was mainly of an administrative nature. Florence Bradley and Iris Pontifex were both qualified shorthand typists and, by virtue of working at and for head office, were on a slightly higher salary (of an extra 2s.6d. per week) than other clerical assistants. Miss Pontifex remembered:

> It was a very happy office, all working a $5\frac{1}{2}$-day week, with exceptionally long hours, as an enthusiastic team ... inspired by the Principal Probation Officer into believing that we were fortunate in having the unique opportunity of shaping, albeit in a small way, the London Probation Service of the future.

During this period Mrs Haberlin was assigned to Clerkenwell Police Court, apparently as the fourth clerical assistant to be appointed in the London Probation Service; and similar appointments soon followed at other London courts, such as North London (Miss Waite), Marylebone (Mrs Skinner), and South Western (Miss Sims), not to mention the juvenile courts. The steadily increasing number of clerical assistants, and the secretaries who followed in their footsteps, made a tremendous qualitative contribution to the capital's probation service, whose professional and managerial capability they helped to enhance. It may be considered no small tribute to the ladies concerned, and no doubt to the probation service as well, that many of these clerical assistants would still be working for the London Probation Service some 20 years after their appointment, and Florence Bradley and Iris Pontifex, for example, would each give over 30 years' service.

On analysis it seems clear that, in terms of posts and grades, appointments in the London Probation Service had been made generally on the basis of a hierarchical structure, from the top downwards: first came the appointment of the Principal Probation Officer (January 1937); then the appointments of the first Assistant Principal Probation Officers (July 1937) and, at the same time or soon afterwards, those of senior probation officers (a surviving London Probation Service minute of 11 January 1938 refers, in passing, to "Seniors Meetings future programme"); and then the formal take-over by the Home Office of the mass of probation officers (July 1938), followed by an increasing number of clerical assistants (a process gathering momentum from about August 1938 onwards).

According to Miss Pontifex's recollection, the head office staff, including the chief clerk and another clerk, totalled six by the end of 1937 and twelve by the end of 1938. This latter figure was accounted for by the appointments of Miss Bradley, Miss Pontifex, two more male clerks, and the arrival of Mr T.W. Marsh and Miss Elizabeth R. Glover in October 1938 as Assistant Principal Probation Officers (of whom there were now five in all). Both Marsh and Glover had previously been missionaries with the London Police Court Mission: the former since about 1926, succeeding the legendary Fred Barnett at Westminster; the latter since 1931, according to her own account[3], after social work training at the Time and Talents Settlement in Bermondsey and seven years' apprenticeship in club work.

Just as internally the structure and organisation of the London Probation Service were expanding, so externally it was beginning to find its role in the criminal justice system. In this process the Service was assisted by the police. At about the beginning of July 1938, Clutton-Brock had a talk with Sir Norman Kendal, Assistant Commissioner at New Scotland Yard, about the problems George Neve had experienced in getting police officers, before they left the court, to see him or his colleagues in "put back" cases at the Old Bailey. Some seven months later Clutton-Brock had a talk with Sir Norman about the police informing probation officers when a probationer was reconvicted (again with reference to the Central Criminal Court), and the Assistant Commissioner promised his co-operation. Just as Alfred Leeding, as a young probation officer, had accompanied the C.I.D. on two night patrols, so Guy Clutton-Brock sometimes went round London at night with the 'Flying Squad', with whom he sat in pubs for informers to sidle up.

In 1938 the proportion of adult offenders appearing in summary courts in the Metropolitan Police District who were placed on probation was 24% (compared with 3% in Liverpool).[4] The courts at the Old Bailey seemed to be making an increasing number of probation orders, with George Neve calculating that 6% of the total number under supervision were recharged during 1938 - almost exactly the same percentage, according to his calculation, as in 1937. Towards the end of September 1938 Clutton-Brock recorded: "Neve tells me that they now have 200 probation cases. He is getting a lot of old lags and the Judges are wanting more and more to place these on probation." (Clutton-Brock had previously visited Neve at the Old Bailey, where he had gone over about half of his cases with him and had suggested to Neve that notes should be kept on the offence, offender, reason for the offence, etc.) Neve and his colleagues visited all probationers in their homes; and Clutton-Brock permitted them to claim travelling and subsistence expenses for not too frequent home visits to probationers outside London: the Old Bailey covered the whole of the Home Counties, and responsibility for supervision of its probation cases had not been transferred to local, or more local, offices. Neve reported: "Those who are unemployed visit us during the day at the Court until we have placed them in work." Clutton-Brock allowed him to claim for his payment of the fares of probationers from the Old Bailey to their homes, if these were a long distance away.

In *Inasmuch: Christianity in the Police Courts,* Sidney Dark reproduced a touching letter to the Old Bailey judge Sir Holman Gregory (who had presided over a Royal Commission on unemployment insurance) in which an ex-offender thanked the judge, who had been assisted by George Neve, for having paid rent and found a job for an apparently reformed friend of his who had just died. The letter-writer then turned to his own situation:

> you advised Mr Neve in my case. But Mr Neve could not find me work, so I put my shoulder to the wheel and found work ... I know that you will be pleased, and so will Mr Neve, to know that there is good in some of us who have been to prison and found out the mistakes which we do when we are young and know no better.

During 1938 Sidney Dark's book (which featured an account of a whole day he spent in an unidentified London police court) had been vetted in typescript by some members of the National Police Court

Mission Executive Committee, which requested the addition of a final chapter pleading for continuation of the work of the Mission.[5] In this chapter (which was included when the book was published in March 1939), Sidney Dark warned of the danger of "a more or less rigid red tapeism" under the new probation system, and he made the questionable claim that "officialdom is inevitably unsympathetic, and it is not the business of the official to be the bringer of comfort and the inspirer of hope". In a somewhat similar vein, Albert Lieck had declared in his book *Bow Street World* (published in 1938): "Now we have a definitely recognized probation system, which has completely justified its existence. It tends, however, to get too officialized, and some of the present day probation officers have slightly swelled heads."

Sidney Dark had visited the London Police Court Mission's boys' home in Camberwell (with its tiny chapel). But he did not mention the London Police Court Mission's hostel for probation students which opened its doors to the first trainees on 1 July 1938, in temporary premises at Lincoln Hall, near Russell Square. Moreover, another response to official suggestions in changed circumstances was marked by the emergence of the Fellowship of St Barnabas. In April 1938 a group had been appointed to consider reorganisation of the Guild of C.E.T.S. Police Court Missionaries. This group - which included the Rev. Harry Pearson and the London probation officers Sidney Boswell, Miss Elizabeth Glover and Ralph Beeson - co-opted Miss Elizabeth Inman, H.E. Norman (who had been a pioneering senior probation officer in South Africa), and Guy Clutton-Brock. As a result of the group's deliberations, the Guild decided on 21 October 1938 that it should be superseded by a new body called The Fellowship of St Barnabas (otherwise known as the Probation Officers' Christian Fellowship). Thus the foundations were laid for the Probation Service Christian Fellowship; it may be noted that the group which, in effect, laid those foundations included one Principal Probation Officer, one future Principal Probation Officer, one Assistant Principal Probation Officer, and one future Deputy Principal Probation Officer, all in the London service.

New foundations were also laid when, on 1 January 1939, Middlesex became a "combined area" with the appointment of a County Probation Committee charged with the duty of appointing, employing and paying probation officers and supervising their work. One of this Committee's first acts was to appoint Mr S.A. Gwynn (a former member of the London Police Court Mission staff) as the new Principal Probation Officer. Although the London Police Court Mission continued to share in the employment and payment of a total of 26 male and 14 female officers attached to the police courts in Middlesex and Hampstead and at the Middlesex Quarter Sessions, it was becoming increasingly clear that its involvement in this field was a diminishing one.

When the London Probation Service came into being in July 1938, London was the largest area in the country with trained juvenile court probation officers; and the new adminstrative structure in the metropolitan area aroused strong feelings of suspicion and resistance - even hostility -among at least some of the older London juvenile court probation officers, as is evident from the Minutes of the Society of Juvenile Courts Probation Officers between June 1938 and January 1942, for example. According to Miss R.M. Braithwaite, many of her early juvenile court colleagues had had a warm relationship with S.W. Harris and his staff at the Home Office, and had suddenly felt cut off from "the source of power" which they used to contact direct until the emergence of the London Probation Service meant that they were expected to go through their own head office. For an appreciable time in the immediate pre-War period S.J.C.P.O. held its meetings at 47 Whitehall - more or less equidistant between St Stephen's House and the Home Office, but in the same street as the latter.

Miss Braithwaite had done two L.S.E. placements: the first at the Time and Talents Settlement (in effect following in Miss Glover's footsteps), and the second at the public library in Blackfriars Road as Nina Blyth's very last student. When, after more than 20 years' service, Miss Blyth had reached retirement age, the exceptional course was taken of prolonging her tenure for 18 months, S.W. Harris describing her at this time as "probably the best probation officer we have ever had in the London juvenile courts".[6] Miss Braithwaite remembered this diminutive woman as "uniquely intuitive", with the gift of broadening one's perspective. Through her, Miss Braithwaite (who would herself become a stimulating teacher) stood in "apostolic succession" to Evelyn Lance and the very first children's probation officers. Referring, it seems, to probation work at about the time of the Home Office take-over, Miss Blyth spoke of "its inevitable standardisation as a social service" and quoted Principal Caird to the effect that "the idea creates the organisation; the organisation destroys the idea". It was perhaps rather ironic, therefore, that Miss Blyth had been a leading light in the formation of two organisations, albeit small voluntary groups: the Society of Juvenile Courts Probation Officers, and later, in January 1926, an Association of Juvenile Courts Probation Officers, of which Association she and her London colleagues Miss Beasley, Miss Crosland, Miss Lindo and Miss Paine were co-founders and of which Margery Fry, J.P., accepted the Presidency.[7]

Contact with London juvenile court probation officers may well have stimulated the conception and preparation of Winifred Elkin's book *English Juvenile Courts* (1938). Winifred Elkin (who was Miss Lindo's cousin) pointed out that these officers

> have themselves to make arrangements for their offices and are provided only with the sum of £40 per annum to cover rent, cleaning, heating and lighting. In other words, they have to search through their district until they find some well-disposed organisation that has one or two unused rooms which they are prepared to let for nothing...

Miss Braithwaite recalled that at least some of the "women of education" furnished their own offices, and that her first office was in a disused public house called "The Horn of Plenty" in Limehouse where she not infrequently worked (like many of her colleagues) till late at night. Individuality and a sense of freedom and independence were qualities prized by probation officers, who generally seemed to show a great sense of dedication and commitment to their work, with "the women probation officers in their 'pork-pie' hats and tweed skirts calling each other by their surnames to show that they were emancipated and 'just like the men' ".[8] The perceived individuality of probation officers no doubt related to a claim, in Laelia Sander's words, that "the probation officer's approach, being an individual one, is always personal". Indeed, Grace Harrison -also in *Probation* for October 1932 - had maintained that "the extraordinary success of Probation is due largely to the fact that it is based on the fundamental principle of individual treatment for the individual, and it is the only part of our penal system which puts this principle into practice".

Miss Braithwaite would declare in 1959: "Probation officers have always tended to feel a sense of loyalty and responsibility to the Magistrates for whom they work, and have never taken kindly to any bureaucratic interference."[9] Many years later, Harold Morton would testify regarding Clutton-Brock's period as Principal Probation Officer for London:

> Perhaps one of the most difficult tasks he had to perform was that of gaining the confidence of the Stipendiary Magistrates who had for many years considered the probation officers very much the officers permanently attached to the courts they had control over. There were many clashes in cases where general staffing considerations necessitated the movement of individual officers.

There seemed a hint of this in the summer of 1939 when Clutton-Brock considered recruiting the part-time probation officer at Hampstead Court, Miss Dorothy Wood - who was "very charming and sensible", according to George Neve - to provide much needed assistance as a female probation officer at the Old Bailey; but although Miss Wood seemed willing to work at the Central Criminal Court, this idea came to nothing after Clutton-Brock had consulted the Home Office (which may have taken into account complications that could have arisen as a result of the fact that Hampstead Court lay outside the area for which the London Probation Service carried responsibility).

The existing female probation officer at the Old Bailey, Miss R.M. Green - whose work was efficiently yet sympathetically assessed by Elizabeth Glover - carried a caseload of at least 60, of whom 19 were bigamists, though she also handled cases of manslaughter, blackmail, attempted suicide, fraudulent conversions, and indecent practices in brothels. In addition, she was always sent for when children or young women gave evidence in indecent cases, and when female witnesses broke down in the witness box. She gave much time and attention to the wives of men sentenced to penal servitude, some of whom were left in a pitiable plight, and to the "wives" of bigamist prisoners. As the probation office had no typist, Miss Green did all her own clerical work, writing about one hundred letters a month; and emphasizing friendship rather than coercion or authority in her relationships, she apparently had extremely flexible reporting times for her clients, some of whom lived some distance away. According to Ada Demer's recollection, Miss Green was known as "The Angel of the Old Bailey"; while C.H. Rolph (C.R. Hewitt of the City of London Police) would remember her as an "accidentally wingless angel. A marvellous creature, loved by everyone."

One of her colleagues was Michael Walsh, who had served at the Central Criminal Court since 1933, and whom Rolph would recall as "a genial, elderly, soft-spoken Irishman", adding: "We became good friends, perhaps because he nourished my ego, soothed my worries, and loved books. He wrote little pieces for the evening papers that might have come straight from Oliver St John Gogarty." Rolph would also recollect occasions when Sir Ernest Wild, the Recorder of London, beamed at "my probation officer" in the witness box (probably George Neve), indicated the defendant in the dock, and asked: "Will you see whether you can do anything about him for me?" According to Rolph: "Only a handful of people would know that my probation officer was already at his wits' end with a case-load like that of Captain Bligh on the *Bounty*."[10] Another perception was provided by Reginald Pestell, who - in his own words -"knew George Neve very well when he was at the Central Criminal Court. He was highly thought of by the judges there for his ability as a Probation Officer. He was very unassuming and always preferred the background rather than the limelight." The probation officer Francis Lister, who joined the service in 1939, would remember Neve as "always kind and helpful". Neve's successors - such as Jack Frost and the monocled Theodore Podger (a heroic wartime naval commander) - would sustain the confidence of Old Bailey judges in the probation service. At the London Sessions, where Sir Robert Wallace had wholeheartedly used the Probation of Offenders Act from its inception, Mr W.J. Watson, who served there between 1913 and 1947 - in C.W. Hornung's words - "had had a great deal to do with establishing probation at Sessions and laid a solid foundation for the rapid expansion of the work".

Clutton-Brock's underlying determination and understanding of human situations enhanced his attempts to organise his staff into cohesive units and secure worthwhile clerical services and other backing for probation officers, who were apparently under pressure to produce more and more social background reports on offenders to assist the courts in imposing appropriate sentences (Miss Braithwaite recalled that the Children and Young Persons Act 1933 resulted in many more children being brought before juvenile courts, reaching a peak in 1938). One of the most time-consuming tasks at head office was the sending out of copies of Form 70 (Metropolitan Police notification of children and young persons charged), which were received daily at St Stephen's House by post from police stations throughout the Metropolitan Police Court District. The addresses of the persons charged - given on the forms - were individually checked on a huge wall map to ascertain which probation office would be dealing with each particular case. The forms were then sent off without delay to the respective offices, accuracy being of paramount importance because of the time factor.

Miss Pontifex regarded the early years at headquarters as

> most exhilarating, a great challenge, and all of us entered into the spirit of making the new department a real success. For instance, getting the huge evening post out was often a communal affair, everyone happily giving a hand - it was not unusual for the Principal Probation Officer being in charge of the stamp sticking.

(Miss Bradley quite independently remembered Guy Clutton-Brock sticking stamps on envelopes for posting.) Clutton-Brock himself amusingly recalled a bright idea he had had as P.P.O.:

> Statistics of crime were thought to be important, so I fell for designing a superb form to meet all requirements. Presenting it to probation officers to complete, they resisted it strongly and wisely. Instead of actually doing the work, they would have been filling up forms. So I tore it up.

Also torn up was a tentative plan for the London Probation Service to act on a consultative basis in an international setting. According to Charles Morgan's recollection, one or two State Governments in Australia, anxious to establish a probation service, approached the Home Office for assistance, and Charles Morgan and Harold Morton were approached through the Principal Probation Officer to see whether they would be interested in so advising these State Governments. But before any response could be given, the Second World War started, and the idea had to be abandoned.

When the War started, the London Probation Service staff totalled 123 (69 men and 54 women); of these, 33 (20 women and 13 men) were attached to the juvenile courts. Already in April *Probation* had announced: "Probation has been scheduled as a Reserved Occupation. This means that the Government realises that the service must be kept as intact as possible in time of war." When war came in September 1939, male probation officers over the age of 30, and all female probation officers, were declared "reserved" (i.e. not called up for military service). The coming of the War and the consequent expectation of air raids on the vulnerable Bethnal Green area forced the closure of the Speedwell Club, which had admitted more than one thousand girls since it opened. Miss Inman would recall: "Several of my own cases were evacuated and re-evacuated four times in the first year of the war... The public air raid shelter does provide a marvellous refuge for anyone who wants to run away. We have boys... who have been living sometimes for weeks in public shelters."

Issues relating to accommodation concerned many probation officers in London and elsewhere from the earliest days of the War. In September 1939 the London Probation Service headquarters were moved from St Stephen's House to offices vacated by the Metropolitan Police Receiver next door. At the same time many young probationers, with other school-children, were evacuated out of London to country areas as part of the Government's precautionary measures (in February 1939 the Sussex Branch of N.A.P.O. had held a conference to consider how the arrival of some 100,000 evacuated children in Sussex would affect their work). To help out, eight London probation officers were sent to the reception areas in September and October 1939: responsible to the local probation authorities and working in close co-operation with schoolteachers and billeting officers, they dealt not only with evacuated probationers, but also with children who were showing behavioural difficulties, but who had not been brought before the courts. As more provision was made for the welfare of evacuees, and as a large proportion of the evacuated children returned when the expected heavy bombing did not materialise, these probation officers were withdrawn as the need for them in London became greater than the demand for their services in the provinces.

It was against this background that in early January 1940 Clutton-Brock sent a circular letter to all his juvenile court probation officers to advise them that in future George Neve intended to contact the appropriate juvenile court officer for him or her to make the necessary enquiries and carry through the case when a juvenile was committed to the Old Bailey, in place of the previous practice of the Old Bailey probation officers to undertake such enquiries themselves. Indeed, wartime conditions and pressures highlighted the need for London probation officers at the higher courts, as elsewhere, to make more effective use of their time. This appeared to be illustrated by a visit by Miss Glover to the London

Sessions, where she told the caring female probation officer (who had fruitlessly sacrificed two days of her leave to provide some kind of moral support for two women standing trial) that probation was becoming more and more a specialist's job, and that the "nursemaiding" of unhappy female witnesses and relatives of sentenced men could be done just as well by women police officers or police matrons, particularly if the London Probation Service were depleted through male colleagues being called up.

Then, in February 1940, the London service (in the authoritative words of R.H. Beeson) "suffered a severe loss" when Guy Clutton-Brock was given special leave of absence to become head of Oxford House Settlement, Bethnal Green, and resigned as Principal Probation Officer at the end of the year. Miss Bradley recalled that his departure was unexpected and rather sudden. Her own recollection tended to confirm an impresssion given by his autobiography that he had felt frustrated in his dealings with the Home Office, admittedly at a time of grave national crisis and of uncertainty for the new London Probation Service and for the civil service generally (his self-deprecating reference, in a letter he sent to the Home Office at the end of June 1939, to "my usual tactless manner" was probably a straw in the wind). Yet he had no doubt helped to enlarge the Home Office's knowledge and understanding of probation work, at least in the adult courts. He clearly made efficient use of his diary, seemed assiduous in following up points, and kept in regular contact with his staff, with appointments at the office at half-hourly intervals towards the end. He later confessed: "I could not see myself enduring to old age as a pensioned civil servant." His persistent desire to be with people "at ground level" - to which he referred both in his wonderfully vivid autobiography (1972) and in a telephone interview (1987) - was clearly a powerful factor in his decision to accept the challenge of being warden of Oxford House in wartime, with some 500 people sheltering and sleeping there night after night to escape Hitler's bombs.

Clutton-Brock evidently had a great capacity to inspire trust in him and confidence in what he was doing: as Principal Probation Officer he allowed a young offender whom he had known from his borstal days to stay many times at his home. In helping to put the London Probation Service on its feet, he had become a much respected and liked Principal Probation Officer; and on his leaving the service, S.J.C.P.O., for example, presented this inveterate smoker with a much appreciated gift of a pipe, pouch and tobacco. He was sadly missed by quite a few London probation officers and Home Office officials, who followed his remarkable career with interest, as he extended his concern for the outcast, the underdog and the suffering from the Service to Oxford House, and from Germany just after the War to colonial Rhodesia, where he would be briefly imprisoned and from which he would be deported for political reasons. He and his wife - and the non-racial community there with which they were identified - would help to sustain the burgeoning African nationalist movement in Rhodesia and to provide a source of inspiration for Robert Mugabe's much praised policy of reconciliation. Whether or not Clutton-Brock's experience with the London Probation Service contributed in any way to his achievement in Africa, he earned a place in the history books describing the transition from Rhodesia to Zimbabwe (just as he had played a significant part in the transition to a fully fledged London Probation Service). Circumstances enabled at least one former or serving London probation officer to meet him in Africa; and he would be remembered by Elspeth Gray as "a great idealist", by Jack Frost as very capable, a delightful personality and "essentially an idealist", and by Miss Braithwaite as "absolutely humble". (A former Middlesex probation officer, Mr B.D. Beecroft, would become Director of Social Welfare in Rhodesia in 1978.)

Clutton-Brock's successor as Principal Probation Officer was Ralph Henry Beeson, who was more closely associated with probation work and perhaps with the Home Office than Clutton-Brock had been: Beeson had been a police court missionary (with the London Police Court Mission) and probation officer since at least 1935, before going to the Home Office Probation Branch, from which he was seconded to act as Principal Probation Officer from 1 March 1940, being formally appointed to that post with effect from 1 January 1941. Beeson had the advantage of direct experience of probation work and of the combined experience of the five Assistant Principal Probation Officers brought in to head office under Clutton-Brock; and he would doubtless have known at least four of these five from the days when they were all probation officers in the field (indeed, he had worked for several years in the same London police court as Miss Glover). According to an illuminating comparison made by Miss Bradley, who worked for both men for some time, the different styles and approaches to their work of Clutton-Brock and Beeson matched the needs of the hour: Clutton-Brock had an informal approach, which was necessary, and worked wonders, at a time when the police court missionaries were suspicious and understandably uncertain in the wake of the Home Office take-over. They needed reassurance, and Clutton-Brock (whose varied experience had included a theological course at Ripon Hall) put them at their ease. Later on, when the probation service seemed more settled, a more civil service-oriented approach seemed to be indicated, and Beeson provided this.

By all accounts Beeson was an earnest and dedicated man who took his responsibilities very seriously. Both Kathleen Hoath (who acted as his secretary for some years) and Jack Frost described him as a "disciplinarian"; and Miss Braithwaite recalled that "he bore the white man's burden, plus, plus". If Clutton-Brock had laid the foundations, Beeson would defend the battlements during the supreme trial of the Second World War, when arguably the Home Office provided a greater measure of protection for probation officers than the Mission could have done. Miss Hoath recalled that Beeson supported a retired probation officer by visiting her and helping her to manage her money. Bill Hornung remembered that during his five years' wartime service in the army (1940-45) - mainly overseas -there were two or three spells of home leave during which he was able to visit the probation head office and was taken out to lunch by Beeson, who took a keen interest in all he was doing and was an assiduous correspondent. Similarly, John Starke was very grateful when, having been dismissed as a probation officer in the provinces because of his stance as a conscientious objector, he was appointed as a probation officer to North London by Beeson, who had been contacted by the sympathetic Miss Rosling. Charles Morgan recalled that Beeson used to come round the probation offices, for example to wish colleagues a happy Christmas.

Probation training was inevitably disrupted in various ways by the War (for instance, the London School of Economics in effect moved out of the London area). But 35 selected probation officers from the metropolitan courts and the counties of Surrey and Middlesex were invited to a "refresher" course of 14 lectures arranged by the London Police Court Mission in consultation with the Home Office and Professor F. Clarke, Director of Education to the University of London. Those who attended much appreciated the course, which was held during 1940, and asked that it be repeated as an encouragement to other probation officers.

The Mission also arranged a course of 52 lectures - including some by the psychologist Dr J.A. Hadfield and the chief clerk A.C.L. Morrison - for probation trainees during the same year.

When petrol rationing came into force, the London Probation Service was able to negotiate a reasonable supply of petrol for each officer, and Mr T.W. Marsh, one of the Assistant Principal Probation Officers, was put in charge of monitoring probation officers' applications for petrol for the official use of their cars. The average mileage claimed in August 1939 was 340; and at the outbreak of war, 40 London officers were authorised to use their cars for official purposes. (At an earlier stage, Miss Inman, for example, had decided not to have a car as "it would have put me on the wrong footing with the children and the families".) Later, when conditions worsened, officers were discouraged from using their cars, in the knowledge that London was generally better served by public service vehicles than most parts of the country; and by September 1943 only two cars would be in use, in particularly scattered districts.

When the "Blitz" or heavy bombing started in September 1940, a large number of London children were evacuated; and Miss Braithwaite found herself, together with two London colleagues, assisting with evacuated London children in Somerset, where she remained for a year or so. She had a caseload of about 120, but relations with the local probation service, to which she and her colleagues were seconded, were good.

During this period London head office was moved back to St Stephen's House (apparently this time to a suite of offices recently vacated by General de Gaulle and his Free French officers); London probation officers in all districts of the capital called on the newly appointed welfare officers in rest centres and offered their co-operation; and Mr A.H. Cole (a London probation officer who was later high in the Middlesex service) was awarded the B.E.M. (Civil Division) for saving the life of the pilot of a crashed aircraft by dragging him clear just before the petrol tank exploded. Because of the bombing, the London Police Court Mission was forced to close Winnington House, which, at the request of many probation officers, it had recently opened as a training home for girls with V.D.; and the Mission lost valuable records when its central offices were destroyed. Similarly, a number of the London Probation Service's offices were totally destroyed or rendered uninhabitable by enemy action: in Whitechapel and Shepherd's Bush (1940), Woolwich and

Peckham (1941). Many London probation officers found their homes wrecked or damaged by blast, and - in the words of Beeson's subsequent report - "in this respect they have shared the experience of those among whom they work". Georgina Stafford recalled that she was visiting a Lambeth woman, who had a babe in her arms, when the air-raid sirens sounded, but the woman, at some risk to herself, insisted on showing her visitor where she needed to go. While there were raids during daylight hours as well as at night, probation officers could not insist on children reporting, in case the clients got killed; and home visiting could also pose problems where many people were legitimately away from home in public shelters or at work, let alone had actually decamped. Although Beeson's 1945 report did not specifically refer to his loss, his house suffered a direct hit, and he had to be dug out of the rubble, but he refused hospital treatment and returned to the office later that day.[11] That was characteristic of the man.

At this time of terrible destruction, the London Police Court Mission finally relinquished its remaining responsibilities for the employment of social workers in the criminal courts. After several abortive discussions with officials associated with the County Probation Committee to ascertain whether the existing relationship between Middlesex and the Mission could be continued, the Mission formally terminated those responsibilities in Middlesex on 31 March 1941, in accordance with the letter and spirit of the Home Office Social Services (Harris) Committee's 1936 Report. Thus, more or less unobtrusively during one of the darkest periods of the War (the Chairman of the Middlesex Quarter Sessions paid an impressive tribute to the Mission two months later), the ministry of light, which the Church of England Temperance Society had begun to bring into the courts some sixty-five years earlier, officially came to an end. The London Police Court Mission noted with pride that, from the earliest years of its history, "the Missionary could be appealed to for advice and assistance by any person in any kind of trouble in the Court".

Perhaps during the 1930s it had become more and more apparent - as Miss Braithwaite later suggested - that the Mission did not have sufficient financial means to meet the steadily increasing demands it had to face in London and Middlesex. Quite probably at least some of the older police court missionaries, because they had lost the Mission and the Rev. Harry Pearson, had some difficulty relating to Clutton-Brock, Beeson and the

Home Office; although the comradeship and sacrifices of the war years no doubt helped in some respects to ease the transition from Police Court Mission to Probation Service. Be that as it may, the London Police Court Mission would continue to assist the London Probation Service and the Home Office in various ways, including projects connected with probation training and residential care. For example, in response to a Home Office request, the Mission opened its first approved school for boys in the summer of 1941, with Beeson's wife as one of the managers: the Cotswold School became well known to London courts. At this time Miss Inman recalled that in London "children are still being brought before the Courts every week who have not been to school since the war started... We are having to make our probationers go to school, whereas their friends are not going, and I think that duty is quite wrong because it changes our relationship with the family."

Rather as the London Police Court Mission and the Church of England Temperance Society were declared legally separate and independent bodies in September 1941; so in June the London juvenile court probation officer Ethel Currant pleaded for the "dissolution" of St Stephen's House, which, in a striking metaphor, she compared to "an artificial branch" blocking out the light needed for the growth of the tree of probation. No doubt highly conscious of the fact that, in the metropolitan area, probation officers were appointed, and the probation service largely controlled, by the Home Office (and not by magistrates, as elsewhere in the country), Miss Currant deplored "the gradual creeping into our service of bureaucracy and red tape, and the lessening of the power of the Courts". She added:

> The Court was our strength and background, to it come the people whom we are appointed to serve, and from the people should spring the life and growth of probation - but this growth is being stifled... I regard St Stephen's House as an artificial branch, and because it is there, the probation service is becoming top heavy, and its foundations are insecure. With St Stephen's came the false idea of promotion... Simplicity of organisation should be the key note of a service whose aim is to help people.

She proposed "that the State relinquish some of its newly acquired power and return it to the Courts, to whom it properly belongs. This would help to do away with the switching over of Officers from Adult to Juvenile Courts."[12]

In June 1941 S.J.C.P.O. endorsed the principle that juvenile court work was specialised, and that probation officers should not be transferred from adult to juvenile courts, or vice versa, against their wishes. There had also been some feeling within S.J.C.P.O. that the appointment of senior probation officers had inhibited the free expression of main-grade opinion at staff meetings; and Miss Paine, for example, openly deplored the creation of seniors (though they appeared to institutionalize the need for support in a demanding job). A somewhat similar view was held by Miss Inman, who, on being approached about becoming a senior, resisted the idea on the grounds that the work was "so intensely individual" and "we were there to work with the children, not look after colleagues". However, by 1942 Miss Inman had agreed to become a senior probation officer (though she was not enthusiastic about the pay differential); and it is difficult to tell how many London officers would have endorsed Miss Currant's views at this time, particularly perhaps when a situation of total war on a global scale seemed to highlight a need for more, not less, bureaucratic control. At the end of the War, Beeson, no doubt quite sincerely, would maintain that "every effort has been made to promote efficient organisation without any appearance of regimentation"; but Miss Currant had raised important issues.

With the London Police Court Mission, Beeson arranged a course of weekly lectures at St Stephen's House in 1941 as part of probation training. Doubtless he was also instrumental in arranging the informal "at home", held monthly from July 1941, for probation officers, working in different parts of London, to meet each other (apparently providing scope for satire in Sewell Stokes's *Court Circular*); though the bombing of London disrupted social life. As Miss Inman testified: "You may go home-visiting and find the whole street evacuated and perhaps have to go and find your family in a rest centre."

The Harris Committee (1936) had suggested that, in London, at least one of any new Deputy Principal Probation Officers should be female. Ethel Crosland had retired, on pension, from head office in September 1941 (by a curious coincidence she would die on the same day in December 1956 as her old friend and colleague Nina Blyth); and in January 1942 Miss Elizabeth Glover became the first, and therefore the first female, Deputy Principal (or Chief) Probation Officer in the London service. Miss Glover was apparently much involved in compiling a central register of lodgings for use by clients, in conducting a survey (at the Home Office's request) of facilities in prisons and other establishments for the treatment of V.D., and in developing the London service's first official children's library (established in 1941, thanks to Canadian and United States donors). According to Miss Bradley, Elizabeth Glover had a knack for describing the lodgings she had inspected; but wartime conditions later made it impossible to keep the register up-to-date. Juvenile court probation officers, and many of the children in their care, were evidently most appreciative of the simply written and profusely illustrated books, made available to encourage the children to read and widen their horizons. At about the same time head office established a lending library for officers of books on probation, criminology, psychology and similar subjects. Over the years this library would be quite extensively used.

In February 1942 Mr T.W. Marsh returned (apparently entirely through choice) to the practical work of the courts as senior probation officer at Clerkenwell Court: he was the first Assistant Principal Probation Officer in London, and almost certainly the first officer of any rank above main grade in the metropolitan area, to be demoted for whatever reason. Of the two established A.P.P.O.s who remained, E.W. Watts would later recall that his close colleague Sidney Boswell - a man of sincere and simple faith, combined with great experience and sympathy, with a joy in his work that nothing could really diminish - was especially happy as an A.P.P.O. when he was called upon to help and advise trainees and the less experienced probation officers; but there were times when Boswell wished to be back in court, in what he called "the front line of the battle against crime and misery". (Bill Hornung had discovered in 1938 that Boswell had left a tremendous reputation behind him at Marylebone Court, where he was still referred to as "the Solomon of Marylebone".) Marsh was temporarily replaced by George Neve, who gave part-time help as an acting A.P.P.O., and whose devotion was suggested by the fact that in the summer of 1940 Beeson had referred to Neve's "great prestige" with the judges at the Old Bailey, where he had some 67 clients under his supervision, and, indeed, where, following his appointment, the number of probation orders made had risen from 11 in 1927 to 110 in 1932.

By February 1942 there was apparently a national total of 18 Principal Probation Officers, one Deputy Principal Probation Officer, five Assistant Principal Probation Officers, and 53 senior probation officers. On the basis of these figures the major growth in the development of a structure for the service had taken place in London, where by early 1942 there was a total of 21 seniors, of whom 14 were men and 7 were women, and where, some three years later, there would be 13 men and 9 women senior probation officers working in the courts at the end of the War: so - in the absence of more detailed information - the general disappearance of men into the armed forces did not seem to affect the respective numbers or proportions of male and female seniors in London to a very significant extent during these years. Miss Bradley recalled that the seniors from all the London courts, adult and juvenile alike, came together for a joint meeting about once a month. But as the war conditions became more difficult, these meetings were held "from time to time" at headquarters to discuss matters of policy and general questions affecting the work. Such meetings doubtless played a vital part in helping to maintain staff morale and ensure a flow of information between officers and Ralph Beeson, who apparently attended the first meeting of Principal Probation Officers (convened by the Home Office on 18 December 1942), which, in effect, laid the foundations of the Principal Probation Officers' Conference.

As a result of an undertaking given by Beeson, case committees (which the London Juvenile Court Panel in 1937 had decided to hold, but which had been in abeyance since the outbreak of war) were revived in 1942, when a total of 31 juvenile court case committees convened, with 37 in 1943, and 38 in 1944. Beeson later reported: "Generally speaking, from May, 1941, until July, 1944, there was a steady increase in the number of children under supervision." On the advice of the Home Office, women officers in the juvenile courts took all the boys up to the age of 14, and all the girls, who were placed on supervision; and Miss Stafford, who remembered this, also recalled some very young children being placed under the care of probation officers, with whole families in some cases being under *de facto* supervision. At Lambeth Juvenile Court (where she worked between 1939 and 1944, Clutton-Brock having transferred her from West London Police Court), she took on 72 children (nearly all little boys), and during the War her caseload went into the nineties, of which about a third consisted of girls. Whereas during the years preceding the War the magistrate Claud Mullins experienced and later recorded[13] a case in which he and the probation officer concerned agreed that a weaning process had to be started at the conclusion of the two years' probation of a client who had become over-dependent, Miss Stafford found that during the War "it was a job holding onto one's caseload". Miss Inman who, like Georgina Stafford, remained in London throughout the War, similarly remembered that the work became fairly chaotic: families got bombed out, her office was bombed, and all records were missing for weeks (being eventually recovered in their steel filing cabinets). But, said Miss Inman, it was "wonderful how the parents kept in touch", and she did not lose track of a single family.

The use of probation by the London juvenile courts between 1937 and 1942 seemed to remain remarkably steady, in terms of the percentage represented by the number of probation orders made in relation to the total number of offences proved annually in those courts taken together. On that basis, probation was used in relation to 37% of offences proved in 1937 and in 1942 (a total of 1,327 and 1,187 probation orders, respectively), the lowest such percentage between those two years being 34% in 1938 and 1939. Francis Treseder Giles, the Chief Clerk of the Metropolitan Juvenile Courts, declared in 1943: "The probation officers in the London juvenile courts are without exception keen and zealous workers, and twelve months under their supervision is no mere nominal punishment." He added that the parents were usually co-operative with the probation officer, who "is never made to feel that a summons for breach is an admission of failure on his part". This was reminiscent of the view expressed by Basil Henriques in 1937:

> The good probation officer is the friend of the whole family, and it is in that capacity that he wields his influence. ...The great weakness of many probation officers is that they wait too long before summoning a child or young person who is failing on probation to be dealt with by the court in another way. They tend to think that the child's failure is their failure, which is far from true.

Of the 191 delinquents against whom proceedings for breach of probation were taken in the London juvenile courts in 1942, 57 were sent to approved schools, and a total of 72 had their probation period extended or varied (Miss Inman had referred to London children put on probation "all over the country").

Interestingly, fewer "care or protection" cases (under the Children and Young Persons Act, 1933) were dealt with by the London juvenile courts in 1942 than in 1937 - a total of 272 as against 295 in 1937 - perhaps largely as a result of the evacuation of many London children. But during these years there was consistently a much higher number of girls than of boys involved in these cases. Many of the girls were found to be suffering from V.D., and some were pregnant. Giles commented that, failing reconciliation with relatives, "the probation officers can put them in the way of finding new friends and wholesome interests which will help them to forget the past". Miss Stafford recalled that, with many girls wanting to go out with American G.I.s, the number of "care or protection" cases rose during the War. "Care or protection" and also "beyond control" cases could be placed under the supervision of a probation officer. There were fewer "beyond control" cases dealt with by the London juvenile courts in 1942 than in 1937 (187 as against 243); but, in contradistinction to "care or protection" cases, there was generally a higher incidence of boys than girls being "beyond control". (Cf. Appendix 17.)

Where possible, care had been taken to place London juvenile courts away from obvious criminal settings (a process that seemed reinforced by the substitution of lay justices for metropolitan police magistrates in the juvenile courts - a change enshrined in the Children and Young Persons Act of 1938); and Giles in 1943 revealed that such courts sat on a weekly basis at Toynbee Hall, Friends House, Lennox Gardens, Southwark County Court, Stamford House, and Lambeth Town Hall. Miss Braithwaite pointed out that, as a rule in the London juvenile courts, probation reports were not read aloud, but were handed round in court by the probation officer, and that the offices of children's probation officers were usually inconspicuous at street level.

A decade earlier, Miss Croker-King advised: "Children's different characteristics can be studied very well by the probation officer playing games with them, and it gives great opportunities of impressing on them the meanness of cheating and unfair play." Though many may not have realised it, the care of quite a few of London's children during these traumatic war years may have owed not a little to Clarke Hall and those inspired by his example; rather as the fact that the general Home Office take-over of probation officers in inner London took place just over a year before the outbreak of war gave time to facilitate the deployment and positive response of probation staff during the War.

Some probation officers were conscientious objectors during the War. Some engaged in Army welfare work, for which Major George Neve would be awarded the O.B.E. and the Highgate (Middlesex) probation officer Sydney Burgess the M.B.E. Quite a few probation officers participated (not infrequently at nights after a full day's work) in civil defence, the national fire service or the Home Guard. Knowledge of local welfare and community resources was doubtless of great assistance to those probation officers in London, as elsewhere, who served on Borough Youth Committees and on the district committees of various bodies such as the Charity Organisation Society and the Air Training Corps; and there were London head office representatives on the Committees of the London Police Court Mission, the Sheriffs' Fund Society, the Royal London Discharged Prisoners' Aid Society, the London Union of Girls' Clubs, the Provisional National Council for Mental Health (casework), and three London hostels. London probation officers also gave talks and lectures on probation and kindred topics to a wide variety of gatherings, including those of church guilds, youth organisations, other social workers, nurses, and the Auxiliary Territorial Service.

Miss Bradley vividly remembered Ralph Beeson carrying her type-writer down into the basement if an air-raid siren sounded, so that she could continue typing. But, fortunately, head office came through the bombing and, later, the onslaught of the flying rockets unscathed. Apparently as a result of a Home Office decision that the Aliens Department should be near Scotland Yard, the London Probation Service headquarters were moved out of St Stephen's House in September 1942 to 35 Lennox Gardens, S.W.1, a large (four-storey) requisitioned private house which was also used to accommodate the Chelsea Juvenile Court, and in which Beeson and his head office staff would remain for the rest of the War. Whereas - according to Miss Bradley's recollection - only the men fire-watched at St Stephen's House, at Lennox Gardens all the staff were on a fire-watching rota, two women being on duty together in a shift. Bill Hornung recalled that, following the outbreak of war, his duties (until he was called up in November 1940) included the necessity to act as air-raid lookout on the roof of the court building where he worked, so that the court could continue to sit for as long as practicable. Similarly, Sewell Stokes was a fire-watcher, according to his satirical book *Court Circular,* which, though based on his experiences as a temporary probation officer at Bow Street between 1941 and 1945, contained relatively few allusions to the impact of the War. So fire-watching by London probation staff would appear to have been the norm.

Despite the ravages of the War, some additional buildings were acquired for use by London probation officers. It is true that by the end of the War no office accommodation had been provided for probation officers in the premises in which the London juvenile courts were held. It was the practice to secure offices in or adjoining the districts served by the different children's probation officers; but in 1942 one large office was taken for the five officers working in the much-bombed area served by Toynbee Hall Juvenile Court. That same year, the London Police Court Mission (of which Beeson was "co-opted probation officer") acquired from Toc H - which had apparently provided recruits for the Mission - the use of 95 Denmark Hill, S.E.5, as a hostel for probation service trainees. The following year, the London juvenile court probation officer Mr C.E. Campin was made warden of this hostel, in addition to his probation duties; and also in 1943 the London Police Court Mission opened Chatfield House, 1025 High Road, Whetstone, N.20, as a hostel for the training of male adolescents on probation, its house committee including George Neve, who was simultaneously a member of the Denmark Hill hostel committee.

Similarly, there were some significant staff changes and developments at head office during 1943. Early in the year the London Police Court Mission decided to discontinue its Employment Department at a time when the nation was becoming more strikingly mobilised for war production; and Mr A.J. Pilgrim was given an office at Lennox Gardens, where he continued his special task of finding jobs for the clients of London and Middlesex probation officers, although in a field mainly restricted by wartime conditions to the Merchant Navy and farming. Miss Glover resigned from the London service in January - she joined the staff of the Home Office Probation Branch - and she was succeeded as Deputy Principal Probation Officer by George Neve, from whom Jack Frost (according to his own recollection) inherited a caseload of 100 at the Old Bailey. Neve's appointment as the first male Deputy Principal in the London service virtually coincided with the appointments, in September and October respectively, of Miss Betty Bromley and Miss Jean Dodds as Assistant Principal Probation Officers. Miss Bromley had been a senior probation officer attached to the juvenile court covering Clerkenwell and North London Districts, and had served as a probation officer in London since 1929; Miss Dodds, who came to the London service from Middlesex, had worked as a missionary with the London Police Court Mission in

North London since 1936. Once again in the appointment of London A.P.P.O.s, a degree of balance had been preserved between juvenile and adult court experience.

No doubt largely through Neve, London probation officers were asked by Army Welfare Officers to investigate 618 cases of domestic difficulty between soldiers and their wives during 1944, apart from a large number of Service cases in which applications were made direct to the courts. The immediate results often seemed disappointing, probably mainly because opportunities were distinctly limited for any matrimonial conciliation work to be undertaken in the presence of both partners together, and because in many cases husband and wife each expected to find the other exactly the same on his return as when he went away. Until the Summary Procedure (Domestic Proceedings) Act, 1937, came into force on 1 October 1937, there had been no legal sanction for the involvement of probation officers in matrimonial conciliation, although this had been an important part, *de facto,* of the work of police court missionaries and probation officers in the adult courts for very many years, at a time when divorce was widely regarded as a rich man's option. In London in 1944 male probation officers dealt with 4,083 matrimonial applications, and female officers with 2,624 such applications, which all contained new grounds for domestic complaint. The metropolitan police magistrates north and south of the Thames who took the keenest interest at this time in matrimonial work at their courts were probably Daniel Hopkin and Claud Mullins, respectively. Some indication of Daniel Hopkin's interest may be discerned in the fact that in just under one year (between 11 April 1944 and 31 March 1945) he made 60 matrimonial orders and 12 orders under the Guardianship of Infants Act - on both counts more than any of his fellow magistrates at North London Police Court during the same period of the War.[14]

Jewish women and girls from all the metropolitan police courts and from the London Sessions were supervised by Miss Yetta Rosenthal, who for some years had been employed as a part-time Jewish probation officer and visitor to Holloway Prison by the Jewish Association for the Protection of Girls, Women and Children before the Home Office appointed her as a probation officer with the London Probation Service. At an earlier stage of the War she was based in the Stepney area; but by 1942 (according to Miss Pontifex's recollection) Miss Rosenthal had an office at 35 Lennox Gardens, apparently to facilitate and support her work not only with Jewish probationers, but also with Jewish aliens and refugees, for which she was awarded the M.B.E. in the King's 1944 Birthday Honours. Although the Nazi persecution, the murder of Jews and others and the brutality of the concentration camps in Germany had been well documented in the book *The Hitler Terror,* which had been published in London barely eight months after Hitler's accession to power in 1933, the full scale and horror of the Nazi mass extermination programme only became universally apparent in the wake of the collapse of Nazism. Although Miss Rosenthal would continue to specialise in supervising Jewish women and girls for a decade or so after the War, her retirement would not result in her being replaced on a sectarian basis.

Miss Rosenthal notwithstanding, London's probation service had a more direct link with the Holy Land. Miss Nina Blyth had spent her early life in Jerusalem, where her father was Anglican Bishop, and where she developed a lasting affection for the Arabs (at least one of her Arab friends subsequently visited her in London). Moreover, Arthur Shields -who had been on the staff of the London Police Court Mission from 1929 onwards - was seconded abroad by the London Probation Service during the War and spent some three years in all as Senior and then Principal Probation Officer for Palestine. By the end of the War, Shields was Principal Probation Officer for Trinidad; just as by 1945, London officers Messrs J.A. Simpson and W.G. Boyce were appointed Principal Probation Officers for Leeds and Hull respectively.

At the end of 1944 the London Probation Service had 46 male and 53 female probation officers. The work was carried out by four-fifths of the staff it had before the War, the reduction in its numbers most marked in the adult courts, where the staff was somewhat depleted as a result of the disappearance of men into the Armed Forces. (It seems that only one London probation officer was killed on active service during the War, and he was killed accidentally in 1944.) In addition to the office staff at headquarters, there were 25 clerical assistants, of whom four were part-time, employed at various courts and offices of the Service throughout London on 31 December 1944: it was hoped that in due course these appointments would be made on a permanent and pensionable basis. As of that date - the only wartime date for which the London Probation Service appears to have pinpointed caseload figures - in both juvenile and adult courts, male probation officers carried somewhat higher average effective caseloads than their female colleagues, and such caseloads were distinctly higher in the juvenile than in the adult courts (up to 57 per officer in the former and up to 38 in the latter).

Ironically in view of their higher caseloads, the male probation officers in the juvenile courts were apparently guilty of making inordinately long written court reports. According to Giles: "The length of some of these reports had to be seen to be believed. ...it was the men who made these very long reports. The women probation officers were far more concise." The provincial probation officer Alfred Leeding had found that transferred files (expected to be "masterly") from London contained very brief entries. In May 1941 S.J.C.P.O. members had "generally agreed that records had their place but that the work of an officer could not be judged by these alone".

When the Camberwell and Stepney probation offices were totally destroyed or rendered uninhabitable by enemy action in 1944, the officers concerned had narrow escapes, with only two of them receiving injuries, fortunately not serious. Most of the score or so other offices were damaged by bomb blast from time to time. During the flying bomb attacks in July 1944, the third and final evacuation of children from London took place, with a proportion of the children returning in the wake of the crisis, as on the two previous occasions. In all, eleven probation officers went on evacuation duty to Bedfordshire, Berkshire, Cornwall, Hertfordshire, Northamptonshire, Somerset, Suffolk and Sussex, for periods varying from four months to over four years. Inevitably some of the London children got into trouble in these country areas; but it seems that on the whole most of the evacuated children, assisted by their supervising London probation officers, local probation officers or other officials, adjusted reasonably well in a situation of great stress and anxiety generally. Certainly Beeson's *Short Survey of the London Probation Service 1939-1944* did not highlight any specific problems posed by the evacuated children in the reception areas.

Equally, Beeson's report noted with pride that during periods of heavy bombing it was difficult to persuade probation officers in London to take any leave, and it was not necessary to take up the generous offer, made in the summer of 1944, by two ex-London officers to spend their leave working in London, so that colleagues there could have a rest. It was indeed a test of faith to pass street after street of shattered dwellings in the course of home-visiting; and some London children, without family life or parental control in any meaningful sense, led a strange twilight existence centred on public air-raid shelters, where some probation officers had to conduct interviews and were appalled by the immorality they observed. No doubt as a counter-measure, the London probation officer Miss Margaret Smith supported the Bermondsey Children's Flats scheme. Launched by the Bermondsey Children's Council in the autumn of 1944, this scheme aimed to provide room for play in rented ground-floor tenement-block flats, so that local children could escape the overcrowding and tensions of their own homes. During its ten years' existence (until the area was redeveloped), the project received financial aid from Basil Henriques and the future London probation officer R. Anthony Forder, amongst others.[15]

In the 1930s Sir Hubert Llewellyn Smith's *New Survey of London Life and Labour* had concluded that generally speaking "the probation system has been of very great advantage both to the community at large and to the individual offender". It acknowledged the "personal influence" of probation officers, but stressed their finding work for offenders.[16] During 1944 A.J. Pilgrim facilitated the entry of one hundred boys into the Merchant Navy, which held a great attraction for youngsters. He was less successful with applications for farm work, at least in 1944, when no less than 26 of the 36 boys and girls he helped to place in such work proved unsatisfactory, perhaps because of the relative lack of selection procedures compared with entry into the Merchant Navy, for example. At about this time the East End juvenile delinquent later known to his readers as Robert Allerton, was asked by Basil Henriques whether he had ever thought of going into the Merchant Navy, after a probation officer had mentioned in court that the boy seemed interested in ships. Pending arrangements to this end being made, Henriques had the boy placed in a Church Army hostel from which he absconded, just as he had previously absconded from another Church Army hostel to which a probation officer had escorted him. During 1944 in London, 187 boys and 118 girls aged 14 or over were placed in hostels, and 33 boys and 132 girls in the same age range were placed in probation homes, under conditions of residence. Between 1943 and 1945, London probation officers expressed concern at the difficulty in placing enuretic boys in hostels and at the shortage of hostels for girls.

In the late autumn of 1944 the metropolitan juvenile court magistrates John Watson and Basil Henriques criticised conditions at Marlesford Lodge, a London County Council girls' remand home in Hammersmith, following a visit they had recently made there. Their criticisms attracted wide press coverage and public discussion, which resulted in the Home Secretary appointing a committee of inquiry into the administration of remand homes by the L.C.C. The committee sat in private at the Royal Courts of Justice, and the quasi-judicial inquiry lasted twelve days between 4 December 1944 and 10 January 1945. The scores of witnesses appearing before the committee included one J.P. who was also a voluntary probation worker in London and 13 London probation officers who, with the arguable exception of Miss Bromley, all served juvenile courts. The 13 officers were: Charles Stanley; Nina Nowell; Kathleen Booth; Nancy Ralli; Margaret Dawkins; William Matthews; Margaret Holland Smith; Valerie Levy; Annie Beasley; Elizabeth Inman; Betty Bromley; Oscarita de Berry; and Rose Mary Braithwaite. In their impressive testimony (which corroborated criticisms made by Watson and Henriques) they gave evidence of lack of segregation of remandees, lack of planned activities for them, and inadequate clothing and accommodation, including inadequate interviewing facilities. It emerged that the Society of Juvenile Courts Probation Officers had adopted a report in April 1944, expressing concern about conditions generally at Stamford House remand home for boys, and, as with the Society's similar report in 1943 on the Shirley remand home, it became known to the Home Office. More than one witness (including Nancy Ralli) drew attention to the L.C.C. ban on probation officers entering its day schools to make inquiries about children on remand who were not already on probation. This was ostensibly because, the L.C.C. claimed, such inquiries would duplicate those made by its own officials, who, it was suggested, enjoyed the confidence of the head teachers, whereas the probation officers did not. Henriques had already publicly criticised the ban in 1937 as "one of the most absurd regulations of the London County Council"; though he had immediately added that probation officers often got round this by visiting the school concerned about some other child who was on probation and then inquiring about the child who was coming before the court.

The committee of inquiry made a number of recommendations, including the establishment of machinery by the Home Office to facilitate consultation between the L.C.C., the magistrates, the probation officers, and the Home Office itself. According to John Watson, the committee's conclusions and recommendations (which broadly endorsed points made by Watson, Henriques, and the probation officers) did help to clear the air and forge a largely successful new partnership in the fight against juvenile delinquency in London. The situation had seemed to require a confrontation to bring about improved working relationships. Presumably in the interests of diplomacy and good relations with the L.C.C., Ralph Beeson's survey of the London Probation Service between 1939 and 1944 did not mention any of the L.C.C. remand homes by name, the appointment of the committee of inquiry, or the fact that some 13% of the London probation officers had given evidence in December 1944 about the remand homes - though the survey (published in August 1945) did refer to events that took place at least as late as mid-January 1945 (the committee of inquiry's report was published towards the end of February 1945, though the typescript evidence on which it was based would remain "under lock and key" for at least a quarter of a century).

In April 1945 the Society of Juvenile Courts Probation Officers - composed of London officers who met monthly - decided to notify the Home Office (through informal discussion with a member of the Probation Branch) that the Society was anxious for the committee of inquiry's recommendations to be implemented. The Society had some outside speakers during 1945, including two women police sergeants on "care or protection" girls, the North London magistrate Daniel Hopkin on the subject of Probation, and Lionel George Banwell (Chief Clerk of the Metropolitan Juvenile Courts) on procedure in the London courts. Also in 1945 the Society received a £10 legacy from the gallant Miss Croker-King, which resulted in the purchase of an oak filing cabinet to which it was agreed a commemorative plaque to her would be fixed: thus in death, as in life, the pioneer juvenile court probation officer gave her mite to further the cause she loved.

Alas, a contemporary supporter or friend of the Society (which claimed that 98% of London juvenile court probation officers were members) could not save Ronald Biggs. Biggs must surely rank as one of the London Probation Service's most notable failures, to be set against its unpublicised successes. Born in Lambeth in 1929, he was evacuated to Devon at the beginning of the War, subsequently returning to London, where he and a friend "spent a lot of our time in air-raid shelters". When Biggs appeared at Lambeth Juvenile Court in February 1945 for his first offence in the eyes of the law, he was placed on probation, as a probation officer had told him he probably would be. He was bound over four months later; and his third and final appearance at Lambeth Juvenile Court was in November 1945, when, once again for theft, he was placed on probation for twelve months, with a condition of residence at MacGregor House approved probation hostel (127 Tulse Hill, S.W.2), where the warden "knew I hadn't reformed during my stay there". While in this last case Biggs was on remand at Stamford House, a young juvenile court probation officer at Toynbee Hall called William H. Pearce was elected a member of S.J.C.P.O. Biggs would go on to participate in the internationally publicised Great Train Robbery of 1963, in the interim breaching yet another probation order, made in 1956 for theft of a bicycle; while Pearce would progress to become Principal Probation Officer for Durham and, thereafter, Chief Probation Officer for the Inner London Probation and After-Care Service.

New developments in probation work, affecting young people and involving London probation officers on a short-term basis, included aspects of the wartime Essential Work Orders and the Daniel Hopkin Scheme. Probation officers assisted the Ministry of Labour in dealing with young people who rendered themselves liable to prosecution under the Essential Work Orders: it was found time and again that a friendly talk with the probation officer, followed by a period of voluntary supervision, brought about a happier situation, and if, as sometimes happened, the probation officer recommended a change of employment, his recommendation was usually considered sympathetically.

The Daniel Hopkin Scheme was initiated by the metropolitan magistrate of that name, no doubt after discussion with the senior probation officer at North London Police Court (on which the Scheme was centred) and perhaps in the light of juvenile court experience. According to the recollection of Georgina Stafford (who worked at North London Court from 1945 onwards), Hopkin quite often used to suggest to the person to whom he awarded custody - almost invariably the mother -that it would be helpful to keep in touch with the local probation officer. Apparently the idea behind the offer of such voluntary supervision and support was for the probation officer to keep an eye on the child or children, so that any problems in child care could be contained, and, at the same time, take into account any possibility of reconciliation between the parents. Although home visiting in most such cases was predictably not very regular, largely because of pressure of work, Miss Stafford could not recall a single case in which the child concerned was known subsequently to have got into trouble with the police. By 21 February 1947, 465 such cases had been placed under supervision since the inception of the Scheme: of these, reconciliation had been effected and supervision terminated in 46 cases, and probation officers had lost contact in a further 25 cases. After Hopkin moved in 1948 to Marlborough Street Court - whose area of jurisdiction seemed to include fewer established families than North London Court - his Scheme, as such, died out[17]; though much of its spirit would appear to survive in the Matrimonial Proceedings (Magistrates' Courts) Act, 1960, section 2(1)(f).

Daniel Hopkin was a probation-minded magistrate. In court (as no doubt elsewhere) he showed "polite concern" and "a warm and round benevolence that glows as brightly as the briefer fires of youth". These descriptions came from *Courts Day by Day* (1946), a volume of selected articles by the journalist James A. Jones, reprinted from his column in the London *Evening News*. Many of these widely read and supposedly amusing articles were about the often pathetic, eccentric or confused people drifting through the London police courts. The probation officers (almost invariably referred to as missionaries) were presented as respectful and helpful to the court, business-like and sincere. Jones told his readers: "the court missionary spoke with a very large understanding of humanity"; "the court missionary, a man who had spent years in studying the very odd behaviour of ordinary human beings"; "the woman missionary's voice had the kindly but dispassionate note that all women missionaries' voices have". Time and again the missionaries, in oral reports to the court, gave useful background information on offenders, some of whom they apparently helped to get work or enter the Army, a convent or hostel, provided with boots, assisted in returning to areas like Suffolk or Scotland, and offered to help on release from prison. Some of those appearing in court were discharged under the Probation of Offenders Act, with no conviction recorded against them; some were placed on probation for one year, perhaps with a condition of residence; and in at least one case reported by Jones, a girl told the magistrate she would rather go to prison than continue on probation (just as in 1950 Basil Henriques would refer to one or two cases known to him in which a boy preferred, or seemed to prefer, paying a fine to being on probation; and Marjory Todd would refer to similar situations).

Jones's book may be compared with Sewell Stokes's *Court Circular* (1950), which, although much more acidulous, was similarly based on experience of the London police court scene during the Second World War. According to Stokes, a magistrate at Bow Street "invariably" put defendants on probation without seeking their consent or explaining the meaning of the order. Stokes suspected that magistrates did not think much of their probation officers, some of whom exaggerated their influence with the bench. "The Work, despite the strides it had recently made, was still the Cinderella of the social services." He began work as a temporary probation officer at "something slightly above starvation wages"; and his book indicated that "it's extremely difficult to get probation officers, particularly at the present time".

To help mitigate wartime difficulties confronting the London Probation Service, London head office made arrangements for "relief officers" - selected from among the probation staff to undertake such duties for up to one year - to cover the absence of colleagues on leave. By 1945 thirteen London probation officers were serving in H.M. Forces: head office kept up a more or less regular correspondence with all of them; their occasional visits were much appreciated; and all 13 were sent the monthly circular, developed by Beeson to keep his probation officers informed and, no doubt, to raise their morale and encourage a sense of professional identity. By the end of the year the London probation officer Miss M. Lucy Tabor (Chairman of the Society of Juvenile Courts Probation Officers) was on the point of joining the Children's Branch at the Home Office, where her erstwhile colleagues Messrs H.M. Morton and W.G. Minn had already been working for some four years as inspectors in the Probation Branch, to which the London Probation Service had seconded them. By 1945 sixteen trainees under the central training scheme had been appointed probation officers in London, and also 18 probation officers from the provinces had been transferred to London, since the beginning of the War, before which there had been comparatively little interchange of staff between the capital and the provinces.

At London headquarters, George Neve was responsible for servicing the Central Criminal Court and the London Sessions (the Sheriffs' Fund

Society at the former and the Probationers' Fund at the latter court provided financial assistance for London clients); whereas E.W. Watts and Miss Bromley were basically responsible for the courts south of the Thames, and Sidney Boswell (the only probation officer mentioned by name in James Jones's book) and Miss Dodds were basically responsible for those north of the Thames. They visited these courts regularly to assist and encourage the probation officers working there. In addition, each member of the head office team took responsibility for certain general matters, such as homes and hostels, approved lodgings, clerical assistance, case committees, travelling expenses, etc. (in January 1944, for example, officers had been authorised to claim a refreshment allowance of 2s.6d. for each evening spent at work until after 7 p.m. for the purpose of visiting probationers or receiving them at reporting centres).

The War stimulated exploration of ways in which social work and related agencies, which had perforce worked together during the War, could more effectively develop their co-operation thereafter. London probation officers contributed to this process. For example, in January 1941 S.J.C.P.O. had hosted a meeting attended by representatives of three different hostels for juveniles: there seemed general agreement that length of residence should not be rigidly limited to six months, but should largely depend on the juvenile's progress at the hostel, which should encourage a family-like atmosphere. Scarcely had the guns fallen silent when the London and Home Counties Branch of N.A.P.O. organised a conference between magistrates, hostel wardens and probation officers to discuss the question of probationers in hostels and their selection, supervision and period of stay. There was some rather inconclusive discussion as to what authority the hostel warden had and should have under a probation order. But it was felt that the probationer should be in a hostel within easy reach of the supervising probation officer; and it was agreed that the hostel chosen should be suitable for the probationer in question, that closer supervision would be facilitated by more hostels (many families had been disrupted and many buildings destroyed or severely damaged as a result of the War), and that there should be a comprehensive, descriptive list of hostels, whether approved or voluntary, which should be classified.

At about the same time the London Police Court Mission arranged a well supported conference of magistrates, justices' clerks and probation officers, and also a conference of representatives of the approved school, borstal and probation services to discuss matters of common interest under Alexander Paterson's chairmanship. The latter was apparently the first occasion on which the members of the three services had met in conference.

In about early March 1946 the Executive Committees of the Society of Juvenile Courts Probation Officers and of the Society of Metropolitan Police Court Probation Officers held a joint meeting to discuss their respective positions vis-à-vis N.A.P.O. By the end of March the Society of Metropolitan Police Court Probation Officers had decided to go over *en bloc* to N.A.P.O. (apparently after the Home Office had accepted N.A.P.O. as the negotiating body for all probation officers); whereas S.J.C.P.O., after a debate followed by a ballot of its members, decided -by 17 votes to 13, with several abstentions - not to apply to become a branch of N.A.P.O., to which it had been affiliated.[18] More than once during the War N.A.P.O. had expressed the view that S.J.C.P.O. should become one of its branches; but the Society of Juvenile Courts Probation Officers would maintain its independence and separate identity for at least another 16 years.

Little is now known of the Society of Metropolitan Police Court Probation Officers, whose records have not come to light. Apparently founded in 1939, it would seem to have established a closer relationship with London Probation Service head office than did S.J.C.P.O., with which the Society also endeavoured to work during the War. The Society's active members appeared to include Reginald Pestell (Chairman in 1941 and 1942) and Tommy Mills. Its long-standing Secretary was Eric A. Cuming. Apart from Cuming (who worked at Old Street and later at the County of London Sessions), those notably involved in that Society's decision to go over to N.A.P.O. included John Starke, who had apparently been Chairman, and Charles Morgan, appointed to North London and Marlborough Street respectively. According to John Starke's recollection of the Society's *raison d'être*, "the difference was mainly regarding our concern that N.A.P.O. should include negotiating rights in its constitution, a move which was for some time resisted by some conservative members and by the President Lord Feversham". (The Earl of Feversham was President of N.A.P.O. from 1930 until his untimely death in 1963.) According to Charles Morgan, the Society had originated as a breakaway group from N.A.P.O., which had been seen - in London at least - as over-identified with the Home Office, and as a quasi-philosophical circle discussing causes of crime rather than as a trade union-oriented organisation adequately representing the interests and promoting the well-being of its members. He recalled that, at its peak, some 95% of London probation officers in the adult courts were members of the Society, and that the Society developed fruitful contacts with bodies like the Institute for the Scientific Treatment of Delinquency (I.S.T.D.) and the Tavistock Clinic, with which the Society held joint meetings.

The Home Office apparently felt compelled to take notice of the Society, as it seemed to speak for a majority of probation officers in London. The existence of two distinct London Societies, catering for adult court and juvenile court probation officers respectively, had seemed to crystallise and perpetuate a dichotomy in the London courts (some adult court probation officers sometimes referred to juvenile court probation officers as "sentimental Peter Pans", despite the fact that most of the latter were female and many of them had been trained in social science). However, the united effort necessitated by the War had partially bridged or masked that dichotomy. With the consciousness of the invaluable contribution of trade unions and professional groups generally to the war effort and at a time when they seemed to be building up their influence, the adult court Society, feeling that unity was strength, decided - by an overwhelming "yes" vote, according to Charles Morgan - that the interests of its members would be most effectively served by one organisation, N.A.P.O., which had modified its outlook and adopted a constitution more in keeping with the spirit of the times.

Meanwhile, in March 1945, the Government had appointed a committee under the chairmanship of the academic and sometime civil servant Miss Myra Curtis (co-author of the report of the committee of inquiry in the Marlesford Lodge affair) to investigate the care of deprived children in England and Wales. The Society of Juvenile Courts Probation Officers submitted evidence to the Curtis Committee by October, in the form of a memorandum prepared by up to seven probation officers working together (Miss Ethel Currant, Miss M.F. Griffiths, Miss Pamela Guest, Miss Elizabeth Inman, Mr D.C. Jones, Mr F.M. Layton, and Miss Lucy Tabor). Receipt of the Society's memorandum - which apparently focused on the institutional experience of adopted children - was acknowledged by Miss D.M. Rosling, one of the Committee's two Joint Secretaries whose "unfailing competence" was praised by the Committee. But when the Committee's report (Cmd.6922) was presented to Parliament in September 1946, it did not even mention the Society or its evidence. Nor did the list of witnesses published in the report refer to the London Probation Service. However, the report did mention Miss Nancy Ralli as one of four officials who gave evidence on behalf of N.A.P.O.; and other witnesses included Miss M. Warner (of the Home Office Children's Branch), who had also been a London probation officer, and notable figures like John Bowlby, Susan Isaacs and Donald Winnicott. The Curtis Committee recommended quite far-reaching changes in the law and in administrative practice affecting children, including the introduction of University training for child care workers; and many of these proposals would be taken into account in the development of children's departments under the Children Act 1948, which in turn would provide a basis for expansion of local authority social services.

At a time when London and indeed Britain as a whole faced immense problems of reconstruction after the trauma of the World War, the London County Council seemed in danger of reopening wounds that were beginning to heal in the wake of the Marlesford Lodge affair. The printed report of the L.C.C. Special Education Sub-Committee for 25 November 1946 - which briefly referred to the Curtis Committee -incorporated detailed statistics regarding juvenile offenders and neglected children brought before the London juvenile courts between 1934 and 1946. Maintaining that "in the last few years there has been a general increase of recidivism" (which it found "disturbing"), the report claimed that lack of vacancies in a suitable approved school or lack of suitable foster-parents, for example, led to a situation in which "the courts may have resorted, against their own judgment, to probation or supervision" (later on, the report played down lack of vacancies in the approved schools). During the period 1934-46 about 27% of all the cases brought before London juvenile courts had been dealt with by probation or supervision, and of such cases the proportion with previous experience of probation or supervision produced an average of 55.8% for boys and 47.4% for girls over the last eight years. The report continued:

> It is extremely rare for London juvenile courts to entrust the supervision to anyone but the juvenile court probation officers, although they have the discretion to appoint any other person whom

they consider suitable and who is willing to undertake the task. The Council itself would undoubtedly be able to help in this matter with its large resources of teachers, school inquiry officers, boarding-out officers, after-care officers, social welfare officers and children's care workers, both official and voluntary.

The Sub-Committee's report concluded, *inter alia:*

> The very high proportion of boys and girls who are again brought before the courts often within very short periods of being placed on probation or under supervision, would appear to indicate that the system of probation or supervision for persons under 17 years of age needs strengthening... the local authority *per se* should come within the definition of "some other person" under whose supervision children and young persons may be placed by the courts, whether on probation or under supervision.

This last, specific recommendation regarding the local authority would be adopted by the full Council and communicated to the Home Secretary. But one reason for doubting whether the Council - at least in 1946 - was in a favourable position to take on new work that would otherwise have been assigned to probation officers is that L.C.C. staff generally already seemed to be fully stretched, as suggested by the fact that a child was kept in a London fever hospital, for which the L.C.C. was responsible, for three months after she was fit for discharge in September 1946, because of a shortage of staff at the hospital, and because of a lack of vacancies in L.C.C. nurseries, which, the Chairman of the L.C.C. Hospitals and Medical Services Committee admitted to a London probation officer, also suffered from "the shortage of staff".

Rather ironically, the Special Education Sub-Committee's report more or less coincided with the publication of an article[19] by Basil Henriques, in which he graphically described some of the disruptive effects of the War on family life and the development of children: "interrupted education due to evacuation"; "many children who remained in the reception areas throughout the war have now come home to find themselves strangers to their own parents"; "the night life in the public shelters has had a deleterious effect on those who remained in the blitzed cities"; the absence on service of fathers and elder brothers; harassed mothers queuing for rations; the temptation to break into bombed or insecure shops and warehouses; the infidelity of one or both of the parents;

the acute housing shortage; the absence of youth leaders on active service.

To try to repair such broken relationships, and to encourage relationships between delinquents and probation officers that would be as natural as possible, Basil Henriques offered the use of a camp site to East London Juvenile Court probation officers, who in 1947 organised the first "Highdown Camp", primarily to provide a holiday for boys who had been placed on supervision by the courts. Although there was no one person who knew everyone, and although there seemed no unifying experience except, so far as most of the boys were concerned, that of delinquency, the camp provided (in the words of William H. Pearce, one of the organisers) "a most interesting and useful experiment". The camp no doubt made a welcome "break" from thought of the inadequate waiting-room accommodation at various juvenile courts, the virtually non-existent hostel facilities for some age groups of maladjusted children, difficulties with boys of very low mentality on supervision for truancy under the new Education Act, and problems in getting boy clients into the Armed Forces - all of which the Society of Juvenile Courts Probation Officers had discussed during 1946 (Florence Bradley vividly recalled working in those days of shortages as a full-time clerical assistant in a two-roomed probation office which had no toilet and no water - at 106 York Street, W.1 - for two juvenile court probation officers).

Pearce's colleague Derek Borboen suggested that an S.J.C.P.O. meeting should be addressed by some psychiatric social workers. Soon afterwards the psycho-analyst Dr Kate Friedlander - who was conducting much appreciated seminars, apparently in London, for probation officers - suggested "an extension of psychiatric social work, by workers attached to a delinquency clinic to the majority of all cases under probation. This would leave the probation officer free to deal with more external problems, of course in close co-operation with the psychiatric social worker dealing with the case."[20] Her thinking may be correlated with the view of Dr Edward Glover, who had addressed S.J.C.P.O. in 1942, and who wrote in 1948 that "the *Probation Service* is by far the most enlightened of all the penal services"; though he added that probation officers were

> handicapped in their individual efforts at re-education and rehabilitation by the excessive case-loads they have to carry and perhaps more decisively, by their divided loyalties. To be a servant of

the Court and at the same time to act as counsellor and friend to the offender is a dual role calling for unusual qualifications. Certainly no trained psychotherapist would relish being put in this emotionally ambiguous situation. Nevertheless we must be grateful for attenuated mercies. There are few psychological workers in the field who have not had occasion to be thankful for the co-operation of an understanding probation officer. As their training is gradually shorn of irrelevant and tedious studies and extended to include clinical instruction in the psychology of delinquency, the status of probation officers will rise rapidly. Already it is an open question whether they should not be recognized as a special branch of the association of psychiatric social workers.

At about the same time the penal reformer C.H. Rolph, writing for the *New Statesman*'s "London Diary", suggested that certain kinds of probationers should be visited by psychiatric social workers.

In 1942 the Society of Juvenile Courts Probation Officers had enlisted the support of psychiatric social workers and hospital almoners in an unsuccessful attempt to affiliate to the British Federation of Social Workers. Although after the War S.J.C.P.O. did not query the basis of its relationship with psychiatric social workers, it did tentatively discuss the possible use of voluntary workers in juvenile courts in view of the shortage of probation officers in early 1947. Ralph Beeson intimated to S.J.C.P.O. that voluntary workers interested in the work could give their services, but would have to be referred to him first. Beeson and head office were not apparently involved when the concern expressed by Derek Borboen about the standard of press reports on juvenile court cases resulted in a meeting (facilitated by the S.J.C.P.O. President and London magistrate, John Watson) between Borboen and the Chairman of the S.J.C.P.O. on the one hand and two senior representatives of the *Star* newspaper on the other. The *Star* representatives (in the words of the S.J.C.P.O. Minutes) "pointed out that inaccuracies in Juvenile Court reporting may in part be due to the fact that, as no names can be published, no libel action can result if facts are slightly distorted to improve their news value". (Some months later, in November 1947, the *Star* was largely instrumental in bringing about Hugh Dalton's resignation as Chancellor of the Exchequer when it publicised Dalton's pre-emptive disclosure to its Lobby correspondent of the contents of his Budget speech.)

A happier relationship with the press seemed to prevail at Marlborough Street Court, where Maurice Wiggin of the *Evening Standard* used fictitious first names, without surnames, in his often sympathetic coverage of social misfits. He respected the probation officers there as "the link between the officialdom of the court and the intense *personalness* of private lives" (his emphasis). For him, Elspeth Stormont (as she then was) and Charles Morgan - both of whom he mentioned by name - were "astute and compassionate", with a knowledge of the inner lives of West End worldlings which was perhaps unsurpassed at the court. The probation officers were "the detectives of the soul: working necessarily in something of the secrecy of the confessional, necessarily with a sense of vocation". What they felt able to say in open court provided "the absorbing ingredient in very many of the stories which appear in this book", he declared in *My Court Casebook* (1948).

The importance for probation officers of psychological knowledge and a sense of vocation was also stressed by A.G. Rose, senior probation officer at North London Magistrates' Court (the name "police court" had now been officially discarded). In an attractively lucid article (*Probation,* November-December 1947) Rose declared:

> religion or no religion, a probation officer must be "called" to his task... Without some powerful impulse and constant renewal from its source, he would be overwhelmed by the welter of misery and disillusionment. ...the test of his influence really begins when the period of probation is ended.

Rose's article - on desirable qualities of probation officers - clearly owed much to a report (of 14 November 1946) by the National Institute of Industrial Psychology for the Home Office Probation Training Board: this report, prepared to advise on the selection of suitable candidates for the probation service, was itself partly based on an analysis of some 50 case histories from London and of a similar number from each of five other representative areas in England and Wales.

Rather like this report, Rose maintained that a prospective probation officer "needs a sound education". By July 1947 a similar point had been made by Eileen Younghusband in her seminal Carnegie *Report on the Employment and Training of Social Workers,* in which she drew attention to "the poor educational background of many applicants" to the probation service. Against a general background of an acute shortage both of trained social workers and of adequate training facilities, Younghusband proposed the establishment of a School of Social Work, attached to a University and perhaps funded by the Carnegie United Kingdom Trust. The following year W.G. Minn, of the Home Office Probation Branch, indicated that many applications for probation training were being received from candidates who had served in H.M. Forces, but that "the general standard of these applicants is disappointingly low". Minn pointed out that by 1948 about one third of probation officers in England and Wales had been formally trained.

With increased emphasis on training, and presumably in an attempt to improve the service in London, Ralph Beeson tried to get seniors to supervise colleagues and scrutinise records, according to Rose Mary Braithwaite's recollection. This marked a significant extension of the role of the early senior probation officers, who, for a differential of about 16s.8d. per week, had often engaged in quite mundane tasks, such as checking the provision of light bulbs, ordering stationery, or totting up expenditure from the poor box.[21] It also meant a change in attitude for independent-minded main-grade officers with intensely personal loyalty to the individual courts they served and a real sense of "sacred trust" vested in them by the bench. In May 1944 S.J.C.P.O. members had expressed some anxiety about the newly defined duties of seniors relating to inspection of main-grade officers' work: Lucy Tabor had claimed that individual probation officers "would no longer be responsible solely to the Magistrate for their work on each case". With the advent of a more professional approach and a bureaucratic structure for the service, arguably the hierarchy of the service - if not the Home Office - was seeking to extend its claim to the loyalty of probation officers in what seemed, in some ways, tantamount to a form of "dual control" (courts still inserted the name of the relevant supervising probation officer in probation orders made under the Probation of Offenders Act, 1907). In retrospect - for *ILPAS '76* - "it seems a pity that at this early stage in the development of the London service more thought was not given to the forging of closer links between administrative and professional needs, as this area has proved to be a continuing source of tension".

Yet Beeson worked hard to promote the service and meet at least some of its growing needs. After discussion among seniors and main-grade officers in the London Probation Service and within the Society of

Juvenile Courts Probation Officers, which seemed to support him, Beeson was apparently instrumental in obtaining modifications to the L.C.C. report, which was eventually adopted by the Council on 16 December 1947, on the alleged rate of recidivism for juvenile offenders and neglected children in London. Beeson pointed out to the L.C.C. that breaches did not necessarily indicate the failure of probation, but he did not appear to have comprehensive facts and figures readily available to refute the statistics used by the Council. In the L.C.C. report, submitted by the Education Committee, it was argued that the increase of recidivism "raises the question whether the methods of treatment available to the courts under existing legislation are sufficiently varied or elastic to be effective" and also "appears to indicate the need for such records to be kept by the Home Office as will enable recidivism to be kept under observation". This point was not lost on the Home Office, which may already have noted the published comments of A.E. Jones or of Dr Kate Friedlander. In 1945, Jones, a magistrates' clerk, had expressed the view that "the probation officer has one mild rival in the juvenile court - the representative of the local authority". He added: "There are no reliable statistics on the real results of probation; the official statistics only cover the actual term of the order." In 1947 (if not earlier), Friedlander declared: "No investigation has so far been carried out to show the results - whether successes or failures - of probation as compared with other methods of dealing with the offender."

It was against this background that the Home Office decided to take action. In 1947 its Probation Branch, in association with the Middlesex Probation Committee and the Criminal Record Office used by the Metropolitan Police, introduced measures, in the London and Middlesex probation areas, for collecting information in preparation for a detailed enquiry into the effectiveness of probation as a method of treatment. This required the keeping of records, built up from January 1948 onwards, relating to juvenile and adult offenders placed on probation by courts in Middlesex, the Metropolitan Magistrates' Court District and also at the Old Bailey, who were supervised by the probation officers of those courts, and whose probation orders terminated in 1948, 1949 or 1950, together with details of convictions, if applicable, recorded during a three-year period following the termination of each order. (The effectiveness of probation evidently concerned the London juvenile court probation officer Miss Lindo, who, in July 1939, in arguing against probation officers officially undertaking after-care work, had maintained that they "ought to concentrate on Probation Work as it in itself was a colossal job".[22]

In May 1947 the Chairman of S.J.C.P.O. had stressed the view that the Society's function was not so much to "interfere" with policy as "to aim to improve our own work and cope with problems arising from it". The parameters of such a distinction were not discussed at that time. But only weeks after publication of the Criminal Justice Bill in November 1947, the Society of Juvenile Courts Probation Officers decided that its Executive should consider the Bill with a view to sending recommendations to the Criminal Justice Bill Sub-Committee of N.A.P.O.'s National Executive. By mid-January the Society had forwarded half a dozen specific recommendations to N.A.P.O. on the Bill: these included naming the supervising probation officer in a probation order (a point also strongly pressed by N.A.P.O.) and an expectation that the court which had made the order would be consulted by the supervising court before any breach of probation were dealt with. Another of these recommendations was that the names and addresses of juveniles appearing in adult courts should not be reported in the press (a concern S.J.C.P.O. had ventilated early in 1939).

An event which could have attracted more attention in the press was the visit by about this time to the South East London Juvenile Court by Princess Elizabeth (as she then was), to whom Pat K. Mayhew, a probation officer attached to that court, had an opportunity to explain his work. Another function towards whose success London probation officers contributed was an amateur dramatic society's performance of Shakespeare's *The Merchant of Venic* in modern dress at the Toynbee Hall Theatre, organised by the London Branch of N.A.P.O. in aid of the Association's Edridge Benevolent Fund: a special word of thanks was due to William Pearce and Derek Borboen, chairman and secretary, respectively, of the committee whose energy and hard work made the performance possible (their adult court colleague Dorothy Hands, who under that name worked as a probation officer in London between 1943 and 1950, would show considerable generosity to the Fund very many years later). A recreational activity also supported by London probation officers was cricket, the London Probation Service fielding a team during 1948 against approved schools like Park House and Banstead Hall. Pamela Guest organised a cricket team in Victoria Park for little boys on her caseload.

Towards the end of May 1948, Miss J.T. Dodds (a high-ranking London probation officer seconded as Assistant Inspector General, Control Commission, Germany) brought a party of five German women prison governors to Britain. In addition to visits to various prisons and borstals, they went to the Central Criminal Court, Tower Bridge Magistrates' Court and Stamford House Juvenile Court. The German visitors were apparently much impressed by the British approach to the treatment of crime; and Miss Dodds and one of the governors gave a broadcast in "Radio Newsreel" in relation to the visit, whose success seems to have been facilitated by the co-operation of the London Probation Service.[23] This visit also appears to have marked one of the earliest official European contacts established by the London Probation Service after the War, when Britain had been largely cut off in a number of fields. Somewhat paradoxically, however, London's position during the War as a centre for governments in exile had resulted in some contact with European criminological thinking under virtually unique circumstances: for example, in June 1942 the Society of Juvenile Courts Probation Officers had held an open meeting on juvenile delinquency addressed by representatives of the Czech and Norwegian Ministries of Justice and the International Save the Children Fund in Geneva, as well as by the Chief Prosecutor in the Netherlands Maritime High Court and the first woman judge in Poland.

It is a striking fact that during the period 1945-50 at least half a dozen men and women who had been or would become London probation officers worked in occupied and devastated Germany on relief and reconstruction projects, whether for the military Control Commission or not. In this context of rehabilitation and reconciliation - themes close to the aims of probation work - may be mentioned not only Miss Dodds, but also: Guy Clutton-Brock (who worked in Germany first for the Control Commission's Education Branch, with responsibilities for youth, welfare and religious affairs, and then for the World Council of Churches); conscientious objectors like Charles Balchin (who went on to join the London Probation Service in October 1948) and Thomas Burke (who joined Middlesex Probation Service by 1951); Miss Rosemary Deane[24] (who, in *Probation* for November-December 1948, presented her impressions of Hamburg Juvenile Court, its female probation officer and "black market" cases); and Derek Borboen, who had studied German at Cambridge during the climacteric 1930s, and who was seconded in

October 1948 to the youth service section of the Control Commission's Education Branch for some two years or so, appealing to London juvenile court probation officers for clothing and footwear for schools in Germany.

Meanwhile, apparently in May 1948, Borboen and his female colleagues Miss M.E. Routh and Rose Mary Braithwaite went to the Home Office to discuss the Society of Juvenile Courts Probation Officers' comments on the Children Bill with an official of the Children's Branch. The Society's comments, which had been published in *Probation* and partly endorsed by N.A.P.O., were tabled in an amended form by Mr C.W. Dumpleton, Labour M.P. for St Albans, at the Bill's Committee stage, attended by Braithwaite and Borboen (the Society's Chairman and Secretary, respectively), who saw their amendments negatived or withdrawn. Miss Braithwaite, moreover, gave evidence at the Home Office to the special committee of enquiry regarding children and the cinema - just at about the time that the London Assistant Principal Probation Officer John Washington was playing the part of the senior probation officer in the Government information film "Probation Officer", which was being made about the efforts of the probation service to help a working class family beset by matrimonial problems and delinquency (criticised in *Probation* for some clumsy and unrealistic touches, the film would be released in 1949, with half an hour's running time). A similar Government information film in which London probation officers had acted during this period was "Children of the City", a praised Paul Rotha documentary about juvenile delinquency, featuring Miss Braithwaite and her colleagues Reginald Peverell, Violet Hunter Craig and apparently Joan Potter.

Probation also published a letter signed by eight probation officers (all of whom worked or would work in London), recording their appreciation of the "breadth of vision" shown in the choice of the pro-Soviet Very Rev. Hewlett Johnson, Dean of Canterbury, to address the 1948 N.A.P.O. Annual Conference. A rather different member of the Anglican clergy was the Rev. Harry Pearson, who had retired as Secretary of the London Police Court Mission in July 1945 after 30 years in harness, though he continued to take an active interest in the social work of the Mission until his death at the end of June 1948, at the age of 74.

The same issue of Beeson's monthly circular dated 1 July 1948 that recorded Pearson's death - referring to him as "affectionately remembered by many of us as our old 'Chief'" - also announced the impending departure of the Principal Probation Officer to become a Grade I inspector in the Probation Branch of the Home Office, with effect from 15 August. Thus, having come from the Probation Branch (presumably, initially at least, as a "stop-gap" or "caretaker"), Beeson returned to it; and, indeed, he would work as a probation inspector for the Home Office during the next 20 years or so. Aline Cholmondeley (whose interest in social work had been stimulated by hearing Pearson preach in his old parish church in Kensington on the Police Court Mission, and who joined the London service in 1943 after some three years as a probation officer in Middlesex) remembered Ralph Beeson as "a real Home Office person". Similarly, Stanley Ratcliffe (who would rise high in the London service, which he joined in 1951) regarded him as essentially a "mandarin".

Whether through necessity or from considerations of broader experience and professional development, Beeson seems to have escalated the process, started by Clutton-Brock, of moving probation officers around, with a greater interchange between juvenile and adult court personnel, for example. This process did not always endear Beeson to officers in the field, according to Miss Cholmondeley (who herself had been transferred from a juvenile to an adult court early in 1947). By the time Beeson left the London Probation Service, the Roman Catholic probation officers on the so-called "Roman roundabout" - a common phrase used originally to denote the peripatetic R.C. probation officers in London - had become absorbed into the state system, though they could continue to take some R.C. clients in addition to the non-Roman Catholic ones they were now expected to supervise. Georgina Stafford - who by 1945 had returned to the adult court from the juvenile court - recalled that for many years there was a form which was supposed to be completed and despatched to headquarters whenever a Roman Catholic was put on probation, so that the client could be visited by a member of one of the Catholic voluntary societies, but that use of this form died of neglect. According to Colette Maitland-Warne's understanding, a Principal Probation Officer at this time was unlikely to be a Roman Catholic. Somewhat similarly, before the War the London Police Court Mission had apparently taken some five years to accept that Norman Grant's Congregationalist beliefs posed no moral impediment to his becoming a court missionary in London.

Beeson does not appear - publicly at least - to have articulated policy proposals for the planned development of the London Probation Service in the post-war era. Perhaps he was forced to concentrate on pressing practical problems and immediate issues in a piecemeal or "crisis management" fashion. Quite probably he saw the service's role and tasks largely defined for the foreseeable future by the long-awaited Criminal Justice Act, which received the Royal Assent just two weeks before he ceased to be Principal Probation Officer. No doubt he felt the time was opportune for a fresher person with a new outlook to guide the service through its next challenging phase. Be that as it may, Beeson had steered the London Probation Service through the storms of war and the immense difficulties of the earliest post-way years; he had seemed determined not merely to hold the service together, but also to improve its tone and raise its morale and status. Miss Alison Allen (who, after training, became a London probation officer in 1946) remembered Beeson as pleasant, yet quite firm and decisive, "the sort of person one would respect, look up to". Her colleague Peter Shervington (who joined the London Probation Service in June 1947 as a direct entrant, with no training) had had no difficulty in gaining a personal interview with Beeson for advice before his appointment as a main-grade officer: he found Beeson very helpful, honest, straightforward, with a dry sense of humour, and "despite the appearance of severity, a very decent fellow". In January 1948, the Chairman of the Society of Juvenile Courts Probation Officers, surveying events of the previous year, emphasized "the great co-operation received throughout from Mr Beeson". Beeson would later help F.V. Jarvis (a prominent probation officer who had joined the London service by 1951) in the preparation of his 1972 history of the service nationally. But as far as direct, day-to-day responsibility for the London Probation Service was concerned, the Beeson years had, in effect, come to an end in 1948. Apparently his last significant act as Principal Probation Officer was to advise London probation officers on 10 August 1948 that the Probation Officers Superannuation Fund was to be wound up, and that they would be subject to the London County Council's Superannuation Scheme.

Now that a measure of recognition had been accorded probation officers, their range of tasks would grow, with an associated perception of a need for more resources.

CHAPTER EIGHT

The Challenge of Change, 1948-59

Beeson's successor as Principal Probation Officer for the Metropolitan Magistrates' Court District, as from 15 August 1948, was Seldon Charles Forrester Farmer. The new man was 43, and was destined to head the probation service in London for the next twenty-two years. In his monthly circular for July, which tersely announced his own departure while expanding on his successor's appointment, Beeson declared that he would hand over to Farmer with every confidence.

Farmer had a cultured background. According to family recollection, his father earned his living as a writer of romantic inclination and with a sense of history, which came into play in his artistic contribution to Charles Kingsley and George Eliot centenaries; while his mother was a promising professional pianist who composed music conducted by Sir Granville Bantock. After attending a grammar school in Sussex and King Edward's School in Birmingham, young Farmer went to work for the Boy Scouts Association in London. He studied shorthand and, later, social science and criminology, in which he gained a recognised qualification, apparently facilitated by some eight months' part-time voluntary police court mission work at Woolwich. Then, on 24 May 1937, he embarked on his probation career in earnest when he was appointed a police court missionary at Thames Court by the London Police Court Mission, to which he had been urged to apply by his friend F.E. Moon (who himself had been a missionary at North London Court since about 1935, and would work as a probation officer in the Woolwich area during the War). According to his widow, Farmer loved his work in the tough Thames Court area; and when the Home Office development of the probation service encouraged him to apply in July 1938 for the job of probation officer in Berkshire, two of his three testimonials came from Thames Police Court magistrates. He got the Berkshire job, at a starting salary of £270 per year, with effect from 1 January 1939 (eight years later, Peter Shervington's starting salary, at exactly the same age when he took up his appointment, was £430 + £15 London allowance per annum). Guy Clutton-Brock congratulated Farmer on his appointment, adding: "There is much pioneering work to be done, and I am sure you can do it." The work was indeed challenging, with Farmer covering virtually the whole county and having to use his home as his office. He was also a chief air raid warden during the War.[1]

In January 1943, Farmer was made Principal Probation Officer for Berkshire; and it was from this position that he moved to London in 1948. When Beeson's successor needed to be appointed, that person was found not in a woman like the redoubtable Miss Kate Fowler of Sheffield (imbued with the missionary spirit and remembered as the first female Principal Probation Officer in the country), but in Seldon Farmer, whose appointment was no doubt facilitated by a number of factors. He already had direct experience of probation work in London, where many probation officers he could have met or heard of before the War were still in post: if not virtually one of the last police court missionaries to be appointed by the London Police Court Mission to the Metropolitan Police Court District, he was certainly the last such police court missionary to become Principal Probation Officer for London. He was already a P.P.O. of some experience (if he had not met Beeson as a police court missionary in London before the War, he would certainly have met him through the Principal Probation Officers' Conference, which had become increasingly accepted by the Home Office as a national forum - and Beeson may have drawn attention to Farmer's undoubted abilities). He had been Chairman of N.A.P.O. since 1946, and he was thanked by the Essex Branch in October 1948 for

> your splendid efforts on behalf of the Association in connection with the passage of the Criminal Justice Act and the Superannuation Act ...your untiring efforts in this capacity in an endeavour to safeguard the Association's interests - and the best interests of the Service - have been crowned with a great measure of success.[2]

Farmer apparently saw no immediate or necessary conflict between his two roles as Chairman of N.A.P.O. and Principal Probation Officer for London, but he stepped down as Chairman at the 1949 N.A.P.O. Annual Conference, held just over eight months after his appointment to London took effect.

It seems it was partly thanks to Farmer's activities that the financial position of probation officers was slowly beginning to improve. When he took office in 1946, he apparently followed up negotiations about a new salary scale, resulting in assimilation of the civil service"war bonus", which by 1944 had risen to a maximum of £49.11s. for men and £40.9s. for women probation officers. The Probation Officers (Superannuation) Act, 1947 – which came into force on 1st July 1948 – brought most officers into the local government superannuation scheme. (Also a survey conducted for the Principal Probation Officers' Conference indicated that by January 1948 London, if not Berkshire, allowed six weeks' annual leave in relation to the recommended minimum of four weeks.)

At London headquarters, Boswell retired soon after the end of the War, and when Farmer arrived, the only officer among the hierarchy who had been there continuously from the beginning of the London Probation Service was "Ernie" Watts (a perceptive, conscientious and widely liked Assistant Principal Probation Officer whose approach to his work was illustrated by the fact that in October 1948 he took a newcomer, Charles Balchin, by tram to Clapham, to introduce him to his first office).

A similar warm welcome awaited Frank Dawtry when, on 1 November, he was met by Seldon Farmer and Nancy Ralli on his arrival at N.A.P.O. headquarters to take up his duties as Secretary. Miss Ralli, who had been made an Assistant Principal Probation Officer, was a London Probation Service representative, along with George Neve, on the house committee of the London Police Court Mission's probation trainees' hostel (which in 1946 had moved from Denmark Hill to 8-10 Draycott Place, Chelsea). She had also been acting as Honorary Secretary of N.A.P.O. for nearly a year, and ten years later Dawtry would admit: "The work Miss Ralli did in her spare time to keep the organisation in being has never, I fear, been fully appreciated by our members" - a judgement reinforced by a reading of F.V. Jarvis's 1972 history.

Seldon Farmer and Nancy Ralli were welcomed by the Society of Juvenile Courts Probation Officers at a meeting in November addressed by Dr Peter D. Scott of Stamford House remand home. A notable forensic psychiatrist who for decades would be a great friend of the probation service in London, Dr Scott indicated he wanted to maintain contact with probation officers over cases, and to encourage close co-operation between probation officer and psychiatric social worker: the former, who visited the child's home, gave a picture of the child's whole background and his relationship to it, whereas the latter was concerned mainly with assessing attitudes in the parents, who were invited for the purpose to the remand home (the parents' attendance rate seemed to be of the order of 66% of cases). He regarded case conferences as essential, but pointed out (at a follow-up meeting in March 1949) that they were available at the child guidance clinic and not at the remand home, which none the less had better liaison with the probation officer than the clinic did. Their subjects doubtless included some future "Teddy Boys".

S.J.C.P.O. members were sensitive about disclosing information, regarded as confidential, to other agencies. However, the Deputy Principal Probation Officer for London seemed less restrained. Writing in *Probation* (March-April 1949), George Neve declared: "Many probation officers fail to realise they cannot do the job alone. Co-operation with other Social Service Agencies of all sorts ... is a duty which is often neglected." A similar point had already been made by A.G. Rose in *Probation* in 1947 and also by W.G. Minn in 1948, and would be repeated by Miss Braithwaite in a radio talk broadcast by the B.B.C. European Service towards the end of 1949.

At this time diverse individuals (mainly community and social workers) and organisations came together to promote the Barge Boys' Club. Among them were Derek Borboen and Peter Kuenstler, who, stimulated by Eileen Younghusband's 1947 Carnegie Report, had suggested the formation of a small group with a view to initiating an experimental facility in the East End for "unclubbable" boys, who were probably, but not necessarily, delinquent. This group first met in November 1947 at Oxford House in Bethnal Green. According to Merfyn Turner in interview, Oxford House was "a power-house of ideas": Guy Clutton-Brock had recently been its head, and his influence remained; two of his friends, Peter Kuenstler and Merfyn Turner, who were members of the group, were residents at "the Oxo" (as it was known). The project for "unclubbables" - supported and assisted by the criminologist Hermann Mannheim - resulted in the acquisition and conversion of the sailing barge "Normanhurst", berthed at Wapping, and the appointment of the vigorously enterprising Merfyn Turner (a youth club leader with practical experience of the East End and of Cardiff's Tiger Bay) as the living-in, full-time warden. By August 1949 - after months of research and enquiry conducted by Turner in conjunction with probation officers and others -eighteen interested London "unclubbables" (whom Clutton-Brock called "a gang of young outcasts") were selected as members, and the Barge

Boys' Club came alive, subsequently winning several racing cups. The impressive array of patrons, largely recruited by Turner, included Basil Henriques, Donald Soper and Eileen Younghusband. The Executive Committee members included Clutton-Brock (according to Merfyn Turner's 1953 book on the project), and also Derek Borboen (from the outset, though he was in Germany much of the time). According to his own recollection, Borboen brought a party of German youths onto the barge for a trip on the Thames; and a quarter of a century later, London probation officers would turn to the river again when they participated in a joint project to provide holidays on a specially refurbished barge for deprived children.

Before sailing for Africa in 1949, Guy Clutton-Brock had clearly inspired Miss Constance Platt to apply to become a probation officer and supported her during her training, after which she was based in Camberwell, later marrying fellow London juvenile court probation officer Huw Rees (who became a lecturer in social work at the London School of Economics).

The importance of co-operation with probation officers was stressed by the new London County Council Children's Officer, Edwin Ainscow, when he addressed S.J.C.P.O. towards the end of May on the scope of the new Children's Department. (Also, the Children Act, 1948, may well have produced the first significant efflux of probation officers to local authority social services: for example, by September 1949 the senior probation officer Richard England resigned from S.J.C.P.O. on his appointment as Assistant Children's Officer for Berkshire.) But the S.J.C.P.O. Chairman had some difficulty in obtaining an invitation to the L.C.C. conference on juvenile delinquency, held on 22 July, resulting in the formation of a committee whose 21 members included one magistrate, but no probation officer: his subsequent letter of protest to the Chairman of the L.C.C. over this omission seems to have been instrumental in persuading the committee to co-opt Seldon Farmer as the representative of London probation officers.

Farmer's deputy, George Neve, maintained:

> In very few courts are thorough social investigations made. ...
> Further the failure to obtain sufficient information regarding offenders results in probation officers lacking enough facts to diagnose the needs of the probationers placed under their care and to build up

intelligent plans for their treatment.

He then criticised "perfunctory" reporting to the probation office "to answer the usual routine questions - 'Still in the same work? Earning how much? All right at home? Everything all right? All right, come again in three weeks' time'." (Miss Madeleine Loring, who had been a London juvenile court probation officer between 1937 and 1942, felt that reporting should have a therapeutic value, enabling study and understanding of the probationer as an individual and the growth of rapport and trust between probationer and probation officer, within a framework of discipline.) Neve also deplored the fact that with wholesale reporting "many undesirable acquaintances may have been made on the stairs or in the waiting room where a dozen or twenty probationers have probably been gathered together". The risk of contamination had also been mentioned in March 1949 by Dr Peter Scott in respect of remand homes, and would be a commonplace observation about prisons. Neve stressed that for an officer to have to interview a client with an extraneous third person in the room (probably a colleague, whether of the same or opposite sex, forced to share the same office) placed the parties involved at a considerable disadvantage.

The views held by Neve on reporting, planning treatment and preparing for meaningful interviews were shared by Elizabeth R. Glover, his predecessor as Deputy Principal Probation Officer for London, in her book, *Probation and Re-Education,* first published in 1949 (Neve regarded probation as "essentially an educational process", and both he and Miss Glover suggested, for example, that busy probation officers should allow at least fifteen minutes per interview for probationers reporting regularly). She commended a central index system of record cards used by a team of officers covering the same district, and she advocated a caseload of 40 to 50 cases, exclusive of other duties, for a full-time officer (in 1955 Basil Henriques would declare that a probation officer's "proper" caseload was "about 40"). Miss Glover's book - a manual on the scope, challenge and difficulties of probation work, enlivened by case examples - seems to have been based, at least in part, on her experiences as Deputy Principal Probation Officer during the War, when her duties included attending case committees, discussing the progress of individual probationers with probation officers all over London, building up a register of approved lodgings, and serving on the committees of two approved probation hostels and one approved probation home (Alison Allen remembered Miss Glover lecturing to probation trainees, of whom she was one, in about 1945: Miss Glover was Joint Secretary of the path-breaking Probation Training Board, which, between 1945 and 1949, apparently took 277 men and women into training).

In the preface to her book, Elizabeth Glover acknowledged her debt to erstwhile colleagues in the London service, Miss O.K.I. de Berry, Miss J.E. Channell, Miss M.F. Griffiths and Mr W.G. Minn, of whom the last-named also helped her by studying certain chapters and offering suggestions, as did the J.P. Eileen Younghusband and the London probation officers Georgina Stafford and William Matthews. The social scientist Barbara Wootton read most of the book in typescript and gave valued criticism.

Elizabeth Glover's book was praised by Basil Henriques as providing "a most excellent description of the work done by probation officers". Henriques was - like Barbara Wootton and Eileen Younghusband - a notable (if childless) Chairman of a London juvenile court; and he proudly related how, at about this time, "the splendid team of men and women who co-operate as friends in the work of the East London Juvenile Court - the police, the magistrates' clerks, the probation officers, the clerical staff, the special officers, and the magistrates - recently dined together" and toasted "our absent friends, the delinquents". Georgina Stafford, who worked at Lambeth Juvenile Court during the War, later recalled that the probation officers there maintained excellent relations with the "special officers" (L.C.C. education officers); and the London court clerk F.T. Giles would declare of a juvenile court case involving a sexually wanton girl: "No doubt one of our indefatigable lady probation officers took her under her wing to such good effect that she may now very well be a respectable wife and mother of a happy family." Other categories of client amenable to help on an unconvicted basis from the probation service before its work-load expanded under the Criminal Justice Act, 1948, included shoplifters, "alcoholists" (whom Dr Norwood East differentiated from alcoholics), and attempted suicide cases.

The Criminal Justice Act, 1948, seemed to offer the prospect of a "golden age" for the probation service. The provisions relating to probation, which came into operation on 1 August 1949, in effect repealed the Probation of Offenders Act 1907 in its entirety and various other enactments, and (together with the Probation Rules of 1949) laid a new foundation, thought to be both stronger and more elaborate, for the administration of the service, while clarifying some accepted ground-rules. In 1987 the Central Council of Probation Committees declared: "The full basis of the present managerial structure of the probation service was not completed until the passing of the Criminal Justice Act 1948." In the same year as the Council's declaration, the retired London probation officer Charles Morgan expressed the view that the 1948 Act set the seal on a complete Home Office take-over of the London service.

Similarly, it could be argued that the death of Harry Pearson in 1948 and the retirement of Mr and Mrs F.A. Green of "Padcroft" at the end of February 1949 marked a definite loosening of the London Police Court Mission's social work ties with the courts (though in Southwark two full-time police court missionaries, Mr and Mrs Samuel Howden, had by the end of 1948 represented the Church in their local court for the last sixteen and five years, respectively). For no less than 30 years (1908-38) Frank Green had simultaneously combined two social work jobs for the London Police Court Mission - as manager of "Padcroft" and as missionary and probation officer at Uxbridge Court - and for some 45 years he and his wife worked as a team in running "Padcroft" until it was closed down at the end of February 1949: surely a record in the annals of the Mission. It was fitting that London probation officers were able to be among those gathered at the Mission's headquarters to thank Mr and Mrs Green for their great work, and that Pearson's successor G.J. Morley Jacob addressed S.J.C.P.O. in March 1950 on the Mission's institutions for the care and rehabilitation of wayward youth.

Under the Criminal Justice Act, 1948, probation hostels and homes were approved, regulated and inspected by the Home Office; and probation officers became responsible for statutory supervision of borstal trainees on their release. Such supervision was undertaken by adult court probation officers, whose average caseloads consistently seemed to total at least 80 (including voluntary cases); while among the London juvenile court probation officers - as Miss Braithwaite explained in her B.B.C. radio talk broadcast towards the end of 1949 - "the women are responsible for all the girls and the boys up to thirteen, and the men for the more emancipated young gentlemen of thirteen to seventeen".

In the words of Basil Henriques: "It is only in London that there are

Juvenile Court probation officers who do no work in the adult courts" - a statement confirmed many years later as historically accurate by the retired probation officer Allen Robins, who, after student placements in Leeds and Norwich and relief work at Houghton le Spring, joined the London service as a juvenile court probation officer not long before Henriques's words appeared in print in 1950. Henriques felt that juvenile court officers "need to have had a good deal of experience in the adult court" (particularly in matrimonial reconciliation work). The division of work in London between the juvenile and adult court probation officers could and did result occasionally in different officers becoming involved with the same family, with no official notification to the juvenile or adult court probation officer that his or her colleague in the other court was also involved (according to Alison Allen's recollection in interview, which independently confirmed a statement to this effect in *ILPAS '76*). Ironically, an officer on relief work - which could be on a day by day basis - could be allocated to both kinds of court, as Miss Allen testified from her own experience as a relief officer in about 1949.

In those days one "clerical assistant" acted as secretary for three officers, as a ratio throughout the London service. In all the London juvenile courts probation reports were invariably typed documents; whereas adult court probation officers followed a practice of giving verbal reports to their own individual courts - usually as a result of "put backs", though sometimes following prison or home visits - and having social enquiry reports typed for other courts. In juvenile courts, reports were not handed or read out to those who were the subject of them, though an understanding had developed that sensitively selected parts of such reports could be read out by the presiding magistrate, who (according to the London probation officer Marjory Todd) could if necessary send the child out of court for a few minutes to facilitate communication between parents and the bench. Under the Criminal Justice Act, 1948, an offender, if aged 17 or over, was entitled to receive a copy of a probation officer's report on him or her; though practice varied regarding the extent to which such a report was read out at the adult courts (on a similar point the probation officer Sewell Stokes was incensed by the alleged habit of a magistrate at Bow Street to read aloud in open court observations made in a confidential prison doctor's report). For Irene Clarkson, the phrase "furnished according to means" in a report often meant "poverty-stricken"; and for Miss Stafford, mention of a client's illegitimacy could be made privately to magistrates by the probation officer. Similarly, according to Mrs Margaret Frost's recollection of work at the London Sessions, a probation officer there, in a verbal report to the judge in open court, would refer to a client's illiteracy in terms such as "the defendant would be the first to admit that he is no scholar".

At a meeting held in about March 1950 between senior probation officers and L.C.C. representatives, the L.C.C. claimed that its education department was "well aware of the problems caused by illiteracy" and was doing all in its power to combat it. At about the same time tentative findings from some research conducted by the Society of Juvenile Courts Probation Officers suggested that probationers - at least those under 17 years of age - were generally below a "normal" standard of education, but were not illiterate. Some months later, the Society, prompted by Basil Henriques, pursued the idea of obtaining disused public library books to interest and stimulate reporting probationers, many of whom were backward in reading, irresponsible, and untidy in their habits. (In a detailed medico-sociological study - in small part based on probation officers' reports - concerning 4,000 borstal boys from the London area, Dr Norwood East had noted in 1942 that "absence from school, especially truancy, was associated with multiple convictions to a significant degree".)

One book which young delinquents might have enjoyed, had they been able to read and understand it, was *Court Circular* by Sewell Stokes (a film and theatre critic whose relatively numerous works included a study of Isadora Duncan and the banned play, *Oscar Wilde*). Published early in 1950, *Court Circular* presented a vivid, engagingly written, and often amusing if caustic account of probation work in London based on the author's experiences as a temporary probation officer at Bow Street for four years from July 1941. (Elspeth Gray remembered him as "quite a character".) In his prefatory Note, the list of "those who helped me on my way" and whom he particularly wished to thank included "Thomas H. Mills (my chief); Miss Joan Woodward (most faithful colleague); R.H. Beeson (then Principal of the London Probation Service)". Whether they appreciated the compliment seems distinctly dubious: for example, Joan Woodward, from all accounts, was far from pleased that she should have provided the model, or primary model, for the probation officer Miss Bundy in the book. Bundy's colleague Mr Gentle (described as having engaged in "The Work" for 40 years) is widely understood to have been modelled on the long-serving Thomas Henry Mills, who in June 1937 had been appointed as the first senior probation officer at Bow Street, where he served until his retirement in 1948, and who may well have found Stokes's book too irreverent for his liking. After his retirement Tommy Mills devoted much of his time to Chatfield House, being for years a member of its managing committee. When Mills died - tragically his two sons predeceased him - a touching tribute appeared in *Probation* for March 1960, penned by Charles Morgan, who had reviewed *Court Circular* in the same journal, and who later maintained in interview that Sewell Stokes had shown him (Morgan) the typescript original of the book before its publication.

Court Circular was dedicated "with affection" to Muriel and Maurice Fenner: according to the clerical assistant Jo Knox, Muriel Fenner did Stokes's typing for him - he was apparently a great family friend of the Fenners - and Maurice Fenner was a warrant officer, later becoming a London probation officer whose concern about the growing number of young people appearing at Bow Street on drug charges led to his being awarded one of the first Churchill Fellowships in 1966 to study drug rehabilitation projects in America.

In 1952 the British film "I Believe in You" was based, very loosely, on *Court Circular* (probably the most enduring of Stokes's books), which in 1955 appeared in paperback form, in an edition "revised by the author". In the film, Cecil Parker played the part of the new probation officer (believed to be modelled largely on Stokes himself), and Celia Johnson that of his female colleague, with Joan Collins and Laurence Harvey acting as delinquents helping to educate him in his new profession. Mr Gentle in the book had become Mr Dove, who seemed to fit perfectly the description of Tommy Mills, given very many years later by Francis Lister, as "a very kind gentleman of the 'old school', always correctly dressed, always most helpful to a 'new boy' and respected by all who knew him"; and like Tommy Mills in real life, the elderly Mr Dove retired on health grounds. The film, rated as moderately good by film critics, was directed by Basil Dearden, whose earlier films "The Blue Lamp" (about the Metropolitan Police) and "Cage of Gold" (about a plausible and unscrupulous crook) - both dating from 1950 - had featured his colleague Harry Kratz as Assistant Director. By 1954 Kratz had himself become a London probation officer, and he would marry his colleague Miriam Routh.

In the London Probation Service of 1948-50, group therapy and camps for probationers were perceived as new techniques in probation work, worthy of investigation. In 1948, not long before he left the London service, William Pearce had collaborated with other Toynbee Hall probation officers in organising the second "Highdown Camp", characterised by careful programme planning to promote team spirit and efficiency.[3] In 1950, Inspector Bissell in charge of the Peel House attendance centre (set up under the Criminal Justice Act, 1948) indicated he welcomed the co-operation of probation officers, and he explained and discussed the centre's use at a meeting attended by Dr Peter Scott and London juvenile court probation officers.

Another area of pioneering work and potential influence for the London Probation Service was provided at the Divorce Court. The former London court missionaries Reginald Pestell (a founder of the National Marriage Guidance Council[4]), Harold Morton (of the Home Office) and Seldon Farmer (representing N.A.P.O.) - as well as the metropolitan magistrate Claud Mullins, who took a particular interest in this field - were among the witnesses appearing before the (Denning) Committee on Procedure in Matrimonial Causes. Mullins had pointed out in 1945 that "ever since 1857 the High Court has exercised its matrimonial functions without any machinery for social advice or investigation"; he maintained that he began conducting a domestic court nearly three years before Parliament made it compulsory; and he appears to have used probation officers regularly as conciliators in his domestic court work. In one such case, which he cited as an example of successful intervention and mediation by the probation officer (whom he preferred to call "court friend" in this context), Mullins received a letter from the reconciled wife thanking him and the probation officer; and the magistrate commented: "Perhaps in this case we prevented the existence of some future criminals."

Following the recommendations of the Denning Committee in its Final Report (Cmd.7024: February 1947), a former London probation officer was seconded to the London Probation Service for an experimental period of six months from June 1950 onwards, and assigned as court welfare officer to the Divorce Division of the High Court, to assist the court, in this pilot project, by enquiring and reporting as required concerning the welfare of children who were the subject of applications for custody or access. The officer chosen for this delicate work was Pat Mayhew, who had been a juvenile court probation officer in South East London for about a couple of years or so until his appointment, in the summer of 1948, as an inspector - later joined by Ralph Beeson - in the Probation Branch of the Home Office (Mayhew's brother Christopher was a promising Labour M.P. who had been Parliamentary Under-Secretary of State for Foreign Affairs between 1946 and 1950).

According to his own recollection, Pat Mayhew attended the Divorce Court daily for several weeks without being used or seriously noticed. Then one day, Mayhew (who was in the Auxiliary Fire Service during the War and, though a conscientious objector, had been awarded the Military Medal for gallant conduct at Dunkirk) was spotted by an ex- wartime colleague turned barrister, who seemed highly amused on hearing what his role was, but soon after mentioned to a judge, before whom he was appearing, that Mayhew's "service" was available. Mayhew was asked to make enquiries and produce a written report on the general circumstances, opinion and wishes of the child involved. He discovered that the affidavits were palpably misleading, and he was able to provide the court with significant information relating to the child's best interests. This seemed to break the ice: he began to be called upon more frequently, and during the next few months he apparently became involved in some twelve custody and access cases. By the time Mayhew returned to the Home Office - before being sent out to New Zealand to try to reorganise the probation service there - it was fairly obvious that there was scope and need for more welfare officers at the Divorce Court in London.

Mayhew's pioneering work was continued and developed by George Neve (contrary to the printed entry in the Home Office's 1951 *Directory of Probation Officers,* Mayhew - independently supported by former colleagues - later maintained that he never was Deputy Principal Probation Officer for London, though presumably he had been seconded by the Home Office at a grade regarded as on a par with Neve's position). On 14 February 1951, Lord Merriman informed the House of Lords that he had had a "long talk" with the officer concerned (presumably George Neve), who was, he said,

> anxious to proceed slowly and to build on sure foundations. For

my part, I am certain that he is right... I am very glad to know from him that, although his jurisdiction is limited, so far as we are concerned, to cases which are heard in London, he can follow a case into the country. Manifestly, as he put it, you cannot present a balanced picture in your report to the Judge unless the same investigating officer sees both spouses.

The Lord Chancellor, who had initiated the experiment, commented: "I hope and believe that slowly, but surely, more and more use will be made of these officers." Indeed, the usefulness of the service would be indicated by the fact that during the 127 days Neve would devote to Divorce Court welfare in 1951, he would deal with a total of 50 custody and access cases and 14 matrimonial conciliation cases.

There was apparently a total of 2,035 juvenile probationers in London in 1950; and by early 1951 a series of meetings between probation officers and psychiatric social workers in the London area had been held under the auspices of the I.S.T.D. in an attempt to improve co-operation between the two groups of workers. At about the same time detailed discussion between representatives of S.J.C.P.O. and the London County Council seemed to herald improved communication and liaison between those two bodies. At the suggestion of Basil Henriques, the Society of Juvenile Courts Probation Officers and the Association of Metropolitan Chief Librarians implemented in 1951 a London-based scheme whereby some probation officers were each loaned 50 children's books for use by their probationers. Another utilised medium of communication was the film: during the same year S.J.C.P.O. arranged for its members to see a number of films (made available by the National Film Board of Canada) relating to social work and psychological themes, including "Drug Addict", described in *Probation* as "a specialised film dealing with a problem that does not arise in any comparable form in this country".

The Canadian contact was one of a number of international professional links established or strengthened by the London Probation Service or by groups or individuals in the London service during the 1950s. For example, three probation officers from Thames Magistrates' Court would separately visit Canada between about 1955 and 1958: Miss C.M. Willis, followed by Leslie Penegar, would study the probation service in Vancouver and elsewhere; and in 1958 Margaret Paterson - who had received sketchy training during the War - left Thames to spend some time in Canada and also the U.S.A. Meanwhile, in the autumn of 1950, Miss Braithwaite (who had travelled to the United States in 1946 and again in 1948 to study social work there) visited Holland, under the auspices of the British Council, to observe Dutch child welfare services and compare notes with Dutch social workers about the treatment of juvenile delinquency in their two countries.

In September 1951 a party of West German judges, visiting England to study the probation system, were entertained at Rainer House (as the London Police Court Mission's hostel for probation trainees was now known, named after the pioneer Frederic Rainer). At the hostel the guests met senior probation officers, magistrates, and Home Office officials. According to Derek Borboen - who assisted in the development of a juvenile criminal justice system in West Germany after the War - these German judges were from the juvenile courts and visited Whitechapel to see the slums which they associated with Edgar Wallace (rather than with Jack the Ripper). The following June, Borboen informed an S.J.C.P.O. meeting that many social workers would be coming from Germany for courses arranged by the Home Office and would doubtless welcome the opportunity to do fieldwork with probation officers. S.J.C.P.O. agreed to assist in any way it could, and Seldon Farmer, who was present, "noted the position".

There was great interest abroad in probation and juvenile courts, and the British Council brought foreign nationals to England for training. In London at least, senior probation officers, who had smaller caseloads than main-grade officers, were expected to help with student training. Elizabeth Inman, for example, had students from France, Italy, Spain, Greece, the Lebanon, Uruguay and Singapore, and found their training very time-consuming, as few of them understood and spoke enough English to be sent out alone. She fondly remembered a Chinese girl from Singapore who was able to do home visiting and was loved by everybody (during 1949 Arthur Shields, the former London probation officer who had largely established the probation service in Trinidad, had been on a visit to Britain, collecting information and recruits with a view to starting probation in Malaya, when he suddenly died). It seems many officers appreciated the stimulation of students.

The international co-operation supported by members of the London Probation Service reached a climax with the European Seminar on

Probation, held in London in October 1952 under the auspices of the United Nations (which in 1951 had published an impressive study of the development of probation throughout much of the world). The Seminar brought together judges, public prosecutors, criminologists, prison officials, administrators, psychiatrists and probation officers from a total of seventeen countries. The speakers included Margery Fry, Eileen Younghusband and Dr Denis Carroll. Miss Fry, an indefatigable penal reformer and memorable London magistrate, spoke of some courageous and apparently successful examples of the use of probation and also distributed some case histories, seemingly drawn, at least in part, from Marlborough Street Court probation records made available through Seldon Farmer. She and Eileen Younghusband stressed the need for the use of full social enquiries as a basis for good casework; and the latter also suggested that the employment of carefully selected and well-trained probation officers led to the recovery of more offenders than would otherwise be the case. Dr Carroll - the Portman Clinic consultant psychiatrist well known to probation students passing through Rainer House - maintained that the introduction into probation officers' training of teaching in the elements of psychiatry had resulted in an incredible improvement in the standard of their casework, and he pleaded for one worker, as a matter of general practice, to deal with a case from court enquiry stage until completion of treatment.

The Seminar guests saw the Government film "Probation Officer" and spent two days visiting institutions and courts. They also witnessed -in the circular Assembly Hall at Church House, Westminster - a dramatised presentation of the work of probation officers during a morning sitting in an English magistrates' court. This presentation, which was organised by the London Probation Service (apparently at the request of the Home Office), featured a total of eight cases designed to illustrate different facets of the court work: placing a young female vagrant in a London hostel pending her return to Manchester; advising on probation for a first offender guilty of larceny; helping a section 4 probationer under the Criminal Justice Act, 1948; returning a young "tearaway" to court for breach of probation; facilitating altering the condition of residence in a probation order; advising on residence in a training home in one case and in a home for inebriates in another; and successfully applying for a probation order to be discharged for good progress.

According to Charles Balchin's recollection, the script was largely written by John Burke (a probation officer at the London Sessions with the name of a dedicatee of Barbara Noble's *Another Man's Life* (1952), her novel about a man who attempted suicide, only to be supervised by a London probation officer). All the parts - those of the defendants, three magistrates, three probation officers, two police officers, the court clerk, the usher, and newspaper reporters - were played by members of the London Probation Service. Stanley Ratcliffe won a special round of applause for his masterly impersonation of a defiant, loudly dressed "spiv". But no doubt fine performances were given by his colleagues who also participated in the "role play": C. Balchin; J.F. Bradley; T.J. Brown; N.W. Grant; Mrs V.H. Grant; D.M. Logan; Miss E.R. Marks; G.C. Morrish; E.G. Pratt; A.G.H. Robins; J.F.D. Selkirk; D.A. Smith; Miss J. Spalding; E.G. Speller; Miss G.M. Stafford; Miss M.M. Thornborough; J.V.C. Washington; Miss C.M. Willis; and Miss W.J. Woodward. Rather ironically, in their dramatic reconstruction of proceedings in an adult court, the largest single group among the actors appeared to be serving juvenile court probation officers. Charles Balchin later recalled being telephoned by Farmer himself to take part in the drama. (A decade later, Balchin gave a comic dramatic performance, assisted by colleagues and court staff, in a closed court at the London Sessions for probation students as the probation officer who did everything wrong during court proceedings.)

While the London Probation Service was forging international links and gaining recognition abroad, there was still widespread ignorance at home about probation officers and their work. When Marjory Todd became an untrained relief probation officer in London - before being accepted for Home Office training - "few people who kept on the right side of the law had heard much about probation officers". At about this time Sewell Stokes's *Court Circular* (1950) was published: this book and then the film "I Believe in You" - Mrs Todd added - "gave probation officers a certain amount of dramatic publicity". In his introductory Author's Note, Sewell Stokes referred to his experiences in "a profession about which the public knows scarcely anything"; and for relations and friends, "learning that I was a probation officer had left them none the wiser". Just as in about 1930 the London magistrate Cecil Chapman had discovered that in a metropolitan court the probation officer was confused with a police nurse; so some twenty years later the London probation officer Marjory Todd discovered that she had been confused with a policewoman. As Rose Mary Braithwaite remarked in her radio broadcast in the B.B.C. European Service towards the end of 1949: "In the public mind here, there is often confusion about what a probation officer is and how he does his job." When Mrs Marjorie Watts was told there was a shortage of probation officers and was asked whether she had thought of becoming one, she asked: "What is a probation officer?" Assisted by the Home Office, she responded to the challenge by, in effect, progressing from pounding a typewriter at 10 Downing Street as social secretary of the Prime Minister's wife, Mrs Attlee, to pounding the streets around Camberwell as a social worker in search of juvenile delinquents (she and Mrs Todd were both elected to membership of S.J.C.P.O. at the Society's meeting in July 1951). Miss Irene Clarkson, who became a London probation officer in 1953, later recalled that "people didn't know what a probation officer was".

This public ignorance was no doubt associated with the veil of secrecy that seemed to be drawn across much probation work, with its confidentiality and delicate nature. Indeed, probation officers seemed a kind of secular priesthood, custodians of the "sacred trust" vested in them by the courts, with probation officers sustained by a sense of vocation if not by religious beliefs as well, and with many of them leading lives as though they were observing vows of poverty, celibacy and obedience (Derek Borboen mock-seriously suggested that they should be a non-smoking, celibate service).

A close relationship between probation officers and magistrates, in London at least, was suggested in 1951, for example, by the fact that in May that year S.J.C.P.O. discussed with L.G. Banwell the Society's views - requested by the magistrates - on use of the power to bind over parents for the good behaviour of their children. Many of a probation officer's duties were outlined by Eileen Younghusband in her Carnegie report, of which an updated edition appeared towards the end of 1951. Although her report surveyed the salaries of probation officers, and although her updated edition was essentially based on information collected up to July 1950, she did not mention the Joint Negotiating Committee for the Probation Service in England and Wales, which the Home Office had initiated to decide on remuneration and conditions of service on a nation-wide basis, and whose first meeting had been held on 9 June 1950. During the first few years the London probation officers' "anchor-man" on the Committee was John Bradley, who in 1944 had criticised the inadequate salaries of London probation officers and had supported the concept of a special London salary scale based on the higher cost of living in the capital.[5]

Up to 1948 probation officers' salaries and conditions of service had been negotiated direct between N.A.P.O. and the Home Office. But on the twenty-one member Joint Negotiating Committee the Home Office had only two representatives, whereas the Association of Municipal Corporations and the County Councils Association had four each, with three from the Magistrates' Association and, on the employees' side, eight from N.A.P.O. This development seemed to suggest some loosening of direct Home Office control in the case of London (where the advisory London Probation Committee was appointed by the Home Secretary and was regarded, rightly or wrongly, as a "Home Office cipher"). A desire in the London service for freedom from direct Home Office control and for staff at field level to play a greater part in management decisions no doubt contributed to the establishment in 1952 of the Staff Consultative Council, which included Home Office representation, the Principal Probation Officer and members of N.A.P.O.'s London Branch appointed by the whole body of London officers.

Another factor in such developments may well have been growing consciousness of the service's more professional role and status. N.A.P.O.'s London Branch held a well attended conference in November-December 1951 to consider a revaluation of probation work and the question of a code of professional standards. Traditional values were represented by Bishop George Bell of Chichester, who told the conference that probation officers were doing religious work. Another speaker was a leading London almoner, who explained the history of her own profession (a Hospital Almoners' Association was formed in 1903, nine years before N.A.P.O.); and at a time when N.A.P.O. was acutely aware of its lack of influence in such matters, Miss Thornborough, the London probation officer reporting the proceedings for *Probation,* commented that almoners, unlike probation officers, "have responsibility for their own selection and training". It was agreed at the conference that "there is nothing incompatible between a good educational and technical qualification and a sense of vocation and both should be insisted upon in the Probation

Service".

At the 1953 N.A.P.O. Annual General Meeting, Rose Mary Braithwaite successfully proposed the creation of a Development Committee to consider the probation service's future development and, in particular perhaps, guidelines for the selection and training of probation officers. Of the original five members of the Development Committee, two - Miss Braithwaite and Georgina Stafford - were from the London service, as was Norman W. Grant, who was one of the three probation officers who were quickly co-opted. The Committee subsequently drew up a report, approved by the 1954 A.G.M. and submitted to the Home Office; but - in the short term at least - it appeared to bear little fruit, largely because of a continued shortage of qualified officers (especially men) and what the Home Office called "Government insistence on the need for the exercise of every possible administrative economy" (the Committee had recommended, *inter alia,* a minimum academic qualification to be required of all candidates for a prescribed training course before appointment, and the prohibition "by law" of the appointment of untrained and unqualified persons as probation officers).

Such concerns about professional standards and training led to a lively discussion - in which London probation officers were prominent - in the columns of *Probation* about the role of experience, desirable personal qualities, and the age factor. Miss Inman (a senior over 50) complained:

> The present tendency in the Probation Department seems to be to consider a probation officer "too old at forty". Senior posts are given to juniors, trainees are sent to those officers who have been trained fairly recently themselves and, when a training course in casework was advertised recently, it was stated that no one over forty should apply.

She added that it would be a disaster for the service if the experienced main-grade officer felt that he or she had become a "back-number". Her comments drew support from her London colleagues John F. Bradley and, to a limited extent, John Burke, though the latter spoilt his case through a mixture of denial and gross exaggeration when he declared: "An adult who must learn virtually unteachable things such as interviewing, learning to work with colleagues, using authority, etc., etc., is unfit for a job as a milk roundsman, let alone a probation officer." In reply to Miss Inman, the Home Office - using Frank Dawtry of N.A.P.O.

as a channel of communication - appeared to rebut some of her points, but maintained, as regards officers as tutors of trainees, that "it is necessary to select for this purpose officers who are conversant with new methods of case-work and new methods of supervising and training. These are frequently found amongst officers fairly recently trained who remember more easily their own period of supervision." These attitudes arguably found expression during the preparatory phase of the formation of that cult of youth which would become such a prominent feature of British life in the 1960s, when the young would be regarded as the innovators, pacemakers and trendsetters needed by society.

During this period of embryonic change there was published the report of the Committee on Discharged Prisoners' Aid Societies (Cmd.8879: 1953), which appeared to envisage greater probation service involvement in work with prisoners before or after their release. At the same time the Society of Juvenile Courts Probation Officers and the L.C.C. decided to make a joint appeal to the Home Office for more remand home places for girls. Before 1952 probation officers had supervised approved school leavers on a voluntary basis; but since that date an amendment to the Probation Rules, in the light of the Criminal Justice Act of 1948, made it their duty to accept such after-care cases if asked to do so by the school managers. (As the Government booklet *The Probation Service,* issued in 1952, explained, probation officers were under a similar obligation regarding borstal trainees, young prisoners released on licence, and persons released on licence from corrective training or preventive detention.) In June 1953 S.J.C.P.O. was told by a Children's Department Inspector that probation officers' reports were highly valued by approved school allocations officers as well as by the approved schools themselves, which were always pleased when a probation officer escorted a boy or girl to the institution ; though a weakness of the reports was that they tended to omit reference to the child's attitude to school. Child development in a London slum area was studied in B.M. Spinley's pioneer work *The Deprived and the Privileged* (1953), whose preparation was assisted by 19 social workers, including an unnamed London probation officer.

A Government photo-poster, issued about a year later - apparently for consumption abroad - featured scenes in the life of a London probation officer (Peter Shervington, mentioned by name), with one of the captions referring to the male probation officer taking a boy to an approved school and another to a female colleague taking a girl to a probation hostel: the other scenes showed Peter Shervington visiting a probationer's parents at home, visiting a boys' club, describing a boy's home life to a juvenile court, reporting progress to magistrates at a case committee meeting, offering advice to a man released from prison, and counselling a married couple.

In response to separate invitations, the Society of Juvenile Courts Probation Officers and N.A.P.O. had given written and oral evidence separately to the Ministry of Education Committee on Maladjusted Children - although sub-committees of the two societies had worked together on a preparatory questionnaire, the one N.A.P.O. witness who was a London probation officer, Miss Miriam Routh, was also a member of the S.J.C.P.O. sub-committee, and there was some co-ordination between the two bodies in giving oral evidence. By about early April 1952 Margaret Dawkins, Nina Nowell and Reginald A. Wright had followed up S.J.C.P.O.'s written evidence with oral evidence to the Committee, which seemed satisfied that the training of probation officers enabled them to recognise maladjustment in children "in, at any rate, some of its manifestations" - though the Committee's recommendations (eventually published in 1955) did not directly involve the probation service.

N.A.P.O.'s General Secretary, Frank Dawtry, was made an honorary member of S.J.C.P.O. in mid-March 1952, and it seems that, largely because of the confidence S.J.C.P.O. placed in him, closer co-operation resulted between the two organisations. In July 1953, S.J.C.P.O. set up a sub-committee (proposed by Rosemary Deane) to examine the question of court proceedings in respect of neglectful parents. This sub-committee's report seems to have been passed on to a N.A.P.O. sub-committee, on which Miss Deane was also asked to serve, and which collated the comments and evidence received to submit a memorandum in July 1954 to a Joint Committee of the British Medical Association and the Magistrates' Association on cruelty to and neglect of children. This N.A.P.O. memorandum proposed *inter alia* the establishment of observation centres to which mothers charged with cruelty or neglect could be temporarily committed, with their young children, for any social enquiries and medical examination to be undertaken. London probation officers doubtless facilitated implementation of the procedure whereby a Bow Street magistrate could grant a licence authorising the transfer of a British child for "adoption" to a British subject resident abroad[6]; and during

1953 S.J.C.P.O.'s comments regarding the law and procedure on adoption were conveyed to Dawtry and used in N.A.P.O.'s evidence to a Home Office committee considering this subject.

As George Neve was beginning to find it difficult to provide an adequate service on his own for the judges at the Divorce Court, Miss Nina Nowell and, later, Miss Alison Allen were both appointed in 1952 to assist him as part-time divorce court welfare officers. Appropriately enough, the court served by each of these two main-grade officers was sited inside Tower Bridge Court in Tooley Street (with the juvenile court long held upstairs and the adult court downstairs), inside the very court building where the pioneer "children's magistrate" Cecil Chapman had worked in wonderful partnership with the pioneer children's probation officer Evelyn Lance. Nina Nowell would serve the Divorce Court for thirty years, and Alison Allen for nearly twenty. Miss Nowell, who had joined the London Probation Service in 1942, came from the South East London Juvenile Court, where she had worked with Pat Mayhew, who became the first divorce court welfare officer. During 1952 and 1953 she was an S.J.C.P.O. representative in respect of the newly formed Association of Workers for Maladjusted Children. Miss Allen, who had joined the London Probation Service in 1946 after a wartime job as Children's Officer in the Ministry of Pensions, came from Tower Bridge Magistrates' Court. According to Miss Allen's recollection, George Neve was asked to report on a custody case which he referred to her as she had already become involved with the family: she did the report, and the judge was satisfied; Neve later asked her if she could do more of this kind of work, and Miss Allen readily agreed.

The two officers began to combine divorce court welfare work with their existing duties in South London (the former was unrecorded in successive editions of the Home Office *Directory of Probation Officers* during the 1950s). Miss Nowell's allocation of her time to divorce court welfare work rose from a total of 52 days in 1952 to 129 days in 1953 and 132 in 1954, while Miss Allen's allocation increased from one day in 1952 to a total of 54 days in 1953 and 89 days in 1954. Together with George Neve, they dealt with a total of 91 custody and access cases in 1952, 105 in 1953, and 104 in 1954, as well as a total of 12 matrimonial conciliation cases in 1952, 15 in 1953, and 5 in 1954. A tribute to their work, and not least the quality of their written reports, was paid by Mr Justice Willmer when he addressed a N.A.P.O. London Branch day conference in February 1954. He indicated that their intervention had "completely revolutionised" the work of the Divorce Court. He added: "The welfare officer can do what the judge cannot - visit the homes of both parties and get the 'feel' of them. Always the reports are of great help and in many cases they are decisive." Of the disputed custody cases, about half were investigated by welfare officers.

Following the reported success of the joint S.J.C.P.O. - Association of Metropolitan Chief Librarians books scheme (on which the Home Office had requested a report), Mrs Marjorie Watts and Derek Borboen were instrumental in establishing an S.J.C.P.O. sub-committee to investigate the problem of backward readers among children and young persons supervised by probation officers. This sub-committee presented its findings in the autumn of 1954 through Mrs Watts (whose interest in literacy was illustrated by the fact that she had been the first secretary of PEN, the international literary movement founded by her mother, of whom she would write an extensive memoir in 1987). Thanks to the co-operation of 27 London juvenile court probation officers, 553 boys and girls between the ages of 8 and 15 were given a reading test (according to the Holborn Reading Scale), and, of these, 276 were found to be retarded to a greater or lesser extent. It was noticed that some boys with low I.Q.s could read quite well, whilst others of at least average intelligence could hardly read at all: because they presented as non-readers, children in the second category were sometimes not recognised as intelligent until they came under the supervision of a probation officer, and there were indications that quite a high proportion of the tested children who were backward readers had not received any particular help for their handicap before they got into trouble. One model of achievement in education was provided by Arthur Robert Duncan, a London probation officer during the 1950s (he died in 1961), who gained a degree in economics, a diploma in social studies, and a diploma in education.

Although there was some division of opinion inside S.J.C.P.O. between those who favoured wider use of E.S.N. schools and those anxious to press for more and smaller classes for backward children in ordinary schools, many of the London probation officers observed a great improvement in their clients when they succeeded in getting them the special help and encouragement they needed to improve their reading ability.

Another scheme to help juvenile delinquents in London was the Redvers Club, which Derek Borboen set up in a Nissen hut in the school playground of a bombed out area in Redvers Street (now no more), N.1, just off Hoxton Street. In a book on a related project[7], Dr Hyla Holden gave 1949 as the starting date of the Redvers Club; but in interview Derek Borboen and Merfyn Turner, quite independently of each other, both said it started in about 1953, which also seems to tally with Jean Moore's recollections; and S.J.C.P.O. Minutes indicate that Borboen - whom Holden acknowledged as the Club's founder - was in Germany between October 1948 and January 1951. It was intended as a youth club for the "unclubbables" (mainly delinquents), as a land-based counterpart of the Barge Boys' Club, though Merfyn Turner recalled that there was some delay in getting it started. When the Barge Boys' Club came to an end, Turner became the first club leader of the Redvers Club, living on the premises in very primitive conditions. The Club was open five nights a week, and the ages of the "drop-in" clientele seemed to range from three to twenty-three. There was a good atmosphere at the Club, where young people could play table tennis or use a gym vaulting-horse if they wished, but mostly they preferred to chat. Derek Borboen and Merfyn Turner both recalled games of hand-ball, which the two of them played with great vigour. A deserter virtually lived there at one stage, and the police, somewhat suspicious, occasionally visited the Club, which more or less became accepted as part of the local community. According to Derek Borboen's recollection, a glue millionaire gave quite a lot of money (which may well have helped to pay the Club leader's salary); and those running the Club aimed, in a delinquent area, to help build up trust in authority and confidence in the community through the development of legitimate recreational activity and group identity. According to Jean Moore, who as a local probation officer was one of a team of helpers encouraging a modicum of discipline at the Club, once a year boys from the Club or otherwise known to probation officers in the area were taken on a wherry for a week, during which the probation officers got to know the boys very well, and no doubt vice versa.

A shorter-term project with similar aims was the Arethusa Camp, organised in 1953 and again in 1954 by the London juvenile court probation officers George Pratt and Stanley Ratcliffe. This was intended to provide a "brief training in social conduct" through the medium of a week's summer camping holiday on each occasion for a party of delinquent London schoolboys aged between 11 or 12 and 15, and both camps were held on the sports ground of the training ship "Arethusa" at Upnor, Rochester, Kent. The first camp was thought to have been generally very successful. In the second, the group was substantially different in composition from the first (though five out of the 25 boys had also attended the camp the previous year); it seems to have been larger (about seven boys more), with a wider age-range, and correspondingly more difficult to manage, with a higher proportion of "severely maladjusted" boys. The second camp witnessed an early, crude and short-lived attempt to divide and manipulate the staff, and highlighted some of the problematical aspects of authority, discipline and their boundaries for those concerned, though a process of integration seemed to emerge after a phase of testing and acting out among the boys.

During 1953 Mr E.R. Guest, a metropolitan magistrate in the West London area familiar to Pratt and Ratcliffe, publicly expressed some doubts about the likely success of section 4 (condition of mental treatment) probation cases; whilst Guest's criticism of psychology and psychiatry in relation to the criminal law provoked a defensive reply from the London probation officer Miss M.M. ("Peggy") Thornborough, daughter of a staunch Liberal who had been Librarian of the National Liberal Club[8]: she drew attention to "two global wars with their shattering impact upon family, social and economic spheres, one of the gravest economic crises ever known, the breakdown of stability in nearly all levels of life, and the insecurity that is part and parcel of this new atomic age". Moreover, in a nation-wide study of section 4 probation orders that were made throughout 1953, Dr Max Grünhut found that 70 per cent of those for whom full medical information was available were discharged with a favourable prognosis after mental treatment, with most of this 70 per cent not being reconvicted within a period of one year after termination of their probation orders, and with some two-thirds of the total number of section 4 probationers completing their probation satisfactorily.

Grünhut acknowledged "the very helpful co-operation of numerous probation officers" in the collection of sufficient data on individual probationers for his survey. No doubt London probation officers were among those who so co-operated, just as they clearly seem to have assisted the research worker engaged by the British Social Biology Council to prepare a sociological study of prostitution in London. Although the Council's committee on prostitution did not include a member of the London Probation Service, it did include a serving Middlesex probation officer (Miss Judith Kennedy). When the research study, in a truncated form, was published in 1955, it did not identify the research worker involved (who was, in fact, Mrs Rosalind Wilkinson, a social science graduate from the L.S.E., which had been associated with the project). Mrs Wilkinson's vivid and illuminating report was based partly on an analysis of police records on 150 known London prostitutes, and partly on face-to-face interviews she conducted with 69 London prostitutes following their appearances at magistrates' courts like Bow Street, Clerkenwell, Marlborough Street and Marylebone. She recorded that in writing up these interviews she was assisted by probation officers who were sometimes "able to give further information or to help in reconciling conflicting histories". She discovered that 18 of the 69 girls interviewed had previously been dealt with under the Children and Young Persons Act, that about 10 per cent of all the girls had at some stage been on probation for soliciting, and that

> if probation enables them to give it up sooner, that is an obvious gain, and the seeing of all prostitutes by probation officers at least for a preliminary talk might be advocated on these grounds, provided the probation officer can take this on. Almost all magistrates at Bow Street court now ask each new prostitute to see the probation officer... While probation officers take comparatively few prostitutes on probation, their initial or occasional talks with the girls are undoubtedly very important.

Sometimes a probation officer could get a girl a job if she wanted one. But generally prostitutes did not want to be put on probation or invited to see a probation officer (Mary Ellison, a former London probation officer, would recall a case in which a "ponce" was opposed to his prostitutes seeking help from a probation officer). The probation service, Rosalind Wilkinson concluded, "can be invoked when the prostitute wishes to co-operate rather than when the court, often unrealistically, judges that she should be prepared to".

After being found at a well-known brothel in Highbury, an unsettled Hoxton girl aged about 15 appeared at Toynbee Hall Juvenile Court before Henriques, who ordered her to report once a week to a probation officer. In later years the young rebel recalled:

> My probation officer was called Miss Cripps, and I believe she was one of the daughters of Sir Stafford Cripps, the Chancellor of the Exchequer in the Labour Government after the war. I think she did her best where I was concerned. Her office was in New North Road, not far to go. The first few weeks I went to see her as regular as clockwork, but then it began to get a bind, and so I stopped. Whenever I did report to her, it was usually after she had been to Jenny to tell her I was not attending. I took to making up some really diabolical excuses... Her answer was always the same: 'I believe you. Thousands wouldn't.'

> Visits to Miss Cripps would last about twenty minutes. I think I was scared to say too much to her - the thought was always at the back of my mind that may be they would take me away from Jenny. I would just answer the questions usually. She always asked me:

> 'How are you and how's the job going? How are you getting on at Jenny's? Has your mother made any contact?'

Both the young rebel and her probation officer became quite well-known: the former as May Hobbs, militant champion of London's ill-paid night office cleaners and founder of the Cleaners Action Group; the latter, after her marriage, as Jean Moore, founder of the N.S.P.C.C. School of Social Work and trainer in child abuse for London probation officers and other social workers. As the very young Miss Cripps -believed to be a distant relative of Sir Stafford's - the latter spent a short period as the first woman probation officer on the Isle of Ely, where she became interested in child sexual abuse (in 1949 the London Police Court Mission maintained Coombehurst as what it called "a home for child victims of incest and sexual assault"). Then, in 1954, she joined the London Probation Service, which she left in 1961 to become senior tutor with the N.S.P.C.C. and to reorganise its training scheme after she had criticised it from a probation officer's perspective (in 1943-44 S.J.C.P.O. had suggested some improvements in the work of the N.S.P.C.C.).

Henriques's sympathetic treatment of the girl May gave no obvious support to the view[9] that his understanding of some of the problems of young girls and women was limited by his experience and imagination. On the other hand, he seems to have conducted his court in a paternalistic, even autocratic fashion. He summoned and questioned Miss Cripps when he heard she had become engaged; and many years later Jean Moore (as she became) recalled that, although she felt she was not among them, "he could be very harsh on probation officers he didn't respect and like, and it was rumoured he had got probation officers removed from his court". Of the exacting standard he imposed on himself and expected of others, Miss Braithwaite (who was attached to his court for years before his retirement in 1955) declared: "Young offenders and officials alike would often quail before his cry of 'This is abominable!' when they had fallen short of this standard, but they would redouble their efforts to do better next time." Miss Braithwaite (who later assisted the preparation of L.L. Loewe's *Basil Henriques*) added that he was "a great believer in the probation system and an inspiring and much loved leader of the team at his Court".[10] Derek Borboen, whose decision to apply to become a probation officer seems to have been largely influenced by Henriques, remembered him as "a very inspiring lecturer" and felt that the enthusiast Clemence Paine was probably one of the probation officers who most deeply influenced Henriques (who in 1943, for example, had addressed S.J.C.P.O. and apparently also the Society of Metropolitan Police Court Probation Officers).

Whatever his limitations and flaws, Henriques seemed a colossus among London juvenile court magistrates. His reputation seemed the more striking in view of the fact that during his thirty years on the London bench his lay associates (as Stanley Ratcliffe would point out) included such forward-looking or able magistrates as Margery Fry, Barbara Wootton, Eileen Younghusband and John Watson. For Henriques, the probation officers with whom he worked were "a sort of hallowed Priesthood". Metropolitan stipendiary magistrates who also held probation officers in high esteem included Frank Powell, Claud Mullins and Frank Milton. Powell (who, in 1954, became the first President of the Probation Officers' Christian Fellowship) had already maintained that it was "indeed difficult" to see how any magistrates' court could function without the aid of probation officers; and in 1959 Milton stated that "one busy London court alone may have as many as eight, and the magistrate would feel hopelessly lost without them". Claud Mullins - who as a magistrate had sought to combine humanity with a scientific outlook - dedicated *The Sentence on the Guilty* (1957) "To all the Probation Officers who worked with me and in special memory of Arthur Shields".

But London probation officers seemed well aware that they could scarcely rest on their laurels, or on those of their colleagues or predecessors. Conscious of a need (in Seldon Farmer's words) "to assimilate the new without devaluing the old", the London Probation Service was taking increasing account of developments in social work orientation and teaching, largely emanating from America and relating to modern concepts of casework and supervision. Farmer had heard his promising young subordinate George P. Newton (who had attended the course) address an S.J.C.P.O. meeting in July 1953 on the Tavistock Clinic Advanced Course in Casework, which had been established in 1951. Although the numbers on the course were restricted to six per year, the different branches of social work which provided students from the earliest days included probation. In 1955 Stanley Ratcliffe took this Advanced Course in Casework, as did his juvenile court colleague Miss M.M. Thornborough, who gratefully recorded that what she had learnt on the course "produces a response within the clients at levels before untouched". Indeed, she and Stanley Ratcliffe constituted the London probation officers in a select group of five Social Work Fellows of the Tavistock Institute. At about the same time, at a N.A.P.O. London Branch week-end conference, held in October 1955, a talk on "Understanding through Casework" was given by Miss Muriel Cunliffe, a Canadian teacher of casework who stood on the threshold of exercising notable influence on British social work education during this decade.

Another milestone in British social work education was the pioneering generic "Carnegie Course", spearheaded by Eileen Younghusband, launched at the L.S.E. in the autumn of 1954, and financed between 1954 and 1958 by the Carnegie United Kingdom Trust in the light of Younghusband's social work reports which it had published in 1947 and 1951. Seldon Farmer would comment in 1963:

> the London Probation Service can claim to have played a pioneer part through its contribution to the first of the courses in applied social studies run by the London School of Economics in 1954. This contribution consisted of providing suitably qualified "supervisors" for students placed with the probation service for a period of integrated theoretical and practical training, and it has continued ever since.

A contribution to the annual course was made on a part-time basis by George Newton, who - in the words of Farmer's secretary Kathleen

Hoath - "came in with the psychiatric movement": a new Assistant Principal Probation Officer of the London service who, according to Miss Braithwaite's recollection, was "a brilliant lecturer", Newton lectured on probation and, in 1955, became a supervisor on this course, of which he wrote that "the Probation Service has been pleased to participate in a professional training of major importance to social work in this country".[11] The probation placements involved fairly complex negotiations with the Home Office, the London Probation Service and a juvenile court, and accommodation for the students was by no means easy to find; but these negotiations were seen as ultimately successful, unlike those involving at least one hospital and, in important respects, the child care placement. The probation supervisors whose services were arranged by the Home Office without any cost to the L.S.E. were Wilfred Oke and Rose Mary Braithwaite, both senior probation officers at the East London Juvenile Court. (Later Miss Braithwaite - who would assist the preparation of Professor Kathleen Jones's 1984 biography of Eileen Younghusband - convened and chaired a working party whose discussions resulted in Alma Hartshorn's notable study, published in 1982, of the genesis and development of the Carnegie Course.)

Simultaneously indeed, the London Probation Service was associated not only with the Carnegie Course from the beginning, but also with a pioneering venture of a different kind in London. In February 1955 Miss Braithwaite's colleague Margaret May began a two year secondment as a full-time social worker in Holloway Prison. Miss May had worked in the London juvenile courts for many years; and as it may seem somewhat surprising that a senior probation officer who had always worked in the juvenile court rather than one from the adult court had been selected for this experiment, it may be presumed that the choice was not unconnected with an appreciation of Miss May's personal qualities or her experience of women separated from their children. Her own subsequent recollection was that, though seconded by the Home Office on the basis of her existing salary, she had been invited to work in Holloway by the reformer Margery Fry, under whom Miss May had worked at Stamford House Juvenile Court, W.12, and who had apparently long wanted to introduce social workers into the prison system.

Half-fascinated and half-repelled by the "curious" atmosphere of the maximum security prison, Miss May started work in her new role with about 60 recidivists serving sentences of between six months and three years (though after eight months she extended her work to include short-term prisoners such as alcoholics, prostitutes and debtors). Of the 115 recidivist women she got to know during the first eight months, only 18 had a home of their own. She tried to relieve some of the anxieties of these women, who often clung "with a sort of frenzied desperation" to their possessions, if not to their children. Miss May felt that a personal relationship developed between social worker and prisoner could encourage the latter to lead a more satisfactory life on release (when, indeed, some evidently kept in touch with her); although for the social worker, "it is hard sometimes to be clear-sighted, realistic, charitable and compassionate all at the same time".

With secretarial assistance already available to the prison, Miss May quickly established contacts with outside agencies, including, wherever possible, any probation officers known to the women. But although Miss May was the only probation officer working in Holloway, she was not the only welfare worker there. Apart from the Governor and the Chaplain, whose role included some welfare aspects, there were a psychiatric social worker and a borstal after-care officer; and from March 1951 onwards, the W.V.S., building on a project it had initiated at Holloway some four years or so earlier, developed a through-care scheme for Holloway prisoners which, *inter alia,* quite often produced beneficial contact with probation officers. Although Miss May's account[12] (published in September 1957) of her Holloway experiences was reticent about her relations with staff, she declared thirty years later: "I would say that the general reaction of the prison staff was friendly; and they did occasionally make use of any service I could offer in the way of help for the women." Miss May appeared to be the first British probation officer, certainly in the London area, to be seconded to work in an English prison. Though it could scarcely have been foreseen at the time, her experimental secondment was a prefiguration of the historic change a decade later, when the probation service would be required to staff prison "welfare" departments.

The names of Margaret May and her colleagues John Bradley, Jean Cripps, John Dunphy and Elizabeth Inman - all, in effect, representing the London Probation Service - appeared on the list of registered members and associates for the Third International Congress on Criminology, held at Bedford College in London between 12 and 18

September 1955. (Another name on the list was that of Margery Fry, described as a member of the Home Office Advisory Council on the Treatment of Offenders.) Although London probation officers did not appear to be associated prominently with the founding in January 1956 of the New Bridge to befriend and help the ex-prisoner, they would become more involved in its work; and in 1988 C.H. Rolph recalled: "to be honest I don't really know where it *would* have got without them." He added that Charles Balchin was one of those who had been specially helpful.

Meanwhile London probation officers continued to participate in and benefit from various international contacts and influences. During 1954 an S.J.C.P.O. sub-committee had worked on a questionnaire for the International Association of Children's Judges, which held a conference in Brussels, attended by S.J.C.P.O. Chairman, Miss U.G. Davies, on an unofficial basis. Arguably officers of the London Probation Service contributed at least as much to the post-war development of youth and social work in West Germany as the members of any other British body of comparable size and resources. German probation officers visited London in 1953 and 1954, and Farmer apparently visited West Germany on an official basis to assess post-war social services developments there. In July 1954 the London probation officer J.F.D. Selkirk visited Finland by courtesy of the United Nations and the Finnish Ministry of Social Affairs to study that country's social services. During his tour he was able to examine the judicial system and child and juvenile welfare work in Finland, where he visited many modern penal and other institutions. He was impressed by the absence of slums and by what he claimed was "the lowest rate of female delinquency in the world", though he acknowledged that alcoholism was a serious problem. Selkirk's colleague Ellen Ruth Marks went to Kenya in 1956 as a community development officer seconded to rehabilitate women in custody and delinquents and vagrants found in Nairobi. Before that, she was seconded to the Gold Coast, to assume responsibility for probation in Accra and for a total of three girls' remand and probation homes during the period 1953-55: she also opened a girls' approved school. At about the time Miss Marks was in Africa, another London probation officer, Miss C.M. Willis, was on a ten-week visit to America, where she renewed acquaintance with one or two ex-clients from the War period and, in Canada at least, visited courts, probation offices and a reformatory for women. No doubt the travelling probation officers reported not only to the readers of *Probation,* but also to colleagues in London on their experiences; and quite a few London probation officers had been shown the American public information film "Angry Boy".

Other angry boys also attracted attention. In February 1955 the Home Office issued a memorandum on approved school after-care. This document had not apparently been prepared in consultation with the probation service, which in 1954 had taken some 14.5% of the boys discharged from approved schools and 30.3% of the girls so discharged; and the Society of Juvenile Courts Probation Officers, which set up a sub-committee under Miriam Routh to study this memorandum, produced a report which was submitted to the Home Office after discussion in September by the Joint Consultative Committee in Child Care, on which Mrs Marjorie Watts and Messrs G.H.D. Borboen and D.F. Tizzard represented S.J.C.P.O. and were, in fact, the only London probation officers present. In this inter-agency committee discussion, regret was expressed that probation officers no longer escorted children to the selected approved schools, and it seemed generally agreed that more frequent visits by probation officers would help to improve liaison with the schools, which often tended, on the one hand, to believe that probation officers should not act as after-care agents for children previously on probation to them, and, on the other, to forget that other children in a family might be under a probation officer's supervision. Not only could representatives of a variety of organisations be appointed as after-care agents; but also the powers of probation officers, acting as such agents, were limited: three years earlier, the Chairman of N.A.P.O. had felt it necessary to point out to a London probation officer that neither the Children and Young Persons Act of 1933, the Probation Rules of 1949, nor the prescribed licence itself, required a discharged approved school child to "report" to a probation officer at his or her office (in July 1939 S.J.C.P.O. members had seemed in favour of probation officers officially undertaking after-care work).

The total of 627 after-care cases held by officers of the London Probation Service as at the end of 1955 no doubt included approved school licences. The total number of after-care cases carried by the London service rose unremittingly between 1950 and the end of our period - as did the total of London probation officers' caseloads, measured in terms of a combination of probation orders, supervision orders, money payment orders and after-care cases (see Appendix 18 for detailed figures relating to the years 1950-62). Needless to say, such case-loads represented only part of the work undertaken by probation officers (Appendix 19 gives annual totals in respect of social enquiries, means enquiries, and divorce court, matrimonial and related work in London between 1950 and 1962).

George Neve, Nina Nowell and Alison Allen devoted a total of 64, 147 and 116 days, respectively, to divorce court welfare work in 1955. Where both spouses lived outside London, whether in the same probation area or in adjoining areas, Neve generally passed the cases on to the local probation service; and in such cases he received assistance from officers as far afield as Cornwall, Devon, South Wales, Anglesey, Lancashire, Yorkshire, or Durham. He dealt with the cases in or near London, while his two female colleagues undertook most of whatever long journeys became necessary from the capital. Cases for investigation were usually referred to him after they had been part heard on the basis of the affidavits; he then attended court, studied the affidavits, made notes, and allocated the cases. With regard to matrimonial conciliation (which, though not officially part of his duties, he found difficult to separate from the welfare of children), he referred cases of special difficulty to persons (psychiatrists, general medical doctors, etc.) he considered better qualified than himself; but by April 1956 he had not yet had occasion to use the Marriage Guidance Council (which, according to Stanley Ratcliffe's recollection, was used largely by the middle class).

In its 1956 report - in which no officers of the London Probation Service were listed as witnesses - the Royal Commission on Marriage and Divorce praised the work of Neve and his two colleagues:

> We have been greatly impressed by the work undertaken by that officer... Increasing use has been made by the judges of his services and, with the growth of his work, he has since 1952 had the assistance of two women probation officers. We consider that this has been a valuable development and that these arrangements should be continued and expanded as part of the system of court welfare officers which we recommend.

It may not be altogether fanciful to suppose that Neve's impressive performance and good standing with the judges could be linked to the Royal Commission's recommendation that the probation service should be the sole statutory social work agency to undertake an extension of divorce court welfare work throughout the country. This recommendation was carried into effect first by the Home Office in May 1957 commending voluntary arrangements for probation officers throughout England and Wales to cover such work, and later by the Matrimonial Proceedings (Children) Act, 1958, and changes in 1959 to the Probation Rules. By the summer of 1956 - soon after publication of the Royal Commission's report - George Neve had received a *de facto* promotion to senior court welfare officer, a title which he now used while retaining the rank of Deputy Principal Probation Officer. In January 1957 he became the first full-time divorce court welfare officer in London (at the Royal Courts of Justice) and, indeed, in England and Wales as a whole; and very soon afterwards he was joined by Miss Stephanie Stevens, who became the first probation service clerical assistant to be based at the Royal Courts of Justice, to undertake the typing of divorce court welfare reports, which had previously been done at the respective probation offices of the part-time officers concerned. According to her own subsequent recollection, Miss Stevens also summarised affidavits reaching the welfare office in Room 550.

At the very end of 1957, Neve expressed the view to his colleague Miss Allen that during the year "not only had the volume of work increased, but... an increasing value and importance was being given to it". This development was no doubt assisted by the newly promoted Lord Denning, who, in his address in London on 4 May 1957 to N.A.P.O., celebrating "Fifty Years of Probation", declared that "the court welfare officers in London have proved invaluable to the courts"; and he instanced a recent case of contested custody where, to his own knowledge, the divorce court welfare officer's report made all the difference to the court's decision.

Other eminent speakers at the Guildhall who addressed N.A.P.O. on the jubilee of the probation service were Lord Samuel and the new Home Secretary, "Rab" Butler. Samuel had moved the second reading of the Probation of Offenders Bill on 8 May 1907; and in the memorable words of *Probation:* "surely it is almost without parallel for a man to bring a Bill to Parliament, and to speak in remembrance of the occasion fifty years later." In the large and enthusiastic audience were Sidney Boswell, Frank Green and J. Bray, who had all been among the first probation officers to be appointed under the 1907 Act: Boswell and Green had also been

London police court missionaries who may well have believed that London's position as a social magnet meant - as *ILPAS '76* would point out - that "the London officer has always felt himself to be in the thick of it, battling with the greatest pressures". On the other hand, to some extent no doubt, London's post-war crime problem was decanted, if not diluted, through the "overspill" facilities provided by at least nine designated New Towns, not to mention Dagenham, described in 1963 as "the biggest housing estate in the world", and some 26 other L.C.C. out-County estates in Essex, Hertfordshire, Kent and Surrey.[13]

Another highlight of these historic celebrations (curiously unrecorded in Jarvis's history, published in 1972) was the reception held on 3 May 1957 at Lancaster House, where London Probation Service staff and Home Office inspectors directed some 5,000 guests, who were received by the Lord Chancellor or his wife. When Queen Elizabeth The Queen Mother arrived at Lancaster House, she was met by the London probation officers Norman Grant (N.A.P.O. Vice-Chairman) and John Bradley (N.A.P.O. Hon. Treasurer) and their respective wives; and she spent nearly an hour talking informally to probation officers from all over the country on subjects ranging from training officers for Ghana to training juveniles in the East End of London.

The London probation officers whose daily work was largely influenced by conditions in the East End at this time included Margaret Christina Paterson. No known relation of Alec Paterson's, though sharing his concern for the outcast, Miss Paterson had been appointed by 1942 to Thames Court, where during the ensuing sixteen years she established a close relationship with members of staff, many of the magistrates entertaining her in their own homes. Together with Father "Joe" Williamson and Miss Edith Ramsay - both familiar figures in East London - Miss Paterson became very concerned about prostitution in Stepney; and all three were members of a small committee in whose name a pamphlet was printed in May 1957 under the title *Vice Increase in Stepney* (in fact written by Edith Ramsay, a veteran East End community worker known to have supported the study of London prostitutes by Mrs Rosalind Wilkinson, who in her research, published in 1955, had sought Miss Paterson's assistance in interviewing prostitutes who appeared regularly at Thames Court). Then in July 1957 - weeks before the publication of the Wolfenden Report - the local press reported a lobby of

M.P.s by a group of East London housewives, led by Edith Ramsay and Margaret Paterson, to tell them about conditions in the vice-land around Cable Street.[14]

Other London probation officers also contributed, from their long professional experience, to the discussion intensified by the appointment and deliberations of the Wolfenden Committee on homosexual offences and prostitution. According to his own recollection, Charles Morgan (who had apparently undertaken some research some years earlier for a B.B.C. radio programme on a century of probation) participated in a B.B.C. radio documentary on the subject of homosexuality as a social problem; and at about this time his Marlborough Street colleague, Mrs Elspeth Gray, took part in a similar radio panel discussion on prostitution. The Wolfenden Committee heard evidence from the London probation officer Miss Mary Hamilton of Bow Street, who, it is believed, had assisted Rosalind Wilkinson's research work on prostitution in London, and who appeared in the Wolfenden Report as having been a witness for the Howard League, and not for N.A.P.O. The Committee did not support the idea (included in N.A.P.O.'s evidence) of an experimental training hostel for young prostitutes. But by the summer of 1958 "Father Joe" had set up Church House, Wellclose Square, E.1, as a hostel and refuge for women and girls who wished to escape an actual or potential life of prostitution.

According to Miss Paterson, prostitution often began in the all-night cafes, which were a considerable problem in Stepney: girls from approved schools found their way to them. Members of the Society of Juvenile Courts Probation Officers discovered that such cafes were causing a problem not only in Stepney, but also in Hoxton, Islington, Camden Town, Paddington and Vauxhall. As a result, in 1958, S.J.C.P.O. agreed to express its concern to the L.C.C. and to try to ascertain the views of the police and youth organisations regarding the cafes. Concern about all-night cafes and, more specifically, "the threat of a disreputable cafe in the area", may well have led Derek Borboen in 1958, after the Redvers Club had burnt down, to propose a cafe project in Hoxton to cater for young people at risk - a proposal that would begin to bear fruit from 1963 onwards, after years of frustrating negotiation.

Problems posed by sexual offenders had already been touched on by Dr David Stafford-Clark, author of *Psychiatry Today,* when he gave a talk to S.J.C.P.O. members in January 1956 on liaison between psychiatrists and probation officers. Two years earlier he had told N.A.P.O. London Branch that clients' relationship with their probation officer could be of great value to them if it was with someone whom they respected and who, they felt, accepted them. (In September 1960 Dr Melitta Schmiedeberg of New York – a pioneering psychiatric writer on menstruation and more recently a Portman Clinic consultant – would address a joint S.J.C.P.O.– N.A.P.O. London Branch meeting on establishing contact with patients.) In October 1957 S.J.C.P.O. held a conference on illegitimacy addressed by the psychiatrist Dr T.C.N. Gibbens and by the barrister Miss Jean Graham Hall, both of whom had given evidence to the Wolfenden Committee (the latter had been a Croydon probation officer). In March 1958 the London probation officer Mrs M.J. Sykes, on behalf of S.J.C.P.O., agreed to find time to study and comment on the Adoption Bill, which, enacted in 1958, would result in the duties of a probation officer as a possible guardian *ad litem* being spelt out in detail. Valerie Haig-Brown, who stood in for Miss Paterson at Thames at about this time, recalled that the probation service received quite a few requests for guardian *ad litem* reports.

Miss Paterson's colleague Aline Cholmondeley remembered "a tremendous amount" of matrimonial work, and similar work under the Affiliation Proceedings Act 1957, at East London courts. She testified that probation officers at one time had been expected to give evidence in court - for example, at Old Street - about the sight of bruises, but that the police matron took over this task as it was felt to be invidious for probation officers to be perceived as taking sides in matrimonial disputes. She added that "Fred" Watts, long-serving senior probation officer at Thames Court, had declined to deal with any sexual aspects mentioned by matrimonial complainants without his first calling in a female colleague to join the discussion with the complainant (in a survey in 1954 conducted exclusively among probation officers outside London, Beatrice Pollard found that the reluctance of probation officers in matrimonial cases to focus on the sexual aspects constituted a special handicap in the effectiveness of marital casework). The London probation officer Geoffrey Parkinson, whose involvement with the London service apparently dated from the days of the 1954 Arethusa Camp, later recorded a debt of gratitude to a healer whose work with disturbed marriages went back at least to 1949:

> Dr H.V. Dicks, the doyen of professional matrimonial workers, held generations of probation officer trainees enthralled by his brilliant case studies of broken and unhappy marriages. We sought to imitate his ways, which to my memory involved assisting husbands and wives to see the errors and inaccuracies of their Oedipal ways by methods so subtle and sensitive that even the most painful of insights came as creative experiences.[15]

On meeting matrimonial clients, however, Geoffrey Parkinson frequently discovered that "in the end all they wanted was a summons or a letter ticking their husbands off". In Miss Cholmondeley's experience of matrimonial cases, "no one took out a summons without seeing a probation officer first". This recollection in interview independently corroborated in large measure Marjory Todd's comment: "Most magistrates like probation officers to see intending complainants first; it saves a lot of time." (Also in *The Probation Officer and His World,* published in 1963, Marjory Todd indicated that the work of probation officers included trying to resolve neighbours' quarrels, on which Georgina Stafford recalled probation officers "could waste an incredible amount of time".) Alison Allen remembered having up to twelve matrimonial applications in one Saturday morning at Tower Bridge Magistrates' Court; and Valerie Haig-Brown, who worked for some years at North London Magistrates' Court after her stint at Thames, had a vivid memory of "the waiting-room full of beaten women with their eyes hanging out". In Irene Clarkson's experience, women with matrimonial problems used the probation office as a "safety valve" and - in South London at least - rarely came back to see the probation officer though advised that they could do so.

According to the separate recollections of Georgina Stafford and the clerical assistant Jo Knox, women probation officers, themselves hard pressed, took on nearly all the London Probation Service's matrimonial work in the magistrates' courts. If this was indeed the case, the situation in London seemed rather different to that elsewhere in the country, where, according to Beatrice Pollard, by 1954 "women probation officers were sharing fairly equally in the burden of matrimonial work. The sample shows no appreciable or significant difference in this respect between the sexes." The situation in London may have been partly due to the surviving tendency for female probation officers to work largely with female clients (and by all accounts matrimonial complainants were nearly all female). But it was probably mainly related to the shortage of male officers and the demands of statutory supervision on those male officers who were available.

Miss Braithwaite recalled that the drain of male officers from London during the 1950s arose largely because men - often from the Forces - coming into the service after the War, married or getting married, wanted to start families, but decided to move out of London because of the higher cost of living there (which no doubt more than offset the addition of London allowances). It was certainly difficult for a married male probation officer to support a family on his salary: Miss Stafford vividly remembered that even before the War one such male colleague was forced to buy a pram on hire purchase. In 1976 the London service declared:

> Records show that the reason most frequently given for leaving Inner London is the difficulty of obtaining accommodation. Another is the pressure of work... The third reason most frequently given for resignation is the distance travelled and the time taken in getting to work, a factor clearly related to the problem of accommodation ... for many officers Inner London will continue to be a kind of transit camp. They come to complete their training and gain substantial experience in a short time. Then they marry but find it is impossible to provide a family home, so they leave.

Such pressing material concerns may have encouraged a practical approach to the job. According to John Wheeler (a Conservative M.P. and former assistant prison governor):

> When the probation service was first expanded in the aftermath of the second world war in the '50s and early '60s many of the then probation officers were hands-on people, they were people who served in the Armed Forces of the Crown, they saw their job very often as doing practical very basic things like ensuring that the probationer got up in the morning and went to work in the job that had been found for him.[16]

Derek Borboen, for example, would recall that "we went to court and spoke for our clients".

Miss Stafford would recollect that in the 1950s two male officers at North London Magistrates' Court were each carrying over 130 cases. In September 1956 Miss Winifred Goode (long remembered as a strong-minded senior civil servant at the Home Office) admitted, as would Miss

Braithwaite many years later, that not all the newly qualified probation officers who wanted to work in London could do so because of the Home Office's obligation to ensure that a sufficient number would be available for appointment by provincial probation committees. Early in 1958 the S.J.C.P.O. Minute Book referred to "the increasing pressure of work" during 1957; and Geoffrey Parkinson later reported that "towards the end of the 1950s the London Service was in a depressed state, probably largely because of the low salary scales".[17]

In 1955 N.A.P.O. had apparently become the first body outside the civil service to apply for the introduction of equal pay after the Chancellor of the Exchequer had announced that he intended to introduce it as a general principle in the civil service; and by the summer equal pay for male and female probation officers had been conceded to the probation service in England and Wales, although clerical assistants were still in the process of getting equal pay when Jo Knox joined the London service in 1958. Whatever relief was afforded by the coming of equal pay, it appears that quite a few female probation officers and a smaller number of their male colleagues, in both the juvenile and adult courts of London, had private means (the probation officers of the London service also included at least one known member of the aristocracy). Some women officers - for example, Miss Inman (who retired in 1957, when she felt the service had become "over-organised") and Miss Allen - had chosen to take a drop in salary to join the probation service; and a similar sacrifice was made by one or more clerical assistants - Florence Bradley, for instance - attracted to probation work.

The pressures of the job seemed to be reflected, at least to some extent, in the long hours that probation officers often worked. Elspeth Gray recalled: "we worked up to 70 hours per week." Miss Stafford affirmed that London probation officers used to work six days a week (including Saturday afternoons), though she was one senior who success-fully negotiated a local arrangement with the magistrates (at North London Court) for her team to have Saturday afternoons off. Mrs Margaret Frost and Miss Alison Allen both remembered having to work the whole of Saturday, not to mention Bank Holidays.

It rather seems, from the testimony of retired members of staff, that the London probation officers working the longest hours tended to be single, usually women: Irene Clarkson said that her colleague Miss

Nowell "worked like stink"; Jo Knox revealed that Miss Hamilton at Bow Street worked till 9 or 10 p.m.; and "Bill" Badger (a bachelor and former London police court missionary) was the senior probation officer who, it was said, answered the telephone when it rang at Lambeth Magistrates' Court one Saturday after 7 p.m. Jean Moore recalled of her time as an East London Juvenile Court probation officer:

> 86 New North Road was our office. We were allowed to use our premises very much how we liked... The secretary Dorothy Cox ran groups for the children while they waited to report. Social conditions were also such that the front door was left open till well after 10 p.m. as reporting went on till that time for the adolescents.

The Principal Probation Officer for London noted that "by 1958 the Service in general was seriously overloaded", with higher caseloads and more and more requests for social enquiries from the courts, and the Home Office training scheme unable to keep pace with the escalating nation-wide demand for probation officers. Seldon Farmer indicated that "the precipitating cause" of this overloading was, in his view, "the unprecedented nation-wide increase in crime which began in the year 1956". Openly acknowledging that "many of the pressures and frustrations felt by the London Service during this period arose from the problem of over-work and under-staffing", Farmer added with great candour in his printed report referring to the period from about 1956 onwards:

> Some of these difficulties arise from the sheer size of the London area and the way in which the Probation Service is scattered in groups; groups that are closely linked with their Courts but traditionally find it hard to feel a real sense of awareness of the London Service as an entity. The problem of housing, and the accompanying problem of the cost in time, money and fatigue of travel from the district where reasonably suitable housing can be found to the part of London where the officer works often impose some hardship. The standard of office accommodation and equipment was only gradually recovering from the effect of the various post-war economy measures; and officers who were hard-pressed to find sufficient time to devote to their cases felt a need for more help than was always available with the clerical side of their work. The historical fact of the separation between adult courts and juvenile courts in London, and the assignment of any individual officer to one or the other type of court at any given time, tended to make more difficult the equitable distribution

of caseloads...

Moreover this so-called "specialisation" by officers in adult court or juvenile court work had come to be a discouragement for recruiting to the London Service. ...

The difficulties and pressures inevitably had a harmful effect upon the morale of the officers in London, and upon the quality of work which it was possible for them to achieve. The sense of frustration experienced by the Service was no doubt accentuated by the knowledge that one result of the pressure had been to slow down or even in some respects to stop the impetus towards a development in the quality of casework, the possibility of which had begun to be generally realised.

While Farmer perhaps quite often had less power, influence or freedom of manoeuvre than he was believed to have, there seemed to be mounting dissatisfaction with the Home Office and its perceived remoteness and lack of sensitivity regarding probation officers, the demands of their work, and their legitimate concerns. This feeling was quite dramatically reinforced in 1957 when the Home Office opposed N.A.P.O.'s claim for higher pay for what was now seen as a skilled professional service which, in Frank Dawtry's words, "has long and irregular hours of work, no overtime pay and no political power". It seems clear that London probation officers in particular felt badly let down by the Home Office in view of its special responsibility for the London service. At the same time N.A.P.O. members generally did not appear to lose confidence in their General Secretary, Frank Dawtry, who showed leadership qualities of a high order.

It was against this background that two significant events, affecting the London service, occurred in 1958. The staff side set out its reasons for thinking that the Staff Consultative Council had not proved effective. In view of the size of the London service and the absence of an executive probation committee, the Council was intended to provide a forum for consultation and discussion between members of the London staff and the Home Office, excepting matters relating to the Joint Negotiating Committee or to individual promotion and discipline. The Home Office response was that the existing system was adequate. In June 1958 the London Branch of N.A.P.O. unanimously resolved that "an Action Committee be set up to remedy the present deplorable position in the

London Probation Service". Among London probation officers the forceful John Bradley, the vigorous Harry Kratz and the strong-minded Frank Langham were then voted onto a N.A.P.O. Action Committee, which, Geoffrey Parkinson later suggested, was largely instrumental in fostering official recognition of the service and the need for a reasonable salary scale.

London probation officers also played a fairly active part in contributing to *The Probation Service,* an influential handbook edited on behalf of N.A.P.O. by the probation officer Joan King, and first published in October 1958. Of the 36 persons - nearly all probation officers - who had supplied material or advice for the book, at least half a dozen were former or serving officers of the London Probation Service, viz.: S.G. Boswell; Rose Mary Braithwaite; Fred V. Jarvis (future author of a manual for probation officers); Frank W. Langham; Margaret May; George P. Newton; and C.H. Stanley. Of the book's eleven chapters - all unsigned - two related directly to casework: Chapter 2 (on "Principles and Methods of Social Casework"), which was specifically praised by C.H. Rolph, and Chapter 3 (on "Casework in Probation and Supervision Cases"). Miss Braithwaite in London and Miss Doris Sullivan in Devon jointly drafted each of those two chapters, apparently with Frank Langham and Margaret May reading through sections of the drafts and making helpful comments. Frank Dawtry recorded that the idea of a new book on probation - in succession to the 1935 handbook edited by Lilian Le Mesurier - had first been pressed upon him ten years earlier by Seldon Farmer and Nancy Ralli (both then probation officers in London) when he started his "sentence" as General Secretary of N.A.P.O.

Publication of *The Probation Service* virtually coincided with that of *The Results of Probation,* which revealed the findings of Dr Leon Radzinowicz and his colleagues at the Cambridge Department of Criminal Science in their study of some 9,336 probationers whose probation orders, made by courts in London and Middlesex, terminated between 1948 and 1950. The adopted "decisive test of effectiveness" of probation was unblemished completion of the probation period together with the absence of any reconviction during a three-year follow-up period in each case. By that test, a success rate was claimed of 70.0% for the adults and of 57.9% for the juveniles. It was also found that the general success rate appeared to be "considerably higher" for females than for males, higher for older than for younger probationers, and that - as might be expected -prospects of "success" diminished according to the number of the probationer's previous convictions. Probation orders containing requirements of residence seemed to be relatively unsuccessful. However, breach of a probation order or commission of a further offence did not necessarily mean that the experience of probation had been completely fruitless. In some cases at least, it could suggest that a probation order had been inappropriately made in the first place, particularly perhaps in view of the fact that some 23.3% of the adults and 14.2% of the juveniles had not been remanded for enquiry before being put on probation. Probation would become a measure for adults rather than for juveniles.[18]

The Radzinowicz study - of 5,020 juveniles and 4,316 adults - was marked by a number of omissions. For example, it did not sustain a rigorous analysis of the effectiveness of probation in terms of a comparison with other methods of disposal, with corresponding follow-up periods. There was no assessment of how the rates of success or failure could be related to or affected by (1) probation officers suggesting probation, or (2) any change of supervising officer (on the second point, Basil Henriques had already reported in 1950 that, regarding the juvenile probationer, "we have in London come to an agreement with the Principal Probation Officer of London that London be considered as one area, and that so long as he resides within the London area he shall be under one officer only"). Indeed, the survey did not concern itself with the causes of "success" or "failure". It did not attempt to evaluate - difficult as that may have been - any effects of probation *per se* upon probationers, whose avoidance of criminal behaviour might conceivably be attributable to factors other than, or no less potent than, their experience of probation.

However, the research did broadly confirm the result of a smaller-scale Home Office enquiry in which it was found that of 2,311 offenders put on probation in 1933, 70% committed no further indictable offence in the three years after their probation ended. (George Neve had reported that of the 405 cases under supervision by the Central Criminal Court Probation Officers' Department during 1940 - for example - only 16, or about 4%, completed their supervision unsatisfactorily during that year.) *The Results of Probation* also tended to support the Cambridge Department of Criminal Science's report *Sexual Offences* (1957), which was based on an enquiry, initiated in February 1950, relating to a total of 3,092 sex cases drawn from 14 areas of England and Wales, including London adult and juvenile courts: this report indicated that 16% of the convicted sex offenders studied were put on probation, and of these probationers 70% were not reconvicted of any sort of offence during a period of four years following the making of the probation order.

Ironically, these generally encouraging findings of the Cambridge Department were published during a period (1938-60) when, as the Morison Committee would point out in 1962, the *proportional* use of probation by the courts was declining in England and Wales. Surveying the treatment of offenders aged 17 or over in the 1938-46 period, Edward Smithies contended in 1982: "Wartime shortages of staff and resources also affected policy applied in the courts; there was a marked shift in sentencing away from probation towards prison in more serious cases and fining in less serious ones."[19] This contention seemed consistent with the finding in *Sexual Offences* that fining was used in about 43% of the cases studied - being the most favoured method of disposal - with 25% of all the convicted sexual offenders sent to prison and 16% placed on probation. In 1956 Hermann Mannheim had pointed out that there was a trend in England away from probation towards fines in relation to indictable offences; and in the same year Max Grünhut commented on the treatment of juvenile offenders in England and Wales: "The outstanding feature in the changing trends of treatment practice between pre-war years and the post-war period is a shifting of the emphasis from probation to fines." The Criminal Justice Act, 1948, restricted the imposition of imprisonment on persons under 21; and the apparent trend away from probation towards fining may have been connected with a perceived rise in living standards on the one hand and, on the other, reluctance by magistrates to add to the burdens of hard-pressed probation officers.

One hard-pressed London probation officer, Anthony Forder, found time to analyse the truancy records of some 54 schoolboys who were under his supervision between April 1956 and March 1959. His analysis suggested that school inquiry officers rarely referred persistent truants to a child guidance clinic; and he argued that more care was needed in selecting cases of truancy for referral to the juvenile court (Forder was a juvenile court probation officer in North London for about six years during the 1950s before he joined the staff of the L.S.E.). He concluded:

> We know that truancy is often associated with delinquency... We

do not know the nature or the degree of that association. We do not know how often truancy... indicates a basic defect of personality or social adjustment. Least of all do we know what are the results of different forms of treatment on different types of truancy.[20]

It is not clear whether these concerns were conveyed to the Society of Juvenile Courts Probation Officers (which Forder represented in 1955 to the Association of Workers for Maladjusted Children), or were ventilated in S.J.C.P.O. discussions with head teachers. As a result of a meeting between the Education Officer and the Principal Probation Officer for London, a gathering of representatives of the London Probation Service and of the Standing Joint Advisory Committee, drawn from L.C.C. teachers and education officers, had been held on 15 March 1950 to discuss matters of common interest on an informal basis. Then, in July 1952, S.J.C.P.O. invited some heads to a meeting with probation officers and juvenile court magistrates to further greater understanding and co-operation between day school head teachers and those engaged in juvenile court work; and later conferences of this kind took place each year up to and including 1958, after which they were held on a more local basis.

Forder (future author of the book *Social Casework and Administration*) observed that probation was frequently successful with delinquents because "the combination of control and understanding helps them to realise that authority can be related to their own needs". In 1958 George Newton, an Assistant Principal Probation Officer for London, declared:

> To the offender, the probation officer is a representative of the authority of society and the offender's past experiences with authority, from childhood onwards, will have shaped his attitude to, and expectations of, other authority figures.

Newton suggested that the probation officer needed to show the probationer that "authority is not only power to punish but power to help", and even that

> to provide for many offenders this new and positive experience with authority while at the same time helping them to clarify their feelings about it, is in itself the key to the solution of their difficulties with society.

Such an approach tested the probation officer's own attitude to authority. As Newton had maintained in October 1956:

The authority of the law for which they work has a disturbing effect upon many officers' own feelings about authority. That this has bothered the Service for a long time is clear from the confusion of thinking around the concept of dual loyalties to court or client. ... Until recently training did little to help with this kind of problem and often what casework theory officers had acquired seemed inappropriate to this job.[21]

Eileen Younghusband (S.J.C.P.O. Vice-President, 1941-43) commented:

In the 1950s probation officers were discovering an accord between casework and authority. ...probation officers and other social workers were struggling to analyse the different meanings of authority, the dangers of its use without adequate self-awareness, and the ways in which it might be used constructively... In any event, probation officers were members of an ill-assorted team of magistrates, clerks, the police, lawyers, local authority officials, and prison officers and borstal and approved school staffs. These people with diverse roles, trainings and attitudes also epitomised society's ambivalent attitudes of punishment, deterrence and reform towards offenders.

The writer Sybille Bedford noted in the London magistrates' courts "the same daily teamwork" and a probation officer's "difficult, balanced duty" in giving evidence about a defendant.[22]

Arguably the attitude of at least some probation officers towards authority in general seemed to be reflected in their attitude to the Home Office. Be that as it may, a fairly conciliatory approach was adopted by Norman Grant, N.A.P.O. Chairman and London senior probation officer, when he told the N.A.P.O. Annual Conference on 25 April 1959:

Some of the frustration we feel in regard to the Home Office is not altogether justified... The Police, the Prison Service and the Probation Service all seem to have suffered in recent years from a shortage of manpower... Another factor which has affected the Police, the Prison Service and ourselves has been the steep rise in the number of offenders. This could not have been foreseen and when we blame the Home Office for the abnormally large caseloads that some of us are carrying, we may not be altogether fair, for some of the blame must be due to those factors in the life of our community which have produced more offenders than ever before.

The seminal Home Office Research Unit was in its infancy.

It was against this background that, on 27 May 1959, the Home Secretary (R.A. Butler) and the Secretary of State for Scotland appointed a committee under the chairmanship of Ronald Morison, Q.C., to inquire into and make recommendations on "all aspects of the Probation Service in England and Wales and in Scotland". Such an enquiry had been advocated for some time by N.A.P.O. and friends of the probation service. The committee members included Eileen Younghusband, who had contributed to *The Probation Service* (1958), and who had just finished chairing the Ministry of Health Working Party on Social Workers in the Local Authority Health and Welfare Services. This Working Party's report, published on 4 May 1959, was later described by Anthony Forder as "an important landmark in the development of the social services of this country" - its recommendations included the setting up of a National Council for Social Work Training - though, perhaps understandably in view of its terms of reference, no identified probation officer or probation service body had submitted evidence to it.

In the future a national body of the kind proposed by Younghusband would be able to examine developing social changes associated with economic factors, religious belief and practice, the collapse of empire, race, sexual roles, the family, discipline in the home, and sources of authority generally. Such changes would provide additional challenges to the role and tasks of the probation officer, living, according to the experienced if gloomy London probation officer Joyce Hotham, in "an age which has lost confidence in its future" and "a world of exciting possibilities and terrifying dangers" (*Children At Risk*, Church Information Office, January 1968).

CHAPTER NINE

Morison and After: Towards Wider Horizons, 1959-65

Possibly spurred on by the announcement of the Morison Committee's appointment, the London Probation Service, on or about 1 September, launched a reorganisation of the work of its headquarters unit on a "regional" basis. Under this system the probation staff of the London courts - higher and lower, magistrates' and juvenile - were regarded as being sub-divided geographically into not less than four regions, for each of which general responsibility was exercised by an Assistant Principal Probation Officer, who acted as the normal channel of communication between headquarters and probation officers and their seniors in that region. Farmer thought that the scheme provided "a clear system of devolution of responsibility to maintain the efficiency of the Headquarters unit". This permitted regional meetings of officers - also attended by Farmer or his Deputy, John Washington - on a scale small enough for useful discussion. Arguably this "regionalisation" contained the seeds of the "integration" that would be set in motion regarding probation work in the London juvenile and magistrates' courts. In Farmer's words: "The regional organisation is not a breaking down of the London unit but a step towards a greater cohesion of the London Service as a whole."

In November, 1967, when the "regional organisation" had outlived the London Probation Service it was intended to consolidate, the Assistant Principal Probation Officer Joan Woodward explained the evolution of the regional system:

> The setting up of a Headquarters with principal officers for a unified Service imposed a new concept of belonging to a large Service rather than only to the probation element in a court and it has taken many years and much constant effort to achieve this unity. ...but as the numbers increased the problems of communication also grew and this, coupled with an acute staffing problem, began to produce a concentration on local loyalties and affiliations and morale was

affected. It was against this background that it was decided to increase the numerical strength at Headquarters and to devise the present Regional system. It was felt that ... if London divided into four regions with one member of the H.Q. staff clearly identified in every way with each region there would be a better chance of establishing a Service loyalty and unity with H.Q. This has in fact proved to be the case... [1]

Another attempt to improve the effectiveness of the London Probation Service was marked by the "direct entry" scheme. It seems clear that from about 1958 onwards - during what Seldon Farmer called "the difficult years (1956 to 1959)" - Farmer and his colleagues at headquarters did make a serious, even imaginative attempt to improve the staffing situation. In this he was doubtless assisted by the good relations he fostered with the Home Office. In 1958 a group of men was recruited specifically for appointment to London after undergoing the usual Home Office training, but with some of their practical training in the London service. Then, in the first half of 1959, the London service initiated its own training scheme with a group of eight men and two women (the so-called "A" Group) recruited for a special pre-service training lasting six months from June, followed by appointment to London and continued training in post.

In November 1959 the Liberal leader "Jo" Grimond claimed in the Commons that the normal caseload of a London probation officer was 150 - Butler, the Home Secretary, replied that the average caseload for men officers in London was in fact about 80, but that it was hoped to ease the pressure through recruitment and training schemes. By this time - according to Miss Stafford's recollection soon afterwards - it had become clear that the London service needed about 40 new officers; so in December 1959 a long-term plan (evolved at London Probation Service headquarters) of direct entry combined with adequate in-service training was quickly passed by the London Probation Committee and the Home Office, and was then discussed with the senior probation officers. Under this special training scheme - which evidently enjoyed Butler's approval from the outset - immediate appointment as probation officers in London was to be offered to men over 28 years old selected by the Probation Advisory and Training Board and given training in post (Miss Braithwaite recalled that Seldon Farmer was a member of the selection board). Accordingly, the first group of "direct entrants" - known as the "B"

Group - was formed between February and May 1960, with a second ("C") group starting in early September 1960 and almost immediately taking up duty in the courts, thereby releasing the "B" Group for a period of full-time training.

In an attempt to reconcile the seemingly incompatible needs of immediate assistance in the courts and adequate opportunities for training (equivalent to the one-year Home Office training course for older entrants), it was decided to plan the training as a whole and spread it over a two-year period. The programme was largely organised with the help of the highly regarded and ebullient Miss Kate Lewis, who had both medical and psychiatric social work training and experience, and who had proved a most successful teacher of casework on the Carnegie Course. By 1958 that Course had engendered a manual for supervisors which, although unpublished, was believed to be the first such manual in Great Britain; its authors apparently included Miss Lewis and Miss Braithwaite. Although there was a background of some resistance by London probation officers to compromise of the principle of pre-entry training, the standard of training for the direct entrants was high; and Farmer later expressed particular thanks to Kate Lewis, "whose knowledge, vision, energy and enthusiasm, both as teacher and consultant, have so much enriched the Training Scheme". According to Miss Braithwaite's recollection, Kate Lewis's participation was suggested by George Newton. (Newton became a probation inspector at the Home Office, but later he was brought by Eileen Younghusband and Miss Lewis into the National Institute for Social Work Training, which, with George Pratt as a Governor, they helped to develop from its foundation in 1961. Newton and Miss Braithwaite were among those who assisted Eileen Younghusband in the preparation of her massive *Social Work in Britain: 1950-1975*.)

After a week's orientation course at headquarters (1A Walton Street, S.W.3), the direct entrants were posted to assist experienced officers with the heaviest caseloads. This gave the new recruits a formative "image" of probation work, while the programme as a whole engaged the skills of many more members of the London service than had ever before taken part in training. A preliminary theoretical course, on one day a week, gave the recruits some background knowledge relating to the social sciences and specific teaching about the law, the working of the courts and the functions of the probation officer. Lecturers - among them members of headquarters staff and other London probation officers - contributed to this course, which also featured special films and visits of observation. Nicholas Rivett-Carnac, who became one of the first direct entrants after years in the Army and the City, remembered his lecturers as including Kate Lewis ("very caring"), George Newton ("able"), and probably Dr Peter Scott. He and his fellow students visited prisons, borstals, approved schools and psychiatric units of hospitals, sat in on some interviews conducted by seasoned probation officers, had about four probation clients each, and took examinations in law and casework.

The direct entrants may also have benefited from seeing the weekly television series "Probation Officer", an Associated Television production transmitted for exactly three years from September 1959 onwards. Set in London, the series dramatised episodes in the lives of three fictional probation officers - two men (a newly joined ex-Army officer and a senior probation officer) and a woman officer (played by the glamorous Honor Blackman). It seemed odd at the time that ATV did not apparently consult the Home Office, N.A.P.O. or the London Probation Service headquarters before putting on the series. Although *TV Times* disclosed that "probation officers have advised on the production of these stories", characterised by "care for accuracy", the identity of these officers was a secret closely guarded by the television authorities. Many years later, Charles Morgan revealed in interview that he and Harry Kratz - both with experience as London probation officers - had been advisers for the programmes. The series generated some criticisms from probation officers, resulting in Frank Dawtry's dissociating N.A.P.O. from the fiction of the programmes and complaining about the presentation of a cynical attitude of probation staff towards a matrimonial problem (at a time when some 75,000 people a year consulted probation officers on marriage problems), and also about the use of notepaper headed "London Probation Service"; while questions were raised in Parliament towards the end of 1959 by Conservative M.P.s who claimed that one of the programmes had denigrated prison officers at Wormwood Scrubs. The London probation officers Marjory Todd and Gunter Lubowski both indicated - quite independently of each other - that probation officers tended to be compared unfavourably with their fictional counterparts in the TV series. But at least the series, in the words of Marjory Todd (who was also a broadcaster for the B.B.C.), "has brought them and their work before a much wider public" and, in Anthony Forder's estimation, "despite some weaknesses seems to have been useful in improving public relations".

A further stage in public education was marked by the Second United Nations Congress on the Prevention of Crime and the Treatment of Offenders. This was held in London between 8 and 20 August 1960; and London Probation Service participants were: Brian Carter, Ronald Davies, Valerie Haig-Brown and Georgina Stafford (all clearly described as from North London Magistrates' Court); Miss Ethel Currant (North London Juvenile Court); John Dunphy (senior probation officer, County of London Sessions); Miss Betty Edelson; Miss Elsie Errington; Donald Houston; Mrs Hazel Houston; Miss Colette Size; and Mrs Mary Westland.

The Congress considered, *inter alia,* questions relating to the origins, prevention and treatment of juvenile delinquency, some of whose aspects, in a British context, also concerned the Ingleby Committee on Children and Young Persons, whose Report was published in October. A Society of Juvenile Courts Probation Officers committee had gone to a lot of trouble in submitting written evidence to the Ingleby Committee (whose members included an Honorary Member of S.J.C.P.O., Dr Peter Scott). Miss Margaret Dawkins had been the S.J.C.P.O. representative on the N.A.P.O. committee preparing evidence for the Ingleby Committee; and the four N.A.P.O. representatives who (unlike S.J.C.P.O.) gave oral evidence included one seasoned London probation officer, E.G. Pratt.

George Pratt had also been Chairman of the sub-committee which prepared the N.A.P.O. evidence for the Minister of Education's Albemarle Committee on the Youth Service in England and Wales. In preparing evidence for the Albemarle Committee - which reported by February 1960 - Pratt had been helped by a memorandum by Derek Borboen, whose influence might be discerned in N.A.P.O.'s appeal to the Committee that special attention should be given to the "unclubbables". The London Probation Service *per se* did not give any evidence to these Committees.

London probation officers had no doubt co-operated with the L.C.C. remand home psychiatrist Dr T.C.N. Gibbens in his study (published in October 1959) of 185 girls placed on probation or otherwise under supervision after being sent to a remand home. His study had led him to the tentative view that an extension in the number and type of alternative homes provided by hostels, residential jobs, foster parents, etc., was preferable to earlier or more frequent committal to approved school for such girls. He concluded: "Wayward adolescent girls seem to need more than any others the supervision of the most experienced, skilful and sympathetic probation officers. Eight years' experience at the remand home certainly convinces one that the London courts are particularly well served in this respect."[2]

However, appearance in a London juvenile court, followed by probation, had seemed an ordeal for Walter ("Angel Face") Probyn: in 1941, at the age of nine, with no previous police record, he had been charged with the larceny of a tin of peas from an abandoned East End cafe and taken to court, where he observed that "some of the children emerged weeping, some screaming, the hard faces of the officials showed no suggestion of sympathy". Up to a point this case seemed to illustrate the Ingleby Committee's recommendation that the minimum age of criminal responsibility should be raised from eight to twelve, with provision for wayward or delinquent children, including those under twelve, to be brought to court as "being in need of protection or discipline" (S.J.C.P.O. apparently favoured raising the age of criminal responsibility to eleven). The Committee also proposed that a unified family service should be developed, and, as regards approved schools, that "the principal agents for carrying out after-care supervision should be the probation service and the local children's authorities".

Another recommendation of the Ingelby Committee was that "every effort should be made to provide more suitable accommodation, including the provision of adequate ancillary accommodation, where juvenile courts are at present inadequately housed". A *Daily Telegraph* reporter who investigated the London juvenile courts in the light of the Ingleby Report found "an appalling hotchpotch of antiquated buildings, including church and school halls and basement premises". At St Mark's Church Hall, Greenwich ("the worst London court I saw"), "probation officers did not have a room in which to meet parents and children. A girl who ran from the court in tears was followed by a woman probation officer, who tried to comfort her under the eyes of a score of peeping parents." (In 1941 S.J.C.P.O. had called for better accommodation at the London juvenile courts.)

In November 1960, Ruth Morrah, a Chairman of the Metropolitan Juvenile Courts, declared: "Since these courts were inaugurated in 1908 not one single juvenile court has been built in London." She added:

In London, at least, the whole system is moving towards crisis and collapse. ...the probation service is already over-burdened and new recruits of the right type are not forthcoming. ... For lack of remand centres and because of pressure on the remand homes, where it is costly both of staff and money to provide maximum security, it becomes inevitable for unruly or depraved young persons to go to prison. ...There is a waiting list for most of the approved schools... Five years ago, when delinquency showed signs of declining, a number of approved schools were closed... The present increase in delinquency has therefore found the Home Office unprepared. ...There is a long delay in obtaining appointments at child guidance clinics. ...Because of the shortage of staff probation officers are carrying intolerable case loads: that one man should supervise from 60 to 80 cases is an impossibility and yet these few dedicated people are everywhere in London trying to cope with the impossible. Even if the probation service was adequately paid probation would still be the cheapest method of dealing with delinquency.[3]

(Some months earlier, the S.J.C.P.O. Chairman, Miss Margaret Muckersie, had written to the Home Secretary to express the Society's concern at the holding of girls under seventeen in Holloway Prison.)

For years the daily "beauty parade" of prostitutes in the London magistrates' courts had resulted in their being fined 40 shillings each (their children sometimes came to the notice of probation officers through "care or protection" proceedings, as Mrs Marjorie Watts would recall).[4] But as a result of the Street Offences Act, 1959, prostitutes seemed to vanish overnight from the London streets; though the British writer John St John noted in 1961 that "there are pockets of semi-amateur prostitution based on the drabber type of private drinking club". Towards the end of 1959 the L.C.C. had sought S.J.C.P.O. support (with evidence of the social evils which undesirable clubs represented) for its proposed legislation for more effective control of drinking clubs. Ronald Howell and Derek Shuttleworth (formerly Borboen) worked hard, in the time available, to collect such evidence - which, in fact, related to Stepney - on behalf of S.J.C.P.O.; and Marie Buxton reported to fellow S.J.C.P.O. members that young girls were being encouraged to become "hostesses" in undesirable clubs.

The research of D.J. West and D.P. Farrington, based on an ongoing study of 41 London working-class lads between 1961 and 1971, suggested that official delinquents tended to come from larger, low-income families, often with parents who themselves had criminal records and whose parental behaviour was considered to be poor. Elizabeth Inman - who felt that many delinquents did not receive the caring they needed, as a consequence of their being in too large families - remembered two boys before Lambeth Juvenile Court: behind them sat their respective mothers, one of whom had 20 children, and the other 19. Maurice O'Mahoney - later known as "King Squealer" after he had informed on "more than 200 crooks" - came from a Paddington family with five children, marked by matrimonial strife and also maternal violence directed towards him: early in 1959 at the age of eleven, he was placed on probation to "Mr McGregor, a kindly Scot who over those two years did all he could to try and help me. ...Mr McGregor soon realised that my family life was a nightmare and he became my first real friend. He was one of those few people who would listen to me." On at least two separate occasions at West London Magistrates' Court during the 1950s Police Constable "Joe" Nixon (later a prison probation officer) was present when it emerged that the father of the young male offender in the dock also had a criminal record and, indeed, was no stranger to prison.

Years before police juvenile liaison schemes could be regarded as in any way widespread in London, P.C. Nixon helped to run a youth club in Clarendon Road, Notting Hill, called the Quest, which enjoyed the support of a West London juvenile court probation officer (and former approved school housemaster) like Anton Wallich-Clifford, who had four of his probationers as members there at the same time. Quest members included lads who were from remand home, approved school or borstal, or on probation. When on the beat, Nixon "would keep a special eye open for boys he knew to be on probation. He would mention the club and invite them to come along."[5]

Nixon resigned from the police force many months before the rioting in Notting Hill and other areas of London during the summer of 1958. The second episode of the TV series "Probation Officer", focusing on "the colour problem in Notting Hill", depicted "Teddy Boys" with a razor tormenting and threatening an unarmed black youth. Of the scores of white thugs and hooligans fined or imprisoned for their part in the disturbances, it is not now clear how many were or had been under statutory supervision by London probation officers (a similar point applies to the rioting with racial overtones in Deptford in July 1949 and to the racial skirmishes in Camden Town in August 1954). From the recollections of interviewees it would appear that these disturbances had no discernible impact on the London Probation Service *per se*, though they probably heightened awareness of racial issues among individual London probation officers, who seemed to have very few non-white clients at this time. A probation officer - thought to be Miss B.K. Crofton, who lived and worked in West London - was among the group of local people (mainly religious leaders and community and social workers) who in November 1960 decided to form the Notting Hill Social Council, in the wake of the 1958 race riots. The Social Council held monthly meetings to provide a forum for the discussion and co-ordinated tackling of local problems[6]; and according to Gunter Lubowski's recollection, its members (who, he suggested, included his West London colleague Mr R. McGregor, as well as himself) joined through individual subscription.

Meanwhile, in May 1960, Mrs Kit Russell, Social Science Department Practical Work Organiser at the L.S.E., had told London probation officers supervising practical work placements for social science students: "it is very important to help these basic course students to get a picture of the area they are working in, of the different elements in the community you serve - new housing estates, movements of population, racial problems, etc."[7] This was at a time when the London probation officer Anton Wallich-Clifford (who had transferred in 1959 to Bow Street Magistrates' Court, with its notably high number of N.F.A., or no fixed abode, cases) realised that "we were only seeing the tip of the iceberg of homelessness... a whole world existed of which only a very few knew anything at all". A visit to the Rev. Bertram Peake's Golborne Centre in the Notting Hill area led to the probation officer's "cramming his unique and never-to-be-forgotten 'hostel-in-a-church' with homeless Bow Street clients". The Roman Catholic probation officer got on very well with the Free Congregational minister, whose Golborne Centre for homeless offenders had in effect started in 1957 as a spontaneous act of charity to provide short-term care for lonely men newly discharged from London prisons. Wallich-Clifford became one of the Centre's trustees; and he became involved in the Golborne River Venture in 1961, when a party of Golborne residents was taken for a week on the Thames in three launches. A fellow Golborne Executive Committee member, Jo Knox, helped Wallich-Clifford by typing the manuscript of his printed pamphlet *One*

Man's Answer (1962) about the exuberant "Bram" Peake and his Centre: with a foreword by J.R.T. Hooper, metropolitan stipendiary magistrate at Tower Bridge, this pamphlet indicated that clients were referred to the Golborne Centre by probation officers at Bow Street, Clerkenwell, Lambeth, Marylebone, North London and West London Magistrates' Courts and the County of London Sessions.

In an apparent attempt "to follow-up the work commenced by Merfyn Turner", whom he admired, Wallich-Clifford in 1961 conceived and helped to set up the Voluntary Hostels Conference (later the National Association of Voluntary Hostels). Indeed, Wallich-Clifford's growing campaign on behalf of the homeless and rootless, "dossers" and "jakies" (meths drinkers), served to complement the endeavours of a social worker like Merfyn Turner on behalf of ex-prisoners and others. In 1961 Turner published two works on Norman House, which he had conceived, named after the "Normanhurst" of the Barge Boys' Club, and opened in 1954 in Highbury as a "friendly community" and home for men who were N.F.A. on release from prison. Initially nearly all the Norman House residents came from Pentonville, where Turner was a prison visitor; and from an early stage Norman House staff worked closely with London probation officers, who referred clients and supplied "well documented reports". Merfyn Turner later recalled that quite a few members of staff or students who came to Norman House became probation officers.

Turner was among those interviewed or consulted on behalf of the Pakenham/Thompson Committee, whose report *Problems of the Ex-Prisoner* was published in 1961. Others who gave evidence to the Committee included the London probation officers Jack Frost (Old Bailey) and Barry Swinney (referred to as based at Old Street). The son of a hospital matron, stepson of a doctor and stepbrother of a nursing sister, Swinney was a leading figure in the London Probation Service's contribution to the campaign against alcoholism. It became apparent to him that problems associated with alcohol had played a major part in the lives of many clients he came across, with inadequate facilities for treatment in most cases; and it is understood that his meeting the Rev. Donald Soper provided a catalyst for the opening in September 1959 of St Luke's House, Wincott Street, S.E.11 - under the aegis of the West London Mission - as, in Swinney's estimation, Britain's first hostel specifically for alcoholics.

At a time when F.T. Giles, the probation-minded Chief Clerk at Clerkenwell Magistrates' Court, noted that a probation order could include a requirement to take the pledge[8], Swinney discovered that there were many alcoholics of both sexes who could be helped without interruption to their employment or home life, provided that they had relatives or friends willing to visit a clinic with them and support their rehabilitation generally. This in turn resulted in Swinney being instrumental in founding the Regent Street Clinic, which was opened in September 1962. The clinic enjoyed the active support of the Chief Metropolitan Stipendiary Magistrate, Sir Robert Blundell, with whom the ever extrovert Swinney discussed alcohol-related cases coming before Bow Street Magistrates' Court, where both men now worked. The clinic was made possible thanks to the generous offer, on a gratuitous basis, of the evening use of premises at the New Gallery Centre in Regent Street and also of the services of a doctor in attendance, later joined by a trained nurse, pharmacist, social workers and voluntary helpers. Regarded as a "family unit alcoholic clinic" offering free medical treatment and social rehabilitation in a receptive and friendly atmosphere, the Regent Street Clinic attracted "a very broad cross-section of cases drawn from widely differing socio-economic backgrounds", with fewer than half the patients having any history of delinquency.

For years the Family Discussion Bureau within the Tavistock Clinic provided in-service training in marital counselling for probation officers and other social workers. Arrangements were made for Lily Pincus of the Bureau to address London senior probation officers on 19 November 1960 on "Psychological Background to the Marriage Relationship". Following a suggestion made by the London Branch of N.A.P.O., an experiment started in 1962 in which a group of London probation officers from both adult and juvenile courts, with consultative help from the Family Discussion Bureau, met to try as a group to extend casework skills in matrimonial conciliation. Divorce was still relatively difficult to obtain; but from about 1962 onwards there seemed to be a progressive decline in the volume of matrimonial conciliation work undertaken by the probation service - a process that Roy Bailey in 1979 would associate in part with "the extension in 1961 of Legal Aid to applicants in summary matrimonial proceedings".[9] However, a growing questioning and debate about sexual behaviour in relation to the law - a feature of British life in the early 1960s - seemed to be reflected in "C" Group discussions (facilitated by the

London probation officer Mr J.D. Houston), which focused, *inter alia*, on issues associated with adultery, masturbation and homosexuality. The only case suggesting transvestism that has come to light regarding a London probation officer during the period under review was one involving the West London probation officer Miss Cecil Barker, who -according to the court clerk Stanley French - unwittingly recommended probation for a prostitute who turned out to be a man. French (who retired in 1967) paid tribute to London's probation officers, who "worked very hard for inadequate pay both at mending marriages and at helping offenders against the criminal law to go straight; they suffered many disappointments and received few thanks but never lost heart."

Home visiting had long been recognised as an important part of a probation officer's work, with its different aspects and purposes being emphasized at different times and under different conditions. Georgina Stafford recalled that during the Second World War home visiting was often limited to enabling probation officers to check on whether clients were living at home or not. In his pilot study of 25 male probation officers (ten from London - drawn equally from juvenile and adult courts - with five each from Middlesex, Hertfordshire and Essex), Anthony Forder made some interesting comments on the practice of home visiting during the early 1960s:

> individual officers also were much less systematic both in the time they gave to visiting and in their policy for it... If the officer had a positive attitude to visiting, he generally spent at least five hours per week in the evening on this. ...Several officers said they visited less than they used to, that they were being more discriminating about whom they visited, and usually spent longer on the visits that they did do. ...the purpose of home visiting was rarely discussed in a positive way with probationers.[10]

For the London probation officer Marjory Todd, "home visiting is an important part of getting to know any probationer... Unless the probation officer can get to know the parents and the home from which the child comes it would be impossible to grasp the reasons for his behaviour in the outside world."

Home visits were facilitated by the provision of motor cars. Service motor cars became available for London officers from 1959 onwards -initially on an experimental basis - with the fleet being increased to 13 to permit official use of a car by officers who did not have cars of their own. From 1961 onwards, London officers wishing to use their own motor cars while on duty benefited both from an "essential user" scale of allowances and from official car loans. By March 1963, 21 London officers had purchased cars with the assistance of these loans, with a total of 122 London officers using their cars for official purposes. At about the same time a scheme was instituted to help officers with the cost of travel between home and work centre.

Under the Metropolitan Magistrates' Courts Act of 1959, the Receiver for the Metropolitan Police District was empowered to hold land and buildings for the probation service in London. It seems that during this period Peter Shervington at head office devised a plan, extending over some 20 years, for continual refurbishment of the London service's office accommodation, tied in with new court building and augmented from other sources. The plan involved consultation with the Receiver's Office, the London Probation Committee and the Home Office. Shervington was determined to improve the standard of office accommodation, bearing in mind that when he joined the London Probation Service just after the War probation offices tended to be in run-down little houses in back streets or over shops. Often the accommodation was cramped and spartan; not infrequently the toilet was the only place to wash a cup or make a pot of tea. Perhaps clerical assistants - who spent more time in such offices than probation officers or clients - were the most conscious of such conditions. Certainly Jo Knox, who worked as a relief clerical assistant in virtually every London probation office between 1958 and 1963, would vividly recall the probation offices of her early days: "offices that gave the overall impression of overcrowding, darkness and black -black tables, black typewriters, dark green filing cabinets, dark lino on the floor and usually dirty dark cream paint on the walls." Frances Finlay, mother of an adolescent delinquent, would describe a London probation office she visited in the early 1960s as "cheerless" and "abysmally bleak".

But already the situation was beginning to improve. Apparently by the end of 1958 the first purpose-built office block for the London Probation Service had been erected at 21 Harper Road, S.E.1, to meet the needs of the probation officers at the County of London Sessions. By 1962 a basic standard of furnishing and equipment for offices had been agreed and was being implemented, with new furniture, more brightly decorated offices, flexibility in painting, in colours, in curtains, and so on. These changes were welcomed by Marjory Todd in *Ever Such A Nice Lady,* published in March 1964 and partly based on her experiences at Bow Street.

To facilitate secretarial assistance, dictation machines were first provided in the London offices in 1958 - by March 1963, 59 such machines were in use - and referring to her time at the 373A Brixton Road office between 1959 and 1963, the clerical assistant Lydia Blackman would recall:

> It was also during this period that the Service introduced the use of Philips' stenorette dictating machines, and I well remember the astonished looks of some of our clients when they peered through our reception window to look at what one of them described as 'four doctors typing' as we listened through our stethoscope-like ear pieces.

During 1961 posts of senior clerical assistant were introduced in the larger offices, thereby relieving senior probation officers of direct or immediate responsibility for the organisation and supervision of the work of the clerical staff. (Appendix 20 lists duties of senior probation officers in London, as agreed by 1959 at an official seniors' meeting.) By about the end of 1962 there were 85 full-time (including ten senior clerical assistants and five telephonists) and 33 part-time clerical assistants. With any shortages being made up by relief or agency typists, the accepted ratio of clerical and secretarial assistance had become one full-time clerical assistant to two probation officers. By February 1965 full-time clerical assistants worked 38 hours per week (exclusive of lunch breaks), were entitled to 13 days annual leave, and received up to about £800 a year.

According to Eileen Younghusband, the probation service during the 1950s experienced "a period of rapid development in staffing ... sometimes achieving a standard of office accommodation and clerical assistance not gained by the other social services until later". To the extent that this was true of the London service, achieving this standard may well have been facilitated by the London Probation Service's special relationship with the Home Office, and perhaps by London's position as the capital. The momentum for new and better office accommodation and resources arose partly from a rising tide of post-war expectations in many fields, and partly from the specific need to cater for the rapidly expanding number of probation staff in London (between 1946 and 1959 the London Probation Service nearly doubled in size).

The need for improved office accommodation was associated in London with the move towards integration of the work of probation officers serving the magistrates' and juvenile courts. Peter Shervington recalled years later that the amalgamation of adult and juvenile courts' probation teams started from considerations of office accommodation; while the Home Office[11] would report that this amalgamation was sometimes "delayed because suitable offices were not available". Integration was discussed in April 1959 by S.J.C.P.O. at a meeting at which Miriam Kratz (Chelsea Juvenile Court) and Eileen Boyland (formerly an adult court officer) played a leading part. This was followed, on 27 May 1960, by Seldon Farmer's address to S.J.C.P.O. on Home Office policy on integration and accommodation, with particular reference to a proposed scheme of amalgamation at Old Street. Then, in December 1961 - the month Sir Basil Henriques died - there began what both Farmer and the Home Office called "an experiment" in the integration of the work of probation officers serving the Old Street Magistrates' Court and the corresponding part of the East London Juvenile Court area. The two teams of officers involved - no doubt with more than a hint of mixed feelings - were amalgamated in a newly acquired, large block of offices at 350 Old Street, E.C.1, under the leadership of two seniors, "Stan" Ratcliffe and "Peggy" Thornborough, who organised the work in the adult court and juvenile court respectively.

This amalgamation was reinforced by a similar reorganisation in November 1962, when probation officers serving North London Magistrates' Court and the corresponding juvenile court area moved from their respective offices into new leased accommodation at 67A Stoke Newington Road, N.16, named Edridge Chambers, after the former Croydon court clerk (whereas the Croydon probation officer and N.A.P.O.'s first Secretary, George Warren, who, according to Lord Feversham, had inspired Edridge, seemed to receive far less recognition from probation officers[12]).

While the courts concerned had to accustom themselves to service from a larger number of probation officers, the integrated method of working was steadily extended to Balham, South Western, Thames and

Clerkenwell Courts. Frank Monk, who transferred from probation work in Derbyshire to London, recalled the atmosphere of excitement at the Commercial Road office (serving Thames Court) in about 1964:

> On my arrival everybody was agog to tell me that they were now an integrated office. I was puzzled upon hearing that the cause of their excitement was that *now* they were dealing with both adults and juveniles and were actually attending both types of court. It seemed unkind not to hail this as a remarkable case of London leading from behind.

C. Roy Barr - who joined the London service in 1966, when the process of integration was still incomplete - recalled that juvenile court probation officers seemed more against integration than adult court officers. (Another incomplete area of integration was that of gender in probation work: Irene Edmonds would recall that when she started work at Marylebone Magistrates' Court in 1962, the male and female probation officers had their rooms on separate floors. However, at Bow Street Anton Wallich-Clifford "dodged continuously" the "regulation" that male officers could not supervise women or girls - a requirement repealed by the Criminal Justice Act, 1967, s.55.)

Years later there was still a feeling among some London probation officers that probation work in the juvenile court called for some degree of specialisation (rather as child psychiatry was a specialised area of psychiatry). On the other hand, the clerical assistant Lydia Blackman would write of the integration she experienced in South London in 1963 that "in many ways this made sense, as so often there was more than one probation office involved in some families" (nor was it unknown for officers to be unaware that others were involved in such cases). Certainly integration seemed to make sense in the light of the Children and Young Persons Act, 1969, which transferred much work from probation officers in juvenile courts to local authority social workers. The integration process was taking place at a time when, in Britain at least, childhood seemed in many ways to be a contracting phase of life. Arguably integration enabled the personal and emotional development of clients to be seen much more as a continuum.

If integration was bringing London into line with practice elsewhere, the Streatfeild Committee was laying the foundations of a national policy regarding the role and status of the probation officer as a professional adviser of the criminal courts at every administrative level. In London at least, the Streatfeild Committee's recommendations, published in February 1961, generated quite a considerable increase in social enquiry work, particularly perhaps as regards pre-trial reports; and its proposal that probation officers should be able to offer opinions on offenders' suitability for various forms of sentence resulted - as George Pratt, an Assistant Principal Probation Officer for London, would point out - in probation officers becoming much more positively involved in the decision-making processes of the courts. Referring to probation officers' tasks, the criminologist Nigel Walker would declare in 1972: "Some of these responsibilities - such as making social inquiries for courts - were acquired between the wars, although they have grown in scope since then."[13]

The Streatfeild Committee seemed attuned to the concept of treatment rather than to that of problem management. It also recommended a handbook for sentencers (first issued by the Home Office in 1964 as *The Sentence of the Court*). Similarly, by 1959 the London Probation Service had issued its probation officers with a staff handbook, presumably in accordance with advice such as that elaborated by *In-service Training in Social Welfare,* published by the United Nations, with which Seldon Farmer had become associated. According to Doris Sullivan's recollection, the handbook was compiled by her colleague Miss Joan Woodward, an Assistant Principal Probation Officer in London, and contained a wealth of information, e.g. on procedure relating to new legislation, borstal licences, conditions of residence, and use of the poor box: it also set out the duties of senior probation officers as interpreted by the London Probation Committee. Such a handbook, which may well have boosted a sense of professional identity, certainly seemed to reflect the growing complexity of the criminal justice system and the bureaucratisation and professionalisation of the probation service.

The influential Streatfeild Report (curiously disregarded in Jarvis's 1972 history of the probation service) was considered by a committee of London seniors. It was evidently published too late to be assessed by John St John in his book *Probation - The Second Chance* (1961), much of which had been drafted by March 1960. Although St John took considerable care to disguise the identity of individuals and courts, his book was in fact largely based on his observations, discussions with probation officers and clients, and unprecedented access to confidential probation case-records at North London Magistrates' Court, where, with official approval, he was based for many months, under the wing of Miss Stafford and her colleagues. His book did not discuss probation officers' working conditions, probation service involvement in the juvenile courts, or the possibilities of integration; nor was it a history of the service. But it gave a generally favourable view of probation. Like Joan King's *The Probation Service,* he suggested that the existence of the Welfare State enabled officers to concentrate more on clients' inner conflicts and emotional problems. This modest, sensitive and lovable man - he was a London councillor with a keen sense of social justice - described probation officers as "determined, often desperate, guardian angels supplied by the Welfare State".

In September 1959 (in an article later used by Eileen Younghusband) Miss Braithwaite had maintained: "Nor, in the public mind, does a court have a welfare function. It exists to punish wrongdoers; it cannot claim to be part of the Welfare State. Probation officers are, therefore, not so easily recognisable as people with a helping function as are almoners or psychiatric social workers." In April 1961 her colleague Doris Sullivan affirmed:

> Increasingly in the minds of enlightened authority the role of the Courts is a reformative one... Even those who are perhaps aware of needing help find that help offered to them by someone who represents the very authority with which they may be in conflict... Many have been the failures of other social agencies ... sometimes it is the worker's warm acceptance and sincere concern which fertilises their capacity to redirect their resources into more desirable channels.

No doubt Miss Sullivan spoke for others in the London service as well as for herself. Certainly the views of many London probation officers were presented in a summarised form by Claude Fubini, Chairman of N.A.P.O.'s London Branch, in October 1961, when he declared: "The authoritarian setting in which we work is unlike that of most other social case-work... We endeavour to assist the development of an atmosphere where anxiety and aggression for instance can be brought by the client without fear of rejection." After noting "a wide measure of discretion" in reporting a breach of probation to the magistrate, Fubini stated:

> ...there is general agreement that the community does expect us to exercise a measure of "control" rather than punishment... We, as

probation officers, know our position is one of authority which we do
not always care to use with our clients but feel no hesitation in using
with other agencies on their behalf.[14]

One test of attitudes to authority was provided by the Committee of
100, which, officially launched in October 1960, aimed to develop a
movement based on non-violent mass civil disobedience as part of a wider
campaign for unilateral nuclear disarmament in Britain. Lord Russell,
Britain's most famous contemporary philosopher - who had supported
the Golborne Centre for ex-prisoners - was sent to prison from Bow Street
at the age of 89. But no evidence has emerged of any specific professional
involvement by London probation officers in unilateralist cases passing
through the courts at this time. However, issues associated with law
enforcement were considered by three official bodies to which London
probation officers made representations, and which published reports
during the first half of 1962. Miss M.D. Samuels gave evidence to the
Royal Commission on the Police; S.J.C.P.O. and N.A.P.O. gave evidence
to the Aarvold Committee, appointed to consider measures to facilitate
integration of the metropolitan magistrates' courts and the petty sessional
courts in London (S.J.C.P.O. condemned "the appalling conditions in
most of the Juvenile Courts in London" and suggested breaking down
court areas, with the opening of more local courts); and in March 1962 the
Morison Report was published.

Although concerned with all aspects of the probation service in
England, Wales and Scotland, the Morison Committee included some
members who had served as London magistrates (such as Harold Sturge,
who, according to Charles Kray, had placed his infamous twin brothers
on probation at Old Street in the early 1950s). Its report featured one
whole chapter on the London Probation Service, which, it pointed out,
was "by a substantial margin, the largest probation service in Great
Britain". Hardly surprisingly, the Committee received separate evidence
from N.A.P.O.'s London Branch, whose representatives - apart from
Frank Dawtry - comprised Charles Balchin, Claude Fubini, Ronald
Howell (who in 1960 became Deputy General Secretary of the London
Police Court Mission), and Georgina Stafford (who at one stage was
appointed to act as spokesman). The Committee also received independent
evidence from London Probation Service senior probation officers,
represented by John Bradley, Rosemary Deane and John Dunphy.

Seldon Farmer gave oral evidence only, and the London Probation Service Clerical Association gave written evidence only. The nine national representatives of N.A.P.O. - which at this time appeared to be the professional social work association with the largest membership in Britain - included the London probation officers Rose Mary Braithwaite (who drafted a history of the London Probation Service for submission to the Committee) and Alison Allen. The four representatives of the Association of Social Workers included its Chairman, the London probation officer George Pratt. Perhaps unwisely, the Society of Juvenile Courts Probation Officers declined an invitation to present evidence to the Morison Committee, "as most S.J.C.P.O. members were serving on N.A.P.O. Sub-Committees preparing evidence".

In its written evidence N.A.P.O. declared: "London officers feel that no positive case can be made for retaining the present position in London whereby the Service comes under the direct control of the Home Office." It added that London Branch firmly recommended the setting up of a London Probation Committee "with full executive powers under the chairmanship of a magistrate who is in day to day touch with the work of the courts". London senior probation officers felt that they had special interests and a point of view of their own, independent of the Principal Probation Officer (seen as a spokesman for the Home Office) and of N.A.P.O. (of which many of the 24 London seniors were apparently not members). A London Probation Committee "with full executive power" was proposed by the London seniors, who also suggested that the Principal Probation Officer should have the duty of publishing an annual report. The seniors, who stressed that their responsibilities were much wider than was commonly supposed, did not propose any new or marked prioritisation, discarding or augmenting of a senior's duties. Their memorandum of evidence did not mention the Assistant Principal Probation Officers (who did not have clients, even if, as Stanley Ratcliffe would recall, A.P.P.O.s in the 1950s "did not have clear-cut functions"), or the seniors' relationship to them or to the Deputy Principal Probation Officer (a second post of D.P.P.O. - with mainly administrative duties -would be created in London in 1961). Their evidence seemed rather more concerned with the senior's authority - in largely conventional terms -than with his or her role as an authority in more than one field.

The seniors associated a deterioration in staff morale with the role of the Home Office in the administration of the London Probation Service. They criticised

> the extent to which the Home Office imposed its will on the service without effective consultation... There is a staff council and there have been regular meetings of the seniors but they have been felt to be ineffective. It was the experience of seniors that with regard to training and in-training their needs, and their position as senior, were not recognised. ... There followed an official policy in which the emphasis appeared to be on the professional superiority of the newer officers which was seen to reflect badly on the seniors and the older officers generally. ... It is felt that the Home Office and headquarters are too remote to be able to understand the day-to-day difficulties of the courts... In courts where a second senior has been appointed, a difficult administrative situation has been created through the failure of the Home Office to designate one as being in charge.

(Margaret Frost would recall that from about 1964 onwards there seemed to be a tendency, if not a policy, for young seniors to be appointed in London - though when Miss Braithwaite became a senior in 1946, at not more than 32, she may well have been the youngest in the country at that time, in joint terms of age and length of service.)

The London seniors added that the salary scale in the probation service "does not sufficiently take into account its skill and importance and the demands made on the time and family life of the probation officer, particularly in London where hours of travelling and the higher proportion of evening work are so common" (though long travelling times, for example, were not, of course, unique to the London service). The senior probation officer "is paid very much less than the executive officer in the clerk's office"; and "the increase of a mere £5 per annum which comes to a probation officer receiving his maximum pay who is promoted to a senior post ... is insufficient recognition of the increase in status and responsibility". At the same time the Receiver for the Metropolitan Police District was criticised for his "exasperating economies".

No doubt conscious of the probation service's roles as a filter and as an agent of reconciliation, N.A.P.O.'s London Branch felt that the service's resources should be augmented and caseloads limited, but that after-care, guardian *ad litem* enquiries and "consent to marry" and affiliation cases exemplified legitimate work for probation officers. The number and functions of probation officers had grown considerably, certainly since the War, and in about the early 1960s Farmer declared: "although fortunately we still have a great many individualists in the Service we are more aware than in the past of being a *Service* with a corporate responsibility" (his emphasis). Believing that administration, communication and casework were very largely interdependent in the service, he felt that a senior probation officer had a responsibility with, to and for his or her colleagues.[15]

From N.A.P.O.'s evidence to the Committee it would appear that, in London at least, the supervisory function of case committees - which at one time seemed to provide the only mechanism for supervising officers' work - was exercised infrequently in many instances. However, case committee meetings were held once every six months for each London juvenile court probation officer. Moreover, case committees met regularly at the Central Criminal Court and the London Sessions, where the attached probation officers undertook social enquiries and direct supervision of probationers in inner London, until at least 1966. Margaret Frost, who worked at the London Sessions in the 1960s, later recalled probationers reporting to 21 Harper Road, S.E.1, though sometimes to more localised reporting centres: she supervised female clients, placed on probation at the Sessions, who lived in London north of the Thames, with a female colleague acting similarly for female clients living south of the river; while each male officer at the Sessions tended to supervise men from a different "patch".[16]

Regarding London, N.A.P.O. added: "Officers value the support and interest of their justices but they are looking increasingly to those in supervisory posts within the Service for professional help with their cases." (A senior's duties included supervision of newly appointed officers, whose "confirmation" by the Secretary of State depended on inspection of their work during or after their first year by Home Office inspectors. The Morison Committee envisaged no radical changes in the inspectors' functions.) The Committee proposed "bold increases in salaries", with higher rates for the higher grades, of probation officers.

The Committee acknowledged that "difficulties" had been created by a perceived sense of the Home Office's "remoteness" from the problems and concerns of London probation officers. It concluded that

to secure the contentment and command the loyalty of the

London service ... the Secretary of State should cease to be probation authority for London: ...the authority should be a London Probation Committee representative of the metropolitan magistrates courts and juvenile courts together with (as representatives of the higher courts staffed by the London Probation Service) the Chairman of London Sessions and one or two judges of the Central Criminal Court, serving *ex officio.*

Financial and technical services for London's probation officers should be provided by the L.C.C., and no longer by the Receiver.

The Morison Report claimed that "when the metropolitan juvenile courts were established, following the Children Act, 1908, there was no body of missionaries which could provide probation officers for them" (para.231). In the light of the known historical facts, this was quite an extraordinary claim. It may be added that in his classic *The People of the Abyss,* Jack London, who attended Thames Police Court in 1902 and was well aware of the work of London police court missionaries, vividly recalled the steady stream of men, women and children in the dock. Referring to the missionaries and also to the Home Office-employed juvenile court probation officers, the Morison Committee declared: "The existence for so long of these two kinds of probation officer with different backgrounds and loyalties appears still to have a legacy today in a lack of cohesion in the London service and a sense of belonging to a particular court rather than to the service as a whole." Rather ironically, the "dual control" of the service by Church and State had been superseded in London by what the Morison Report called the "dual responsibility" of the Home Office as both the central authority for the service in England and Wales and the local probation authority for a part of that service.

The report gave a somewhat misleading or over-optimistic success rate for probation. From the Cambridge Department of Criminal Science's *The Results of Probation* the Morison Committee quoted a probation success rate of 73.8% for adults and 62.4% for juveniles, though it failed to mention the Department's caveat that these figures included offenders "found guilty of a breach of the order or the commission of a further offence while under supervision". According to the criterion of offenders who "kept a clear record from the time they were put on probation up to the end of the follow-up period", the Cambridge Department's findings were 70% for adults and 57% for juveniles, which the Morison Committee did not refer to. However, these generally encouraging findings - from a study of cases in the London area - lent some weight to the witty remark (remembered by Lydia Blackman) of the London probation officer George Morrish that the Probation Service should have a coat of arms, bearing knuckle-dusters rampant and the motto "Honi soit qui maladjusted"!

In August 1962 the Morison Committee published its second (and less famous) report, which was devoted to the approved probation hostel system. Although there were some five approved probation hostels for boys and two for girls in the London area (excluding Middlesex), which had liaison probation officers, no such London probation officers seem to have appeared as witnesses before the Committee. The report accorded the liaison probation officer only a few lines and made no strikingly radical proposals. Yet the recollections of Bill Hornung and Georgina Stafford suggest that the liaison probation officer could, and sometimes did, play quite an important part in helping to ensure the smooth running of the hostel.

Hornung, who for a short time just after the War was liaison probation officer for the Boys' Shelter Home (later Ellison House), 134 Camberwell Road, S.E.5, would recall that he supervised a comparatively small number of boys (aged over 17) on probation at the hostel. This was because most London officers, and some from outside London, retained supervision of their own cases at the hostel in those days; and Hornung's cases there were mainly from probation officers outside London. He visited his clients at the hostel on a regular basis and "shared an evening meal with them and joined them in their leisure activities. By arrangement with the hostel warden the boys reported to me at my Lambeth office."

Miss Stafford liaised in North London with two approved probation hostels for girls, Elizabeth Fry (then in Highbury) and Katherine Price Hughes (run by the West London Mission), which were financially supported and to some extent regulated by the Home Office under the Criminal Justice Act, 1948. She would recall that the girls in residence contributed to their keep in a predetermined fashion from their wages, but that teaching them the art of money management proved to be more of a challenge. Sometimes girls were placed unsuitably at the hostels: she would remember one girl from Suffolk who had stolen some hens' eggs, but who was apparently corrupted by contacts she made in London. The liaison probation officer tended to have a close relationship with, and to be supportive towards, the hostel warden, with recourse to the authority of the court if a resident's behaviour warranted it. Miss A.C. Cholmondeley, and, it seems, other London probation officers, quite often placed girls in convents during their probation. Later, the Criminal Justice Act of 1972 (s.53) would empower probation and after-care committees to provide bail hostels and probation hostels - a development that would appear largely to fulfil representations directed at the Home Office by Anton Wallich-Clifford in about 1961.

By about this time the practice of female probation officers and clerical assistants wearing hats in court had appreciably declined in London, though it seems to have lingered on in other areas. With the apparent exception of a personal arrangement negotiated by Miss Cecil Barker with magistrates at West London, the practice of women wearing hats in court was, by all accounts, the norm until the Second World War. Even so, the experience of Miss Stafford as a holiday relief worker at Thames Police Court in the summer of 1937 could suggest that already the custom of women wearing their own hats was beginning to co-exist with female social workers resorting to wearing a general office or court hat available to probation staff. From the independent testimony of the clerical assistant Jo Knox and of the delinquent Maurice O'Mahoney it would appear that hat-wearing was still a regular occurrence in some London courts in about 1959. However, Mrs Maitland-Warne (then Colette Size) would recall that when she joined the London Probation Service in 1957, she noticed that "women officers had ceased to wear hats in their own courts, though if you went to juvenile courts, higher courts or anywhere away from London itself you were still expected to wear one. Some officers even then still wore hats in their own courts."

It may be, as Miss Braithwaite believed, that the decline in hat-wearing was largely due to shortages associated with the War. Bill Hornung cited the War, but stressed a somewhat different aspect of it:

> The war brought about the change. There was greater freedom and relaxing of protocol and regulations. Fashions change and more and more men and women were going hatless in public and this spilled over into the courts and churches. By the time I returned from the Forces, all but a very few of the older ladies were hatless in court and there were no raised eyebrows or caustic comments from the bench.

Sybil Campbell - understood to be London's first female stipendiary magistrate - sat at Tower Bridge Court, which had provided one of the first women juvenile court probation officers, the first two women divorce court welfare officers in London, and apparently the first late adolescent or adult male offenders on statutory supervision for lady probation officers in London. The London probation officer Carol Martin would testify:

> As one of my early assignments, during 1958-59, I was sent to Tower Bridge where John Bradley was S.P.O. ... Probation Service policy at that time was that female P.O.s worked only with women and children... This usually meant that Courts had to be manned by one P.O. of each sex. John Bradley thought this wasteful of wo/man power - so, along with everyone else, I did court duty plus any work arising from it on my own. This often necessitated interviewing men in the cells - at the time an unprecedented thing for a woman to do... I certainly worked equally with male and female clients during the short time I was at Tower Bridge M.C. and believe I was one of the first to do so.

Alison Allen would recall that in about 1959 Tower Bridge Magistrates' Court gave her her first male probationer (a tramp who had been drunk and disorderly). When Miss Allen left quite soon afterwards to work full-time at the Divorce Court in London, her successor at Tower Bridge was apparently Irene Clarkson, who then started taking on male clients, initially to the horror of prison officers. Conversely, male probation officers were not allowed into Holloway Prison to prepare reports (e.g. on children); although such prohibitions did not extend to male officers dealing with females in matrimonial work at court (e.g. in the celebrated case of McTaggart v. McTaggart - mentioned by Morison - which involved Norman Grant at Hampstead Court in 1943, and which in 1948 clarified a point of law regarding a probation officer's "privilege").

Such developments in the breakdown of gender separation in London probation work did not feature in Marjory Todd's book *The Probation Officer and His World,* published on 2 May 1963, when the B.B.C. broadcast a radio interview with her about her work. Apparently aimed mainly at school-leavers considering a career, Mrs Todd's book presented a vivid picture of the varied day-to-day work of a probation officer in an urban area - in this case, London - in about 1962. She persuasively stressed the value of home visiting and of family contacts in probation work (Lydia Blackman would recall that "Toddy" "had a wonderful gift for recording her home visits and reporting in the shortest possible pithy sentences that said everything"). Yet she did not surpass the perception of the "subtle, searching and exacting" role of probation officers or clients' assessment of them presented in *The Delinquent Child and the Community* (1957), which Donald Ford of the L.C.C. partly dedicated to her colleagues. She did not refer to Elizabeth Glover, whom John St John had called one of the few British probation officers to have written on the techniques of the job. Nor did Mrs Todd cite Jack London's *The People of the Abyss*, a graphic account of East End slum life in which the American writer quoted with approval from Thomas Holmes's *Pictures and Problems from London Police Courts*, which was also not mentioned by her. However, in this last case Marjory Todd made some amends, for, on later discovering Holmes's book, she participated in a radio programme (broadcast by the B.B.C. on 14 January 1964) in which she drew attention to his pioneer work.

In describing the various facets of the work of probation officers, her book alluded to their involvement in "neighbours' quarrels" - an involvement that the metropolitan police court magistrate Henry Turner Waddy had placed on record in 1925. She also briefly delineated "time-absorbing and diverse" demands of casual caller or office duty - a duty that Anton Wallich-Clifford and Irene Edmonds, who had both worked as London probation officers, would vividly record. (Georgina Stafford would maintain that the police court missionaries had taken on whatever was asked of them, so as to gain acceptance and trust, especially as far as the courts were concerned.) Mrs Todd realistically portrayed a need for a probation officer in court - in Miss Clarkson's words - "to think on one's feet, like a barrister". Marjory Todd paid some attention to the role of the probation officer as a facilitator, but did not explore complex issues of confidentiality; and she said relatively little about the officer as an authority figure, even less about proceedings for breach of probation. She did not reveal that probation officers worked at the higher criminal courts; and she did not refer to any Assistant or Deputy Principal Probation Officers. The basic grade (significantly known as "main grade") probation officer and all the other ranks of probation officer in London were alluded to by Seldon Farmer in his *Principal Probation Officer's Report 1960-1962* concerning the service in London, which appeared at virtually the same time as Marjory Todd's unofficial account.

Farmer's report opened with a brief survey of developments from the 1950s onwards which affected the London Probation Service: the increased range of duties expected of the service, largely as a result of legislation, from the Criminal Justice Act, 1948, to the Matrimonial Proceedings (Magistrates' Courts) Act, 1960, and the Criminal Justice Act, 1961; the rise of casework and its effect upon officers "of widely differing training and experience", with "a new meaning to the concept of supervision of probation officers' work by senior colleagues"; and associated organisational changes for the London service (the Central Council of Probation Committees, formally established in 1961, and the Principal Probation Officers' Conference, for instance, were not mentioned). According to Farmer: "The work of the London Service was substantially increased in 1948-9, when it took over from the Borstal Association the after-care supervision of all persons released to their homes in London on discharge from Borstal training." Although the second, revised edition of Joan King's *The Probation Service*[17] would give a somewhat conflicting version of responsibility for borstal after-care in London, there seems little doubt that from about 1948-49 onwards may be dated a period of continuous growth for the probation service in London. Arguably associated with this growth were some characteristics of a "front line organization", with a formal hierarchy of authority combined with a dispersal of "power" and location of organizational initiative and services in scattered units with local loyalties as strong as attachments to head office or to the London Probation Service as a whole. Farmer is not known to have penned any general policy statement, as such, for the London Probation Service. Probably he felt that policy was predominantly the responsibility of the Home Office, with which he needed to work harmoniously; possibly he was too absorbed in day-to-day problems; and his actions generally appear to have been reactive rather than pro-active.

Understandably those London probation officers most involved in community-oriented projects tended to be main-grade officers, closest to the "grassroots" and furthest from hierarchical considerations. Examples could include officers like Derek Shuttleworth, Barry Swinney, Anton Wallich-Clifford, Margaret Paterson, Katherine Crofton, and Mary Hamilton, none of whose names or projects was mentioned in Farmer's report.

Miss Crofton -a dependable member of the Notting Hill Social Council - actively participated in a West London area committee, formed in 1961 by representatives of the Standing Joint Advisory Committee (teachers and L.C.C. education officers) and of S.J.C.P.O. for the area covered by Chelsea Juvenile Court, so as to promote co-operation between teachers and those engaged in metropolitan juvenile court work.

For years during the 1960s, if not earlier, Mary Hamilton ran "Christmas shop and parcels schemes" (as Wallich-Clifford called them), with her office crammed with goods - foodstuffs, toys, clothing, etc. - which were solicited gifts from scores of firms to be distributed to local people in need, families suffering hardship, and long-standing clients all over Britain. *The Probation Officer and His World* was dedicated to this colourful Bow Street probation officer, who, according to her secretary Jo Knox, had apparently been involved in the setting up of the David Isaacs Fund for the disadvantaged. Miss Hamilton also became an Executive Committee member of the Circle Trust, which in May 1964 opened its first club at 16 Moreton Street, S.W.1, as a centre for ex-offenders; and in *Five Women* (1965) the criminological writer Tony Parker would thank Mary Hamilton for her assistance.

According to Dr Hyla Holden, its historian and one of its major supporters, the Hoxton Cafe Project "owed its existence to the dogged persistence and devotion of one man, Derek Shuttleworth, a local probation officer whose life was largely dedicated to attempts to better the lives of young Hoxtonians": intended as a successor to the Redvers Club, "the probation cafe" (as it became known) opened in March 1963, and although delinquent behaviour forced its closure between June 1963 and March 1964, it would provide a warm, accepting environment, encouraging a sense of belonging and, ultimately, of responsibility, for hundreds of young people over a period of some six years. Its supporters included Rose Mary Braithwaite, Jean Moore, Merfyn Turner, Dr Peter Scott, and also Edith Ramsay of the Stepney Women's Institute whose retirement ceremony in 1960 was attended by 600 people, with probation officers among the speakers.

Similarly, S.J.C.P.O. probation officers expressed interest from an early stage in the work of Michael Duane, headmaster of Risinghill comprehensive school, Islington; and when eight London probation officers protested to the L.C.C. at the suggested closure of Risinghill

School, the *Guardian* for 12 January 1965 devoted a front page article to their protest under the heading "Probation officers want school kept open". At Risinghill under Duane the number of children on probation fell from 98 in 1960 to 9 in 1964. At the same time London officers worked to improve co-operation with the L.C.C. Education and Children's Departments.

Farmer's 1963 report referred briefly to the London Probation Service's interest in research and willingness to participate in it. But, for some reason, he did not mention any specific completed piece of research where the London service had rendered assistance - for example, the study of shoplifting, published in June 1962, by Dr T.C.N. Gibbens and Joyce Prince, who had been greatly helped by Mrs Elspeth Gray (Marlborough Street), not to mention Farmer himself. In addition, for their psychiatric study, published in February 1963, of 200 borstal lads, mainly from London, Dr Gibbens and two assistants made use of relevant probation officers' reports. Nor did Farmer allude to any published articles -perhaps involving some research - by London probation officers: for instance, P.M.W. Voelcker's "Juvenile Courts: The Parents' Point of View" in the *British Journal of Criminology* for October 1960, or "Comments on Special Problems of Delinquent and Maladjusted Girls" by Margaret May, Margaret Dawkins and Miriam Kratz in the *Howard Journal* for 1963. Moreover, London probation officers almost certainly assisted with the study, emanating from 1958 onwards, by the doctors John Cowie, Valerie Cowie and Eliot Slater of 318 delinquent girls admitted to the Magdalen Hospital Classifying Approved School in London. Wallich-Clifford (1962) did some research on Golborne Centre clients.

According to a then current Home Office comparative study (published in 1966) to which Farmer briefly referred, London was the region of England and Wales in 1961 with the highest proportion of one-year probation orders, and also with the lowest number of persons put on probation as a proportion of those found guilty of indictable offences. London in 1961 had the highest regional proportion of probationers of whom the probation officer lost trace or whose supervision became impracticable for some other reason (this was thought to be related to "characteristics peculiar to London"). At the same time London had the lowest regional figure - also 5% - of probationers given another probation order when they committed a breach or further offence. Yet statistically

London in 1961 had the second highest regional success rate (69.6%) for probation orders, in terms of normal completion or early completion for good progress. In the same study London appeared to be the region with the lowest average caseload (defined in terms of probation, supervision, money payments supervision and after-care cases) per whole-time probation officer: 48 for men and 36 for women. This may be compared with Farmer's provisional and independent calculation that the average number of persons supervised by London officers ("other than those in the supervisory grades") was 60 for men and 39.5 for women at the end of 1962 (by November 1963 four of the five permanent, main-grade female probation officers at North London carried caseloads ranging from 52 to 76 each).

Farmer reported that the total number of clients supervised by London officers increased by over 50% between 1955 and 1961, while the number of probation officers in post and of social enquiries for the courts both rose by about 40% during the same period. The growing work-loads and numbers of "clerical assistants" were doubtless factors in the London Probation Service Clerical Association becoming a branch, by early 1963, of the National Association of Local Government Officers - it seems largely thanks to the clerical assistant Miss Cope - with branch members attending meetings at the L.C.C.'s County Hall.

As for training and supervision, Farmer's report mentioned *inter alia:* the groups for potential student supervisors run by Miss Vera Taylor and Miss Barbara Abraham in 1960, and by Miss Kay Brown in 1962; the discussion groups for social science students run by Margaret May and Ronald Howell; and the course in 1962 (against a background of intensifying "integration") run by Georgina Stafford and Rosemary Deane for officers who, attached to either adult or juvenile court, wished to learn more about the work of the other type of court. Over a period of at least three years, assistance for the national training scheme was provided by the London officers Barbara Abraham, Rose Mary Braithwaite, John Simmonds (who, in Miss Braithwaite's words, "had a considerable following among young officers"), Doris Sullivan and Vera Taylor, who all conducted seminars on casework for Home Office students at Rainer House.

Another development was the pioneering course in 1961 organised by the Home Office in conjunction with the University of London, the Regent Street Polytechnic (base for the theoretical studies), and the London Probation Service (which supervised practical work placements in the courts): this was a two-year pre-service course for candidates aged 25 and over, leading to the University of London's External Diploma in Social Studies and to appointment as London probation officers. Also in 1961 steps were taken to recruit a further ("D") group of "direct entrants"; and by early 1963 a total of 43 direct entrants - nearly all of whom were men - had joined the London service. (Appendices 21 to 23 give details relating to establishment and staffing levels, officers entering and leaving the London Probation Service, and qualifications and age distribution of London probation officers in and/or before 1962: the one recorded male death was apparently that in 1960 of George Neve, concerning whom Farmer's sensitive obituary in *Probation* recorded that as P.P.O. he had been "immeasurably helped by his knowledge and experience, his wise and candid comment, his unfailing equanimity and his complete loyalty as a colleague".)

During the years 1960-62 so many courses - often organised or sponsored by the Home Office - seemed available to London probation officers that much of the credit for this atmosphere of dynamic movement was almost certainly due to Rose Mary Braithwaite and Doris Sullivan, who carried training duties at headquarters. Miss Braithwaite "first taught me to be a probation officer", declared Marjory Todd[18] in about 1963; and in 1970 Dr H.V. Dicks would list a dozen or so former or serving London probation officers trained by the Tavistock Clinic over the years. Both Margaret Paterson and Margaret Frost remembered the challenging nature of the extensive and intensive course led by Dr Pierre Turquet of the Tavistock Clinic. In 1963, in response to a Home Office invitation, Dr Turquet became chairman of a working party (which included nine probation officers from London and neighbouring areas who had already undertaken some group work with probationers) to examine what might be the place for group work in the probation service, what form it should take, and what training for it would be required: at this time group work by British probation officers was still a relatively rare phenomenon (see King's *The Probation Service,* 1964, p.98).

In 1961 London had apparently constituted the region of England and Wales with the second smallest proportion (27%) of full-time probation officers untrained before appointment. Among such officers appointed in 1963 was the esteemed musician and club warden Leslie Thompson, who began work in September that year as a temporary probation officer assigned to North London Magistrates' Court. Turned 60 and "unsure what I was going to do", he had been advised by the Registrar of London University to apply for social work:

> So in 1963 I got in contact with a Miss Braithwaite, and I had an interview at the Home Office ... I had to answer questions on all manner of subjects for an hour, and that was that. But I got in. In that way I joined the probation service in London... It was quite extraordinary that I had no formal training... I had to see it all in action. So I was put at different tasks to see how it was done at the magistrates' court. I don't know if there was a deliberate policy to recruit coloured probation officers; certainly there was a shortage of probation officers, and that's why I think I got the job.

As a black probation officer, Leslie Thompson had been preceded in the Greater London area by John Fraser, who was established in Willesden by March 1953, and by Mrs Maud Ivy ("Bel") Alleyne, who had begun work for the London Probation Service in March 1963 as its first known black female probation officer (Farmer does seem to have supported the appointment of black probation officers in London). After wartime service with the A.T.S. followed by social science studies at Liverpool University, "Bel" had worked as a probation officer in Leicester City between 1951 and 1957 - undoubtedly one of the earliest black probation officers in England - and then as a welfare officer for West Indians in Britain. As a probation officer in South London, she apparently encountered little racial hostility, as did Leslie Thompson, who vividly described his experiences in North London:

> We had to deal with all sorts of people: young and old, men and women, drunks, intellectuals, the lot. The hours were from nine until four, with some nights. We worked in the locality. Sometimes the people would report to us, and we had to chat to see how they were getting on, and check that they were not misbehaving. And I had to visit their homes, generally in the evening. There was a pool of cars and you put your name down and off you would go. There wasn't any trouble over colour. 'Probation Officer' was enough. Of course the families were a bit careful, for I was an officer of the law. No uniform, but with the authority of the magistrates behind me.

> There were some West Indians on probation, and their families were a bit friendly...

> Most of the charges were like that: basically decent chaps who had been tempted. If they had been sent to prison their families would have really been in difficulties. Most of my contacts were White, but there were Blacks, too. Foolish little crimes, like stealing a motor car, breaking into a gas meter, or breaking and entering.

London probation officers had contacts with people of Greek Cypriot, Chinese or West Indian origin, for example. Yet Farmer's report did not offer an assessment of the London Probation Service's contacts with any of the capital's diverse ethnic groups. Nor did he refer to the professional visit to England by twelve Greek probation officers in July 1962, when they were largely based in London and were looked after by the London and Middlesex Probation Services. Such omissions may seem the more surprising as Farmer was sensitive to international perspectives. Assisted by his linguistic skills (he was fluent in French), he had participated in quite a few criminological conferences with international implications - sometimes under the auspices of the United Nations - whether in Austria (1954), France (1955), Belgium (1956 and 1960), or Japan (1957). Moreover, he made professional visits to Singapore and Hong Kong at the request of the Colonial Office; and in 1961 he broadcast in French on crime, punishment and public opinion for the B.B.C. Farmer also omitted from his report any reference to his being awarded an O.B.E. in the New Year Honours List for 1961.

By all accounts, Farmer was a modest, dedicated, kind and very intelligent man with a courteous manner, conciliatory approach and ready sense of humour. Exercising a stabilising influence, he made a point of welcoming new officers and maintaining face-to-face contact with officers through meetings at head office or visits to the London courts, at a time when the London service was still small enough for most of the officers to know each other. While his style of quiet diplomacy and careful preparation may have been misconstrued in some quarters, he introduced and presided over far-reaching changes for the London service. As with other British probation officers of his generation, his life was guided by a sense of public service; and in Peter Shervington's words, "he made a big contribution".

Seldon Farmer and S.J.C.P.O. had expressed support in general terms for the kind of non-residential treatment provided by the Citizen Training Centre in Boston, Massachusetts, U.S.A., which the British Advisory Council on the Treatment of Offenders considered though largely rejected in 1962. But neither Farmer nor any of his London colleagues would be publicly listed as having submitted evidence to the A.C.T.O. in its 1961-63 review of after-care for persons released from prisons, borstals, detention centres and approved schools. In August 1961 a N.A.P.O. London Branch sub-committee had revealed that the total number of borstal after-care cases under supervision in London had risen from 393 in April 1958 to 665 in September 1960 (the number of borstal cases carried by the London Probation Service would rise to a total of 852 in 1963). The sub-committee maintained that "there is no provision for communication between London probation officers and institutions", and suggested that, to ease the over-loading of officers in some adult court areas, all London officers, including women, should accept borstal after-care cases, and that "an after-care unit be established at Walton Street to study and give guidance on the special techniques required for effective after-care and to co-ordinate supervision and allocation of cases in London".[19]

Published in October 1963 as *The Organisation of After-Care,* the A.C.T.O. (Barry) Report held out the prospect of "even faster expansion" for the London service, as the Assistant Principal Probation Officer George Pratt told London seniors the following month. The report recommended, *inter alia,* that "the single service which would undertake both compulsory and voluntary after-care in the community should be an expanded and re-organised 'probation and after-care service' ", which would accordingly need "to build up new machinery of collaboration with the social workers in penal institutions and with voluntary agencies". There were some striking if unnoticed similarities between recommendations in the Harris (1936) and Barry (1963) Reports: both proposed an extension of state or public control, with suitable volunteers assisting probation officers and with religious bodies and voluntary organisations helping to establish hostels for ex-offenders.

One voluntary organisation striving to establish grassroots "houses" for ex-offenders and homeless people was the Simon Community, which Anton Wallich-Clifford conceived in September 1963, soon after he left the London Probation Service, "a service I had tried to honour". Rather like Guy Clutton-Brock, he had embraced life at "ground level":

My case-load at Bow Street taught me in weeks what I had not
learnt in years. It brought me face to face with the hard facts about
dossing and skippering ... other officers (not only in London) and
even our own headquarters began referring difficult N.F.A. placements to me for possible help in recommending facilities.

The man who set up a club for the isolated and lonely in his own
home used to meet some of his clients in cafes and "pubs" by Charing
Cross. At Bow Street he was a pin-striped probation officer by day and "a
dosser by night", changing into "skipper gear" at his office and venturing
out, sometimes with magistrates or others, into the twilight world of
London meths drinkers and "down and outs". His colleague Mary
Hamilton supported and encouraged him in the plan to launch Simon
(named after Simon of Cyrene, who had carried the cross of Jesus), and
she became one of the first members of the Simon Community Trust; just
as their secretary Jo Knox was inspired to found, by March 1964, the
London regional branch and the Brighton branch of the Trust.[20] His
identification with the needs of the social outcast was doubtless a potent
force in the opening, in May 1964, of the Simon Community's first house,
St Joseph's, at 129 Malden Road, N.W.5, which was soon familiar - for
example - to the London probation officer Geoffrey Parkinson (whose
articles in *New Society* and elsewhere seemed to shock, stimulate or amuse
his readers). In 1964 Marjory Todd suggested[21] that guilt could be a
motivating factor in social work (*A Sense of Guilt* would be the title of
Andrea Newman's 1988 novel about a London probation officer). This
certainly seems to have been true of Anton Wallich-Clifford, thanked for
his assistance by Tony Parker in *The Unknown Citizen* (1963), while
countless unknown citizens would have cause to appreciate Wallich-
Clifford's example of dedication to the care of the homeless and rootless.

Meanwhile N.A.P.O.'s London Branch set up a sub-committee to
assess the implications for the London service of the implementation of
the 1963 A.C.T.O. (Barry) Report. Members of the sub-committee
included Stan Ratcliffe (the Old Street senior who in 1962 had prepared
social enquiry reports on John Orton and his homosexual partner
Kenneth Halliwell, who were both sent to prison for stealing and defacing
scores of public library books, though Orton became famous as a
playwright and Halliwell became notorious as his murderer). When the
sub-committee reported in August 1964[22], it expressed somewhat lukewarm

acceptance of the general principles of the report. This sub-committee recommended that probation officers should receive training regarding "the particular needs of the various categories of people under after-care" and also regarding the use of volunteers and "the means by which they were to be supported and guided by members of the Service". It was proposed that there should be a central register for London of after-care cases ("presumably at Home Office level"), and that inmates who were homeless at the time of admission to an institution should initially be contacted by the probation officer covering the "place of origin", who would subsequently transfer the case to an officer for the area in which the offender was to settle on release. It was felt that early pre-release visits and the sharing of information with institutions by probation officers were desirable. At the beginning of 1964 probation officers had assumed responsibility for statutory after-care supervision of those released from detention centres; and in 1964 the London Probation Service carried 292 detention centre cases, which constituted 20% of its total after-care caseload for that year. The sub-committee suggested that "women officers could supervise men and boys subject to after-care ... in view of the staffing problems of the Service". This was at a time when probation in England and Wales apparently cost £20 per head per year compared with £490 per head per year for prison[23] (like the Morison Report and the later *ILPAS '76,* Farmer's 1963 report gave no figures for the overall cost of the probation service in London or in England as a whole).

It was against this background that the service witnessed the establishment of the After-Care Unit at Borough High Street on 1 January 1965. Certainly the A.C.T.O. Report had recommended: "Because of the concentration of discharged prisoners in London, the organisation of after-care in London should be given priority" (para.217: para.174 said "high priority"). Following consultation with the Home Office and other agencies in the light of this report, the London Probation Service was instructed near the end of 1964 to take over the offices, with their existing functions and staff, at 289 Borough High Street, S.E.1, which housed the National Association of Discharged Prisoners' Aid Societies (N.A.D.P.A.S.) and the Central After-Care Association. The staff of the new unit - which would appear to have been the first functioning, official probation service after-care unit in England - comprised officers of these two organisations who had been working on the premises, and who, at a stroke, were appointed full-time probation officers in the Metropolitan Magistrates'

Courts Area on 1 January 1965 (subject to confirmation of appointment after one year), and half a dozen already appointed London probation officers, who moved into the building.

All these officers came under two seniors and an Assistant Principal Probation Officer. One of the two seniors, R.B. Robinson, who had formerly worked for the Central After-Care Association in a senior position, seems to have been the first, and last, senior probation officer with the London Probation Service who had not previously worked as a probation officer (Clutton-Brock seemed to provide the closest analogy). Robinson's new colleague, John Pannell, had joined the London service in 1949 and, by 1965, had been a senior for at least five years. The previously appointed probation officers - from juvenile and magistrates' courts in more or less equal numbers - came from working in some of the toughest areas of London and were more or less equally represented in terms of gender, but had not apparently worked together as a team before. From the recollection of Peter Barnes, who was one of them, it seems that these already appointed probation officers had been individually asked to go to Borough High Street at the instigation of George Pratt, the A.P.P.O. responsible. (Appendix 24 outlines Pratt's duties as of March 1963.) Remembered as an organisation man, credited with having designed some of the documentation and records of the London service, George Pratt had maintained in November 1963:

> the only major administrative changes since headquarters were set up in 1938 seem to have been regionalization and the appointment of an administrative deputy principal ... there are 7 courts with staffs of 11 or more, and large units are likely to become the rule rather than the exception... More and more we are leaving behind that rugged individualism which characterised casework up to only a few years ago; more and more we are accepting the value of client-centred teamwork.[24]

Fusing the three groups - each with its own history and identity -seems, in some respects, to have resembled the situation nearly thirty years earlier when the London Probation Service was born. While court missionaries had reacted more in sorrow than in anger to the severance of ties with the London Police Court Mission, some London probation officers seemed distinctly unenthusiastic about the prospect of what Patrick Emerson and R.M. Lewis in December 1964 called "the after-care chore added to our functions", though the probation service was facing a rising tide of after-care cases (and on 1 January 1966 the service would take over responsibility from N.A.D.P.A.S. for staffing prison welfare departments). The fact that the assimilation of Central After-Care Association staff at Borough High Street took place at least a year before the Association nationally ceased to carry any responsibility for the after-care of prisoners no doubt added to any tensions of assimilation in London.

It seems that when the After-Care Unit was born, the London probation officers who entered the building for the first time had only a vague idea of what was expected of them. Perhaps largely for this reason the Unit perpetuated the different work patterns already established by the Central After-Care Association and N.A.D.P.A.S., with the former generally working by appointment with longer known or regular clients, many of whom were or had been on compulsory after-care supervision; while the latter received voluntary clients without appointments as casual callers. Albert Raisbeck of the C.A.C.A. had dealt with "lifers"; and as one of the "instant" probation officers, he was quite probably the first London probation officer to be in touch with "lifers" on a more or less regular basis. The number of "lifers" was at that time very small: nine were released during 1962, and it seems there was a total of 365 "lifers" in prison at the end of 1964. However, the number of life sentence prisoners in Britain would grow inexorably following abolition of the death penalty soon after the end of the period under review (between 1946 and 1948 Frank Dawtry and Miss Clemence Paine had been Secretary and an Executive Committee member, respectively, of the National Council for the Abolition of the Death Penalty[25]).

Probation officers at the Unit were assigned to cover and, as appropriate, visit specific penal institutions (Peter Barnes, for example, would recall that his function was to look after homeless detention centre boys discharged to the London area). Many of the voluntary male clients who came to the Unit with pressing material needs or demands seemed to be single, homeless and often alcoholic recidivists just released from prison. The Home Office detected a paradox that while the Unit provided a service that seemed largely focused on material needs, its material resources were comparatively few. From her experience at the After-Care Unit from February 1966 onwards, Georgina Stafford would maintain that the mentally ill, the mentally sub-normal, the physically handicapped, the drug addict, the alcoholic and the elderly needed "a specialised after care which is not at present available".[26] At various times and in various ways London probation officers had tried to help such people.

Anton Wallich-Clifford, Marjory Todd and Irene Edmonds were conscious that callers at probation offices included people with mental health problems. Lydia Blackman would recall that London probation officers quite often referred clients to a specialist agency like the Portman Clinic. Dr Max Grünhut had found that magistrates' courts in the Metropolitan Police District generated no less that 32% of the section 4 probation orders made in England and Wales during 1953. Probation officers at two central London magistrates' courts co-operated in Richard F. Sparks's study of remands at those two courts in 1961 for mental examination.[27] Also in 1961 Professor Titmuss, based in London, had warned that community care for the mentally ill could result in "more expenditure on the police forces, on prisons and probation officers". As early as 1927 Clarke Hall had begun to put the occasional child on probation on the understanding that the child would attend Dr Emanuel Miller's East London Child Guidance Clinic[28]; and during the Second World War Beeson was apparently a Committee member of the Central Association for Mental Welfare, which merged with two other bodies in 1946 to form the National Association for Mental Health. Over the ensuing years the North London probation officer John Barter would hold an important position in the National Association; and from March 1965 onwards George Pratt was a member of a steering committee sponsored by the Association to support young women and adolescent girls without any effective home, family or friends.

Jo Knox knew of clients placed on probation for attempted suicide. The Suicide Act of 1961 - an act of decriminalisation - may have both reflected and stimulated the development of more positive attitudes towards mental illness in England.[29] The London probation officer Stanley Ratcliffe was very involved in the formation of the Reigate branch of the Samaritans in 1964; and his colleague Peggy Thornborough - to be followed by Philip Pestell and Doris Sullivan, who had both been London probation officers - gave her services to the recently founded Highgate Counselling Centre, whose clients no doubt included people feeling depressed, even suicidal. Probation officers certainly made referrals to the Hampstead Young People's Consultation Centre in the years after it opened in 1961.[30] The Maudsley Hospital also offered help.

Anton Wallich-Clifford and Valerie Haig-Brown would both recall a meeting at which London probation officers expressed concern to Home Office officials about the increasing drugs problem in London at a time -apparently the early 1960s - when for Whitehall there seemed to be virtually no cause for any such anxiety. It seems clear that drug addicts had not yet emerged as a client group for London probation officers, and that the latter had not yet explored the dilemmas for representatives of the criminal justice system in working with this group (Anton Wallich-Clifford, with his knowledge of the problem, would describe the period 1965-70 as representing "the peak of the 'addict explosion' in Britain"[31]; the Institute for the Study of Drug Dependence would be established in 1968).

Despite the likelihood that many offences were drink-related, and despite the notable endeavours of probation officers like Wallich-Clifford and Barry Swinney in working with alcoholics (Swinney helped to set up a special clinic at Pentonville Prison for alcoholics), the general focus of the work had extended beyond alcoholics.

An individual (Frederic Rainer) had identified a need to tackle a distressing social problem. A newly established body - the Church of England Temperance Society - had taken up the challenge, providing agents with considerable zeal, but no statutory powers. As the scope of the work broadened and its usefulness became more widely accepted, the State became increasingly involved and, in time, took over from the Church to create a unified public service that itself would become an institution; a mission of mercy had developed an aura of authority. A personal initiative to confront the problem of alcoholism had generated purposive responses to a range of anti-social and criminal behaviour; and a largely male-dominated and all-white service had moved towards a non-sexist and non-racial orientation. In 1961 Doris Sullivan suggested that the "intuitive and 'setting an example' approach of the early police court missionaries" had been replaced by the modern probation officer's perception of his or her task as establishing a relationship within which the client could achieve greater self-understanding and be assisted to adapt.

In February 1963 there was some expansion of the work when

Charles Balchin, senior at Tower Bridge, became the first Liaison Probation Officer at the Court of Criminal Appeal, albeit on a part-time basis. Then, soon after mid-March 1965, he handed over to Bill Hornung, who became the first full-time probation officer at the Court of Criminal Appeal, with an office and typing facilities on the premises.

The recollections of Charles Morgan and Irene Clarkson would tend to suggest that by about this time oral use of the term "court missionary" had finally died out in those very areas where it had evidently been in circulation longest: parts of South East London and of the West End. The retirement in September 1964 of Mrs Gray after 39 years' service at Marlborough Street Court may have marked the beginning of the end of a long period in London when it was not unknown for probation officers to work for decades at the same court or office. Her retirement came at a time of growing social mobility, when the probation service, endowed with a sense of professionalism, was moving into an increasing number of areas within the criminal justice system (the 1938 edition of the H.M.S.O. booklet *The Probation Service: Its Objects and Its Organisation* commended "a sense of vocation" - a phrase omitted from the 1952 edition, which highlighted training). The emergence of rules, regulations and bureaucratization had not apparently stifled a sense of freedom in the job or the distinctive contribution of colourful probation officers, animated by qualities of caring, sharing, understanding and trust.[32]

Now, once again, the agents of change were themselves affected by it: for, following the London Government Act, 1963, the Administration of Justice Act, 1964, and ancillary orders and instructions, the London Probation Service died on 31 March 1965, and the next day its probation officers were reborn as members of the Inner London Probation and After-Care Service. In keeping with the recommendations of the Morison Report, which the Government had accepted, direct responsibility for the London service would pass from the Home Office to a new Inner London Probation Committee. Over the years all the endeavours and contributions of individual probation officers and police court missionaries were streams flowing unseen into a surging river that, like the Thames in London, had come a long way, but was moving towards wider horizons.

References and Notes

(Where references are given in an abbreviated form, they generally relate to entries in the Select Bibliography)

CHAPTER ONE

My main sources for this chapter are: Ayscough(1923); Bochel(1976); Edward William Cox, *The Principles of Punishment*(1877); information provided by Gordon Cullingham; Heasman(1962); Holmes(1900); Jarvis (1972); King(1964); Le Mesurier(1935); Lieck(1938); McWilliams(1983 and 1986); Potter(1927); Purcell(1916); The Rainer Foundation, *Annual Report 1975;* Timasheff(1941); Waddy(1925); Young and Ashton(1956).

Other sources, or sources that merit highlighting, are:-

1 *Windsor Express,* 10.12.1926.
2 Information provided by Captain John Sedgwick (Regimental Headquarters Coldstream Guards).
3 See the Rev. J. Dennis Hird's *Guide to C.E.T.S. Work in the London Diocese* for September 1889 and September 1890, and also *C.E.T.S. Annual Report* for 1892.
4 According to Jarvis(1972), p.3.
5 Cited by McWilliams(1983), p.133.
6 E.W. Cox, *op. cit.,* pp.164-5, his italics; also pp.44,163,161,45-7.
7 Matthew Davenport Hill, *Suggestions for the Repression of Crime* (1857), pp.346-7,350-2,118.
8 Bochel, p.5; Rosamond and Florence Davenport-Hill, *The Recorder of Birmingham*(1878), p.156; Purcell, p.58.
9 Potter, p.9.
10 Inner London Probation Service (I.L.P.S.) archives.
11 Jarvis, p.5.
12 Enid Huws Jones, *Margery Fry*(1966), p.240.
13 Holmes (1908), pp.3-4.
14 St. Giles(1891), p.45.
15 Mills(1887), pp.34-6.

CHAPTER TWO

Main sources: Ayscough; Babington(1968); Church of England Temperance Society *Annual Reports* for 1892-1900; Heasman; Holmes(1900); Howard Association *Annual Reports* for 1896-1901; Jarvis; London Diocesan Branch of the Church of England Temperance Society (London Police

Court Mission) *Annual Reports* for 1893-1901; McWilliams(1983); Potter; Purcell; St. Giles(1891).

Other sources, or sources that merit highlighting, are:-

1 From leaflet entitled *1876-1956: 80th Anniversary of the National Police Court Mission*(Lambeth Palace Library archives).
2 *C.E.T.S. Annual Report* for 1896, p.28 (see opposite page for picture of wood-chopping yard).
3 See, for example, *The Reformer* (London), 15.7.1897, p.149, and Frederick James Gould, *The Pioneers of Johnson's Court*(1929), p.48.
4 According to *Windsor Express,* 10.12.1926, p.9, and unsigned hand-written note on the back of a photograph (in the Rainer Foundation archives) of Batchelor and Nelson: I am indebted to Gordon Cullingham for his assistance with copies of this source material. The retired London probation officer Charles Preece has revealed that his great-grandmother had been a drunkard who had contemplated suicide in London in the 1860s before she found salvation in Christianity and temperance and became an ardent police court missionary and pioneering probation officer in Wales (*Woman of the Valleys,* 1989 edition, p.50 *et seq.*). It seems to me that this story is remarkably similar to the one concerning George Nelson, with corresponding psychological and sociological implications.
5 See *The Reformer* (London), 15.2.1899, p.68, and 15.1.1899, p.39.
6 Monger(1969), p.5.
7 Rainer Foundation, *Annual Report 1975,* pp.10-11; point independently made to me by Elizabeth Wilford (most helpful) of the Church Army head office staff. 8Holmes(1908), pp.25, 26-7.

CHAPTER THREE

Main sources: Ayscough; Babington; Bochel; Church Army archives; Church of England Temperance Society *Annual Reports* for 1902-7; Gamon(1907 and 1908); Holmes(1900); Home Office files at the Public Record Office (Kew); Jarvis; Le Mesurier; London Diocesan Branch of the Church of England Temperance Society *Annual Reports* for 1901-8; London (Diocesan) Police Court Mission, *Handed Over to the Police Court Missionary*(1913?); Milton(1959); Timasheff(1941); *Toynbee Record* for June 1907; United Nations(1951); Williams(1891).

Other sources, or sources that merit highlighting, are:-

[1] See the London Police Court Mission's *Report* for 1948-49, pp.14-15, and the Rainer Foundation's *Annual Report 1975,* pp.11-12.

[2] Information kindly provided by Mr. C. Tucker; see also Gamon (1907), p.viii.

[3] C.H. Denyer in the *Toynbee Record,* June 1907, p.125.

[4] Information from: F.V. Jarvis; interview with Mrs. Elspeth Gray, 16.4.1987; interview with Gunter Lubowski, 22.4.1987.

[5] From George Newton's article "Trends in Probation Training": *British Journal of Delinquency,* October 1956, p.123.

[6] Playfair and Sington (1965), p.192.

[7] Public Record Office (Kew), H.O.45. 10503/125632.

[8] P.R.O. (Kew), H.O.45. 10311/123946/72.

[9] Information from the Church Army archives: Committee Minute Book no. 4, entry for 31.5.1906; *Church Times,* 27.7.1906; Church Army *Annual Report* for year to 30 September 1906, p.58.

[10] *Hansard* (Commons), 8.5.1907, cols.295-8.

[11] *Hansard* (Commons), 26.7.1907, cols.373-4; Bochel, p.37.

[12] Letter in Howard League for Penal Reform library, with Parliamentary extract attached; see also G. Rose (1961), p.82.

[13] Recollection of London probation officer Mr. W.E. Hill; see also Home Office *Directory of Probation Officers and Approved Probation Hostels and Homes - 1964* (H.M.S.O.,1964), p.55.

[14] P.R.O., H.O.45. 10369/159319/21.

[15] (relating to this paragraph and the preceding one) P.R.O., H.O.45: 10369/159319/31; 10367/156623/27; 10367/156623/1.

[16] (relating to this paragraph and the preceding two paragraphs) P.R.O., H.O.45: 10369/159319/29; 10369/159319/31; 10369/159319/28. See also: J.M. Robertson, *A History of Freethought in the Nineteenth Century*(1929), pp.423-4; Ethel Croker-King's death certificate (re: 8.10.1944).

[17] P.R.O., H.O.45: 10369/159319/21; 10369/159319/51 (incl. Ivimy letter of 30.1.1909). Also Bochel, p.42.

[18] Bochel, pp.41,44; Jarvis, pp.9,19-20; George Smithson, *Raffles in Real Life*(n.d.), p.9; W. Norwood East *et al., The Adolescent Criminal* (1942), p.272; *Hansard* (Lords), 5.8.1907, col.1487.

CHAPTER FOUR

Main sources: Ayscough; Bailey(1987); Benney(1936); Blyth(n.d.: leaflet); Bochel; Cairns(1922); Cancellor(1930); Chapman(1925); Church of England Temperance Society *Annual Reports* for 1908-19; (Home Office) Departmental Committee on the Probation of Offenders Act, 1907: *Minutes of Evidence* and *Report* (published 1910); Gamon (August 1908); Holmes(1908); Jarvis; Leeson(1914); Lieck(1938); London Diocesan Branch of the Church of England Temperance Society *Annual Reports* for 1908-21; London (Diocesan) Police Court Mission, *Handed Over to the Police Court Missionary* (1913?) and *The Quality of Mercy* (1922?); A Middlesex Magistrate(1911); *National Association of Probation Officers* (April 1913 to July 1928); Rose (1961); Walton(1975).

Other sources, or sources that merit highlighting, are:-

[1] See Stan Shipley, *Club Life and Socialism in Mid-Victorian London* (1971?), p.26 et seq.; Rainer Foundation, *Annual Report 1975,* p.9.

[2] Pp. 34-5.

[3] Information about Miss Adler from: Bochel; *Who Was Who, 1941-50*; London School of Economics Library Catalogue.

[4] For Paterson, see *inter alia:* Departmental Committee *Minutes of Evidence (op. cit.),*pp.47-8; Bailey, pp.9,241n.,290n.; Attlee, *As It Happened* (1954), p.24.

[5] See, for example, obituary of Annie Hayden, who had worked in London, in *NAPO Newsletter* for February 1988, p.11.

[6] See Rose (1961), pp.84-5, and Bochel, pp.54-5.

[7] P.R.O., H.O.45. 10369/159319/21.

[8] Information from: *National Association of Probation Officers* for April 1913, p.5, and July 1928, p.661; *Probation* for September-October 1952, p.198; Jarvis, pp.28-9,45; Leeson, pp.135-6; Walton, pp.48-9.

[9] Biron(1936), pp.267-8,249.

[10] Information provided by Lydia Blackman and Derek Shuttleworth independently of each other.

[11] From George Nelson's death certificate.

[12] *National Association of Probation Officers,* July 1916, p.115.

[13] See Biron, p.285.

[14] *Probation,* January 1934, p.284.

[15] See Hilary D.C. Pepler, *Justice and the Child* (1915), pp.64-5.

[16] See Clarke Hall(1917), pp.107-11,114-16,119,122,126-30,190.

17 Walton, p.97, and Church Army, *Our Bi-Monthly,* May 1916, p.14.
18 Jarvis, p.33; Bochel, pp.69-71; *National Association of Probation Officers,* September 1919, p.194.
19 Penal Reform League *Record,* July 1919, pp.78-80; *National Association of Probation Officers,* March 1920, pp.224-5, 232.
20 *Report of the Departmental Committee on the Training, Appointment and Payment of Probation Officers* (Cmd. 1601,1922), pp.14-15 (for probation orders, see pp.5-6).
21 Waddy(1925), pp.79,83-4; *National Association of Probation Officers,* September 1919, p.194 (for Barnett on training, see p.195).
22 S.J.C.P.O. Minute Book, entry for 23.4.1948.
23 Bailey, p.24.
24 Information from interview with Mrs. Edith Farmer, 16.12.1987.

CHAPTER FIVE

Main sources: Bailey; Blyth; Bochel; Chapman; Mrs. Cecil Chesterton, *Women of the Underworld* (1931); Clarke Hall(1926); R.E. Corder(1925); Ellison (1934); interview with Mrs. Elspeth Gray (née Macpherson, later Mrs. Stormont), 16.4.1987, and documents supplied by her; interview with Elizabeth Inman ("A Lovely Job", *Sideways,* Autumn 1984, No.4, produced by Avon Probation Service officers); Jarvis; Lieck(1938); London Diocesan Branch of the Church of England Temperance Society *Annual Report* for 1922; London Police Court Mission (formally established with effect from January 1923) *Annual Reports* for 1923-30; *National Association of Probation Officers* for April 1913, March 1920, December 1923, February 1925, July 1925, February 1926, September 1926, and February 1927; *Probation* for December 1929, October 1931, April 1933, January 1934, and March 1957; *Report of the Departmental Committee on the Training, Appointment and Payment of Probation Officers* (Cmd. 1601,1922); Treherne(1987); Waddy.

Other sources, or sources that merit highlighting, are:-

1 Walton, p.49.
2 See Cairns, pp.250-5.
3 Lieck(1938), p.211 (see also p.88).
4 According to information kindly provided by D.H.O. Owen, Registrar of the Privy Council Office, Downing Street: Dr. John Treherne (1987),

and certainly my own research, appeared to point to the same conclusion regarding Miss Porter as a witness.

[5] These are detailed in my review (South Place *Ethical Record,* October 1988) of Dr. Treherne's book on the Wakeford Case.

[6] From interview with Mrs. Elspeth Gray, 16.4.1987.

[7] See Cairns, pp.162-4.

[8] From MS. 2060 in Church of England Temperance Society (C.E.T.S.) records in Lambeth Palace Library archives.

[9] London Police Court Mission, *The London Police Court Mission and Charles Dickens* (1924), p.15.

[10] Waddy, pp.79,123,167-8.

[11] *National Association of Probation Officers,* December 1923, p.443.

[12] *National Association of Probation Officers,* July 1925, pp.539,543.

[13] R.E. Corder, p.82 (see also pp.74,105); Bailey, p.215; Sydney Moseley, *The Truth about Borstal* (1926), pp.1,4,5, and 10.

[14] S.J.C.P.O. Minute Book, entry for 24.10.1938.

[15] *National Association of Probation Officers,* July 1925, pp.530-4.

[16] London Police Court Mission *Annual Report* for 1924 (pp.5,15) and 1925 (pp.7,17); Rainer Foundation *Annual Report 1975,* p.14; Mark Monger(1969), p.5.

[17] For unemployment in Britain at this time, see Rainer Foundation, *op. cit.,* p.13, and R.C. Birch, *The Shaping of the Welfare State* (1974), p.37; and for Alfred Pilgrim, see *Crockford's Clerical Directory* for 1963-64.

[18] *National Association of Probation Officers,* February 1927, pp.612-15. See also the 1965 *Annual Charities Digest,* p.235.

[19] *National Association of Probation Officers* for February 1926 (pp.574-5; also p.567) and September 1926 (p.594); Babington(1968), p.123.

[20] See pp.130-5.

[21] Interview with Mrs. Elspeth Gray, 16.4.1987.

[22] I am indebted to Mrs. Gray for sight of R.E. Corder's article "Clothes and Character" (newspaper cutting giving no date or title of the journal from which it was taken) and of her Summary of Evidence (undated) for the Street Offences Committee.

[23] The provincial missionary was Robert - not Thomas - Holmes. See his *Them that fall* (1923), pp.288-9, and also Potter(1927), p.98. Their public clamour for castration or sterilisation of certain types of "degenerate" was, in effect, echoed some 60 years later by James

Anderton, Chief Constable of Greater Manchester, and by Lord Denning, former Master of the Rolls (*The Scotsman,* 9.11.1987, p.2).

[24] See Cyril Burt, *The Young Delinquent* (1925), pp.ix,180n.,193,196n., 610,611; also "Report of Investigation by the National Institute of Industrial Psychology for The Probation Training Board of the Home Office on The Work of the Probation Officer 1946" (typescript, dated 14.11.1946: e.g. para.15).

[25] Bochel, p.102; information from Mrs. Elspeth Gray, 16.4.1987. Handwritten, outline records were known as "coffin cards".

[26] William Tallack, *Penological and Preventive Principles* (second and enlarged edition, 1896), pp.367-9.

[27] See Mary Ellison (1934), pp.xi-xii,xvi,111; also *Probation,* October 1931, p.136.

[28] According to Mrs. Elspeth Gray and Miss Ada Demer, respectively. Virtually all the other information in this paragraph came to me from Miss Georgina Stafford.

[29] My principal sources for this paragraph and the preceding two paragraphs were the following issues of *Probation:* December 1929, p.24; April 1933, p.235; January 1934, p.284; March 1957, p.75.

[30] J.B. Sandbach (1950), p.67; Stanley French (1976), pp.151-2.

CHAPTER SIX

Main sources: information from Cecil Barker, Rose Mary Braithwaite, Guy Clutton-Brock, Ethel Currant, Ada Demer, Jack and Margaret Frost, Elspeth Gray, Bill Hornung, Elizabeth Inman, Charles Morgan, Iris Pontifex, and Georgina Stafford; Bailey; R.H. Beeson/London Probation Committee, *A Short Survey of the London Probation Service 1939-1944* (1945); Bochel; the British Broadcasting Corporation; Eric R. Calvert and Theodora Calvert, *The Lawbreaker* (1933); Chapman (1932); Mrs. Cecil Chesterton, *Women of the London Underworld* (1938); Church. Army archives; Guy and Molly Clutton-Brock, *Cold Comfort Confronted* (1972); Sidney Dark (1939); Mary Ellison, *Sparks beneath the Ashes* (1934) and *Missing from Home* (1964); Cyril Forster Garbett, *In the Heart of South London* (1931); Henriques (1937); Inner London Probation Service archives: file no. 742/1, entitled "Central Criminal Court: Work and Court Meetings: 19.4.37 - 10.3.41"; R.M. Jackson (1940; 1942 reprint); Jarvis; MS. 2062 in C.E.T.S. records, Lambeth Palace Library archives;

Alfred Leeding, *Community Care,* 30.8.1978; Le Mesurier (1935); Lieck (1938); L.L. Loewe, *Basil Henriques* (1976); London Police Court Mission *Annual Reports* for 1930-38; William McWilliams (1983,1985,1987); Hermann Mannheim (1940); Milton (1959); W.G. Minn (1948); Claud Mullins (1945 and 1948); issues of *Probation* between 1929 and 1962; *Report of the Departmental Committee on the Social Services in Courts of Summary Jurisdiction* (Cmd. 5122, 1936) - i.e. the Harris Committee Report; Sandbach; Various Contributors, *Guy and Molly Clutton-Brock* (Zimbabwe, 1987).

Other sources, or sources that merit highlighting, are:-

[1] *The Young Delinquent,* p.192n.

[2] According to Elizabeth Inman (*Sideways,* Autumn 1984, No.4, p.1); Cyril Burt (*op. cit.,* p.194n.) in 1925 referred to 12 London juvenile court probation officers, "all women".

[3] Henriques (1937), p.253.

[4] Grace Harrison's comments were reported in *Probation* for January 1932 (p.149) and for October 1932 (p.201), respectively (see latter issue, p.194, for Laelia Sander).

[5] For Barnett, see London Police Court Mission *Report for 1931* (p.5; p.6 for Henry Robinson), *Probation* for July 1931 (p.125), Chapman's *From the Bench* (1932), pp.78-9; for Fitzsimmons, see London Police Court Mission *Report for 1931* (p.5), French (p.150), *Probation* for April 1933 (p.236), Lieck (1938), p.87.

[6] See Cyril Burt, *The Young Delinquent* (1925), pp.71-4, and C.F. Garbett, *In the Heart of South London* (1931), pp.17,142-3.

[7] Chapman, 1925, p.306, and 1932, p.85. See also *Probation* for April 1933, p.235, and for November 1938, p.42.

[8] Sources for this paragraph: *Probation* for October 1931, p.136; Ellison (1934), p.188 (see p.xv for the increasing interest in psychology and medicine in relation to criminological study); Calvert (1933), pp.164, 178 & n.

[9] Bailey, p.81.

[10] L.L. Loewe, *Basil Henriques* (1976), pp.72,73-4; *Probation* for October 1933 (p.258), October 1932 (p.196), January 1933 (pp.211-12), November 1938 (p.42), and March 1962 (p.13).

[11] See *Probation* for April 1933 (p.235), March 1957 (p.75), January 1934 (p.284), November 1938 (p.42).

[12] Mullins (1948), pp.194-5 (see pp.103-4 for probation orders); Chapman

(1932), p.79; Ellison (1964), pp.117-18; *Probation* for October 1933
(p.258); London Police Court Mission *Report for 1933,* pp.6-7,17.
13 Dark, pp.32-5.
14 Biron, p.246; Sandbach, p.74; Milton, p.76.
15 See Tom Cullen's biography *The Prostitutes' Padre* (1975), pp.72,172-4.
16 See Mullins (1948), pp.109-11,188,191,183-4. For information about
the Institute (I.S.T.D.) and its work I am much indebted to Dr. David
Rumney.
17 *Probation* for September-October 1948, p.221.
18 *National Association of Probation Officers,* March 1920, p.231.
19 *National Reformer,* 9.6.1889, p.358.
20 Central Council of Probation Committees, *The Probation Committee*
(1987), p.4.
21 *Guy and Molly Clutton-Brock* (1987), p.8; also p.7.
22 *Cold Comfort Confronted,* pp.24-5 (see also pp.13,15,16,19 *et seq.*).
23 I.L.P.S. archives: file (no. 742/1) on the Central Criminal Court, letter
of 19.4.1937 to George Neve, and typed note of 15.6.1937.
24 From Reginald Pestell's obituary of her in *Probation* for June 1961,
p.152.
25 From Ethel Currant's typed memorandum of "Feb 5th, 1937" (addressee
unidentified) among her papers to which she kindly gave me free
access.
26 *Probation* for February 1942, p.240.
27 For background to the South London and Ridley Road clashes, see,
for example, Harry Cole's *Policeman's Prelude* (1984) and Robert
Skidelsky's *Oswald Mosley* (1975), respectively.
28 Information from: Henriques (1937), p.253; Charles Morgan; *Probation*
for April 1930, p.45; London Police Court Mission *Report for 1938,*
pp.7-8; Crockford's; and S.J.C.P.O. Minutes for 22.10.1943.
29 As regards "re-education", see Bailey, p.161n., and *Probation* for
October 1932, p.196 (Laelia Sander), and for August 1938, p.24 (Guy
Clutton-Brock). Secularisation, professionalisation and bureaucratization similarly befell University teachers.

CHAPTER SEVEN

Main sources: information from Alison Allen, Charles Balchin, Florence
Bradley, Rose Mary Braithwaite, Aline Cholmondeley, Guy Clutton-
Brock, Ethel Currant, Ada Demer, Jack and Margaret Frost, Kathleen

Hoath, Bill Hornung, Josephine Knox, Francis Lister, Colette Maitland-Warne, Pat Mayhew, Charles Morgan, Reginald Pestell (Lord Wells-Pestell), Iris Pontifex, Allen Robins, C.H. Rolph, Peter Shervington, Derek Shuttleworth, Georgina Stafford, and John Starke; Bailey; R.H. Beeson/London Probation Committee (1945); Blyth; Bochel; Kenneth Brill, *John Groser* (1971) and "Brill looks back", *Community Care,* 6.7.1977, p.23; Carr-Saunders, A.M., Mannheim, H., and Rhodes, E.C. (1942); Guy and Molly Clutton-Brock (1972); Dark; Winifred Elkin, *English Juvenile Courts* (1938); French; Francis Treseder Giles, *Report on the Work of the London Juvenile Courts, 1942* (1943: typescript) and *Open Court* (1964); Dr. Edward Glover, *The Roots of Crime* (1960: the passage quoted by me is from a section originally published in 1949); Alma Hartshorn (1982); Henriques (1937 and 1950); Home Office *Directory of Probation Officers* (etc.) for 1941/2 and 1947, and *Inquiry into the administration of Remand Homes by the London County Council: Minutes of Proceedings* (4.12.1944 - 10.1.1945: typescript); *ILPAS '76;* Elizabeth Inman, "Juvenile Court Work" *(Probation* for May 1941, pp.194-6) and "A Lovely Job" *(Sideways,* Autumn 1984); Inner London Probation Service archives: file no. 742/1 on the Central Criminal Court and file no. 542 on the Morison Committee; Jarvis; Jewish Welfare Board archives: Jewish Association for the Protection of Girls, Women and Children, General Purposes Committee Minutes for 29.4.1936 and 15.11.1938; James A. Jones, *Courts Day by Day* (n.d.,1946); MS. 2060 and MS. 2063 in C.E.T.S. records, Lambeth Palace Library archives; Alfred Leeding, *Community Care,* 30.8.1978; Lieck (1938); London County Council records; London Police Court Mission *Annual Reports* for 1938-48; W.G. Minn (1948); Tony Parker and Robert Allerton (1962); issues of *Probation* between 1929 and 1963; C.H. Rolph (1974); Society of Juvenile Courts Probation Officers Minute Books covering the period June 1938 to August 1948; Sewell Stokes, *Court Circular* (1950); Various Contributors, *Guy and Molly Clutton-Brock* (1987); Walton (1975); Watson (1969); Wiggin (1948).

Other sources, or sources that merit highlighting, are:-

[1] "Mental defectives" are discussed in Beeson (1945), p.21, and in S.J.C.P.O. Minutes for 20.6.1938, 25.7.38 and 26.9.38 (in the care of the Rainer Foundation).

[2] W. David Wills, *The Hawkspur Experiment* (1941), p.188.

[3] Elizabeth Glover, *Probation and Re-Education* (1949), p.x. (Gwen

Rawlings, who joined the London Probation Service after the Second World War, was also associated with Time and Talents: see Marjorie Daunt, *By Peaceful Means: The Story of Time and Talents 1887-1987*, 1989, p.88.)

4 W. Norwood East, *Society and the Criminal* (1949), pp.177,291.

5 MS. 2063, Lambeth Palace Library (MS. 2060 touches on the genesis of the Probation Officers' Christian Fellowship).

6 *Probation* for March 1957, p.75.

7 Blyth (n.d.), pp.1,3.

8 *ILPAS '76*, p.11.

9 "The History of the London Probation Service", p.4: typescript forming part of N.A.P.O. evidence to the Morison Committee (copy in file no. 542, Inner London Probation Service archives).

10 Rolph (1974), pp.272-3; *Probation* for December 1958, p.185.

11 Information from Iris Pontifex. S.J.C.P.O. Minutes for 21.10.1940 referred to Beeson's "accident" in the context of his being "the victim of bombing".

12 From Ethel Currant's (typed) letter of "23.6.41" to "Mr Mathews" (quite probably William Burton Matthews, a London juvenile court probation officer since April 1939: he was a former teacher).

13 *Why Crime?* (1945), pp.99-101.

14 According to statistical information from Georgina Stafford.

15 Information about the scheme from Miriam Kratz, Marjorie Daunt, *Bermondsey Children's Flats* (Committee) *Annual Report 1950-1951* and *Annual Report 1951-1952*, John Watson (1965), and R.A.D. Forder (1966).

16 Vol. IX, p.369; Vol. I, p.399.

17 Information from Georgina Stafford.

18 S.J.C.P.O. Minutes for 22.3.1946 and 26.4.46.

19 In the *Journal of Criminal Law and Criminology* of Northwestern University, Vol. 37, No. 4, November-December 1946 (Evanston, Illinois, U.S.A.).

20 Dr. Kate Friedlander, *The Psycho-Analytical Approach to Juvenile Delinquency* (1947), p.255 & n.

21 *ILPAS '76*, pp.11-12; information from Margaret Frost.

22 S.J.C.P.O. Minutes for 16.7.1939.

23 London Probation Service Monthly Circular for 1 July 1948.

24 Inner London Probation Service Circular 13/1983 indicated that Rosemary Deane received a foreign honour for her relief work in Germany.

CHAPTER EIGHT

Main sources: information from Alison Allen, Charles Balchin, Florence Bradley, Rose Mary Braithwaite, Aline Cholmondeley, Irene Clarkson, Katherine Crofton, Edith and Mary Farmer, Margaret Frost, Elspeth Gray, Valerie Haig-Brown, Kathleen Hoath, Bill Hornung, Jo Knox, Francis Lister, Margaret May, Pat Mayhew, Frank Monk, Jean Moore, Charles Morgan, Margaret Paterson, Stanley Ratcliffe, Constance Rees, Allen Robins, C.H. Rolph, Peter Shervington, Derek Shuttleworth, Georgina Stafford, Stephanie Stevens, Doris Sullivan, Ellen Ruth Susskind (formerly Marks), Merfyn Turner, Marjorie Watts, and Lord Wells-Pestell; The Barge Boys' Club Annual Reports; B.B.C. Written Archives Centre; Bochel; Cambridge Dept. of Criminal Science (1958) and *Sexual Offences* (1957); *Case Conference* between 1954 and 1962; Mary Ellison, *Missing from Home* (1964); Farmer (1963); Giles (1964); Glover (1949); Grünhut (1963); Hartshorn (1982); Henriques (1950) and *The Home-Menders* (1955); Hobbs (1973); *ILPAS '76;* Elizabeth Inman, "A Lovely Job" (*Sideways,* Autumn 1984); Inner London Probation Service archives: Divorce Court Welfare papers at the Royal Courts of Justice, file no. 742/1 (Central Criminal Court) and file no. 542 (Morison Committee); Jarvis; Joint Consultative Committee in Child Care, Minutes of meeting held at L.C.C. County Hall on 21 September 1955; Joan King (ed.), *The Probation Service* (1958); Jo Knox, "Carry On Typing" (dated 30.9.85: a typescript history of the secretary in the probation service in London); London Police Court Mission *Annual Reports* for 1948-59; Milton (1959); Morison Report (*Report of the Departmental Committee on the Probation Service,* Cmnd. 1650, 1962); Morris (1950): this includes W.G. Minn's paper on "Probation Work"; Mullins (1945) and *The Sentence on the Guilty* (1957); Pollard (1962); Frank Powell, *Justice in Magistrates' Courts* (1951); issues of *Probation* between 1948 and 1961; Rolph (1974); Rose (1961 and 1967); Dr. P.D. Scott, "Selection of Cases in Juvenile Courts for Psychiatric Examination" (undated pamphlet reprinted from *Proceedings of the Royal Society of Medicine* for April 1948, Vol. XLI, No.4, pp.201-206); Society of Juvenile Courts Probation Officers Minute Book covering the period 1948 to 1959; Stokes (1950); Todd (1963); Various (1987); Walton (1975); Wilkinson (1955); Younghusband (1978).

Other sources, or sources that merit highlighting, are:-

[1] From letters to Farmer of 18.10.1938 from Guy Clutton-Brock and of

4.8.1948 from F.E.Moon, respectively, and other information provided by Edith and Mary Farmer.

2 Letter to Farmer of 18.10.1948 from V. Nigel Godfrey, Hon. Secretary, Essex Branch of N.A.P.O.

3 W.H. Pearce, "Probationers in Camp", *Probation,* March-April 1950, pp.15-16. *Probation* for November-December 1947 (p.165) indicated that a camp in August 1947 for probationers was the third such annual camp organised by Birmingham probation officers. The erstwhile provincial delinquent "Tony Grestone" related how, in about the late 1950s, his probation officer suggested he went camping with some other boys on probation (*They Put Me Inside,* 1973, p.23).

4 *Who's Who 1990,* p.1918 (under "Wells-Pestell").

5 Information on John Bradley's role vis-à-vis the Joint Negotiating Committee from the Public Record Office, Kew (ref. LAB 10/952), and N.A.P.O. head office. In 1946 John Bradley had proposed, albeit unsuccessfully, the quite skilfully worded motion that S.J.C.P.O. should apply to become a branch of N.A.P.O. The S.J.C.P.O. Minutes for 22.7.1944 and 22.9.44 indicate his critical attitude regarding London probation officers' remuneration.

6 Inference drawn from Margaret Kornitzer's *Child Adoption in the Modern World* (1952), pp.54,234-41.

7 *Hoxton Café Project: Report on Seven Years' Work* (March 1972: Youth Service Information Centre, Leicester, Report 3), pp.4,55.

8 Facts concerning her father supplied by Miss Thornborough and others in the course of my researches into the life and work of John Mackinnon Robertson.

9 Expressed in Sarah McCabe's article on Henriques in the *D.N.B.* for 1961-1970, p.508.

10 From Miss R.M. Braithwaite's unsigned obituary in *Probation* for March 1962, p.13, partly reproduced, in an amended form, in L.L. Loewe's *Basil Henriques* (1976), pp.73-4.

11 In his article "Recent Developments in Probation", *Case Conference,* February 1958, p.224.

12 "The Social Worker in Prison", *Case Conference,* September 1957, pp.99-102.

13 See, for example, Frank Schaffer's *The New Town Story* (second edition, 1972, pp.278-93) and Peter Willmott's *The Evolution of a Community* (1963, pp.4,121).

[14] Information from Margaret Paterson, Sokoloff (1987), Williamson (1963) and Rolph (1974). Miss Paterson was a co-author of the London Probation Service Women's Hostels and Homes Committee *Handbook of Hostels and Homes, Shelters and Refuges for Children, Girls and Women other than Approved Hostels and Homes* (printed July 1953). The handbook's other co-authors (all female) included the London probation officers Miss A.M. Born, Mrs. E.M. Dashwood, Miss M.E. Dawkins, Mrs. Margaret Garlick (later Frost), Mrs. V. Grant, Mrs. Elspeth Gray, Mrs. K. Hill, Miss Elizabeth Inman, Miss A. Kerridge, Miss Ellen Ruth Marks, Miss Nina Nowell, and Miss Joan Woodward (as well as Superintendent E. Smith of the Metropolitan Women Police and probation officers from Essex, Kent, Surrey, and Middlesex).

[15] *Social Problems of Modern Britain* (1972, eds. Eric Butterworth and David Weir), p.87.

[16] *NAPO News,* October 1988, p.5.

[17] Inner London Probation and After-Care Service Circular 7/1979, p.35.

[18] *Trends in British Society since 1900* (1972, ed. A.H. Halsey), p.516.

[19] E. Smithies, *Crime in Wartime* (1982), p.199. Very largely the same pattern regarding the period 1938-60 as a whole was discerned by Hugh Klare in *The Twentieth Century* for Winter 1962, p.15.

[20] *Case Conference,* April 1960, pp.246-7,252-3,256.

[21] The George Newton quotations are drawn from *Case Conference,* February 1958, pp.222,223, and *British Journal of Delinquency,* October 1956, pp.131,126.

[22] Younghusband (1978), Vol.1, pp.100,101; Sybille Bedford, *The Faces of Justice* (1961), pp.45,60.

CHAPTER NINE

Main sources: information from Alison Allen, Maud Ivy Alleyne, Charles Balchin, Peter Barnes, Roy Barr, Lydia Blackman, Rose Mary Braithwaite, Aline Cholmondeley, Norah Clarke, Irene Clarkson, Ron Conn, Katherine Crofton, Ethel Currant, Irene Edmonds, P. Engleman, Edith and Mary Farmer, E.A. Fleming, Margaret Frost, Tony Goodman, Norman Grant, Elspeth Gray, Valerie Haig-Brown, Bill Hornung, Elizabeth Inman, Jo Knox, Gunter Lubowski, Colette Maitland-Warne, Carol Martin, Charlotte Mitra, Frank Monk, Charles Morgan, Joe Nixon, Margaret Paterson, Stanley Ratcliffe, M.A. Richman, Nicholas Rivett-Carnac, Peter Shervington,

Derek Shuttleworth, Georgina Stafford, Doris Sullivan, Dorothy Swinney, and Merfyn Turner; *The Annual Charities Digest* for 1965; Hugh Barr and Erica O'Leary, *Trends and Regional Comparisons in Probation (England and Wales)* (Home Office, 1966); Barry Report (*The Organisation of After-Care*: Report of the Advisory Council on the Treatment of Offenders, 1963); B.B.C. Written Archives Centre; Leila Berg, *Risinghill: Death of a Comprehensive School* (1968); the Circle Trust; Farmer (1963); Finlay (1969); Forder (1966); French (1976); Glass (1960); Grünhut (1963); Dr. H.M. Holden, *Hoxton Café Project* (1972); Home Office, *Report on the Work of the Probation and After-Care Department 1962 to 1965*, Cmnd. 3107, 1966); *The Hoxton Café Project*, Report No. 1(1964) and No. 2(1965); *ILPAS '76;* Independent Broadcasting Authority; Inner London Probation Committee; Inner London Probation Service archives: especially file no. 542 (Morison Committee); King (1964); Jo Knox, "Carry On Typing" (typescript dated 30.9.85); Morison Reports (*Report/Second Report of the Departmental Committee on the Probation Service*, Cmnd. 1650 and 1800 respectively, both 1962); O'Mahoney (1978); issues of *Probation* between 1959 and 1965; Martin Silberman *et al., Explorations in After-Care* (Home Office, 1971); S.J.C.P.O. records; Gilbert Smith, *Social Work and the Sociology of Organizations* (1970); Sokoloff; St. John (1961); Leslie Thompson (1985); Marjory Todd (1963 and 1964); Turner, *Norman House* (1961); Wallich-Clifford (1962 and 1974); West Midlands Probation Service; Younghusband (1978).

Other sources, or sources that merit highlighting, are:-

[1] From "The Inner London Probation and After-Care Service", p.1 (dated 14.11.1967: typescript by W. Joan Woodward, who used the initials "WW" to distinguish her from her colleague John Washington, also at head office).

[2] *British Journal of Delinquency,* October 1959, pp.99-100.

[3] The quotations in this paragraph and the previous one referring to the London juvenile courts are drawn from the *Daily Telegraph and Morning Post* for 28.11.1960, p.18 (article by Guy Rais), and for 25.11.60, p.12 (article by Ruth Morrah).

[4] See, for example, Stokes (1950, pp.63-4), Bedford (1961, pp.76-7) and Todd (1964, p.131); also information from Jo Knox and Marjorie Watts.

[5] Anthony Richardson (1965), pp.53,170,150,122,120.

[6] Stokes (1950, p.61) described a London colleague's client as "a coloured boy". For the formation and early days of the Social Council, see David Mason *et al., News from Notting Hill* (1967), pp.18-19.

[7] "Practical Work Placements for Social Science Students", p.4 (typescript of address to London probation officers on 31.5.1960).

[8] F.T. Giles, *The Criminal Law* (1961 edition), p.156.

[9] In *Pressures and Change in the Probation Service* (1979, ed. Joan King), p.115.

[10] "Pilot Survey on Probation Officers Interviewing Sessions", pp.13,14 (undated typescript circulated on non-confidential basis to probation officers in London and elsewhere).

[11] Cmnd. 3107 (1966), p.19.

[12] Lord Feversham in *Probation* for June 1962, p.18; see also *The Probation Service* (ed. Joan King), p.227, 1964 edition. N.A.P.O.'s Benevolent Fund was named after Edridge.

[13] *Trends in British Society since 1900* (1972, ed. A.H. Halsey), p.523.

[14] The Braithwaite, Sullivan and Fubini quotations are drawn from "The Probation Officer, His Training and Skill" (*Probation* for September 1959, p.32), "The Probation Officer - His Function and Role" (typescript dated 28.4.61, pp.3,4,5,6), and "Re-assessing the Work of Probation Officers" (typescript dated 13 October 1961, pp.1,3,4), respectively.

[15] Farmer's perceptions found expression in his papers "What I Expect of a Senior" (typescript dated October 1960) and "The Role of the Senior Officer in His Setting" (undated typescript, emanating from about 1962?): the direct quotation is drawn from the latter, p.10.

[16] Irene Clarkson, in interview, independently recalled that probation officers attached to the London Sessions "borrowed" rooms at local probation offices for reporting purposes.

[17] King, p.118, 1964 edition.

[18] From Marjory Todd's signed inscription (undated) on fly-leaf of Rose Mary Braithwaite's copy of *The Probation Officer and His World.*

[19] Information gleaned from the sub-committee's interim report (typescript dated 21 August 1961, especially pp. 2 and 3).

[20] Jo Knox's contribution was indicated in the *Brighton and Hove Gazette,* 20 March 1964, p.11.

[21] *Ever Such A Nice Lady,* p.16.

[22] The ensuing quotations are drawn from this sub-committee's report

(typescript dated 17 August 1964,5pp.), drawn up by Seldon Farmer (representing headquarters), Mr. J.S. Ferguson (Old Street Court), Claude Fubini (West London), Stanley Ratcliffe (Old Street), and Miss Doreen Yardley (Thames).

23 Playfair and Sington (1965), p.330. The 1990 White Paper *Crime, Justice and Protecting The Public* (Cm 965, p.39) exaggerated in suggesting that the Morison Committee, which reported in 1962, had undertaken a major review of the financing of the probation service (as distinct from probation officers' salaries and conditions of service).

24 "Group Situations in the Service of the Client", pp.4,6 (undated typescript relating to seniors' conference on 8.11.1963).

25 Information from the National Council's 1946 to 1948 Annual Reports. *Licensed To Live* (1985, p.12) by J.B. Coker and J.P. Martin, the Barry Report (1963, p.81), and the Inner London Probation Service "Life Sentence Working Group Report" (typescript dated 16.2.83) provided some interesting historical data concerning "lifers".

26 "After Care in the Penal System", *Case Conference,* March 1968, p.432.

27 "The Decision to Remand for Mental Examination", *British Journal of Criminology,* January 1966, pp.6-25. No information has come to light regarding the extent - presumably minimal - to which London probation officers up to 1965 supervised clients discharged conditionally from special hospitals, given the Mental Health Act 1959. Years later the Government appointed the former London probation officer George P. Newton, Sir Carl Aarvold and Sir Denis Hill as a committee to review procedures for the discharge and supervision of psychiatric patients subject to special restrictions.

28 Walker and McCabe, Vol. II, 1973, p.64. For Titmuss, see the proceedings of the 1961 Annual Conference of the National Association for Mental Health.

29 Personal communication from Dr. Doris Hollander (consultant psychiatrist).

30 Mary Morse, *The Unattached* (1965), p.211. In 1954 Hampstead had the highest suicide rate in England and Wales (D. McCormick, *The Unseen Killer,* 1964, p.83).

31 *Caring on Skid Row,* 1976, 1982 reprint, p.93.

32 Norah Clarke remembered London probation officers as "very kind and dedicated".

Appendices

Appendix 1

Messrs Batchelor and Nelson, ex-guardsmen who became the first two Police Court Missionaries

Source: *Rainer Foundation*

Appendix 2

Source: *London Police Court Mission Annual Report for 1893*

Appendix 3

LONDON DIOCESAN POLICE COURT MISSION C.E.T.S.

Summary of Preventive and Rescue Work done in the Police, Petty Sessional and Sessions Courts of the Diocese of London by the Police Court Missionaries during 1900.

Nature of Work Done	Total	Mr. F. W. Burrett, Westminster Court	Mr. P. Carslake, West London Court	Mr. W. J. Plaithwaite, Thames Court	Mr. G. Hall, Bow Street Court	Mr. T. Holmes, North London Court	Mr. A. Kirby, Marylebone Court	Mr. R. Marshall, Brentford Court	Mr. G. Nelson, Mansion House and City Courts	Mr. H. Robinson, Dalston Court	Mr. W. S. Frame-Falkner, Enfield, Tottenham and Wood Green (In-2 Sessions)	Mr. C. A. Gough, Hampstead and Harlesden Courts	Mr. J. E. Sampson, Highgate Court	Mr. S. Billington, Barnes, Sunbury and Teddington Courts (9 months)
Visits to Police Courts	3431	297	801	278	292	298	288	299	294	308	266	178	291	51
House visits to and re Cases	8777	739	741	1079	552	751	1574	911	719	327	353	431	291	359
Workhouse, Hospital, and Infirmary visits	343	33	9	98	7	18	36	35	14	25	73	7	5	19
Visits to employers	450	63	19	73	10	48	48	36	2	6	101	27	6	21
Successful in averting loss of employment	169	14	10	4	7	8	21	30	6	4	54	3	1	1
Visits to Missionaries at home or at the Police Courts	8319	846	363	282	775	662	1378	1464	530	160	681	248	91	659
Pledges taken	1430	131	64	67	149	92	262	152	95	73	196	46	22	91
Persons met at Prisons	105	22	28					21	1		18	1	2	16
Persons received into Missionaries' House	56	4	1		*		1	40		1	1			
Persons sent to Convalescent Home	113		1	7	6	18			27	14	8	3		
Persons furnished with clothing, blankets, food, coals, &c.	1546	169	65	124	80	62	171	236	374	170	31	45	6	18
Situations found for (a) men	201	24	11	2	7	30	4	84	15	3	19	3		9
(b) lads	190	24	5	7		29	7	71	7	1	22	4		4
Situations found for (a) women	198	22	8	4	10	17		104	8	6	7	7	2	1
(b) girls	150	14		14	6		3	74	2	5	11	7	2	2
Women and girls taken or sent to Homes	394	57	35	25	37	80	22	36	66	58	96	3	5	4
Women and girls restored to friends	264	30	23	5	47	1	30	49	35	12	14	9	1	8
Families set up with homes (whole or in part)	46	2	1		3	6		33	1					1
Rent and lodgings paid	545	72	64	24	71	37	14	65	20	86	63	6	2	15
Helped with tools or stock, &c.	649	133	20	11	29	41	2	65	137	34	189	21	9	8
Men sent to Homes	143	22	8	6	22			11	7	52	13	2		2
Lads sent to Homes	343	30	10	12	75	6	24	33	43	62	43	1	3	
Lads provided with outfit and sent to sea	50	10		14	2		7	9		6	2			
Lads restored to friends	275	25	33	2	38	22	34	42	54	6	17	1		
Letters written by Missionaries	6661	540	611	572	424	826	629	1040	611	360	424	335	171	188
Special cases from Magistrate	1469	234	149	148	40	9	165	199	201	132	121	12	43	41
Remand cases dealt with by Missionaries	1782	207	204	65	64	No Return	289	323	273	118	85	15	46	33
Cases referred to local Clergy, &c.	333	96	87	24	11	46	3	33	25	11	27		4	6
Money received	£1605 6 4	487 9 1½	167 9 1½	175 0 0	180 16 10	146 0 0	84 8 6	300 12 6	123 1 0	64 0 0	75 5 8	19 18 9	15 5 0	13 0 0
Money expended	£1784 2 7	452 19 10	167 9 0	174 0 0	174 3 4	136 2 6	60 19 11	295 18 6	127 18 3	64 0 0	78 9 4	19 9 11	16 3 0	12 9 0

Source: *London Police Court Mission Annual Report for 1900*

Appendix 4

No. 15 PROBATION OF OFFENDERS ACT, 1907.

_____Police Court.

Date_____190___

I HEREBY CERTIFY that_____
released on probation for_____months, has during that time been under the supervision of
_____who has fulfilled the duties of Probation Officer
during that period to my satisfaction, and the period of probation being completed, the said
Probation Officer is now entitled to be paid

				£	s.	d.
Fee in respect of such supervision	...	...	...			
Allowance for out of pocket expenses	...	...				
		Total	...	£		

Magistrate.

NOTE.—This Certificate is to accompany the Account, which must be presented for payment at the Office of the Receiver for the Metropolitan Police District, New Scotland Yard, S.W., immediately after 31st March, 30th June, 30th September or 31st December.
Payments are made daily (Saturdays and Public Holidays excepted) between 11 a.m. and 3 p.m.
No payment will be made in respect of this Certificate unless presented within twelve months from the date of issue.

Drake, Driver & Leaver, Limited, London, E.C.

Source: *Inner London Probation Service archives*

Appendix 5

TABLE A.—POLICE-COURT MISSION REPORT 1901-1908.

	Situations found for				Cases dealt with at Request of the Magistrates.	Women and Girls placed in Homes or restored to Friends.	Employers persuaded to reinstate Persons charged.	Men and Lads restored to Friends, sent to Sea or to Homes.
	Men.	Women.	Lads.	Girls.				
1901	170	259	175	143	2,012	958	134	900
1902	174	284	162	136	1,768	1,052	113	865
1903	171	301	164	157	1,737	1,004	115	929
1904	173	247	141	151	2,019	1,164	108	916
1905	196	211	189	141	2,293	1,108	117	954
1906	245	217	167	113	2,521	1,041	125	1,007
1907	265	261	203	180	3,466	1,113	157	1,185
1908*	351	231	277	192	4,403	982	173	1,127
	1,745	2,011	1,478	1,213	20,219	8,422	1,042	7,883

* Probation work started in this year.

Source: *Report of the Departmental Committee on the Probation of Offenders Act, 1907 (1910, Cd. 5002)*

324

Appendix 6

DEPARTMENTAL COMMITTEE ON PROBATION OF OFFENDERS ACT, 1907 :

RETURN with regard to the Persons against whom Probation Orders were made at the CENTRAL CRIMINAL COURT, the NORTH and SOUTH LONDON SESSIONS, the COURTS of SUMMARY JURISDICTION of the CITY of LONDON, and the METROPOLITAN POLICE COURTS during the Year 1908.*

Court.		
COURTS OF RECORD.		
Central Criminal Court		
London Sessions { North		
{ South		
TOTAL (*Courts of Record*)		
COURTS OF SUMMARY JURISDICTION, CITY OF LONDON.		
Mansion House Justice Room		
Guildhall		
TOTAL (*City of London*)		
METROPOLITAN POLICE COURTS.		
Bow Street		
Clerkenwell		
Greenwich		
Lambeth		
Marlborough Street		
Marylebone		
North London		
South Western		
Thames		
Tower Bridge		
West London		
Westminster		
Woolwich		
Old Street		
TOTAL (*Metropolitan Police Courts*)		

Source: *Departmental Committee on the Probation of Offenders Act, 1907*

325

Appendix 7

DEPARTMENTAL COMMITTEE ON PROBATION OF OFFENDERS ACT, 1907 : [*Continued.*

29 *March* 1909. Mr. H. C. BENNETT.

PADCROFT HOME.

	Placed in Situations.	Absconded.	Miscellaneous Occupations.	Died.	Hospital.	Navy.	Army.	Farms.	House Boys.	Page, Pantry, Kitchen Boys.	Grocers, Bakers, or Butchers.	Apprenticed to Trades.	Yorkshire Mines.	Stable and Garden Boys.	Errand or Van Boys.	To Shoemakers, Carpenters, Engineers, or Printers.	Emigrated.
1902 (six months)	62	15				2	1			13							
1903	92	19	15	2	2	5	4	7		10	13	11	16				
1904 (Home burnt down)	110	25	30					14		35	13	4	3	2			
1905	60	18	13			5		2		20	4	5	3	2	6		
1906	146	22	43			10		4		34	8	3	12	12	7	12	1
1907	174	21	39			6		6		43	8		15	12	19	21	5
1908	202	14	35			3		22		44	25		27	12	4	28	2
	846	134	175	2	2	36		55		199	71	23	76	40	43	61	8

Source: *Departmental Committee on the Probation of Offenders Act, 1907*

Appendix 8

NUMBER of PERSONS with respect to whom PROBATION ORDERS were made during the year 1912, the NATURE of the OFFENCES for which made and the DISPOSAL of PERSONS who APPEARED for SENTENCE, after RELEASE on PROBATION.

Table headings:
- Persons with respect to whom Probation Orders were made — Total Number; Sex (Males, Females); Age (Under 12 years M/F; 12 to 14 M/F; 14 to 16 M/F; 16 to 21 M/F; Above 21 M/F)
- Disposal of Persons who appeared for sentence after release on Probation Order — Total Number; Discharged; Committed to Industrial School; Sentenced to Imprisonment; Place of Detention; Committed to Reformatory School; Dealt with for a fresh offence; Otherwise disposed of

Offence	Total No.	Males	Females	Und.12 M	Und.12 F	12–14 M	12–14 F	14–16 M	14–16 F	16–21 M	16–21 F	Abv.21 M	Abv.21 F	Disp. Total	Discharged	Comm. Industrial Sch.	Sentenced to Impris.	Place of Detention	Comm. Reformatory Sch.	Dealt with fresh offence	Otherwise disposed of
INDICTABLE OFFENCES TRIED SUMMARILY.																					
Simple larceny and offences punishable as simple larceny	1,038	854	184	76	1	149	6	189	20	342	77	148	80	60	23	2	21	—	2	8	4
Larceny from the person	22	17	5	1	—	—	—	3	1	9	3	4	1	1	1	—	—	—	—	—	1
Larceny as a clerk or servant	322	310	112	—	—	4	1	42	18	93	51	71	42	8	1	—	3	—	3	2	—
Embezzlement	119	118	1	—	—	1	—	20	—	47	1	50	—	3	—	—	1	—	—	2	—
Obtaining goods, &c., by false pretences	21	12	9	1	—	—	—	1	—	7	4	3	5	—	—	—	—	—	—	—	—
Receiving stolen goods	11	6	5	—	—	—	—	1	—	3	—	2	5	—	—	—	—	—	—	—	—
Indecent assault upon female person under 16	1	1	—	—	—	—	—	1	—	—	—	—	—	—	—	—	—	—	—	—	—
Other indictable offences committed by children or young persons, viz.:— Malicious wounding and other like offences (misdemeanours)	1	—	1	—	—	—	—	—	1	—	—	—	—	—	—	—	—	—	—	—	—
Defilement of girls under 13	1	1	—	—	—	—	—	1	—	—	—	—	—	—	—	—	—	—	—	—	—
Burglary	2	1	1	—	—	—	—	1	1	—	—	—	—	—	—	—	—	—	—	—	—
Housebreaking	10	10	—	4	—	2	—	4	—	—	—	—	—	—	—	—	—	—	—	—	—
Breaking into shops, warehouses, &c., and stealing	30	30	—	8	—	10	—	12	—	—	—	—	—	1	—	—	—	1	—	—	—
Attempts to break into houses, shops, warehouses, &c.	2	2	—	2	—	—	—	—	—	—	—	—	—	—	—	—	—	—	—	—	—
Entering with intent to commit felony	3	3	—	—	—	2	—	1	—	—	—	—	—	—	—	—	—	—	—	—	—
Possession of house-breaking tools	1	1	—	—	—	—	—	1	—	—	—	—	—	—	—	—	—	—	—	—	—
Arson	1	1	—	—	—	1	—	—	—	—	—	—	—	—	—	—	—	—	—	—	—
Forgery and uttering (felony)	2	2	—	—	—	—	—	2	—	—	—	—	—	—	—	—	—	—	—	—	—
Uttering or possessing counterfeit coin	1	1	—	—	—	1	—	—	—	—	—	—	—	—	—	—	—	—	—	—	—
TOTAL	1,588	1,270	318	92	1	170	7	228	41	502	136	278	133	73	24	3	25	—	4	12	5
OTHER OFFENCES TRIED SUMMARILY.																					
Assaults: Aggravated	1	1	—	—	—	—	—	—	—	—	—	—	—	—	1	—	—	—	—	—	—
On constable	2	2	—	—	—	—	—	1	—	1	—	—	—	—	—	—	—	—	—	—	—
Common	19	18	1	—	—	—	—	1	—	3	—	14	1	—	1	—	—	—	—	—	—
Betting and gaming	2	2	—	—	—	—	—	—	—	2	—	—	—	—	—	—	—	—	—	—	—
Brothel keeping	3	—	3	—	—	—	—	—	—	—	1	—	2	—	—	—	—	—	—	—	—
Cruelty to children	5	2	3	—	—	—	—	—	—	—	1	2	2	1	1	—	—	—	—	—	—
Education Acts, offences against	1	1	—	—	—	—	—	—	—	—	—	1	—	—	—	—	—	—	—	—	—
Indecent exposure	4	4	—	—	—	—	—	2	—	2	—	—	—	—	—	—	—	—	—	—	—
Intoxicating Liquor laws, offences against: Drunkenness simple	38	6	32	—	—	—	—	—	—	—	—	6	32	4	2	—	—	—	—	—	2
Drunkenness with aggravations	65	19	46	—	—	—	—	—	—	3	1	16	45	7	1	—	—	—	—	2	4
Malicious damage: To trees, shrubs, &c.	1	1	—	—	—	1	—	—	—	—	—	—	—	—	—	—	—	—	—	—	—
Other offences	17	14	3	5	—	1	—	1	—	5	2	2	1	1	1	—	—	1	—	—	—
Merchant Shipping Acts, offences against	1	1	—	—	—	—	—	—	—	1	—	—	—	—	—	—	1	—	—	—	—
Military and naval law, offences against: Army	2	2	—	—	—	—	—	—	—	1	—	1	—	—	—	—	1	—	—	—	—

Appendix 8 (continued)

NUMBER of PERSONS with respect to whom PROBATION ORDERS were made during the year 1912, the NATURE of the OFFENCES for which made and the DISPOSAL of PERSONS who APPEARED for SENTENCE after RELEASE on PROBATION—*continued.*

Offence	Total Number	Males	Females	Under 12 yrs M	Under 12 yrs F	12 to 14 M	12 to 14 F	14 to 18 M	14 to 18 F	16 to 21 M	16 to 21 F	Above 21 M	Above 21 F	Total Number	Discharged	Committed to Industrial School	Sentenced to Imprisonment	Place of Detention	Committed to Reformatory School	Dealt with for a fresh offence	Otherwise disposed of
OTHER OFFENCES TRIED SUMMARILY—*cont.*																					
Parks, commons, and open spaces, offences in relation to	4	—	4	—	·	—	—	—	—	—	2	—	2	1	—	—	—	—	—	—	1
Pawnbrokers Acts, offences against: Unlawful pledging	6	2	4	—	—	—	—	—	—	—	1	2	3	—	—	—	—	—	—	—	—
Police regulations, offences against:																					
Metropolitan Police Acts	28	8	20	—	—	—	—	2	1	4	12	2	7	5	2	—	1	—	—	1	1
County Byelaws	1	—	1	—	—	—	—	—	—	—	1	—	—	1	1	—	—	—	—	—	—
Local Acts and Byelaws	1	1	—	—	—	—	—	—	—	1	—	—	—	—	—	—	—	—	—	—	—
Poor Law, offences against: Neglecting to maintain family, &c.	3	—	3	—	—	—	—	—	—	—	—	—	3	—	—	—	—	—	—	—	—
Misbehaviour by paupers	3	1	2	—	—	—	—	—	—	1	1	—	1	2	1	—	—	—	—	—	1
Stealing or destroying workhouse clothes	2	2	—	—	—	—	—	—	—	1	—	1	—	—	—	—	—	—	—	—	—
Prostitution	74	—	74	—	—	—	—	1	—	34	—	39		3	—	—	1	—	—	—	2
Railways, offences in relation to	7	5	2	—	—	1	—	1	1	3	—	—	1	—	—	—	—	—	—	—	—
Stealing and attempting to steal:																					
Animals	3	3	—	—	—	—	—	—	—	2	—	1	—	—	—	—	—	—	—	—	—
Growing fruit, plants, vegetables, &c.	44	42	2	10	1	7	—	16	—	7	—	2	1	—	—	—	—	—	—	—	—
Unlawful possession	40	39	1	2	—	2	—	8	—	21	1	6	—	1	—	—	1	—	—	—	—
Vagrancy Act, offences against:																					
Begging	81	73	8	20	—	6	—	12	—	28	1	7	7	1	—	—	—	—	—	1	—
Sleeping out	27	19	8	—	—	2	—	8	2	8	3	1	3	3	—	1	1	—	—	—	1
Gaming, &c.	9	9	—	—	—	—	—	5	—	4	—	—	—	1	—	—	—	—	—	1	—
Found in enclosed premises, possessing picklocks, &c.	41	39	2	2	—	1	—	8	—	20	1	8	1	3	—	—	—	3	—	—	—
Frequenting	33	33	—	—	—	2	—	2	—	19	—	10	—	4	1	—	2	—	—	1	—
Living on prostitutes' earnings	2	2	—	—	—	—	—	1	—	1	—	—	—	—	—	—	—	—	—	—	—
Other offences	5	2	3	—	—	—	—	1	—	1	2	—	1	1	1	—	—	—	—	—	—
Other offences, viz.:																					
Offences under:																					
Pedlars Act, 1871	1	1	—	—	—	—	—	—	—	—	—	1	—	—	—	—	—	—	—	—	—
Post Office Act, 1908	2	2	—	—	—	—	—	—	—	1	—	1	—	—	—	—	—	—	—	—	—
Total	578	356	222	30	1	22	—	70	5	139	64	86	152	39	10	1	10	—	—	●	12
Grand Total for all offences	2,166	1,626	540	131	2	192	7	296	46	641	200	364	285	112	34	4	35	—	4	18	17

Source: *Report of the Commissioner of Police of the Metropolis for the Year 1912* (1913, Cd. 7108)

Appendix 9

Offenders Released on Probation, shewing Age and Sex and Number subsequently Sentenced.

Metropolitan Police District and London City.

Year.	Total Number.	Sex.		Number who were under 16.		Number of Persons who appeared for Sentence after release on Probation Order.
		Males.	Females.	Males.	Females.	
1908 ...	1,411	1,047	364	321	41	88
1909 ...	1,458	1,078	380	302	37	96
1910 ...	2,005	1,535	470	447	44	91
1911 ...	1,844	1,363	481	421	41	100
1912 ...	2,210	1,676	543	638	56	116
1913 ...	2,544	1,844	700	694	75	118
1914 ...	2,535					
1915 ...	2,659					
1916 ...	3,459	⎫ Particulars not available for these years. (Returns				
1917 ...	3,618	not collected.)				
1918 ...	3,593	⎭				
1919 ...	3,148	2,106	1,042	994	109	175

No persons were placed under **Probation** by the *Central Criminal Court* during the years 1917 to 1919.

Source: *Report of the Departmental Committee on the Training, Appointment and Payment of Probation Officers* (1922, Cmd. 1601)

Appendix 10

SHOREDITCH JUVENILE COURT FIGURES.

Table Showing the Nature of the Offences Charged.

Boys.

Year	Larceny Act.	Suspected Person.	Wilful Damage.	Indecency.	Assault.	Gambling.	Found Wandering.	Beyond Control.	Begging.	Immoral Surroundings.	Falling on Probation.	Petty Offences.	Totals.
1912	299	15			3	14	83	25	54	22	3	27	546
1915	554	5	2	4	0	22	77	43	0	30	0	46	813
1916	623	18	14	1	0	13	110	50	1	34	4	55	944
1921	300	8	4				27	25	6	7	16	9	402
1922	272	4	2				23	16		1	1	14	333
1923	239	14	5				20	20		5	2	30	341
1924	172	12					18	21		7	8	25	263

Girls.

Year	Larceny Act.	Suspected Person.	Wilful Damage.	Indecency.	Assault.	Gambling.	Found Wandering.	Beyond Control.	Begging.	Immoral Surroundings.	Falling on Probation.	Petty Offences.	Totals.
1912	13						29	7	4	7	1	1	62
1915	40						23	17	4	6	1	1	05
1916	39	1			1		32	18		12			103
1921	12						13	7		12	3		47
1922	14						27	5		5	2	1	54
1923	13						16	3		8			40
1924	14						9	5		10	1		48

Source: *W. Clarke Hall: Children's Courts* (1926)

Appendix 11

SHOREDITCH JUVENILE COURT FIGURES.

Table Showing the Way in which Charges were Dealt With.

Year	Discharged Forthwith	Discharged after Remand	Bound Over	Put on Probation	Fined	Whipped	Industrial School	Reformatory	Poor Law	Custody Transferred	Unfinished	Adjourned Sine Die	Total
Boys.													
1912	91	50	64	90	38	67	124	29	3	—	—	—	540
1915	104	88	160	129	80	63	155	27	3	—	—	—	813
1916	86	208	129	130	141	36	177	21	11	—	—	—	944
1921	38	—	33	182	24	2	08	23	—	1	19	12	402
1922	52	—	15	181	6	—	43	14	—	1	10	11	333
1923	36	—	13	170	12	—	48	20	—	—	5	21	341
1924	27	—	14	136	5	—	50	10	—	—	10	5	263
Girls.													
1912	5	6	2	5	1	—	35	3	3	—	—	—	62
1915	10	5	14	18	2	—	31	2	13	—	—	—	95
1916	6	20	10	20	2	—	31	2	12	—	—	—	103
1921	2	—	1	13	—	—	21	1	—	1	4	4	47
1922	6	—	—	10	—	—	28	1	—	2	4	3	54
1923	—	—	—	7	—	—	18	2	—	1	1	5	40
1924	1	—	—	17	—	—	24	1	—	1	2	2	48
Total Percentage 1924	9	—	4·5	50	1·5	—	23·5	6·5	—	0·3	4	2	—

Source: *W. Clarke Hall: op. cit.* (1926)

Appendix 12

PROBATIONER'S NAME
(Surname first)

PROBATION EXPIRES ON 14 - 6 - 28

Guildhall

Probation completed satisfactorily

Probation Records.

Cover.

LONDON :
PUBLISHED BY HIS MAJESTY'S STATIONERY OFFICE.
To be purchased directly from H.M. STATIONERY OFFICE at the following addresses :
Adastral House, Kingsway, London, W.C.2 ; 120, George Street, Edinburgh ;
York Street, Manchester ; 1, St. Andrew's Crescent, Cardiff ;
15, Donegall Square West, Belfast ;
or through any Bookseller.

1926.

Source: *Inner London Probation Service archives*

Appendix 12 (continued)

Probation Records.	............*Guildhall*............Court.
Particulars.	RECORD OF PERSONS PLACED ON PROBATION.

Magistrates....*Alderman*............ Probation Officer....*C. Mornaday*

........*Howell*........ Police Officer....*P.C.*............

1. Probationer's Name	
Address	
Sex	*Male* Religion....*C.E.*
Aged	*12 yrs* on ....*29 - 11*............19.*26*.
2. Charge	*Larceny (automatic machines)*
3. Date and Duration of Order (for any variation of the order see 14 infra.)	*14 - 6*....19.*27* to ....*14 - 6*....19.*28*
4. Condition of recognizance	*In the sum of £5*
5. Special conditions	—
6. Surety	—
7. Previous offences (if any)	—
8. Occupation and Wages	
9. Name and address of Employer	
10. Name of School	*Burston Rd. L.C.C. school*
11. School attendance during Probation	
12. Family	*Both parents 5 children (Boys 16 yrs 14 & 11 yrs Girls 8 & 10 yrs)*
13. Number of visits 1. paid, 2. received	
14. Result of Probation. Any Order varying the original Order should be specially noted here.	

[OVER.

333

Appendix 12 (continued)

Special remarks and Particulars (if any) continued from overleaf.

Fair home occupy 4
rooms pay 18/- per week.
Respectable parents.
attends Hoxton Mission,
Pitfield St,
E.C.
Father a worker in Whitbread

LONDON:
PUBLISHED BY HIS MAJESTY'S STATIONERY OFFICE.
To be purchased directly from H.M. STATIONERY OFFICE at the following addresses:
Adastral House, Kingsway, London, W.C.2; 120, George Street, Edinburgh; York Street,
Manchester; 1, St. Andrew's Crescent, Cardiff; 15, Donegall Square West, Belfast; or
through any bookseller.

1927.

Price 3d. net per 25; 5d. net per 50; 9d. net per 100.

Printed under the authority of His Majesty's Stationery Office by
Jas. Truscott & Son, Ltd., Suffolk Lane, E.C.4.

(*2290) Wt. 23042—1548. 10,000. 2/27. T.S. 138

Appendix 12 (continued)

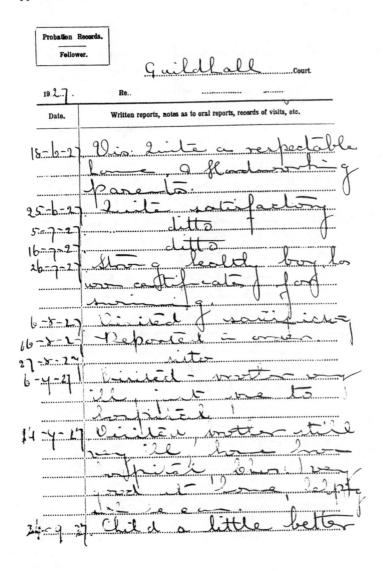

Probation Records.

Follower.

Guildhall ....Court.

19 2 7. Re.. ....

Date.	Written reports, notes as to oral reports, records of visits, etc.
18-6-27	Was quite a respectable home, a hardworking parents.
25-6-27	Quite satisfactory
5-7-27	ditto
16-7-27	ditto
26-7-27	Was a healthy boy but was certificate for swimming
6-8-27	Visited & satisfactory
16-8-27	Reported — own
27-8-27	ditto
6-9-27	Visited — matter
14-9-27	Visited, matter still
24-9-27	Child a little better

Appendix 12 (continued)

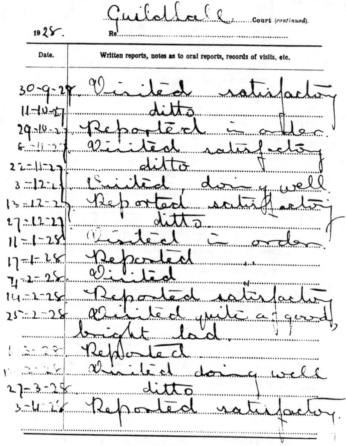

Guildhall.................Court (*continued*).

19 2 8 . Re...

Date.	Written reports, notes as to oral reports, records of visits, etc.
30-9-27	Visited satisfactory
11-10-27	ditto
29-10-27	Reported in order
6-11-27	Visited satisfactory
22-11-27	ditto
3-12-27	Visited doing well
13-12-27	Reported satisfactory
27-12-27	ditto
11-1-28	Visited in order
17-1-28	Reported
7-2-28	Visited
14-2-28	Reported satisfactory
25-2-28	Visited quite a good, bright lad
1-3-28	Reported
1-3-28	Visited doing well
27-3-28	ditto
3-4-28	Reported satisfactory.

LONDON :
PUBLISHED BY HIS MAJESTY'S STATIONERY OFFICE.
To be purchased directly from H.M. STATIONERY OFFICE at the following addresses
Adastral House, Kingsway, London, W.C.2; York Street, Manchester ;
1, St. Andrew's Crescent, Cardiff ; or 120, George Street, Edinburgh ;
or through any Bookseller.

1926.

Price 3d. net per 25 ; 5d. net per 50 ; 9d. net per 100.

Printed under the authority of His Majesty's Stationery Office by
Jas. Truscott & Son, Ltd., Suffolk Lane, E.C.4.

Appendix 12 (continued)

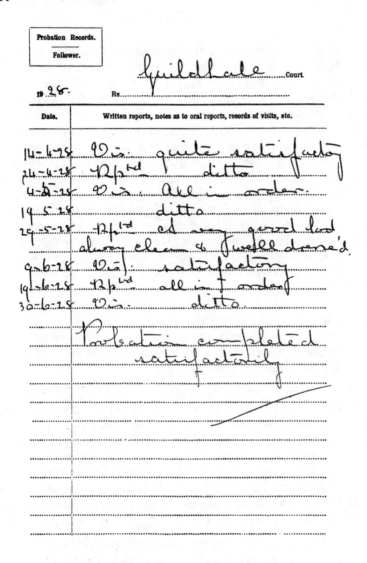

Source: *Inner London Probation Service archives*

Appendix 13

MIKE

Mike was one of the first friends Miss Crane made through her work; he was one who taught her a great deal and one to whom she was eternally grateful, because he taught her never to despair of anyone. When she was first appointed she inherited Mike, who was twelve, and already on probation, from her predecessor. His home was one of the most wretched in the district, a tumbledown, dirty, four-roomed cottage. His parents were Liverpool Irish; his father, a casual dock labourer, was in and out of prison. Both parents were sodden with drink; they ruled the home with kicks and blows; all the older children had left as soon as they could keep themselves; there remained only Mike, who was the youngest, and his sister Sally, who was a year older, and to whom he was devoted. They were good-looking children, with grey Irish eyes and dark, curly hair. They could truant and steal as they pleased as long as they were not caught, but if they brought attendance officers or police to the home their parents set about them with righteous wrath. It was not surprising that Mike's hand was against every man. He had not been long on probation when he was caught stealing from a shop and brought before the Court again. His school attendance was almost nil and, in view of the bad reports of his home, the magistrates decided to send him to an approved school. Mike did not mind going; he thought he might be much better off, but he minded dreadfully leaving Sally.

He was reasonably happy at school; he was intelligent and, when there was no opportunity to truant, he made rapid progress, and he was good at games. He was better clothed and fed than ever in his life and he put on weight rapidly. He would have been quite happy if he had had news from home, but his parents never wrote or sent him parcels like other boys' parents, and they never bothered to visit him. They were bad parents but they were all Mike had and he fretted for them and still more for Sally. After two months' silence he ran away and came home to see what had happened to everyone.

The headmaster sized up the situation correctly; he rang up Miss Crane and explained that Mike had had no visit or letter since he came and he felt sure he was worrying and had run off home. He did not want to send the police after him and asked Miss Crane if she would try to get

Appendix 13 (continued)

him back. She had hardly put down the receiver when there was a knock at her door and an indignant Mrs O'Brien appeared, holding Mike by the collar. "Look at him, Miss", she said, "With 'is lovely clothes an' all - 'e don't know when 'e's well off. 'e'll get 'is Dad an' me 'ung, so 'e will, with 'is goings on." Mike was tearful and sulky and it was plain that there was nothing to be done with the pair of them together, so Miss Crane told Mrs O'Brien that she had done right to bring Mike to the office and that she herself would take him back and she sent her off home. Mike had then to be reassured that there would be no trouble if he went back at once, and a telephone call put through to the school. This done, Miss Crane was free to give Mike her full attention. He had calmed down and was ready to talk; he told her how bad he felt when other boys had letters and parcels and visits from their families and he had none. It was not only that he missed them but he felt that he lost face with the others; he "didn't 'arf feel a fool". This was the first important lesson that he taught Miss Crane, who was young and inexperienced. She took him back to the school, where he was received with kindness and understanding; she tried to get his parents to write to him regularly and, when this failed, wrote to him herself, so that at least he should have letters, and visited him when she could, taking Sally with her.

Mike left school when he was fifteen and joined the army in boys' service. He found the life came easily to him, accustomed as he was to the discipline of an approved school, and for a year he was happy. Then, most unfortunately, he had an accident while fooling about with a rifle, and shot off the first finger of his right hand. After a spell in hospital he was discharged as unfit for service and returned home. Here he found tragedy; Sally had run away some months before and Mike had not been home very long when he discovered that she had gone on the streets. This nearly broke his heart and filled him with increased bitterness towards his parents. He would not work regularly, he began to steal again, got into very bad company and before long was concerned in breaking and entering. This time he was sent to Borstal. Institutional life now came easily to him; he was always clean, smart and respectful; he worked and played well and had uniformly good reports. He was never popular with his fellows, but got on well enough, as they respected his ability to keep himself out of trouble without being really on the side of the authorities.

Appendix 13 continued)

After eighteen months he was discharged on licence: superficially satisfactory, fundamentally unchanged; he had not yet made a real relationship with any other human being; he still distrusted them. He went home and resumed his drifting, casual life. He was under the supervision of a Borstal after-care officer and also often visited his old friend Miss Crane, whom he was as near to trusting as he trusted anyone. He was always full of bright ideas, most of which depended on someone lending him money, and Miss Crane had to harden her heart. "If I just had £10 for the uniform, Miss, I could get into the Merchant Navy for sure, and then I would be seeing the world and I wouldn't get into trouble." Or his idea might be more modest: "I've a friend who'll give me a lend of a barrer, Miss, and if you could just lend me £1 to buy some apples, sure, it would be a start for life." He once succeeded in getting to sea but deserted his ship at the first foreign port and made his way back to London. His after-care officer found him jobs and he lost them and before long he was in trouble again and was sent to prison.

For two or three years Mike was in and out of prison for short sentences. He was always a good prisoner and always earned the maximum remission. When he came out he always visited Miss Crane; he had never been a drinker, having a horror of it from his childhood, and he remained clean and smart in spite of threadbare, shiny clothes. There was no vice in him; he was just a drifter.

Then one day he brought a shy girl to see Miss Crane, saying, "Miss, I want you to meet Jenny - we're getting tied up on Saturday." Jenny was not particularly attractive; she was not overclean or tidy beneath the usual layer of makeup; she had worked in a factory since leaving school and had no idea of home-making. The speed with which the first baby arrived suggested that Mike had married her from necessity rather than from choice, but marriage had a steadying effect on him. He adored his children and was determined to give them all the chances he had not had himself; he poured out on them the love he had only been able to give to Sally in his childhood. When his first child, a girl, was a few weeks old, he brought her, a white woolly bundle, to be introduced to Miss Crane. Gazing at her proudly he said, "I'll never tell that kid a lie. Kids have got to be able to trust you." Where had Mike, dragged up in a family ruled by threats and bluff, acquired such wisdom?

Appendix 13 (continued)

Jenny contributed little to the marriage except the children, but they were everything to Mike, and Jenny was their mother. He went to work regularly, as never before, and when he came home he washed and ironed and cleaned, for Jenny never came up to his standards, removed safety pins from the children's clothes and sewed on buttons. When the war came he had the three children, all under five, evacuated to a nursery in the country. Jenny returned to the factory; Mike, unfit for military service, joined the Civil Defence. Both were now earning and the children were costing them very little. After a time Mike managed to buy a little house and garden in one of the nearer suburbs and, as the children reached school age, they had them home one by one.

After the war Mike could not find work for a time and Miss Crane trembled for him, but she need not have worried. Jenny stayed in the factory while Mike looked after the house and worked in the little garden and enjoyed his children, and they managed. Then one day Mike, whose smart appearance and excellent handwriting always stood him in good stead, visited Miss Crane in a smart navy blue uniform with black buttons and said "Miss, you know that big new block of offices they're building for the Ministry of....? Well, I've got the job of security officer on the site!" "Oh, Mike", said Miss Crane, "How lovely!"

Source: *Elizabeth Inman*

CRIMEFIGHTERS OF LONDON

Appendix 14

6th October, 1930.

Dear Madam,

The Selection Committee by whom you were interviewed
on Friday last have decided to recommend you for
appointment to one of the two vacancies open to women
under the Home Office Scheme for training candidates
for the Probation Service. It is proposed that you should
be attached to one of the London Courts for training,
and if the Committee's recommendation is accepted
arrangements will be made as soon as possible for your
appointment as an Assistant Probation Officer in the
Metropolitan area.

Before the Committee's recommendation can be laid
before the Secretary of State it will be necessary for us
to verify your date of birth and to be assured that you
are in a fit state of health to undertake the duties of a
Probation Officer. I shall be glad, therefore, if you
will send to me as soon as possible a certified copy of
your birth certificate, and a medical report (preferably
from your own doctor) on your state of health.

Miss D.M.Cecil Barker,
  Gable Cottage,
    Connaught Avenue,
      Chingford,
        Essex.

/It

342

Appendix 14 (continued)

- 2 -

It would be convenient if you would let me know at the same time when you will be at liberty to relinquish your present employment and take up an appointment under the training scheme.

The original testimonials which you forwarded with your application will be returned to you later.

Yours truly,

Norman Brook.

Source: *Cecil Barker*

Appendix 15

The Police Court Mission

OF THE

CHURCH OF ENGLAND TEMPERANCE SOCIETY

——— Diamond Jubilee ——— 1936

1876

In this year of the Diamond Jubilee of the Police Court Mission the Officers and Committee desire to express their warm appreciation of the Service of Elspeth Macpherson Stenuart faithfully rendered over a period of Eleven years.

They remember with deep gratitude all those who during the past Sixty Years have, by their devotion to its ideals, their gifts, and their loyal personal service, furthered the work of the Mission.

They return thanks to Almighty God for His enabling power in that united effort to raise the fallen, to protect the tempted, to reclaim the backsliding, to raise up those who stumble, to encourage the weary and to strengthen the weak; for His directing Spirit which gave the vision to His Servant Frederick Rainer, and the courage to respond thereto resulting in the present nation-wide and permanent service in which Church and State are in co-operation.

Signed on behalf of the Police Court Mission.

William Ebor;

Rollo F. Graham - Campbell

Cosmo Cantuar;

A. F. London;

Source: *Elspeth Gray*

344

Appendix 16

The London Police Court Mission

Chairman of Committee—	*President—*	*Hon. Treasurer—*
Bertrand Watson, Esq., J.P.	The Rt. Hon. Viscount Hailsham, P.C.	J. Jefferson Hogg, Esq., O.B.E., D.L., J.P.
Secretary—		*Assistant Secretary—*
The Rev. Harry Pearson, O.B.E., M.A.		G. J. Morley Jacob, Esq.

Cheques should be drawn to the order of THE LONDON POLICE COURT MISSION.

Boys' Home—Padcroft, Yiewsley.
" Speedwell Club "—for Girls
(East London).
Employment Department.

80 Missionaries working in the Police Courts (50 Men and 30 Women).

27, GORDON SQUARE, W.C.1.

Telephone : EUSTON 3756 (2 lines)

Copy

24th September 19 37.

HP/VRS.

Letter of Appointment.

Dear Miss Stafford,

The Committee, as you know has given you an appointment on our staff as a Missionary, on the following conditions:—

1. The Missionary will serve in any Court or Courts within the sphere of the London Police Court Mission as the Committee may at any time direct, and will be liable to transfer from one Court to another if required.

2. The Missionary will give her full time to the Missionary and Probation work of the Court or Courts. The commencing salary will be at the rate of £220 per annum with yearly increments of £10 until the maximum of £320 is reached.

3. This salary is to cover all services carried out in connection with work in the Court whether as Missionary or as Probation Officer. It is understood that if the Missionary should receive from any person any gift or remuneration other than salary in respect of such services, it will be paid over to the Committee for the purposes of the Mission.

4. It will be necessary for the Missionary to reside at an address within reasonable distance of the Court.

5. The Missionary must not undertake any duties, paid or voluntary, other than those connected with the Court except with the consent of the Committee.

6. The Missionary will be allowed four weeks holiday on full pay in

Source: *Georgina Stafford*

345

Appendix 16 (continued)

-2-

each year at such time as can best be arranged.

7. In case of absence from duty through sickness for more than two days, a medical certificate must be sent to the Secretary and in the case of continued sickness, further medical certificates will be required at appropriate intervals.

8. The present engagement is for a period of three months as from November 1st, after which it is hoped you will receive an appointment as Probation Officer. In the event of your failing to obtain such an appointment, your engagement as a Missionary will come to an end. If you receive an appointment as a Probation Officer, this engagement will be continued and you will then become subject to the conditions mentioned in this letter. (A copy of the Probation Rules is enclosed.)

9. Subject to the provisions in the preceding paragraph, this engagement may be terminated by either party giving one month's notice in writing to the other.

10. On appointment as Probation Officer, the Probation Officers' Superannuation Rules 1926/37 will apply to you; these provide for retiral on Pension at the age of 65. You will be required to pay, by deduction from your salary, the appropriate contributions, and you will be entitled to the benefits under the Scheme. A copy of the Superannuation Rules is enclosed.

Yours very truly,

Secretary.

I accept the appointment on the conditions set out in the above letter.

Signed _____

date _____

Source: *Georgina Stafford*

Appendix 17

THE LONDON PROBATION SERVICE

Report by Miss G. . Stafford. , Probation Officer. Date 12 : 11 : 1943.

Name	Age	Born	Rel.	Address
R , A	15		C/E	London, S.E.

Offence BEYOND CONTROL.

Previous Offences Nil.

FAMILY

Name	Age	Occupation	Income	Remarks
J		Butcher	5.0.0	
D		Butcher's cashier		
D	17	Navy		
A	15			
H	10			

Home: They occupy a 5-roomed flat in a good neighbourhood. Rent 18/3
Beautifully furnished and well kept.

I have had a long talk with Mr. and Mrs. R   who tell me
that they have found A   difficult almost from birth. Many of
their difficulties arose from her refusal to do what was required
of her. She would not take the bottle, she would not crawl, she
refused to walk much until over 3 and if forced to do so sat down
and screamed until picked up. She had very dirty habits until she
was over 4 and to some extent her unpleasant ways recurred when she
was older.

As a small child she never seemed to laugh, or to play with
her brother or sister. She was very jealous of them and of a
younger brother who died. She never chattered about what she was
doing, thinking or feeling, and any information had to be coerced
from her by specific and persistent questioning. She would not
help in the house and if forced to wash up would smash most of
the china. She never returned from school until long after she
should have done, and a variety of punishments failed to alter the
habit.

She pilfered small things such as fruit and sweets and on

Appendix 17 (continued)

two occasions took money. She twice stole from people other than her family. She lied when in trouble and sometimes lied imaginatively. She practically never brought her friends home but was seen out of doors with numbers of small boys. When she left school and went to evening classes, she used to be seen "hugging the wall with ~~her~~ boy"(to use Mr. R   's phrase) after the classes were over. She once came in at 11.30 p.m.

She went to school when she was 4.9/12ths. ~~Owing to the fact that her family moved.~~ Owing to the fact that her family moved several times and that she was evacuated to Cornwall for a period, she ~~has~~ had six changes of school. The parents say that she missed her chances of scholarships because she would not try, and in the second case because she refused to sit for the exam. A   denies these stories absolutely.

When she left school her ambition was to be a hairdresser. On making enquiries her mother found that she could be trained for this near home, receiving a nominal wage of 3/6d a week. Mrs. R   told A   that out of this she would have to pay her fares of 2/-. A   therefore decided against training. As she was already receiving 3/- per week pocket money at school, this decision is not surprising.

She was placed in a baby linen shop. She did well for a time but then became very rude and unmanageable. A   herself says that she was bored with the work and did not feel that she was fairly treated in it. Her next job was in an office. Her mother reports that she there flirted outrageously with the men, sitting on their knees, smacking their faces etc. A   indignantly denies all this although she admits a little mild flirtation. Her third job was an office one, from which she was dismissed the week that she was brought to Court for bragging of her experiences and for larceny from the petty cash.

Mr. and Mrs. R   give one the impression of being an unusually thrifty couple who have been very ambitious for their children. I think they have formed very high standards of behaviour and appearances and have tried to mould their children to conform to these standards. It is clear that a great deal of pressure has been brought to bear on A   towards this end. I think the result has been that almost from the beginning A has, in her own way, fought to establish and maintain her own independence and her right to be herself as an individual and not as a creation of her parents. There are obviously a number of very deep-seated emotional difficulties in her relationships with them. She heartily dislikes her mother and says that not only does her mother hate her, but has told her that she does so. In view of Mrs. R   's admitted hysterical tendencies, this is quite possible. Mrs. R   told me that had there been ~~in any~~ loophole for doubt, she would not have believed that A   was

Appendix 17 (continued)

her own child. A   herself seems to feel that she has
no real place in the family. I think she has a genuine
affection for her father. She has little good to say of
her brother and sister, although she declares she is fond
of them.

Her story of the two nights she spent away from home
is that she and another girl spent the evening with two
sailors. When they all separated to go home, it was very
late. She knew that there would be a row if she returned
home. so she spent the night on the common on a seat. She
met her friends again the next day and spent the next night
in a similar fashion. As the physical examination has shown
her to be virgo intacta one must accept her story.

A   had pneumonia four times before she was 7. The
last attack appeared to leave her with some ear trouble
which has never fully cleared up. She appears to be very
deaf in one ear and slightly deaf in the other. I think
this is a matter which should perhaps be gone into more
fully.

A   still wants to do hairdressing. I hesitate to
make any definite suggestion about future plans until I have
had the opportunity of discussing the matter with the
psychiatrist and seeing his report.

G. M. Stafford.

G.M.Stafford.
Probation Officer.
12th November,1943.

Source: *Georgina Stafford*

Appendix 18

TOTAL OF PROBATION OFFICERS' CASE LOADS—AT 31st DECEMBER

Year	Probation Orders	Supervision Orders	Money Payment Orders	After Care Cases	Total
1950	4,247	373	103	533	5,256
1955	4,041	696	225	627	5,589
1960	5,224	902	603	1,053	7,782
1961	5,438	1,034	698	1,256	8,426
1962*	5,837	1,064	828	1,345	9,074

*Provisional figures.

Source: *London Probation Service: Principal Probation Officer's Report 1960-1962* (1963)

Appendix 19

ENQUIRY, MATRIMONIAL AND MISCELLANEOUS WORK : ANNUAL TOTALS

| Year | Social Enquiries | | | Matrimonial Work | | | | Means Enquiries | Adoption | | Divorce Court Enquiries | Enquiries under Guardianship of Infants Acts | Enquiries under Sec. 4 Matrimonial Proceedings (Mags. Crts.) Act, 1960 | Other Work |
| | Magistrates' Courts | | Quarter Sessions and Assize Courts | Conciliation | Cases Closed | | Other Domestic Work | Magistrates' Courts Act, 1952 Sec. 60 | Guardian ad litem Duties | Other Enquiries | | | | |
	Juvenile	Adult			Parties known or thought to be living together as husband and wife	Other Cases								
1950	3,835	9,134	1,025	6,354	2,307	1,588	12,107	545**	–	–	–	–	–	12,194
1955	3,662	7,464	972	4,304	2,251	1,575	10,829	591	56	71	103	–	–	10,830
1960	5,469	8,863	1,601	4,090	2,451	1,386	3,805	48	50	109	253	792	–	22,504
1961	5,193	9,509	1,497	4,744	1,835	1,293	4,893	113	73	123	296	672	92	26,298
1962*	5,878	9,564	1,584	4,476	2,607	1,572	4,636	63	53	172	312	522	79	27,193

*1962 figures are provisional only. **Domestic Proceedings Act, 1937

Source: *London Probation Service: op. cit.* (1963)

Appendix 20

<u>SENIORS' DUTIES</u>

These duties are laid down in Rules 49 (1) and (2) of the Probation Rules 1949 and so far as London is concerned were defined and approved by the London Probation Committee (see L.P.S. Handbook). The following is a detailed list of duties of varying importance which are the responsibility of all seniors in London. If the suggestions outlined in the report above were adopted, some of these duties would become the special responsibility of the senior-in-charge in courts where new second appointments are made:-

I. ORGANISATION

Court staff meetings and local interpretation of Service policy.
Arrangements for providing staff for all court duties.
Allocation of typing facilities.
Sick and annual leave arrangements for colleagues, clerical assistants, office cleaner, and arranging for their work to be covered.
Distribution of work between officers.
      "   " caseloads.
      "   " districts.
Arrangements for case committees.
Arrangements for appeals.
Requests for reports and enquiries from other courts.
C.A.C.A., B.A. and other agencies involving supervision, home leave or other matters.
Reports, enquiries and correspondence relating to cases handled by officers who have left the court.
Collecting and collating reports on cases under supervision to outside courts.
Filing and correspondence and case records both current and expired.
Index system.
Circulation of periodicals, circulars, etc.

II. ADMINISTRATION

Account keeping; handling of official moneys, poor box and other charitable funds and quarterly check of colleagues' accounts.
Monthly expenses - checking and countersigning of expenses claims and reimbursement where customary.
Payment of wages and insurance of cleaner.
Preparation of monthly statistics.
      "   " annual statistics.
      "   " annual progress reports as required.

III. LIAISON WITH:-

Judges and Magistrates.
Clerks' Department.
Warrant Office.
Gaoler's Office.
Police.
Barristers and solicitors.
The P.P.O's office (including consultations, routine Seniors' Meetings and with the general office).
Visitors.
Visiting students etc.
Research workers.
Local community (social agencies, committees, talks, etc.).
Prisons for Remand and other cases.
C.A.C.A.
B.A.
Approved Schools and Remand Homes.

Appendix 20 (continued)

- 2 -

IV. <u>IN RELATION TO COLLEAGUES</u>:-

Review of case records.
Assistance with legal and other problems.
Dissemination of new knowledge.
Assistance with casework, individually and by organising group
  discussions.
Supervision of unconfirmed officers.
Supervision of temporary and relief officers.
Reports on officers (as required).
Students' training arrangements.

In addition to this list of specific duties there are equally important
aspects of a senior's duties which cannot be tabulated. These stem from his
position as leader of a team responsible for encouraging and preserving the
best traditions of the Service and of the court. The senior shares with the
administration, of which he also is a representative, the responsibility for
providing, so far as practicable, the best possible working conditions for his
colleagues, and for anticipating and discerning their needs. He has to take
an active interest in their welfare and professional development. The senior
has an important supportive role to play; colleagues should be able both to
admit their mistakes and failures to him and come to him at any time for advice
and encouragement. The senior should set the standard for the work of his
colleagues and try to ensure that each officer works to the best of his
capabilities, and is enabled to develop his skills to the full, subject only to
the limitation of the setting.

Finally, the senior should help each colleague to find his place in, and
make contribution to, the team of probation officers at the court so that a
high standard of work is reached and maintained.

Group relationships have a bearing on this and it is the senior's duty
to make allowance for individual differences in working method and preserve
harmony in the relationships within the group.

Source: *London Probation Service file on the Morison Committee*

Appendix 21

ESTABLISHMENT AND STAFFING AS AT 31st DECEMBER

Year	Establishment			In Post			Vacancies			Notes
	Men	Women	Total	Men	Women	Total	Men	Women	Total	
1950	78	57	135	76½	54	130½	1½	3	4½	
1955	87	63½	150½	81¼	66	147½	5½	(+2½)	3	Additional women officers helping with men's work.
1960	121	80	201	121	79	200	—	1	1	Including 44 men and 2 women in London Training Schemes and carrying modified case loads.
1961	121	80	201	125	83	208	(+4)	(+3)	(+7)	Including 10 men and 1 woman in London Training Scheme carrying modified case loads. The additional women were helping with men's case loads.
1962	127	82½	209½	113	84	197	14	(+1½)	12½	The additional women were helping with men's case loads.

Source: *London Probation Service: Principal Probation Officer's Report 1960-1962* (1963)

Appendix 22

OFFICERS ENTERING AND LEAVING THE LONDON PROBATION SERVICE

	Entering			*Leaving*	
	Men	*Women*		*Men*	*Women*
1955	8	6		5	7
1956	4	5		5	10
1957	4	10		9	8
1958	16	8½		5	3½
1959	15	12		12½	4
1960	41	10		9	6
1961	16	11		12	7
1962	2	15		14	14
TOTALS	106	77½		71½	59½

From Home Office Training	41	52½	Transfer to other probation areas	35	7
From London Training	46	2	Resignation to enter other work	25½	24
Transfer from other probation areas	16	21	Resignation for domestic reasons	–	22½
Re-appointment	1	2	Retirement	8	5
Secondment from Prison Service	2	–	Return from secondment	2	–
			Death	1	1
TOTALS	106	77½		71½	59½

Source: *London Probation Service: op. cit.* (1963)

Appendix 23

(a)

Qualifications of whole-time officers employed in the London Probation Service on 31st December, 1962.

	Numbers	Percentage
Degree or certificate in social science or mental health after a course of whole-time study at a university followed by Home Office training or university applied social studies course	63	31.8
Home Office training only	58	29.5
London Training Schemes	46	23.4
Social science degree or certificate after a course of whole-time study at a university without Home Office training or university applied social studies course	10	5.2
Teachers' training course or university youth leaders' course	1	.5
No relevant university qualifications (so far as is known) or Home Office or other training	19	9.6
	197	100.0

(b)

Distribution by age of London probation officers as at 31st December, 1962 :—

Age	Men	Women
under 25	–	8
over 25 but under 30	9	9
over 30 but under 35	19	3
over 35 but under 40	18	15
over 40 but under 45	17	8
over 45 but under 50	13	18
over 50 but under 55	23	5
over 55 but under 60	10	10
over 60	4	8
	113	84

Source: *London Probation Service: op. cit.* (1963)

Appendix 24

CHART SHOWING ALLOCATION OF HEADQUARTERS DUTIES

Principal Probation Officer and Deputy Principal Probation Officer (General) each maintain general contact so far as possible with all Courts and officers, and attend regional meetings of officers.

Principal Probation Officer	Deputy Principal Probation Officer (General)	Deputy Principal Probation Officer (Administrative)
General Policy and organisation. Communications and staff relations. Contacts with other Services	Deputy covering as required all aspects of Principal Probation Officer's work. Staffing allocation. Relief Officers. Temporary Probation Officers. Borstal and other After-Care. Men's Hostel and Home liaison. Regional duties in respect of South-East Region.	Deputy covering "administrative" aspects of Principal Probation Officer's work. Headquarters' office organisation and records. Accommodation and Furniture. Finance and Statistics.
General responsibility for all matters concerning the region; and for fostering and developing standards of work.	Staffing needs. Relief arrangements within region as possible.	Accounts and Expenses claims.
Maintaining contact with Seniors, Probation Officers and Clerical Assistants in the region.		
Regional Meetings.		
Clerical Assistants: Pay and conditions of service. Library and Periodicals.	Women's Hostel and Home Liaison. Relief Officers (Women)	Clerical assistance allocation. Superannuation.
London Training Scheme.	Home Office Students (Men and Women). University Students (Men and Women).	
Juvenile Court Questions.		Cars, motor cycles and cycles (including Service Cars).
Assist with London Training Scheme.	Case Committees—General. Probation Officers taking Courses.	

Regional duties:

MR. WASHINGTON (Deputy Principal Probation Officer): South-East

MISS WOODWARD: West and Central

MR. PRATT: North and East

MISS SULLIVAN: South and South-West

Central duties of Assistant Principal Probation Officers

MISS WOODWARD

MISS BRAITHWAITE

MR. PRATT

MISS SULLIVAN

Source: *London Probation Service: op. cit.* (1963)

Select Bibliography

(excluding H.M.S.O. publications, annual reports, and non-printed material)

ADLER, Nettie: *Probation and Probation Officers* (1908)

AYSCOUGH, H.H.: *When Mercy Seasons Justice. A Short History of the Work of The Church of England in the Police Courts* (no date: 1923)

BABINGTON, Anthony: *The Power To Silence* (1968)

BAILEY, Victor: *Delinquency and Citizenship: Reclaiming the Young Offender, 1914-1948* (1987)

BAZELEY, E.T.: *Homer Lane and the Little Commonwealth* (1928)

BEDFORD, Sybille: *The Faces of Justice* (1961)

BEESON, R.H./LONDON PROBATION COMMITTEE: *A Short Survey of the London Probation Service 1939-1944* (1945)

BENNEY, Mark: *Low Company, describing the evolution of a burglar* (1936)

BIGGS, Ronnie: *His Own Story* (1981)

BIRON, Sir Chartres: *Without Prejudice* (1936)

BLYTH, Nina M.P.: *Society of Juvenile Courts Probation Officers* (n.d.)

BOCHEL, Dorothy: *Probation and After-Care: Its Development in England and Wales* (1976)

BRIDGWATER, Thomas Rawling: *Origin and Progress of the Probation System* (1909)

BRILL, Kenneth: *John Groser* (1971)
(and Ruth Thomas): *Children in Homes* (1964)

CAIRNS, John Arthur Robert: *The Loom of the Law* (1922)

CALVERT, E.R. and T.: *The Lawbreaker* (1933)

CAMBRIDGE Department of Criminal Science (Director, L. Radzinowicz): *The Results of Probation* (1958)

CANCELLOR, Henry Lannoy: *The Life of a London Beak* (n.d., 1930)

CARR-SAUNDERS, A.M., MANNHEIM, H., and RHODES, E.C.: *Young Offenders* (1942)

CHAPMAN, Cecil: *The Poor Man's Court of Justice: Twenty-Five Years as a Metropolitan Magistrate* (n.d., 1925)
:*From the Bench* (1932)

CHESTERTON, Mrs Cecil: *In Darkest London* (1926; 1930)
:*Women of the Underworld* (1931)
:*Women of the London Underworld* (1938)

CLUTTON-BROCK, Guy and Molly: *Cold Comfort Confronted* (1972)

CORDER, R.E.: *Tales Told to the Magistrate* (1925)

DARK, Sidney: *Inasmuch...Christianity in the Police Courts* (1939)

ELLISON, Mary: *Sparks beneath the Ashes: Experiences of a London Probation Officer* (1934)

FARMER, S.C.F./LONDON PROBATION SERVICE: *Principal Probation Officer's Report 1960-1962* (1963)

FINLAY, Frances: *A Boy in Blue Jeans: A Woman's Story of Her Delinquent Son* (1969)

FORD, D: *The Delinquent Child and the Community* (1957)

FORDER, R.A.D.: *Social Casework and Administration* (1966)

FRENCH, Stanley: *Crime Every Day* (1976)

FYVEL, T.R.: *The Insecure Offenders* (1961)

GAMON, Hugh R.P.: *The London Police Court To-day and To-morrow* (1907)
:"The Probation of Offenders Act, 1907: An Appreciation and a Criticism" (*The Law Magazine and Review,* August 1908)

GARBETT, Cyril F.: *In the Heart of South London* (1931)

GILES, Francis Treseder: *Open Court* (1964)

GLASS, Ruth: *Newcomers* (1960)

GLOVER, Elizabeth: *Probation and Re-Education* (1949; 1956)

GRÜNHUT, Max: *Juvenile Offenders before the Courts* (1956)
: *Probation and Mental Treatment* (1963)

HALL, W. Clarke: *The State and the Child* (1917)
:*Children's Courts* (1926)

HALMOS, Paul: *The Faith of the Counsellors* (1978 edition)

HARTSHORN, Alma: *Milestone in Education for Social Work* (1982)

HEASMAN, Kathleen: *Evangelicals in Action* (1962)

HENRIQUES, Basil L.Q.: *The Indiscretions of a Warden* (1937)
:*The Indiscretions of a Magistrate* (1950)

HOBBS, May: *Born To Struggle* (1973)

HOLMES, Thomas: *Pictures and Problems from London Police Courts*
(first edition, 1900)
:*Known to the Police* (1908)

HOWARD ASSOCIATION: *Probation Officers and the Gift of Guidance*
(1901)

INNER LONDON PROBATION AND AFTER-CARE SERVICE:
ILPAS '76 (n.d., 1976?)

JACKSON, R.M.: *The Machinery of Justice in England* (1940; reprinted
1942)

JARVIS, F.V.: *Advise, Assist and Befriend* (1972)

JONES, A.E.: *Delinquency and the Law* (1945)

JONES, James A.: *Courts Day by Day* (n.d., 1946)

KING, Joan (editor): *The Probation Service* (1958; second edition, 1964)

KRAY, Charles: *Me and My Brothers* (1976)

LEEDING, Alfred: *"Leeding looks back: Pioneering probation with
missionary zeal" (Community Care,* August 30, 1978)

LEESON, Cecil: *The Probation System* (1914)

LE MESURIER, Lilian (editor): *A Handbook of Probation and Social
Work of the Courts* (1935)

LIECK, Albert: *The Justice At Work* (1922)
:*Bow Street World* (1938)

LOCK, Joan: *Marlborough Street: the Story of a London Court* (1980)
:*Tales from Bow Street* (1982)

LONDON, Jack: *The People of the Abyss* (1903)

LONDON (DIOCESAN) POLICE COURT MISSION: *Handed Over to the Police Court Missionary* (1913?)
:*The Quality of Mercy* (1922?)
:*The London Police Court Mission and Charles Dickens* (1924)

LONDON PROBATION SERVICE: *Handbook of Hostels and Homes, Shelters and Refuges for Children, Girls and Women other than Approved Hostels and Homes* (1953)

MANNHEIM, Hermann: *Social Aspects of Crime in England between the Wars* (1940)

McWILLIAMS, William: "The Probation Officer at Court: From Friend to Acquaintance"
:"The Mission to the English Police Courts 1876-1936"
:"The Mission Transformed: Professionalisation of Probation between the Wars"
:"The English Probation System and the Diagnostic Ideal"
:"Probation, Pragmatism and Policy" (*The Howard Journal* for 1981, 1983, November 1985, November 1986 and May 1987, respectively)

MIDDLESEX MAGISTRATE, A.: *The Justice of the Peace and His Functions On and Off the Bench* (1911)

MILLS, J. Grant (editor): *Church of England Temperance Society Jubilee Book* (1887)

MILTON, Frank: *In Some Authority* (1959)

MINN, W.G.: "Training for the Work of a Probation Officer in England and Wales" (*The Journal of Criminal Science,* Vol.1, 1948)

MONGER, Mark: *The English Probation Hostel* (1969)

MORRIS, Cherry (editor): *Social Case-Work in Great Britain* (1950)

MORRISON, A.C.L., and THACKRAY, E.L.: *Outlines of Law for Social Workers* (1948)

MULLINS, Claud: *Why Crime?* (1945)
:*Fifteen Years' Hard Labour* (1948)

NOBLE, Barbara: *Another Man's Life* (1952)

O'MAHONEY, Maurice: *King Squealer* (1978)

PARKER, Tony, and ALLERTON, Robert: *The Courage of His Convictions* (1962)

PARKINSON, Geoffrey: "Casework and the Persistent Offender" *(Probation,* March 1965)

PATERSON, Alexander: *Across The Bridges* (1911)

PLAYFAIR, Giles, and SINGTON, Derrick: *Crime, Punishment and Cure* (1965)

POLLARD, Beatrice: *Social Casework for the State* (1962)

POTTER, J. Hasloch: *Inasmuch: The Story of the Police Court Mission 1876-1926* (1927)

PROBYN, Walter: *Angel Face* (1977)

PURCELL, Edmund: *Forty Years at the Criminal Bar* (1916)

RICHARDSON, Anthony: *Nick of Notting Hill* (1965)

ROLPH, C.H.: *Living Twice* (1974)

ROSE, Gordon: *The Struggle for Penal Reform* (1961) *:Schools for Young Offenders* (1967)

ST. GILES' CHRISTIAN MISSION: *A River of Mercy and Its First Spring* (1891)

ST. JOHN, John: *Probation – The Second Chance* (1961)

SANDBACH, John Brown: *This Old Wig* (n.d., 1950)

SOKOLOFF, Bertha: *Edith and Stepney: The Life of Edith Ramsay* (1987)

SPENCER, Walter: *The Other Side of the Prison Gate* (1938)

SPINLEY, B.M.: *The Deprived and the Privileged* (1953)

STOKES, Sewell: *Court Circular* (1950; revised ed. 1955)

THOMPSON, Leslie: *An Autobiography* (1985)

TIMASHEFF, N.S.: *One Hundred Years of Probation* (U.S.A.: Part I, 1941; Part II, 1943)

TODD, Marjory: *The Probation Officer and His World* (1963)
    :*Ever Such A Nice Lady* (1964)

TREHERNE, John: *Dangerous Precincts* (1987)

TURNER, Merfyn: *Ship Without Sails* (1953)
    :*Norman House: The First Five Years* (1961)
    :*Safe Lodging* (1961)

UNITED NATIONS: *Probation and Related Measures* (U.S.A., 1951)

VARIOUS CONTRIBUTORS: *Guy and Molly Clutton-Brock*
    (Zimbabwe, 1987)

WADDY, Henry Turner: *The Police Court and Its Work* (1925)

WALKER, Nigel, and McCABE, Sarah: *Crime and Insanity in England*
    (Vol. II, 1973)

WALLICH-CLIFFORD, Anton: *One Man's Answer* (1962)
    :*No Fixed Abode* (1974)

WALTON, Ronald: *Women in Social Work* (1975)

WATSON, John: *The Child and the Magistrate* (January 1965 edition)
    :*Which is the Justice?* (1969)

WIGGIN, Maurice: *My Court Casebook* (1948)

WILKINSON, Rosalind/British Social Biology Council: *Women of the
    Streets* (1955)

WILLIAMS, Montagu: *Later Leaves* (1891)

WILLIAMSON, Joseph: *Father Joe* (1963)

WILLMOTT, Phyllis: *Consumer's Guide to the British Social Services*
    (1974 ed.)

YOUNG, A.F., and ASHTON, E.T.: *British Social Work in the
    Nineteenth Century* (1956)

YOUNGHUSBAND, Eileen: *Social Work in Britain: 1950-1975* (2 Vols.,
    1978)

Index

Reformer, 30
Regent Street Clinic, 271
Regent Street Polytechnic, 292
"regionalisation", 261-2, 298
Reigate, 300
relief officer(s), 130, 155, 195, 219, 227, 285; see also 83, 273
religion, aspects of, 27, 52, 120-1, 134, 146-7, 150, 151-2, 157-8, 203, 228, 229, 260, 295
remand centres, 267
remand home(s), 73, 94, 152, 191-2, 213, 214, 216, 231, 243, 265-6, 267, 268
remands in prison, 33, 116, 145, 300; see also 219, 286
reporting (by clients), 61, 76, 88, 127-9, 140, 170, 178, 196, 216, 244, 253, 282, 287, 293
Report of the Departmental Committee on the Social Services in Courts of Summary Jurisdiction, 146 *et seq.;* see also 178, 180
Report on the Employment and Training of Social Workers (Younghusband), 203
research, 290
resources, probation service, 210, 281, 299
Results of Probation, The, 255-6, 283
retirement, retiring age, 79, 105, 110, 118, 140, 188
Reynolds, B.J., 148
Richmond, 25, 39, 86
Risinghill School, 289-90
Rivett-Carnac, Thomas Nicholas, 158, 264
Robeson, Miss, 41
Robins, Allen G.H., 219, 227
Robinson, Henry, 136
Robinson, R.B., 298
Rochester Diocesan Branch (C.E.T.S.), 11-12, 16, 25-8, 30, 35, 39; see also

2, 13, 236
Rolph, C.H. (Cecil Rolph Hewitt), 170-1, 202, 243, 255
Roman Catholic clients/probation officers, 62, 76, 103, 111, 114-15, 126-7, 134, 137-8, 146, 159, 209, 269
Rose, A.G., 203, 214
Rose, John, 66-7, 69, 76
Rosenthal, Miss Yetta, 187-8
Rosling, Miss D.M., 148, 176, 199
Rotha, Paul, 208
Routh (later Kratz), Miss Miriam E., 208, 222, 232, 244
Royal
    Commission on Marriage and Divorce, 245-6
    Commission on the Police, 279
    Courts of Justice, 191, 246
    London Discharged Prisoners' Aid Society, 185
    Society for the Assistance of Discharged Prisoners, 139
Ruggles-Brise, Sir Evelyn, 20, 55
Russell, Lord (Bertrand), 279
Russell, Mrs Kit, 269
Russell, R., 103

St Giles' Christian Mission, 15, 19-20, 63, 70, 75
St John, John, 267, 277-8, 287
St Luke's House, 270
St Stephen's House, 150, 153, 163, 164, 168, 171, 173, 177, 179, 180, 185
salaries, 14, 24, 41-2, 54, 60, 68, 77, 92, 95, 105, 107, 110, 129-30, 155, 163, 164, 213, 229, 252, 254-5, 267, 272, 281, 282
Salvation Army, 62, 111
Samaritans, 300
Samuel, Herbert, 55, 56, 58, 62, 65, 78, 246